P9-DTL-002

CONSUMER GUIDE®

1982 CONSUMER BUYING GUIDE

Contents

1982 Consumer Buying Guide

EFFECTIVE BUYING depends on having the right information at hand when you shop. Yet no one person can know enough about every product available. With this in mind, CONSUMER GUIDE® magazine introduces you to *1982 Consumer Buying Guide,* an indispensable guide to buying the best for the least.

We have no ties to manufacturers or retailers, we accept no advertising, and we're not interested in selling products. Our sole purpose is to provide consumers with the information they need to make intelligent purchases at the best prices. Our experts examine and evaluate all sorts of products—everything from cars to kitchen appliances—and select those that offer exceptional value. In most areas, there's a trend toward smaller, higher-quality products. The "Best Buy" isn't necessarily the cheapest buy; it's the highest-quality product and, if applicable, the one with the lowest energy use.

To make the most of this book, first review the section that describes the product you want. It contains important information on trends and features. Then study our "Best Buy" selections carefully. They've been chosen for their usefulness, durability, high quality, and overall value; all electrical products are UL listed. Product selections under each category are listed alphabetically or by size; the introduction to each section will tell you which. And keep in mind that a "Best Buy" designation applies only to the product listed; it doesn't necessarily apply to other models by the same manufacturer, or to an entire product line.

"Also Recommended" selections are products that didn't meet our "Best Buy" criteria in some way. They may have features that probably won't appeal to most buyers, they may carry a higher price than our "Best Buy" selections, or they may have some deficiency. For example, a major appliance may be a fine product in all respects except that it uses more energy than a "Best Buy" selection. "Also Recommended" products have been included because they may give some buyers an alternative or meet the special needs of some consumers.

Finally, shop at your local retail stores, comparing prices and models. If a dealer quotes a price close to the "Low Price" we give for each "Best Buy" and "Also Recommended" selection, you can be sure that you're receiving first-rate value for your money. The prices listed here were accurate at the time of printing; however, due to currency fluctuations and manufacturers' changes, both retail and low prices may vary.

New Cars

THE OUTLOOK FOR an upturn in the U.S. auto market is part good news, part bad news. The good news is that Detroit's products keep getting better in both quality and design. Also, industry leaders see a pent-up demand that could make 1982 one of the biggest sales years on record. The bad news is that buyers won't come out of hiding unless interest rates come down and inflation eases. At least that's the view in Motown. Meantime, it's new model time again, so—if we can—let's forget the economy and high prices for a moment to review the highlights of the '82 model year.

American Motors Corporation

AMERICA'S SMALLEST automaker mostly marks time this year. A new five-speed manual transmission arrives as an option for all the firm's domestic products, which are mostly unchanged. The four-wheel-drive Eagles get the "Select-Drive" system as a new standard feature. Introduced as an option mid-way through '81, Select-Drive allows the driver to switch between two- or four-wheel operation from inside the vehicle just by moving two dash-mounted levers. Following its weight-paring last year, AMC's optional 4.2-liter (258-cubic inch) straight six gets a single-belt engine accessory drive said to reduce power losses and simplify servicing. Six-cylinder models with automatic get more widely spaced gear ratios as an aid to fuel economy, and low-drag front disc brakes are adopted across the board for the same reason.

You can't talk about AMC these days without mentioning Renault. The giant state-owned French automaker now owns a controlling interest in the U.S. firm. For 1982, the little front-drive Renault Le Car stands pat, and the mid-range 18i returns for a second season following a disappointing sales record in its debut year. A diesel engine will be offered in the 18 for mid-'82, followed next April by the curvaceous Fuego hatchback coupe built off the 18 floorpan. The Fuego is expected to boast a turbocharged rendition of the 18i fuel-injected 1.6-liter (100-cid) four-cylinder engine.

AMC Concord

There's only so much you can do with a 13-year-old design, so don't expect much mileage improvement from this former "compact." Not as spacious inside as more newly designed front-drive competitors, and heavier, too. Performance depends on the engine chosen. The four doesn't give much, especially with automatic. The problem is weight. The six is peppier, but you pay at the pump. Against this, Concord is a known quantity, and its build quality is now among the best in Detroit. Comprehensive drivetrain and no-rust warranties are value bonuses. Refinement is a strong point, and ride is pretty good. Not the best choice for space- or fuel-efficiency, but price is attractive against that of rear-drive rivals of similar size. On the way out, probably by 1984.

AMC Eagle

Four-wheel drive makes Eagle unique among domestic cars. It also makes it easier to overlook the shortcomings of what is now a very old body/chassis design. A rather crowded cabin, disappointing mileage, and dated control layout are the main debits. Not intended for serious off-roading. If you try to use it that way, you'll pay for it with very costly repairs. The standard four gives surprisingly lively pickup and decent economy with manual shift in the smaller Eagles. Stick with the six for the bigger models. Workmanship is first-rate, heating/ventilation/air conditioning top-notch, and factory-applied rustproofing reassuring. Select-Drive doesn't boost mileage much, but the new five-speed manual gearbox and higher gearing for all models may yield a small mpg improvement. Main appeal is still for buyers in the snowbelt, who will appreciate 4WD's superior on-road traction in foul weather. Remains an enigma: advanced engineering in an old-fashioned package.

AMC Spirit

A cut-down derivative of the larger Concord, with all the compromises that implies for interior and luggage room, performance, and economy. Wheelbase length puts Spirit in the same league with such mileage marvels as the VW Rabbit, Mazda GLC, Honda Accord, the domestic Ford Escort/Mercury Lynx, and Chrysler's L-body Omni/Horizon. Against these, Spirit has only marginal four-passenger seating, limited cargo space, an old-fashioned driving position and controls, and mpg ratings that trail the pack by a wide margin. Old design is actually a plus for workmanship, which benefits from decade-long production. The rear-drive layout also helps keep service costs lower than for some front-drivers. Can be quite plush if you spend enough for the right options.

Chrysler Corporation

THE NATION'S best-known welfare recipient has two new models at the start of the '82 campaign, and will bolster these with several mid-year offerings. The newcomers are the Chrysler LeBaron and Dodge 400, essentially more luxuriously trimmed and equipped variations of the front-drive Dodge Aries/Plymouth Reliant K-cars. Most engineering refinements developed for LeBaron/400 also apply to the less expensive models. These include self-propping hood, revised front suspension and steering geometry for better cornering control and road noise isolation, and (as a running change) roll-down rear door glass for sedans and wagons. The standard Chrysler-built 2.2-liter (135-cid) "Trans-4" engine comes in for tweaks to induction system and emissions control electronics aimed at better driveability and quieter operation. At mid-year a Town & Country edition of the five-door K-wagon joins the LeBaron line, along with a two-seat convertible under both nameplates.

The smaller front-drive L-body models, the five-door Dodge Omni/Plymouth Horizon sedans and their 024/TC3 sisters, stay mostly the same, but get a linkless front swaybar like the K-cars. The lines are regrouped into three price-and-equipment classes. All but the top-line sporty coupes revert to the 1.7 liter (105-cid) Volkswagen-based four as standard, with the Trans-4 as an option. Last year's "Euro-Sedan" option package for the five-doors is renamed "E-Type," and becomes a full-fledged model. Debuting soon is a front-drive pickup built on a stretched L-body platform and wearing the sloped 024/TC3 front-end treatment. It will be marketed as the Dodge Rampage.

On the import side, Chrysler's Japanese partner, Mitsubishi, will send over a five-door version of the familiar front-drive Dodge Colt/Plymouth Champ hatchback. It's built on a slightly longer chassis but differs little in other ways from the familiar three-doors. Also due is a 4WD version of the Dodge Ram 50 minitruck.

Chrysler Cordoba/Dodge Mirada

The personal-luxury field is stagnant this year, so these cars' ranking stays the same. Outmoded next to GM's G-body coupes like Chevy Monte Carlo, and lacks their diesel option. Looks better against the Thunderbird/Cougar XR7 twins from Ford, but doesn't offer a four-speed overdrive automatic like they do, and is bulkier. Probably at its best carrying two people on a long trip over interstate highways. That's where you can enjoy a spacious front cabin, hushed cruising ability, nice ride, and creature comforts. Advanced age of design shows up in decidedly cramped rear quarters, soggy handling, and relatively high fuel consumption. With standard six-cylinder engine mileage is on the wrong side of 15 mpg. The optional V-8 won't do better, but has more torque for swifter passing on two-lane roads or merging in fast-moving traffic. If these models have any saving graces they are construction quality that's much better than it used to be and the proven dependability of a body and chassis that have been around since the mid-1970s.

Chrysler LeBaron

We have yet to put the new front-drive LeBaron through a full road test, but first impressions are mostly positive. Chrysler has done a nice job of upgrading the sensible K-car, and there are several worthwhile improvements. The suspension changes work. LeBaron takes dips and chatter bumps with good control and little suspension noise. Handling is not in the sports-car realm, but it's quite good for the class. On bumpy crests taken quickly the back end can hop a little, but it's not serious. Driveline vibration is minimal, and noise from all sources is low. Interiors are plush, seats comfortable, and standard equipment fairly complete. We'll have to reserve comment about fuel economy and workmanship until we test an actual production model. Things we'd change include adding more punch off the line (neither engine gives really quick pickup), reducing assistance on the power steering, and opening up the sedan's quarter windows for better over-the-shoulder vision. All in all, shapes up as a strong contender in the little-limousine market.

Chrysler New Yorker

Chrysler may have been too clever in making this year's New Yorker out of last year's LeBaron. As a full-size car, New Yorker is smaller and more maneuverable than its GM and Ford opposition, but suffers a tighter interior, less trunk room, and a choppier ride. It's also not that much lighter than a Chevy Caprice or Ford LTD, and offers similar low-calorie engines, so it has no advantage in performance or economy, either of which ought to be better than on its larger rivals. Considered as an intermediate, New Yorker would be compared with GM's G-body rear-drive cars like the Buick Regal or Olds Cutlass and Ford's Granada/Cougar. Against these, the Chrysler lags in almost all areas, except maybe opulence. To be sure, it's a thoroughly developed, if dated, design, but it's sturdy and proven. Workmanship is now quite good, and getting better. Standard equipment is generous, and some people will like the styling.

Dodge Aries/Plymouth Reliant

A first-rate design, as it had to be to pull Chrysler back from the financial brink. This year's sprucing up improves the K-car further. Scores for interior room, cargo space, nice ride on most surfaces, and quietness (except in full-bore acceleration). Economy doesn't lead the compact class, but it's in the ballpark. Performance is adequate—but no more than that—with either engine. The Chrysler-built four is laid out with the do-it-yourselfer in mind, a big plus for keeping down maintenance costs. A few distractions remain: road manners are uninspired, the dash is too glittery, and workmanship, though getting better, needs to be better still. No major owner complaints or recalls since introduction, unlike the problem-plagued GM X-cars. Verdict: capable all-around family car and Chrysler's best effort in years. We like it.

Dodge Challenger/Plymouth Sapporo

A very pleasant sporty car, equal in most respects to the Datsun 200-SX. Not as frugal with fuel, however, and subjectively less lively. Performance tails off noticeably with automatic, so take the manual unless you can't do without no-shift convenience. Mitsubishi's 2.6 still suffers some harsh throbbiness associated with large-displacement four-bangers despite the claimed vibration damping of its Silent Shaft design. Good if not great handling and road hugging ability. Major controls are nicely spaced, stylish dash is thoughtfully arranged. Back seat is meant for only short-haul use by adults. Trunk isn't large, but the car is better used by two people on a long trip anyway. Impressively well made, equipped, and furnished. Sum-up: surprisingly good and sadly overlooked.

Dodge Colt/Plymouth Champ

One of the smaller economy cars, which sets its practical limits as all-around transportation. We haven't tried the longer-wheelbase five-door yet, but we doubt it will have noticeably more interior space than the three-door. Room in back is in very short supply, which is just as well because cargo volume isn't great when the fold-down seat back is in place. Diminutive size is an asset in urban work, along with commanding outward vision and tight turning circle. Steering a mite heavy at parking pace, though. Ride is good for the class, but performance of the standard 1.4-liter (86-cid) engine isn't, even with the extra flexibility of the eight-speed Twin-Stick gearbox. We think you'd be happier with the larger 1.6-liter (98-cid) engine, which is peppier, smoother, and quieter. Rather basic trim and appointments in base and Deluxe models, though workmanship is tidy and tight. Mileage a bit below that of competitors like the Mazda GLC, Honda Civic, and Toyota Tercel. Price is attractively low, and reliability/durability record looks good (design was new for 1979). Judgment: a good alternative to the Honda Civic, but not as refined or frugal.

Dodge Diplomat/Plymouth Gran Fury

A boring, anonymous car, but nice enough if you like mid-'70s engineering. Modest performance with standard slant six is balanced somewhat by mileage that's acceptable for a car of this size and weight. Ride too soft, and the simple leaf-spring/live-axle rear end is prone to hop uncomfortably on rough patches. Road noise spoils an otherwise peaceful interior, which is well finished and adequately roomy for five adults. Driving position a bit cramped for those with long legs, mostly due to lack of rearward seat travel. Dash quite old-fashioned and too fussy. Standard power steering rather dead, though effort isn't as feathery light as in the past. Trunk floor uneven, luggage space unexceptional. Assessment: outclassed as an intermediate, yet doesn't fare well as a full-size, either.

Dodge 400

A nicely integrated package that successfully takes the intelligent K-car design up a notch in prestige and refinement. We particularly like the reduced driveline vibration compared to early K-cars, the tastefully appointed interiors, and detail changes like reclining backrests for the optional bucket seats and a more precise manual shift linkage. The softer suspension improves the 400's ride comfort over bumps at some expense in vertical wheel control, but road shocks are much better damped. Handling has not been the K-car's forte, so it's not the 400's either, but for a luxury intermediate the car is easy to maneuver and its handling is stable and vice-free. Engine and wind noise levels are both low, so the sound-deadening work seems to have paid off. The 400 shares the basic K-car dash, which isn't to our taste, and over-the-shoulder vision is hindered by the formal-look roof styling. Workmanship can't be assessed yet, but Chrysler knows it's got to be good to win sales. In all, one of the year's happier developments.

Dodge Omni/024 and Plymouth Horizon/TC3

The first American-built front-drive small cars still compare favorably against newer rivals, foreign and domestic. Main difference between sedan and coupe is in rear seat accommodation, where the coupe sacrifices space for its swoopier styling. Both body styles offer above-average front seat room and a good ride. Easy to drive, though we prefer the sedan's higher seats and more useful outward glass area for tackling city traffic. Not cured on the '82s, however, are awkwardly placed pedals, a steering wheel set too high and close to the chest, and very low-geared manual steering. We'd also like more supportive, better-shaped seats. Economy is up there with the best in class, the Miser models especially so. However, the smaller 1.7-liter (105-cid) four sounds busy and buzzy in hard acceleration, and lacks the lazy open-road cruising ability of the optional 2.2-liter (135-cid) Trans-4. We recommend the latter unless maximum mpg is your prime concern. Workmanship is improving, but it'll need to be better to satisfy today's pickier shoppers. Competitively priced, and well worth a look. Less fussy to drive than the Escort/Lynx and roomier than the dull old Chevette.

Imperial

The past model year proved to be the wrong time for launching a big personal-luxury coupe. Impressive standing still, but betrays its humble origins on the move. The simply located live rear axle thumps and bumps too much for a luxury liner. The standard power steering is almost devoid of feel, and the long nose makes you think you're piloting the Queen Mary. There's unseemly body roll in turns, and the power brakes can be touchy in panic stops. In fairness, the car handles pretty well for its size and weight. But weight—excess weight—is the rub. The big V-8 just isn't strong enough to move all that mass very quickly, and conspires to keep fuel economy uncomfortably close to single-digit averages. Chrysler boasts extra quality-control measures for this car, but we felt a disturbing looseness on bumpy streets, and heard a few rattles, too. Exceptionally well equipped and loaded with snob appeal. Scorecard: a poor third in this year's "battle of the bustlebacks."

Ford Motor Company

DEARBORN ROUNDS OUT its successful "world car" lineups with a five-door hatchback sedan. Otherwise, the front-drive Ford Escort and Mercury Lynx are changed only in detail. Due later in the year is a close-ratio four-speed manual transmission for better off-the-line snap, plus an optional high-output version of the 1.6-liter (98-cid) "CVH" (Compound

Valve Hemispherical) four-cylinder engine. The two-seat EXP/LN7 coupe derivatives of these models debuted last spring as '82s, and are unchanged except for a slightly longer list of standard equipment.

At the other end of the price-and-size scale is the new "baby" Lincoln, the Continental. It's built off the 108.5-inch-wheelbase stretch of the familiar rear-drive Fairmont/Zephyr platform. It's offered in three versions, all richly equipped four-doors sporting "bustleback" trunk styling in the manner of Cadillac's Seville. Features include standard electronic digital instrumentation with on-board trip computer, and the first use of gas-pressurized shocks and puncture-sealant tires as factory-installed items.

The mid-size Ford Granada and its Mercury Cougar clone debuted last year as upscale versions of the Fairmont/Zephyr. For '82, Ford transfers the Fairmont/Zephyr wagon to the higher priced lines to join the returning two- and four-door notchback sedans.

Most of Ford's other cars have been left alone, except for the usual shifting of powertrains and final drive ratios for higher fleet-average fuel economy numbers. The firm has a new "corporate" engine this season—a 3.8-liter (232-cid) V-6, with thinwall cast iron block and aluminum cylinder head. It will be an extra-cost item for the Granada/ Cougar and the personal-luxury Thunderbird/Cougar XR-7 coupes, and will be a no-cost alternative to the standard 5.0-liter V-8 in the new Continental. The V-6's lightweight construction makes it only a few pounds heavier than Ford's 2.3-liter four, and output compares favorably against Buick's similarly sized V-6. Also new is a reworked three-speed "Select-Shift" automatic with lockup torque converter effective in all forward gears. It will be offered as either standard or optional in all Ford Motor Company lines except the Escort/Lynx, the full-size Ford LTD/Mercury Marquis, and the big Lincoln and Mark VI.

Ford Escort/EXP and Mercury Lynx/LN7

Escort/Lynx is a generally competent car with two main flaws. An unhappy ride/handling compromise is one. The rather limp springs and shocks make for a disturbingly floaty ride over undulations, yet the car can jolt over sharp bumps. There's also too much body roll. Without power assistance, the steering is unduly heavy for easy parking. In the credit column, interior room is good, the upright driving position and large glass area aid maneuvering, and mileage is good but not great. The world car's other problem is shared by the EXP/LN7 which shares its drivetrains and floorpan. The much-ballyhooed CVH inline four isn't very powerful, so performance is dull even with the shorter 4.05 final drive. It's also a rough-running engine except at modest rpm, and suffers from a boomy exhaust. The engine installation on both models is crowded. The coupes have a less comfortable ride. Sunken seats and lower roof impede forward vision, and the lack of a back seat is also a minus. The coupes' stiffer chassis does give better handling, though. Some interior design details on both models are clumsy, and workmanship could stand some tightening up. We basically like Ford's minis, but they deserve a smoother, quieter engine with more zip.

Ford Fairmont Futura/Mercury Zephyr

A solid, reliable, relatively simple car now in its last year. (For 1983, Ford will replace the Fairmont and Zephyr with a stretched version of the front-drive Escort/Lynx.) Seems a bit old-hat next to most competitors, but has attractions. The main ones are its less complicated rear-drive layout, sturdy (though not refined) engines, and generally pleasant seating for up to five. This year's new deep-well trunk is a sensible change for utility. Ride mostly good except on closely spaced bumps, which the live rear axle doesn't cope with well. Handling and roadholding predictable but ordinary. Mileage won't win prizes, but is respectable. We dislike the rough-and-rude 2.3-liter (140-cid) standard four, and recommend you opt for the smoother and more liveable 3.3-liter (200-cid) straight six.

Ford Granada/Mercury Cougar

Mostly the same as the '81 model. Main competition comes from GM's G-body intermediates like the Chevy Malibu and Olds Cutlass. They're about the same size and weight, are also rear drive, and offer engines of similar displacement and power. The Ford cars have about the same passenger space and an edge in trunk room among sedans. They're also marginally quieter except with the boomy big four. Over the road, Granada/Cougar is softer and a bit clumsier than the GM cars, so the optional handling package or TRX suspension is recommended. The optional, antiquated straight six has the same horsepower as the four, but its greater torque means safer passing and less fussy operation. We haven't fully tested the new 3.8-liter (232-cid) V-6 yet. Both models' fuel economy is still on the wrong side of 20 mpg, and a diesel option is conspicuously absent. Sum-up: remains a pleasant resolutely conservative design with no outstanding virtues or vices.

Ford LTD

Still rates in a virtual dead heat overall with the Chevrolet Caprice/Impala. While the Ford can't boast the advertised mpg figures of the diesel-powered Chevy, it does have better low-end performance when base-engine models are compared. Both are similar in passenger accommodation, trunk space, and ride quality, the Ford being perhaps a tad silkier and quieter on the boulevard. Chevy gets the nod for handling, though neither of these cars is meant to be a cornering fool. In all, the choice of one over the other will probably come down to personal taste and the deal you can get.

Ford Mustang/Mercury Capri

As always, these are tricky to rate because they can be equipped so many ways. Handling, roadholding, and maneuverability are all average with the limp standard chassis; much better with either of the two upgraded suspensions. Interior accommodations naturally favor front seaters. Dash has neatly styled full instrumentation and handy minor controls. Hatchback offers a measure of practicality with its fold-down back seat; notchback's trunk is small. Choosing an engine is frustrating because none are very satisfactory. The standard four is rough, noisy, and not very responsive. Its available five-speed overdrive manual gearbox has an awkward shift pattern that's a trial to use. The six gives only modest performance and not much better mileage. That leaves the small V-8 as our choice. We appreciate the gesture toward efficiency in the lockup converter automatic. But look at the EPA ratings: 21, 20, and 19 mpg, respectively, for the four, six, and small V-8. The hot GT and RS will be as thirsty as they are fast. Takes dressing up to be liveable, so not as good value-for-money as import competition.

Ford Thunderbird/Mercury Cougar XR-7

Ford has been too busy with its smaller cars to do much with its coupes this year. There's nothing wrong with them that a couple hundred fewer pounds and more carefully matched drivetrains wouldn't cure. Rides well, and offers good front seat accommodation. Rear seat space is tight, though, aggravated on the formal-roof models by semi-blind rear quarters that severely hamper vision to the right rear. The driving position is comfortable, and controls are where they should be. Noise levels are quite low. Not as nimble perhaps as GM competitors like the Buick Regal or Olds Cutlass and not clearly superior in either performance or economy. The new 3.8-liter (232-cid) V-6 may change our minds, but we doubt it in view of its 19-mpg EPA city rating. The standard six is woefully slow and best avoided because of that. In brief: okay for what it is, but growing old rapidly.

Lincoln Continental

A good car in some areas and not so good in others. Smaller size (more than a foot shorter overall than the four-door Mark) makes things easier in parking and city driving. Though the suspension is basically what you'd find under a Fairmont, extensive modifications (notably gas-filled strut/shock units) yield decent handling and road grip. Feel through the power steering is pretty good, as are steering effort and precision. For a unit-construction car, the Continental is impressively quiet, and rides with all the marshmallow smoothness of the bigger Lincolns. Interior decor is a bit too boudoir for us, and back seat space could be better. Performance is leisurely with either standard V-8 or optional V-6 engine, the formal roof styling makes the cabin dark and confining, and rated mileage barely hits the Mark's—in fact, the 5.0-liter Continental has the same EPA city rating as the bigger Lincolns. Hardly a great advance in small luxury cars, but a step in the right direction.

Lincoln Town Car and Mark VI

Unchanged for the second straight year, and still quite close to the big DeVille/Fleetwood in virtually every area of comparison. Cars like these don't make much sense to practical folk like us. Of course, buyers in this price bracket can afford to be extravagant, so mileage is relatively less important here. Still, the Cadillac's optional diesel V-8 does have a certain snob appeal, even if its poor reliability record so far doesn't. Lincoln has a slight edge in performance because its smooth, fuel-injected 5.0-liter (302-cid) V-8 has more muscle than any Cadillac engine this year. The Lincolns are also perhaps a bit quieter. There's little in it when it comes to room, ride, features, and price. In fact, the choice between these traditional rivals ends up as very much a matter of personal taste. Trouble is, a growing number of buyers are finding big luxury liners quite distasteful. And that explains why Lincoln has cast its new smaller Continental in the role of division flagship for '82.

Mercury Marquis

The upmarket LTD stays mostly the same for '82. Still without the appeal of a diesel option or, indeed, any real gain in mileage over 1981 levels. Remains attractive for some buyers because of its roomy interior, soft ride, low noise, and plush appointments. But many smaller cars offer those qualities plus much better economy and tidier road manners. Competes with B-body GM biggies like Buick LeSabre and Olds Delta 88, and a good alternative to them if you need a car this large.

General Motors Corporation

CARRYOVER MODELS from the General came out in the fall, but the country's biggest automaker has some brand-new cars still to come. Due in January are the redesigned A-body intermediates based on the front-wheel-drive, 104.9-inch-wheelbase body/chassis structure of the X-car compacts. They'll be marketed as the Buick Century, Chevrolet Celebrity, Oldsmobile Cutlass Ciera, and Pontiac 6000. External sheet-metal is different and suspensions slightly softer to set this quartet apart from the corresponding X-cars. Body types are limited to two- and four-door notchback sedans. All models have standard power steering and brakes and three-speed automatic transmission.

Also arriving in January is the third-generation Chevrolet Camaro/Pontiac Firebird. Both now share a 101-inch wheelbase, and are considerably shorter and lighter than their predecessors. Styling is all-new, and features a lift-up hatch rear window for extra cargo carrying versatility. The chassis is still rear drive, but updated by a switch to MacPherson struts for the front suspension and a torque-arm/coil-spring arrangement to locate the live rear axle. Steering is now rack-and-pinion, and all-disc brakes return as an option for the first time since 1969.

GM's workhorse four-cylinder engine, the 2.5-liter (151-cid) "Iron Duke" unit built by Pontiac, acquires the firm's new throttle-body fuel injection (TBI) system this year. TBI is said to result in a slight horsepower gain over last year's carbureted powerplant, and to improve driveability, particularly cold starting. The TBI 2.5 will see wide use at

GM, being standard on the base Camaro/Firebird, the A-body intermediates, and the X-car foursome. Other engine developments include a new diesel V-6 from Oldsmobile. With a displacement of 4.3 liters (262 cid), it's essentially a cut-down version of the 5.7-liter (350-cid) "smoker" V-8. It's available as an option in the new A-cars and in the rear drive intermediates, which are now called G-body in GM parlance. From Buick comes a 3.0-liter (181-cid) derivation of that division's well-tried 3.8-liter (231-cid) gasoline V-6. There are several internal changes, however, including a shorter stroke. For now, it will be limited to the Century and Ciera as the top power option.

Cadillac has a new engine, too—a 4.1-liter (250-cid) aluminum-block V-8, which becomes standard for all models except the little Cimarron. Last year's highly touted "V-8-6-4" is restricted to limousine service.

GM's other lines are basically unchanged except for minor exterior trim and drivetrain revisions. Lockup torque converters come to the big E-body front-drive coupes (Buick Riviera/Cadillac Eldorado/Oldsmobile Toronado) for the first time, and diesel power is now optionally available in all the G-body sedans, coupes, and wagons. Pontiac drops its full-size B-body Bonneville and transfers the name to what used to be the LeMans. At Buick, the former Century sedans and wagons become Regals, while Oldsmobile tags all its rear-drive intermediates Cutlass Supreme.

Buick Century

This year's new front-drive Century is essentially a softer, quieter, plusher extension of the Buick Skylark. See Oldsmobile Cutlass Ciera.

Buick Electra/LeSabre

A fine choice for those who want or need big-car virtues and can put up with (and afford) the vices. Main attractions are ride comfort, mechanical refinement, and convenience. Interiors are roomy enough for up to six, and the trunk will take their travel luggage with ease. Size and weight now seem more conspicuous. Not very practical for city use because of bulk and wide turning circle. Performance adequate with the gas engines, but borders on the sluggish on diesel models. Mileage is as you'd expect: 20 mpg or less overall with any of the gas engines, maybe 25 or so with the diesel. Can be expensive to maintain because of numerous power assists, and GM's diesel engine has a checkered repair record at best. Not as good value-for-money as the less expensive B-body Chevrolet Caprice/Impala or Ford's LTD unless the Buick name means something special to you.

Buick Regal

Basically the same car it has been since GM unveiled this series (redubbed G-body for '82) for 1978. Adding last year's Century sedans and wagon to the Regal line is an interim step to pave the way for the new front-drive Century. Regals offer stylish, comfortable accommodations for four (five, if you squeeze) in a reasonably sized, well-built package. Limited versions are the most luxurious. The turbocharged Sport Coupe has the most interesting performance and the best road manners. Diesel economy is balanced by a poor service record to date. Buick's V-6s are sturdy and reliable, however, and give smooth if not brilliant acceleration. Mileage figures are average. About as roomy but more refined than the Ford Granada/Mercury Cougar, and thriftier than Chrysler's New Yorker or the Dodge Diplomat/Plymouth Gran Fury.

Buick Riviera

Hardly the best example of front-wheel-drive efficiency, and slightly pretentious. A big, handsome, quiet car that's surprisingly well behaved on twisty roads. Handling is better with the optional Gran Touring suspension, but the standard chassis isn't bad, aside from marked body roll in tight corners. Heavy, so mileage and performance are both weak. The turbo engine delivers good straightline go. All-independent suspension absorbs the rough stuff with ease, and interior comfort is high despite a rather confined rear cabin. Wide roof pillars can be a nuisance at times. Trunk space is ample but not generous in relation to overall size. Upkeep can be costly, particularly on the turbo version. Diesel engine aids economy, but costs too much for what you save in fuel unless you drive a good many miles each year.

Buick Skylark

Potentially excellent family car of modern design spoiled for us by nagging reliability doubts. After more than two years on the market, all the X-cars, including Skylark, are still the subject of disturbing callbacks. The latest involves 245,000 1980-81 models for possible excess slippage in the self-adjusting clutch linkage and potential loss of braking control. Such bugs should have been worked out long ago, and do nothing to inspire owner confidence. Workmanship still varies quite a bit, and can't match that of the best-selling imports. Also, the drivetrain packaging seems to contribute to service costs, especially on V-6 models. Still appeals for interior space, decent economy, fine ride, and smooth road manners. New fuel injection system for '82 may help four-cylinder's modest performance and economy. Sum-up: Nice car despite flaws, and getting better. Skylark probably the best-looking member of the X-car foursome.

Cadillac Cimarron

Like its less expensive Chevrolet Cavalier and Pontiac J2000 relatives, quite good as it stands. However, there's still room for improvement. The biggest drawback is leisurely performance due to the wide-ratio gearing adopted for both the standard four-speed manual or optional three-speed automatic in the interest of mileage. We also suspect the output of the 1.8-liter (112-cid) four is a mite weak for the car's weight. Mileage isn't spectacular, except by Cadillac's yardstick, and the Cimarron's road manners won't threaten price competitors like the Audi 4000 or BMW 320i. On the plus side, noise levels are low, space utilization good (though the narrow front footwells feel confining), seats comfy, dash and control layout thoughtfully done, and appointments tasteful. Fit-and-finish quite high for a domestic. Startling price against Cavalier/J2000, but not far above that of the cheaper models comparably equipped. Only one question, though: who's the intended buyer?

Cadillac DeVille/Fleetwood

New standard 4.1-liter (250-cid) V-8 has the same power but less torque than the Buick V-6, so Cadillac's engineering efforts hardly seem worth it. We doubt the V-8 will prove any more efficient than the V-6. Remembering, too, that last year's injection system caused numerous owner servicing headaches, we wonder whether this year's digital setup will be any more reliable. All this may not matter much, because big luxury cars are out, small luxury cars are in, judging by the sales charts. If you must have a DeVille/Fleetwood, we think you should get the relatively simple carbureted V-6. The optional diesel is second choice, primarily because its service record is none too good to date. As for the rest of it, the full-size Cadillacs remain what they've always been: roomy, quiet, comfortable, and luxurious carriages, with tolerably good road manners and a silky ride. Workmanship seems to have slipped lately, however.

Cadillac Eldorado

Our comments on the new V-8 under DeVille/Fleetwood also apply to the swanky Eldorado. Briefly, we're skeptical this engine will do much, if anything, for this heavy car's dismal mileage despite a sophisticated (and potentially trouble-prone) design. In other respects, our previous assessment of the Eldorado still holds. For a cushy coupe, handling and roadholding are surprisingly agile, due mainly to front-wheel drive and a well thought out all-independent suspension. Ride is in the Cadillac tradition, as are the sybaritic interior furnishings and numerous comfort and convenience gadgets. The V-6 offers the best blend of performance and economy, though neither are noteworthy. The diesel ups mpg at the expense of pickup, which is laggardly and annoying in change-of-pace city/suburban driving. We see no reason for preferring the Eldorado over the less costly Riviera or Toronado unless you must ride behind the Cadillac crest.

Cadillac Seville

Faces a direct competitor in the new lookalike Lincoln Continental. The Cadillac offers the superior traction and space utilization of front-wheel drive, while the Lincoln has the simplicity of conventional rear drive, which may prove to make it the cheaper car to maintain. Last year's quirky "V-8-6-4" powerplant tarnished Cadillac's reputation for engineering excellence, and makes us wonder about the reliability of its aluminum-block successor, particularly its electronic injection system. Both cars offer all the opulence anyone could want. The Lincoln may have the edge in roadability, and perhaps quality control, too. Neither is very economical, which probably won't bother most buyers in this lofty price bracket. The Seville has a plus in its diesel V-8, and a minus in that engine's higher-than-expected incidence of repairs over the years.

Chevrolet Camaro

Much more agile and handy over the road than its hulky predecessor, and a bit more practical. Performance with standard four-cylinder engine is sedate. The V-6 gives reasonable off-the-line dig and smooth if not really quiet cruising ability with automatic. Too bad the four-speed manual shift linkage is stiff and clumsy and the clutch heavy. The carbureted V-8 will probably be the compromise choice for most buyers. The injected version on the Z-28 feels very strong. All Camaros have a firm ride and hang on very well in corners with minimal body lean, especially the Z-28. Brakes a little touchy on a couple of the cars we tried, and hard stops produced more nosedive than expected. Feels more spacious inside than the old model, though the rear seat is still mainly for show. At least it now flips down to enlarge the cargo area. Jazzy dash is laid out well. Comfy front seats, good outward vision.

Chevrolet Caprice/Impala

Virtually unchanged this year. Continues to swap points with the Ford LTD. Despite its size, can be surprisingly well behaved off the straight and narrow when equipped with the low-cost F41 suspension package. Performance lackluster with any available engine, especially the diesel, which we recommend only if you're a high-mileage owner who puts economy above all else. Remains a fine example of the fast-dying big car breed.

Chevrolet Cavalier

Off to a strong start, despite prices that make buyers grumble. The most completely equipped Chevy in history, but many imports deliver comparable features for less money. Intelligent design makes good use of available interior room, though all the J-cars are best considered four-seaters. Smooth-running engine and tight construction keep noise levels refreshingly low for the class. Handling and roadholding okay with standard suspension; budget-priced F41 package improves both markedly without upsetting ride. Attractive interior decor, fine outward vision in the notchbacks and wagon, good cargo space, comfortable driving stance, convenient controls. Even though hampered by an automatic, our test car returned a gratifying 27 mpg, besting the EPA estimate by one mpg. Complaints are few. Acceleration is lazy, particularly with automatic. Assembly quality is high for a domestic, but still short of Japanese levels. Conclusion: not top value-for-money, but practical, refined, and well made.

Chevrolet Celebrity

New front-drive mid-size destined to replace the rear-drive Malibu. Behaves much like a Citation, but is quieter and softer-riding. On some surfaces, especially gently rolling waves, it's almost too soft. Body lean not excessive for a family car, but we'd prefer slightly firmer springs and shocks than the standard chassis provides. The power-assisted rack-and-pinion steering is geared up fairly high for minimal wheel flailing and has good accuracy, but it's too light and lacks adequate feel in the straight-ahead position. Chevy claims quietness is in the Caprice league, but we noted marked tire roar on coarse surfaces and a bit too much fan noise from the four-cylinder engine. Not a strong performer in any form. Interior has room for three adults in the rear providing front-seaters give up some legroom. Outward vision is good, and the driving position well chosen even without power seat or tilt wheel. Serviceability with Chevy's narrower-angle gas V-6 a little better than with the 90-degree engine on Olds Ciera and Buick Century, but still no prize. Verdict: competent, modern replacement for Malibu and its ilk.

Chevrolet Chevette

Low price, good mileage, and fine durability record keep Chevette sales strong despite its old-fashioned engineering. The new diesel engine earns a laudable 40-mpg EPA city rating, and serves up smooth, if leisurely, performance. It should sell like hotcakes despite a steep price. The overdrive gearing of this year's optional five-speed transmission should help highway cruising ability with either engine. Outmoded rear-drive layout and aging body/chassis design mean a jiggly ride, limited interior room, and only so-so handling and roadholding. Not well equipped (even less so as the Scooter) to keep the price down, and finish is crude in places. Makes a certain amount of sense as low-cost urban transport, but not for all-around use.

Chevrolet Citation

We're less enthusiastic about the X-cars now, including the top-selling Citation. The main reason is continuing owner complaints of mechanical problems that still occasion recalls after two years of production. It's unclear whether such defects are due to insufficient engineering development or poor work on the assembly line, but they can't be ignored. Too bad, because on paper the Citation and its relatives are admirable. Front-wheel drive gives good roadholding and easy handling. The compact drivetrain also means a roomy interior for the overall size. Economy is good, though not exceptional, and performance is sprightly with the optional V-6. With its hatchback body, Citation can be a versatile, commodious load carrier for a family vacation. The car is pleasant to drive, offers splendid visibility, and doesn't bounce you around on rough roads. But being good on paper and in practice are two different things. GM apparently needs a bit more practice.

Chevrolet Corvette

Not a rational car, nor one that's fairly judged by common sense. Chevy wants to gain field experience with this year's four-speed-overdrive automatic and "Cross-Fire" fuel injection before introducing the rest of the 1983 design. Both contribute to fuel efficiency, but talking about that in a car like this is silly. As always, Corvette's appeal is to the young and young at heart, who can put up with a cramped interior, bouncy ride, ludicrous luggage provisions, and cop-stopping style.

Chevrolet Malibu/Monte Carlo

Newly available 5.7-liter (350-cid) diesel V-8 will cheer mileage-minded buyers, but its drawbacks won't. These include messy refueling, lower performance, noisier operation (though GM's diesel isn't loud or harsh), and a substantial price penalty. Otherwise, these mostly unchanged models offer relaxed highway performance, good comfort for front seaters, passable rear seat room (though entry/exit on the Monte Carlo isn't easy), and safe if uninspired road manners. The F41 suspension option costs peanuts, brings a welcome improvement in handling control, and doesn't ride like a mechanical bull. The Malibu sedan and wagon are preferred for their better passenger accommodation and utility. Overall, a bland bunch, but good value.

Oldsmobile Cutlass Ciera

Very nice smaller mid-size model, Oldsmobile's version of GM's front drive A-car. Floorpan and central passenger cell shared with the compact X-cars, so about as roomy as an Omega and not far behind the bigger Cutlass Supreme in most dimensions. Attention to body and chassis isolation results in modest wind, road, and engine noise. Suspension tuning favors ride, but front-drive pull helps the car take corners without theatrics. Some front-end mushiness over wavy roads suggests springs and shocks could be usefully firmer. Standard power steering too light, but gearing is right for car to be jockeyed around easily. Good control spacings and clear outward vision. Ample trunk space, but high rear sill makes loading heavy items awkward. Economy very good on diesel, but crowded underhood area implies costly extra labor time for routine servicing. That also applies to the gas V-6, particularly with air conditioning. Performance only leisurely with the diesel or standard gasoline four, adequate with the V-6. In all, a symbol of today's priorities.

Oldsmobile Cutlass Supreme

One of the country's consistent best-sellers. Coupes sacrifice a little legroom for sportier looks. Front seat room and comfort rates high in all Cutlasses, as do ride and general running refinement. Diesel models are predictably noisier than gas-engine versions, and have more leisurely acceleration. Substantially higher cost makes us leery of recommending the diesel except to those who drive at least 20,000 miles or more a year. Even so, the troublesome repair history of the 5.7-liter V-8 brings up the subject of false economy. We hope the new-for-'82 diesel V-6 proves more reliable. The usual pillowy Detroit ride and rather modest handling and roadholding. Nice interior decor, except for some of the velour fabrics. Apart from diesel dithers, repair record pretty good since this series appeared for 1978. Conclusion: aging well.

Oldsmobile Delta 88/Ninety-Eight

GM's current full-size cars seemed quite daring five years ago, but now seem just as out of proportion to most customer needs as their outlandish predecessors did. In fairness, big cars don't come much better than this. Both 88 and Ninety-Eight offer full six-passenger room and comfort, smooth if sometimes queasy ride motions, and very low overall noise levels. Ninety-Eight approaches Cadillac standards of luxury. Fuel economy is reasonable for the size and weight of these models, particularly in diesel form. Beware, however, persistent complaints of clogged fuel injectors, as well as fuel pumps that pack up early and dealer service that ranges from bone-headed to brilliant. As in most cars of this sort, roadability is let down by too-soft springing and too much unsprung weight. Acceleration adequate with the gasoline engines, but the diesel will seem too slow for some. Good but not astounding quality control in light of today's much higher prices. Deserves consideration if you put a premium on king-size comfort and are willing to pay it.

Oldsmobile Omega

Omega and its corporate cousins are easy-to-like, practical family cars, but we recommend them with less conviction than we used to because of troubling mechanical bugs GM can't seem to squash. That apart, a virtual twin to Buick Skylark. Opinion: still thoroughly up-to-date, but unsolved mechanical ills take the luster off a basically sound concept.

Oldsmobile Toronado

Little changed since the first 1979 model in this series. Front wheel drive alone does not make a paragon of engineering efficiency—Toronado is too big and heavy for that. However, it gets around surprisingly well, mainly because of the sophisticated all-independent suspension. Ride is butter-smooth on all but the roughest roads, and cornering is poised and stable, providing you don't ask the car to do things it was never intended to do. What it does best is transport four people in opulent peace over long distances on the highway. The rear seat feels closed in because of the formal-look roof, which also hampers the driver's view over-the-shoulder when parking or changing lanes. Acceleration is merely adequate with either available gas engine. The diesel seems downright slow, but returns more acceptable mpg. Continuing complaints of clogged diesel fuel injectors, though, make this engine our third choice.

Pontiac Bonneville/Grand Prix

This year's Bonneville is a mid-size, essentially a retitled LeMans. As before, there's little to choose between this Pontiac and the equivalent Buick Regal, Olds Cutlass, and Chevy Malibu for performance, economy, or passenger space. Engine offerings are more alike than ever. All are smooth-riding, pleasantly appointed cars of reasonable proportions, with decent handling, middling mileage, and adequate acceleration. Similarly, the G-special Grand Prix is much like the Regal, Cutlass, and Chevy Monte Carlo coupes under the skin. We prefer any of these over Ford's Thunderbird/XR-7 duo or the Chrysler Cordoba/Dodge Mirada.

Pontiac Firebird

Downsized and virtually all-new. Should be a lot more liveable as day-to-day transportation than the overweight, impractical second-generation design. (See Chevrolet Camaro.)

Pontiac J2000

Assessment: promising new small car that needs only more go, a lower price, and a less plasticky feel to be top-notch buy. (See Chevrolet Cavalier.)

Pontiac Phoenix

As appealing as ever because of compact size, ample passenger space, and successful ride/handling blend. The switch to fuel injection this year may clear up two blemishes common to four-cylinder X-cars—erratic engine running under peak accessory load and rather slow throttle response. Horsepower is up slightly, but pickup with automatic will probably continue to be modest. Pity no development work has been done on the balky manual shift linkage. Like other X-cars, has a history of mechanical troubles and worrisome recalls. Plus points include comfortable driving posture, good outward vision (especially in the five-door sedan), and ample luggage space. Standard equipment not generous; rather utilitarian in base form. Our view: now lags behind Chrysler's rapidly improving K-cars for mileage and overall value-for-money, but has the performance edge with its optional V-6.

Pontiac 6000

A solid improvement over its rear-drive predecessor, which lives on as this year's Bonneville G. (See Chevrolet Celebrity.)

Pontiac T1000

What goes for Chevette goes for its clone. In brief: worth considering because of price, but down on refinement, interior room, and finish compared to most rivals. (See Chevrolet Chevette.)

Imports

Audi 4000

One of our favorites since it debuted two years ago, the 4000 line just seems to get better and better. This past year we tested the now-discontinued 5+5 sedan and the new Coupe, both with injected five-cylinder engine from the larger 5000. Both offer lively performance, crisp handling, fine road grip, excellent front seating and driving position, and a smooth, supple ride. Construction quality is first-rate, as expected of a German product, and enhances the smooth-running engine and slick manual shift linkage. Negatives include interior furnishings that may seem too plain for some buyers and mileage that's only in the low 20s overall. Four-cylinder models are more economical but less punchy. Visibility in the Coupe suffers because of bulky rear-quarter roofline, but it is superb in the sedans. Repair record now confirmed as much better than that of the 4000's trouble-prone predecessor, the Fox. A bit pricey, but well worth the money.

Audi 5000

Regardless of engine, a sophisticated, well-mannered machine offering a roomy interior, high-quality craftsmanship, and very un-sedan-like roadability. Performance is adequate with the normally aspirated gas engine, snail-slow with the diesel, but smooth and brisk with the turbo. Excellent driving position and big windows aid town driving. Interior a bit austere by U.S. standards, but nicely finished. Complex mechanical layout discourages home maintenance, and dealer service can cost a mint. Unlike its predecessor, the balky 100LS, the 5000 enjoys a good reliability record so far. Fuel economy only fair on Turbo, average to very good on other models. Expensive compared to most domestics, but reasonably priced next to other premium Europeans. Pleasant to drive, satisfying to own.

Datsun Maxima

Both gas and diesel Maximas disappointed us. The diesel proved pretty quick for an oil-burner, with little vibration and tolerably low noise levels. Start-up waiting time is commendably brief. Perhaps because of its automatic transmission, the Maxima Diesel wasn't all that hot for mileage, though. This leaves us wondering why anyone would pay extra for the loss in performance with no significant gain in economy. Despite its extra horsepower, the gasoline model wasn't all that peppy either, though again refinement was high. Even though the Maxima is fairly large, its interior accommodations are limited, particularly headroom. Trunk space is below expectations, and the ride is unexpectedly lumpy for a luxury model with all-independent suspension. Road manners are only adequate, and the long snout makes garage maneuvering tricky. The dash looks impressive, but has too many separate pieces that don't line up properly. Workmanship is generally below the usually high Japanese standards. Judgment: average in too many areas.

Nissan (Datsun) Stanza

New front-wheel-drive replacement for the rear-drive Datsun 510. Follows now-customary industry thinking with transversely mounted four-cylinder engine, standard five-speed overdrive manual gearbox, all-independent suspension, and rack-and-pinion steering. Known as the X-Series in corporate lingo, the Stanza engine is an all-new overhead cam design incorporating NAPS (Nissan Anti-Pollution System) features like crossflow cylinder head with two spark plugs per cylinder plus swirl induction ports. Not yet tested by us. On paper, looks like a solid improvement over the 510, primarily because of more efficient packaging that should result in a much roomier interior than the 510's. Front drive may also benefit roadability, not a big attraction on the previous model. No doubt mileage will be very good, though just how good remains to be seen. Could well be a top contender among small to middle-size economy cars.

Datsun 200-SX

Toyota has a completely new competitor for the 200-SX this year, but the Datsun should still compare favorably against the '82 Celica. A thoroughly pleasing little sportster offering smooth performance, fine mileage, good overall visibility, a comfortable driving position, beautiful instruments, loads of convenience features, and solid assembly. The extra torque of this year's larger 2.2-liter (133-cid) engine should enhance flexibility in city driving, which was good already. Refinement is a strong suit, the 200-SX being generally restful and not too buzzy in most situations. Easy to drive thanks to light, high-geared steering and compact size. Handling and roadholding only average; the main problem is a tendency to break rear-end traction in tight turns taken quickly in the rain. Puny fresh-air ventilation remains a shortcoming, and the extremely limited back seat accommodations are literally that. Overall, still a very enticing, high-style package.

Datsun 210

Untouched for '82. A rather ordinary small car with several drawbacks that keep it from being good all-around transportation. Sluggish acceleration (even with manual transmission), a bouncy ride, and poor rear seat accommodations are the biggest sore points. Handling is marked by lots of understeer and low limits of grip in hard cornering, but steering is light and reasonably accurate. A good driving position and typical Japanese control layout enhance driving ease, but feeble ventilation detracts from passenger comfort. Fuel economy is still near the top of the list, and simple mechanicals imply lower maintenance costs than for some front-drive rivals. In short, a serviceable commuter car, but not one of the best. An enviable durability record helps offset design limitations.

Datsun 280ZX

Comes off more as a luxury cruiser than as a sports car. The last ZX we tested, the '81 Turbo two-seater with automatic, was spoiled most by an annoyingly jiggly ride on patchwork city streets and by a cabin that is adequately spacious but feels cramped. The turbocharged engine gives brilliant performance and predictably spendthrift fuel consumption. Body roll is controlled well, but the power steering is numb, and the car too heavy to be really agile. Sumptuous interior, but seats curiously mediocre. Not much luggage space, mostly due to the sloping roof. Back seat in the longer-wheelbase 2 + 2 is only a token gesture. Workmanship on the last few Datsuns we've sampled isn't as good as we've come to expect from this maker, paint finish in particular. Despite the turbo engine's greater complexity, service access is quite good. One of our testers described it as "the Ford LTD of sports cars," which pretty well sums it up.

Datsun 310

Datsun's second attempt at a front-wheel-drive minicar is not up to the best in this hotly competitive field. This year's new E-Series engine may answer two of our previous criticisms—noisy operation and rather dull performance. The rest of the design is unchanged, however, so this will remain a rather cramped small car with a stiff ride and only average handling and roadholding. Small size, tight turning circle, and quick steering are a help in congested traffic and in parking. Hatchback convenience is a plus, though the high rear sill on the curiously styled three-door coupe means you have to heave heavy objects a long way off the ground. Standard-guise models are adequately but not generously equipped; the GX models have more no-cost extras. Finish leaves something to be desired, especially the interior, which comes off a bit cut-rate. Still strikes us as not as thoroughly developed as opponents like the Honda Civic, but should be frugal and cheap to maintain.

Honda Accord

One of our favorite—and most highly rated—cars of the past year, so we're eager to see the effects of this year's body revisions. We haven't examined the new model yet, but it appears Honda has rebodied the Accord even though styling is much the same as before. The extra 2.8 inches in wheelbase length and one-inch greater overall width should mean slightly more leg and shoulder room compared to the first-generation model, which wasn't noted for an overabundance of passenger space. Honda also says the Accord's 1.7-liter (107-cubic inch) four has been given some subtle refinements. We hope they won't detract from the 1981 model's easy-revving, smooth-running nature. Suspension design and mechanical layout are mostly the same, so this should remain one of the better handling and riding small cars. It should also continue to be one of the best built, barring any gaffes in Honda's usually meticulous quality control. Well-equipped, but not a bargain.

Honda Civic

Largely unchanged from last year, and still at the head of our small-car list for pep, mileage, refinement, and solid construction. The Civic's main drawback for some buyers will be passenger room limited by the car's small external dimensions. Front seat room is adequate in all models, due mainly to long-travel seat tracks. The three-door has a shorter wheelbase than the sedan and wagon, however, so its back seat is very cramped for adults unless front seaters share some of their space. In other respects the Civic is hard to fault. It's zippy without being buzzy, and squeezes lots of miles from each gallon. Other pluses include nimble handling, relaxed highway cruising (with five-speed), first-rate assembly quality, nicely tailored interior, neat dash, and good all-around visibility. Still some torque-steer reaction through the steering; attention to tire pressures a must to keep this minimal. Last test car suffered a notchy shifter and a carburetion fault that made smooth driving difficult, especially going around corners. Still a model of small-car excellence.

Honda Prelude

Billed as "the sports car for adults," but more a sporty Civic with less usable passenger room. The car will take four adults, but those in front must move their seats up far enough to be in fetal position. Trunk is small but boxy; a pity the back seat doesn't fold down. Otherwise, a very refined little car. Pleasant to drive, with light and direct steering, smooth cornering, and a comfortable ride for its size. New gauge layout is much easier to read, though dash still looks busy. Driver's seat rather buried, but outward vision still very good. Long-travel seat track allows nearly legs-out posture for taller pilots. Noisy on the highway with the optional automatic, mostly because of the low final gearing that keeps the engine turning over frantically. Also rather sluggish, because the slushbox has two fewer gears than the five-speed. Mileage unexceptional, too. Loaded with goodies, but hardly cheap. Built like a fine watch. Conclusion: pocket-size personal car. Far more pleasant than the domestic Ford EXP/Mercury LN7, but a Mazda RX-7 it isn't.

Mazda GLC

Tested most recently by us in newly available four-door sedan form. Our real-world mileage worked out to 32.9 mpg, which confirms the 35 mpg EPA city rating. Engine delivers adequate pickup, but feels and sounds harsh going up through gears. Tire roar and some exhaust-induced body resonance mar refinement in highway driving. Easy to whirl around in tight spaces. Ride not too firm except over sharp bumps. Seats could stand some additional padding and better shaping. Logical, well-arranged dash; good major control relationships. Sedan's trunk borders on the cavernous, and the split-back rear seat can be flopped down to increase load space as on the hatchbacks. Feels structurally less solid than Honda's Civic, and there's some evidence of cost-cutting in the grade of interior trim used. Against this, price is very competitive and reliability/durability so far appears very good. Opinion: an appealing car at an appealing price.

Mazda RX-7

Very well-designed and quite snappy two-seater. High-winding rotary engine has finally earned its stripes for reliability/durability, according to reports reaching us. Its strong performance is enhanced by the well-spaced ratios of the five-speed manual gearbox. Refinement marred mainly by exhaust boom at high rpm. Cantankerous to start in sub-freezing weather. Ride firm but not jolting like the Porsche 924 can be. Takes corners like a go-kart except in the rain, when the rear end can slide readily under sudden power application. Steering heavy at parking pace, pleasant on the move. First-class placement of major and minor controls, but cockpit is snug for those approaching six-foot height. Mazda's usual thorough and tidy assembly, but door panels look decidedly low-buck. Only fair mileage (around 19 mpg) puts a damper on our enthusiasm. The best sports car value around, in our opinion.

Mazda 626

Comparable to the Toyota Corolla and the now-discontinued Datsun 510 in size and design. Main detractions are a buzzy, harsh-sounding powerplant and mileage that's below par for this size, weight, and engine displacement. Other shortcomings are tediously heavy steering and sharp suspension reaction over frost heaves, transverse ridges, and the like. Cabin features nicely tailored seats, sufficient room for four medium-size adults (though headroom is a bit tight), and carefully applied trim of good quality. Well-chosen control spacings and a neatly arranged dash make things comfortably convenient behind the wheel. Fold-down asymmetrically split rear seatback is great for utility in a notchback design. Generous no-cost standards. Reliability record to date much better than average, and conventional drivetrain layout should reduce repair downtime and cost. Sum-up: lacks mechanical refinement, but excellent value-for-money.

Subaru

Generally sound value-for-money package. Rather dull performance but good fuel economy from somewhat harsh engine. Firm but not bouncy ride, though big bumps and dips are felt. Braking marred by premature rear-wheel lockup in panic stops and a fair degree of nosedive. Tire noise resonates through the body on coarsely paved roads. Easy to whirl around in traffic, though manual steering a bit heavy for parking. Outward vision poses no problems. Interior a bit small for large adults, and fore/aft front seat travel could be usefully longer. Good major control spacings. Dash neatly organized, but has a slight jukebox look. Interior trim not rich-looking, but assembly and detail work carefully done. Prices are reasonable, and equipment pretty generous, particularly on GL models. Repair record very good.

Toyota Celica and Supra

Fully redesigned this year, so firm evaluation awaits a full road test. The four-cylinder Celicas shouldn't be too much different on the road than their '81 counterparts given the mostly carryover chassis and drive-trains. Toyota's 22R four is heavy for its displacement and doesn't produce a lot of power, but does give a reasonable blend of performance and fuel economy. The more extensive changes in the Supra should make it a real road-burner, notably the independent rear suspension and twin-cam six-cylinder engine. Colleagues who've driven the new models in Japan report both have very fine road manners, seat comfort, furnishings, and ride. Prediction: Supra will be stronger competition for Datsun's ZX even without a turbocharged engine. Celica should continue its winning ways, provided the new styling goes over.

Toyota Corolla

An orthodox rear-drive economy car that's average in most ways, better than average in a few. Capable little engine delivers spunky performance for the class plus excellent mileage. Small size and light steering combine with good outward vision and handy turning circle to make light work of parking and city traffic. Road manners nothing special, with a bit too much body roll and a simply located rear axle that can hop slightly if the corners are bumpy. Ride okay, subject to occasional fore/aft pitching and sharp vertical bounce. Braking effort needs better front/rear proportioning; rear end hops in hard, anchors-out stops. Like most cars in this size class, Corolla has limited rear seat room for adults. Front seat room is adequate without being generous. Seat comfort not a strong point on previous models, may be better with redesigned chairs on the '82s. Simple, sturdy drivetrain. Very good workmanship. Verdict: a safe bet for reliability and mileage, but not the most space-efficient or smooth-riding small car around.

Toyota Corona

A posh little family car stays mostly the same this year. Strong points include very refined engine and well-insulated passenger compartment with ample front seat space and plush trimmings. Suspension is set up to favor a soft ride, which it delivers at the expense of handling and road grip. Rear end can be thrown off line occasionally by sharp bumps. Easy to drive, the engine being exceptionally well behaved during cold start and warmup. Performance not really zippy, but satisfactory in most situations. Mileage now rates very good. Driving position comfortable despite crowded front footwells. Well-organized if slightly busy dash, clear instruments, handy minor controls. Versatile heating/ventilation system. Liftback sedan's foldable rear backrests a boon for cargo space in a little luxury liner. Finish rates high marks. Price now a bit high relative to size and passenger accommodation. In brief: boring but capable. High price offset some by numerous standard features and the terrific reliability/durability record of this Corona series.

Toyota Cressida

Completely revamped last year, little changed for '82. Toyota's answer to the Datsun Maxima. Size pits Cressida against U.S. compact/mid-size models, yet the Toyota is heavier and has lower fuel economy. Usable rear seat space comparable to that of GM's G-body cars or the Fairmont/Zephyr. Headroom is restricted for taller adults front and back. Smooth straight-six engine and unobtrusive overdrive automatic transmission plus well-sealed cabin. Ride is soft but a tad floaty, handling soggy. Sumptuous cabin appointments matched by thorough attention to detail assembly. Driving position and outward vision okay. Dash design more restrained than Maxima's, and trunk space is better, too. Underhood layout is tidy, but complexities of injection and emissions plumbing will deter home mechanics. Not unreasonably priced considering all the standard goodies.

Toyota Starlet

Chevette-like rear-drive minicar new last year. Designed mainly for high mileage. Our overall mpg for a 60/40 mix of hard city/highway driving worked out to 36 mpg (last year's city rating was 39), and a spot check showed a phenomenal 52 on the highway. Small and light, so moves in and out of tight spots with ease, aided by pleasantly direct steering and clear outward vision. Handling is agile, panic braking causes no unwanted rear-axle hop. Ride is not so hot, a function of the fairly stiff springing and petite 90.6-inch wheelbase. Rather limited passenger room. Modest luggage space and high load floor. Well-built. Clean engine installation will delight do-it-yourselfers. In all, strictly a commuter car, but a very nice one.

Toyota Tercel

A successful design despite ungainly styling. Front-drive packaging provides surprising interior room for the short overall length. The front compartment is not particularly spacious, but satisfactory for adults on long trips. The rear is cramped, and the seat too short and thinly padded. Terrific handling, roadholding, and maneuverability thanks to quick steering, front-drive "pull," and a well-balanced suspension. Performance adequate considering only 62 horses are available. Superb all-round visibility. Luggage space meager on two-door sedans. Liftbacks and four-doors offer extra versatility of fold-down back seat. High standard of workmanship, though cheaper versions show some bare metal inside, and look built down to a price. Our view: a beautiful buy at an attractive price.

Volkswagen Quantum

The renamed, rebodied successor to the Volkswagen Dasher. Wheelbase is slightly longer (100 inches versus the previous 97.2) for a claimed gain in passenger room. Just out, so we'll reserve final judgment for now. Inherits much of the Dasher's mechanicals and chassis design, so Quantum performance, handling, roadholding, and braking should all be similar—which is to say very good. Most of the extra wheelbase length has apparently gone into providing more back seat space. Despite slightly greater size, Quantum is supposed to return 33 mpg in combined city/highway driving. Engineered for light weight like the Dasher, and this together with super-long gearing in the standard "4+E" overdrive manual transmission helps mileage. Curiously, the Dasher's diesel option isn't continued, but may arrive later.

Volkswagen Rabbit/Jetta

Still good buys, though not top value for money because of steadily rising prices. Biggest plus points are good interior space utilization (though the back seat is a bit cramped for adults), fine assembly quality, good all-around vision, and nimbleness. Earns average marks for noise, though both engines run smoothly. Sparse instrumentation and slightly awkward "sit-up-and-beg" driving posture. Ride firm, jolts only over really big bumps and heaves. Rabbit has hatchback versatility, Jetta has deceptively huge trunk. Service access easy as pie with the diesel, okay on gas models. Diesel mileage is astounding, performance not too good. Gasoline mileage much lower, pickup much better. Dealer service can be costly. Sum-up: once the standard of minicar design, but eclipsed in space- and fuel-efficiency by some newer competitors. Still recommended, with reservations about the diesel because of oil leaks.

Volkswagen Scirocco

We haven't driven this year's restyled Scirocco yet, but it would appear the all-new body has not diminished the fun-loving nature of the previous model. Road manners are reportedly still sharp and poised, and comfort is said to be improved due to revised front seats and a more compliant ride. The '82 is also said to be quieter, thanks to extra sound-deadening and the new body's smoother shape that produces less wind noise. Performance should be about the same as last year's car, because weight is up only a little and could be offset by minor changes to engine tune or transmission gearing. Mileage should be little different also, though reduced air drag may show up as a tiny gain in EPA-rated highway fuel economy. Assessment: a little more practical and refined version of a sporty coupe favorite.

Volvo

Roomy, practical, and solid as a rock. All models retain the familiar, old-fashioned, boxy body that gives comfortably upright seating, good outward vision, and ample passenger space all-around. Sedans have decent trunk space; wagon cargo bay is cavernous. Firm, supportive seats. Easy to park thanks to light, accurate power steering, standard on all models. Handling and roadholding only average, but hold no unpleasant surprises. The GLT rates above average because of its stiffer suspension and grippier tires. However, its ride is thumpier and noisier. All models have all-disc brakes that are powerful and reassuring. Good control layout and commanding driving position, too, but we dislike the way the radio is buried just above the transmission hump in front of the shifter. Performance and mileage depend on engine. The V-6 disappoints on both counts. The turbo-four is very strong low down, but feels harsh and has a boomy exhaust. The diesel six is hard pressed to provide much pickup off the line, but it's fine for the highway. The standard four is smooth-revving, tolerably quiet, surprisingly muscular. All Volvos a bit expensive, but still good value.

 New Cars

Audi 4000 is our pick among what might be called the "premium" imports. Though not as luxurious as the similarly priced Datsun Maxima or Toyota Cressida, it rivals the costlier BMW 320i for handling and roadholding ability. Like the BMW, the 4000 is made in Germany, and build quality is topnotch even though interior decor seems austere at this price. Delightful to drive thanks to front-wheel-drive pull, excellent steering, and supple suspension that also gives a comfortably controlled ride. Thriftier than almost all class competitors except the Volkswagen Jetta, which uses the 4000's standard 1.7-liter (105-cubic inch) four-cylinder gasoline engine. New for the 4000 this year is a diesel option, also from VW, with an impressive 38-mpg EPA city mileage rating. For spirited performance there's the recently announced Audi Coupe, a high-style fastback derivative of the 4000 bodyshell powered by the five-cylinder engine from the larger 5000 series. Other pluses include picture-window vision in sedans, relaxed driving position, great front seats, and cleanly styled dash. Minuses are rather slim rear seat room, so-so engine access, and rather pricey parts and service. In all, a true sports sedan and something of a bargain in its class.

Buick Century, Chevrolet Celebrity, Oldsmobile Cutlass Ciera, and Pontiac 6000 make up GM's new A-body family of front-wheel-drive family cars. They're being marketed as intermediates even though their wheelbase and central body structure are shared with the "compact" X-cars (Buick Skylark, Chevrolet Citation, et al). Because the A-cars aren't due until next January, prices weren't set at this writing. Nevertheless, we'll give them a conditional "Best Buy" endorsement based on our early test drives of pre-production models. All have slightly less interior room than the larger G-body rear-drive cars they'll eventually replace, but their ride and refinement are at least as good, if not better. Other virtues include capable (though not sporty) handling, nice cabin appointments, ample trunk space, and good outward vision. Fuel economy is attractive with the standard four-cylinder gas engine or optional diesel V-6. Performance is adequate with either of these, and there's an extra-cost gas V-6 for more spirited go. Our main reservations concern a crowded engine bay, which may aggravate maintenance costs, and prices likely to be higher than for GM's old-style intermediates. In all, this is a very capable quartet that takes the sensible X-car design up a class in comfort and style. Let's hope prices aren't out of sight and reliability woes don't crop up.

Chrysler LeBaron and **Dodge 400** could easily be dismissed as simply more luxurious renditions of the front-drive K-car, but that's selling them short. Chrysler has made important revisions to the basic platform— enough that LeBaron/400 emerges with a personality all its own. Among the most noticeable changes are better sound isolation in the body and suspension that results in very low levels of noise from all sources, plus tighter construction and a less thumpy ride compared to earlier K-cars. Other praiseworthy features of the Dodge Aries/Plymouth Reliant are retained, like the roomy interior, commanding driving position, deceptively large trunk, and pleasing mileage figures. The standard Chrysler-built "Trans-4" engine doesn't provide neck-snapping getaway, but it's smooth and reasonably quiet. It's also one of the best engines anywhere for service accessibility. Prices are attractive, and the convertible coming at mid-year is sure to be a showroom draw.

Datsun 200-SX again gets the nod as the "Best Buy" in a small sporty coupe. It's stylish, well-appointed, and quite refined. Its principal drawbacks are a hobbit-size back seat and (in the notchback hardtop) a trunk to match. In other respects, the 200-SX is still as impressive as it has been since the current design appeared two years ago. For 1982, Datsun has boosted engine displacement a little to gain more torque, which makes for a less busy engine (especially with automatic) and slightly quicker acceleration. Despite this, mileage remains in the minicar league. The suspension isn't sophisticated, but works very well. Ride is smooth on most roads, and the handling nimble. The front seat area is roomy and comfortable, instrumentation is neat and complete, and handy convenience features abound. Quieter, smoother-running, and more economical than the Dodge Challenger/Plymouth Sapporo; trades points with Toyota's redesigned four-cylinder '82 Celica. All in all, the 200-SX remains a real charmer despite stronger competition from Datsun's arch-rival.

Dodge Aries and **Plymouth Reliant** were new last year, and sold well enough to keep Chrysler from going under. For 1982, the emphasis is on detail refinements. Useful changes include a self-propping hood, roll-down rear door glass in sedans and wagons, a reworked front suspension for a softer ride and better cornering stability, and additional big-car options like power windows and reclining bucket seats. Mileage and performance are in the same league with GM's X-car foursome, but the K-cars have proven more trouble-free, at least so far. Because of that, the Chrysler products look like a better bet if you're looking for a front-wheel-drive car suitable for all-around family transportation duty. The standard equipment list was lengthened for mid-'81, and Chrysler's hold-the-line pricing on base '82 models is a refreshing change from the usual hikes that occur with depressing regularity these days. Assembly quality is better now, too, though there's still room for improvement. Last year we said Aries/Reliant deserved to succeed. This year, they deserve top honors for value in the compact-car class.

Dodge Omni and **Plymouth Horizon** have been appealing small cars ever since their 1978 debut. This year, Chrysler has made them better still, with chassis changes like a linkless front sway bar and lower-rate springs that smooth out the ride. The manual transmission linkage has been tightened up, but spongy clutch action makes swapping gears less pleasant than in, say, a VW Rabbit or Honda Civic. Mileage isn't at the top of the heap, but it's hardly shabby, particularly the no-frills Miser models. The compact transverse-engine/front-wheel-drive mechanical layout makes good use of available interior space, which is ample for both people and cargo. The optional domestically made "Trans-4" engine gives these cars suprisingly relaxed highway cruising ability plus nippier acceleration. This year's new performance models, the Dodge Charger 2.2 and Plymouth Turismo coupes, are quite lively, but we prefer the greater practicality of the boxy sedan body over the eye-appeal of the coupes. Quality control is getting better, but still falls short of import standards. Competitive pricing and a sound basic package make the "Omnirizon" a must-see for small-car shoppers.

Ford Escort and **Mercury Lynx,** the so-called "world cars," scored a sales hit in their debut year despite 1981's depressed market. For '82 the big news is an additional body style—a five-door sedan—a claimed improvement in fit and finish, and chassis alterations for better steering and handling. Coming soon are a close-ratio four-speed manual gearbox and a high-output version of the Escort/Lynx four-cylinder engine. These new driveline options will be welcome, because in standard form the Escort/Lynx is frustrating to drive. The CVH engine doesn't give much go, particularly noticeable with automatic transmission. The engine is also harsh-sounding and noisy at higher rpm, aggravated by a boomy exhaust note. In other respects, a competent "import fighter" sized along the lines of the Mazda GLC, Honda Civic, and Volkswagen Rabbit. The Escort/Lynx has front-wheel drive, transversely mounted engine, and all-independent suspension like they do. It's somewhat roomier but not as thrifty with fuel, has a softer ride and slightly clumsier handling. On the plus side, there's good front seat room, clear outward visibility, a comfortable driving stance, and enough options to suit almost every taste and budget. The lineup also includes the Ford EXP/Mercury LN7 two-seat coupes, but we don't like them as much as the sedans and wagon. Their sportier styling sacrifices passenger and cargo space, and results in a "bathtub" seating position we find annoying. Also, their stiffer springs and shocks sacrifice ride comfort over rough roads in exchange for more responsive handling, a tradeoff some buyers won't like. Nevertheless, the "world cars" have much to recommend them, and that makes them "Best Buys" in our book.

Ford Granada and **Mercury Cougar** compete in the intermediate class, even though they're based on the "compact" Ford Fairmont/Mercury Zephyr body/chassis structure. These conventionally engineered rear-drive twins are about the same overall size as GM's comparable G-body cars (like Chevrolet Malibu and Buick Regal) but are a bit lighter. Passenger room is about the same in all cases, but the Granada/Cougar now has the edge on trunk space among sedan models thanks to this year's new deep-well design. Lighter and more economical than the Dodge Diplomat/Plymouth Gran Fury from Chrysler, and also quieter, more elegantly appointed, and better-handling. Fuel economy is nothing special, and last year's optional V-8 engine has been replaced by Ford's new lightweight V-6 of about the same power and efficiency. Granada/Cougar lacks the appeal of the GM cars' diesel option, but does offer somewhat more agile handling and roadholding when equipped with one of the available upgraded suspension packages. This year's new wagon is essentially last year's Fairmont/Zephyr model with the Granada/Cougar front sheetmetal and interior. Overall, Ford's middleweights aren't state-of-the-art cars—just pleasing, thoroughly proven, and polished. And you can't ask for much more than that.

Honda Accord has been rebodied this year. The '82 model's slightly longer wheelbase brings a needed gain in back seat room. There are also front suspension geometry changes and minor internal engine alterations. None of these should alter our assessment of this excellent little front-drive car. The smooth-revving engine delivers brisk performance plus fine economy, yet isn't boomy or buzzy at highway speeds. The well-developed chassis takes bumps and dips without jarring your teeth, aided by a reassuring absence of squeaks and rattles that results from Honda's meticulous attention to quality control. The variable-assist power steering (standard on the notchback sedan and LX hatchback) is quick, has plenty of feel, and complements the car's precise handling. Tastefully designed and trimmed interior is a little short on room for taller occupants, but the standard equipment list is as long as your arm. All this plus an enviable reliability/durability record and strong resale value will keep the '82 Accord as much in demand as previous models, so don't expect dealers to discount much. Despite this, excellence is hard to ignore, and that's what makes the Accord an outstanding value.

Honda Civic again heads our list of small, front-drive economy cars. It's a Scrooge with a gallon of gas, especially this year's new FE model rated at an eye-popping 41 mpg city by the EPA. The Civic also impresses with its eager performance, turn-on-a-dime maneuverability and handling ease, no-nonsense control layout, comfy front cabin, and a level of assembly quality that wouldn't be out of place in a Mercedes-Benz. A natural for negotiating congested traffic, the Civic is equally at home on the highway where it can cruise without fuss for hours on end. Unfortunately, the small size limits the car's usefulness for those who need adult-size back seat room, but that's why there's the Accord. Against its main rivals, the Civic is better built and more refined than Mazda's GLC, peppier and easier to drive than the Dodge Colt/Plymouth Champ, more reliable and better-equipped model-for-model than the Volkswagen Rabbit. In short, the Civic does everything expected of a small car and then some.

Lincoln Continental displaces the Cadillac Seville as this year's "Best Buy" luxury car. It's exceptionally well-equipped, with standards like digital instrumentation, on-board trip computer, cruise control, and power everything, yet sells for slightly less than the Caddy. The Continental also has the edge in performance from its larger-displacement engine yet equals or slightly betters the Seville in EPA-rated mileage when gasoline models are compared. The baby Lincoln is a little smaller and weighs substantially less than the Seville, yet offers similar passenger room and is a bit more maneuverable. The Continental lacks the outright mileage potential of the diesel-powered Seville, as well as the traction advantage of front drive. Yet the Lincoln's straight-forward rear-drive chassis should make for less costly upkeep. We've never been big on domestic luxury liners, especially the boat-like Lincolns of old, and we're still not. But if luxury is what you crave, we think this swanky, smaller Continental should be your choice.

Mazda RX-7 is not only the "Best Buy" among two-seat sports cars, it's about the only one left with prices starting under $10,000. Even so, this nifty little coupe still compares favorably against much costlier machines. Though it can't outcorner a Porsche 924, it has a much more comfortable ride, and is quieter besides. The cockpit is a bit tight for larger adults, but no more so than the Porsche's or a Corvette's. Major controls are properly spaced for serious driving, the dash cleanly styled and intelligently arranged. The smooth-revving rotary engine provides lively acceleration, aided by a slick-shifting five-speed gearbox that's a delight to use. The RX-7 is also built like a tank, and comes with a number of useful comfort and convenience features. A short list of faults includes difficult cold-weather starting, tricky wet-weather roadholding, and mileage that's on the wrong side of 20 mpg. But at the price, who can complain? RX-7 is far and away the top value in driving fun.

Toyota Corolla is the world's top-selling car line, according to the company. Popularity, of course, doesn't necessarily mean something's good, but in this case it does. The Corolla is a smallish car with a familiar rear-drive chassis and conventional suspension design. The engine is a sturdy, economical four-cylinder unit that provides decently quick acceleration for the class without making a lot of noise. Parking or threading through dense city traffic is easy thanks to a comfortable driving stance, good outward vision, and steering that's light and direct. Small size and the rear-drive layout mean back seat space is limited for adults, but it's fine for kids. The interior is fully trimmed in pleasant materials of good quality, and close attention to detail assembly has become a Toyota hallmark. So has reliability, the Corolla having one of the most trouble-free service records among the imports. If something does go wrong there's lots of room to work around the engine, and there's a Toyota dealer around most every corner. Good mileage, simple engineering, and hassle-free ownership are all a lot of people need, which explains the Corolla's mass appeal—and its selection as a "Best Buy."

Discount Price Guide

American Motors Corporation

CONCORD	Retail Price	Dealer Cost	Low Price
2-Door Sedan	$5954	$5210	$5610
4-Door Sedan	6254	5472	5872
4-Door Wagon	7013	6136	6636
DL 2-Door Sedan	6716	5877	6277
DL 4-Door Sedan	6761	5916	6316
DL 4-Door Wagon	7462	6529	7029
Limited 2-Door Sedan	7213	6311	6811
Limited 4-Door Sedan	7258	6351	6851
Limited 4-Door Wagon	7959	6964	7464

OPTIONAL EQUIPMENT:

	Retail Price	Dealer Cost	Low Price
4.2-liter (258-cid) 6-Cylinder Engine	$150	$125	$127
3-Speed Automatic Transmission	411	341	345
5-Speed Manual Transmission	199	165	167
Twin-Grip Differential	75	62	63
Power Steering	199	165	167
Power Brakes	99	82	83
Power Decklid Release	37	31	32
Power Driver Seat	171	142	144
Power Left & Right Seats	281	233	236
Power Windows & Door Locks			
2-Doors	275	228	231
4-Doors	391	325	329
Convenience Group	71	59	60
Air Conditioning	679	564	570
Air Conditioning Package w/A/C, Tinted Glass, & Power Steering	973	808	817
Tinted Glass, All Windows	95	79	80
Electronic Cruise Control	159	132	134
Tilt Steering Wheel	99	82	83
Digital Electric Clock	59	49	50
Light Group	59	49	50
Dual Horns	16	13	14
Rear Window Washer (Wagon)	119	99	100

Prices are accurate at time of printing; subject to manufacturer's change.

CONSUMER GUIDE®

	Retail Price	Dealer Cost	Low Price
Electric Rear Window Defroster	$125	$104	$106
Roof Rack, Wagon	105	87	88
Sunroof	279	232	235
Halogen Headlamps	41	34	35
Luxury Steering Wheel	35	29	30
Extra-Quiet Insulation Package			
(std. DL, Limited)	59	49	50
Protection Group			
Concord	128	106	108
DL, Limited	78	69	70
Bumper Guards	50	42	43
Locking Gas Cap	10	8	9
Heavy-Duty Engine Cooling System	75	62	63
Heavy-Duty Battery	23	19	20
Cold Climate Group	56	47	48
Handling Package	46	38	39
Automatic Load Leveling	163	135	137
Heavy-Duty Shock Absorbers	17	14	15
Trailer-Towing Package	101	84	85

EAGLE

	Retail Price	Dealer Cost	Low Price
3-Door SX/4 Liftback, 50	$ 7451	$6669	$7169
2-Door Kammback Sedan, 50	6799	6085	6585
DL 3-Door SX/4 Liftback, 50	7903	6915	7415
DL 2-Door Kammback Sedan, 50	7369	6448	6948
2-Door Sedan, 30	8719	7629	8229
4-Door Sedan, 30	8869	7760	8360
4-Door Wagon, 30	9566	8370	8970
Limited 2-Door Sedan, 30	9166	8020	8620
Limited 4-Door Sedan, 30	9316	8152	8752
Limited 4-Door Wagon, 30	10013	8761	9361

OPTIONAL EQUIPMENT:

	Retail Price	Dealer Cost	Low Price
4.2-liter (258-cid) 6-Cylinder Engine	$150	$125	$127
3-Speed Automatic Transmission	411	341	345
5-Speed Manual Transmission	199	165	167
Air Conditioning			
Eagle 50	609	506	512
Eagle 30	679	564	570
Heavy-Duty Battery	23	19	20
Bumper Guards	50	42	43
Cold Climate Group	56	47	48
Electric Clock, Eagle 50 (std. DL)	59	49	50
Convenience Group	71	59	60
Heavy-Duty Cooling System	56	47	48
Maximum Cooling System	68	56	57
Cargo Cover, Eagle 30	68	56	57
Cruise Control	159	132	134
Console	56	47	48
Power Decklid Release	37	31	32
Rear Window Defroster	125	104	106
Eagle Sport Package			
Eagle 50	499	414	419

Prices are accurate at time of printing; subject to manufacturer's change.

	Retail Price	Dealer Cost	Low Price
Eagle 50 DL	$394	$327	$331
Eagle 30, ex. 4-Door Sedan	333	276	279
Fog Lamps	79	66	67
Locking Gas Cap	10	8	9
Gauge Package			
Eagle 50	147	122	124
Eagle 50 DL, Eagle 30	88	73	74
Tinted Glass			
Eagle 50	82	68	69
Eagle 30	95	79	80
Halogen Headlamps	41	34	35
Insulation Package,Eagle 50 (std. DL)	56	47	48
Light Group	59	49	50
Automatic Load-Leveling System,			
Eagle 30	163	135	137
Power Liftback Release,			
Eagle 50 Liftback	37	31	32
Parcel Shelf	26	22	23
Protection Group			
Eagle 50 ex. w/Sport Package	92	76	77
Eagle 50 w/Sport Package	42	35	36
Eagle 30 ex. w/Sport Package..................	92	76	77
Eagle 30 w/Sport Package	42	35	36
Roof Rack			
Eagle 50 Sedan	85	71	72
Eagle 30 Wagon	105	87	88
Power 6-Way Driver Seat	171	142	144
Power 6-Way Driver &			
Passenger Seat	281	233	236
Front Skid Plate	75	62	63
Rear Spoiler, Eagle 50 Liftback	101	84	85
Steering Wheels			
Leather-Wrapped			
All ex. 30 Limited or 50			
w/Sport Package	58	48	49
Eagle 30 Limited	23	19	20
Eagle 50 w/Sport Package	19	16	17
Luxury Woodgrain	35	29	30
Vinyl Sport, Eagle 50 Liftback	39	32	33
Tilt	95	79	80
Sunroof (NA wagon)	279	232	235
Extra-Duty Suspension, Eagle 50	40	33	34
Extra-Duty Suspension, Eagle 30	75	62	63
Trailer-Towing Package A,			
Eagle 30	101	84	85
Trailer-Towing Package B,			
Eagle 30	215	178	180
Rear Window Wiper/Washer, Wagon,			
Liftback	119	99	100
Woodgrain Bodyside Panels, Wagon	189	155	157

SPIRIT—43 STATES

3-Door Liftback Coupe	$5576	$4991	$5291

Prices are accurate at time of printing; subject to manufacturer's change.

	Retail Price	Dealer Cost	Low Price
2-Door Sedan	$5476	$4902	$5202
SPIRIT—AZ, CA, ID, NV, OR, UT, WA			
3-Door Liftback Coupe	5455	4882	5182
2-Door Sedan	5355	4793	5093
SPIRIT DL—43 STATES			
3-Door Liftback Coupe	5959	5214	5614
2-Door Sedan	5859	5126	5526
SPIRIT DL—AZ, CA, ID, NV, OR, UT, WA			
3-Door Liftback Coupe	5838	5108	5508
2-Door Sedan	5738	5021	5421

OPTIONAL EQUIPMENT:

	Retail Price	Dealer Cost	Low Price
4.2-liter (258-cid) 6-Cylinder Engine	$145	$120	$122
3-Speed Automatic Transmission			
Column Shift	390	324	328
Floor Shift	390	324	328
5-Speed Manual Transmission	199	165	167
Power Assists			
Steering	199	165	167
Brakes	99	82	83
Door Locks, DL	106	88	89
Liftback Release	37	31	32
Windows & Door Locks	275	228	231
Air Conditioning System	609	506	512
Air Conditioning Package	890	739	747
Air Deflector	32	27	28
Heavy-Duty Battery	23	19	20
Electric Clock, Spirit	59	49	50
Cold Climate Group	56	47	48
Console w/Armrest	89	74	75
Convenience Group	71	59	60
Heavy-Duty Cooling System	69	57	58
Cruise Control	148	123	125
Rear Window Defroster	120	100	102
Twin-Grip Differential	79	66	67
Extra-Quiet Insulation (std. DL)	56	47	48
Gauge Package			
w/o GT Package	147	122	124
w/GT Package, DL	88	73	74
Tinted Glass	80	66	67
GT Package			
Spirit	399	331	335
Spirit DL	288	239	242
GT Rally-Tuned Suspension Package	129	107	109
Halogen Headlamps	41	34	35
Light Group	59	49	50
Sunroof	267	222	225
Protection Group			
DL	78	65	66
w/GT Package	42	35	36
Others	128	106	108
Roof Rack, Sedan	85	71	72

Prices are accurate at time of printing; subject to manufacturer's change.

	Retail Price	Dealer Cost	Low Price
Handling Package	$ 46	$ 38	$ 39
Rear Spoiler, Liftback	101	84	85
Leather-Wrapped Steering Wheel			
w/o GT Package	58	48	49
w/GT Package	19	16	17
Tilt Steering Wheel	95	79	80
Rear Window Wiper/Washer, Liftback	119	99	100

Chrysler Corporation

CHRYSLER CORDOBA	Retail Price	Dealer Cost	Low Price
2-Door Hardtop	$9197	$7920	$8420
LS 2-Door Hardtop	8258	7369	7869

OPTIONAL EQUIPMENT:

	Retail Price	Dealer Cost	Low Price
Engines			
5.2-liter (318-cid) V-8 2-bbl. (NA Cal.)	$ 70	$ 60	$ 61
5.2-liter (318-cid) V-8 4-bbl. (Cal. only)	70	60	61
Landau Roof, LS	158	134	136
Tape Stripes			
Bodyside & Decklid (std. LS)	82	70	71
Hood (NA LS)	111	94	95
Interior Trims			
Cloth & Vinyl Bucket Seat, LS	104	88	89
Leather Buckets w/Center Armrest &			
Passenger Recliner, ex. LS	501	426	431
Light Package	153	130	132
Basic Group (AO4)			
Cordoba	1048	891	900
LS	1205	1024	1035
Protection Package	138	117	119
Cabriolet Roof Package			
LS w/oAO4	709	603	610
LS w/AO4	552	469	474
Cordoba	554	471	476
Air Conditioning	731	621	628
500-amp. Long-Life Battery	43	37	38
Electronic Digital Clock	61	52	53
Console	125	106	108
Maximum Cooling	142	121	123
Electric Rear-Window Defroster	125	106	108
Triad Horns	25	21	22
Cornering Lights	57	48	49
Illuminated Entry System	65	55	56
Power Assists			
Power 60/40 Split Bench, Left	197	167	169
Power Windows	165	140	142
Power Door Locks	106	90	91
Power Decklid Release	49	42	43

Prices are accurate at time of printing; subject to manufacturer's change.

	Retail Price	Dealer Cost	Low Price
Conventional Spare Tire...........................	$ 44	$ 37	$ 38
Automatic Speed Control	155	132	134
Steering Wheels			
Sport	50	43	44
Tilt	95	81	82
Leather-Covered.............................	50	43	44
"T" Bar Roof	790	672	679
Heavy-Duty Suspension	31	26	27
Trunk Dress-Up	60	51	52
Undercoating	39	33	34
Deluxe Windshield Wipers	47	40	41

CHRYSLER LEBARON

	Retail Price	Dealer Cost	Low Price
2-Door Sedan	$8143	$7267	$7767
4-Door Sedan.................................	8237	7350	7850
Medallion 2-Door Sedan	8408	7500	8000
Medallion 4-Door Sedan	8502	7583	8083

OPTIONAL EQUIPMENT:

	Retail Price	Dealer Cost	Low Price
2.6-liter (156-cid) 4-Cylinder Engine	$171	$145	$147
3-Speed Automatic Transmission (required w/2.6 engine)	396	337	341
Interior Trim			
Vinyl Bucket Seats w/Dual Recliners, LeBaron	92	78	79
Cloth & Vinyl w/Dual Recliners, Medallion	151	128	130
Leather Bucket Seats w/Dual Recliners, Medallion	415	353	357
Light Package, LeBaron	79	67	68
Mark Cross Package, Medallion	861	732	740
Two-Tone Paint Package	171	145	147
Air Conditioning	676	575	581
500-amp. Long-Life Battery	43	37	38
Bumper Guards F or R	27	23	24
Console	100	85	86
Maximum Cooling	141	120	122
Rear Window Defroster, Electric..................	125	106	108
Tinted Glass, All Windows	88	75	76
Cornering Lights	57	48	49
Halogen Headlamps	15	13	14
Power Assists			
Power Bench Seat or 60/40 Split Bench Seat, Left..................................	198	168	170
Power Windows			
2-Door	165	140	142
4-Door	234	199	201
Power Decklid Release	32	27	28
Conventional Spare Tire	51	43	44
Automatic Speed Control	155	132	134
Steering Wheels			
Sport	50	43	44

Prices are accurate at time of printing; subject to manufacturer's change.

	Retail Price	Dealer Cost	Low Price
Tilt	$ 95	$ 81	$ 82
Leather-Covered	50	43	44
Sunroof, Glass.................................	275	234	237
Heavy-Duty Suspension	26	22	23
Trunk Dress-Up (std. Medallion)	51	43	44
Undercoating	39	33	34
Deluxe Wiper Package	47	40	41

CHRYSLER NEW YORKER

4-Door Sedan	$10781	$9267	$10267

OPTIONAL EQUIPMENT:

Engines

	Retail Price	Dealer Cost	Low Price
5.2-liter (318-cid) V-8 2-bbl. (NA Cal.)	$ 67	$ 57	$ 58
5.2-liter (318-cid) V-8 4-bbl. (Cal. only)	67	57	58
Fifth Avenue Edition Package	1525	1296	1309
Long-Life Battery	43	37	38
Power Decklid Release	32	27	28
Power Door Locks	152	129	131
Illuminated Entry System	72	61	62
Illuminated Visor Vanity, Right	58	49	50
Power Seat, Left or Bench	197	167	169
Conventional Spare Tire	51	43	44
Automatic Speed Control	155	132	134
Steering Wheel, Leather-Covered	50	43	44
Tilt Steering Column............................	95	81	82
Heavy-Duty Suspension	26	22	23
Power Glass Sunroof	982	835	844
Undercoating	39	33	34
Deluxe Wipers	47	40	41

DODGE ARIES/PLYMOUTH RELIANT

	Retail Price	Dealer Cost	Low Price
2-Door Coupe	$5990	$5552	$5852
4-Door Sedan	6131	5680	5980
Custom 2-Door Coupe	6898	6171	6771
Custom 4-Door Sedan	7053	6308	6908
Custom 5-Door Wagon	7334	6555	7155
Special Edition 2-Door Coupe	7575	6767	7367
Special Edition 4-Door Sedan	7736	6909	7509
Special Edition 5-Door Wagon....................	8101	7230	7830

OPTIONAL EQUIPMENT:

	Retail Price	Dealer Cost	Low Price
2.6-liter (156-cid) 4-cylinder Engine	$171	$145	$147
3-Speed Automatic Transmission	396	337	341
Air Conditioning (power brakes required)	676	575	581
Long-Life Battery	43	37	38
Power Brakes (std. Wagons & Spl. Edn.)	93	79	80
Bumper Guards Front or Rear	27	23	24
Cabriolet Roof Pkg., 2-Doors	696	592	598
Digital Clock, Base models	61	52	53
Console (bucket seats required)	100	85	86
Maximum Cooling (NA w/air conditioning)	142	121	122

Prices are accurate at time of printing; subject to manufacturer's change.

	Retail Price	Dealer Cost	Low Price
Power Decklid or Tailgate Release	$ 32	$ 27	$ 28
Electric Rear-Window Defroster	125	106	108
Tinted Glass	89	76	77
Halogen Headlamps (std. Spl. Edn.)	15	13	14
Dual Horns, Base models	12	10	11
Light Group			
Coupes	89	76	77
Sedans, Wagons	98	83	84
Lower Body Protection	39	33	34
Luggage Rack	106	90	91
Seats			
Bench Cloth & Vinyl, Base	31	26	27
Bucket Vinyl			
Custom ex. Wagon	132	112	114
Custom Wagon	151	128	130
Special Edition	NC	NC	NC
Bucket Cloth			
Custom ex. Wagon	250	213	216
Custom Wagon	270	230	233
Special Edition	99	84	85
Power Seats, Left or Bench	197	167	169
Special Sound Insulation	87	74	75
Conventional Spare Tire	44	37	38
Power Steering	195	166	168
Steering Wheels			
Luxury, Base	40	34	35
Sport			
Base	90	77	78
Special Edition, Custom	50	43	44
Tilt (deluxe wipers required)	95	81	82
Heavy-Duty Suspension	26	22	23
Automatic Speed Control	155	132	134
Sunroof (NA Wagon)	275	234	237
Rear Tonneau Cover, Wagons	64	54	55
Trunk Dress-up (NA Wagon)	50	43	44
Undercoating	39	33	34
Vinyl Roof			
Full, 4-Door Sedans	158	134	136
Landau, Coupes	158	134	136
Deluxe Wipers	47	40	41
Tailgate Wiper/Washer, Wagons	117	99	100
Woodgrain Delete, Special Edition Wagon	NC	NC	NC

DODGE CHALLENGER/PLYMOUTH SAPPORO

	Retail Price	Dealer Cost	Low Price
2-Door Coupe	$8036	$7229	$7829

OPTIONAL EQUIPMENT:

	Retail Price	Dealer Cost	Low Price
Air Conditioning	$620	$533	$539
Speed Control	138	119	121
3-Speed Automatic Transmission	303	261	264
Trunk Dress-Up	41	35	36
Road-Wheel Package	382	329	333

Prices are accurate at time of printing; subject to manufacturer's change.

DODGE COLT/PLYMOUTH CHAMP

	Retail Price	Dealer Cost	Low Price
3-Door Sedan	$5543	$5089	$5489
3-Door Deluxe Sedan	5794	5315	5715
3-Door Custom Sedan	6116	5605	6005

OPTIONAL EQUIPMENT:

1.6-liter 4-cyl. Engine (std. Custom)	$ 88	$ 76	$ 77
Air Conditioning	620	533	539
California Emission System	NC	NC	NC
Electric Rear-Window Defroster, Base	103	89	90
Tinted Glass, Base	56	48	49
RS/LS Package, Custom	571	491	496
Luggage Rack	96	83	84
Roadwheel Package	295	254	257
Sunroof	250	215	218
3-Speed Automatic Transmission (w/1.6-liter engine)	300	258	261
Rear-Window Wiper/Washer	64	55	56

DODGE DIPLOMAT/PLYMOUTH GRAN FURY

Salon 4-Door Sedan	$7750	$7077	$7577
Medallion 4-Door Sedan	8799	7582	8182

OPTIONAL EQUIPMENT:

Engines			
5.2-liter (318-cid) V-8 2-bbl. (NA Cal.)	$ 70	$ 60	$ 61
5.2-liter (318-cid) V-8 4-bbl. (Cal. only)	70	60	61
Vinyl Roof, Full, Salon	157	133	135
Vinyl Bodyside Moldings	46	39	40
Hood Tape Stripe	109	93	94
Interior Trim			
Vinyl Bench Seat, Split Back w/Center Armrest, Salon	58	49	50
60/40 Split Bench w/Center Armrest & Passenger Recliner, Leather, Medallion	416	354	358
Light Package			
Salon	139	118	120
Medallion	106	90	91
Basic Group			
Salon	1143	972	982
Medallion	923	785	793
Protection Group	124	105	107
Automatic Temp. Control Air Conditioning	731	621	628
500-amp. Long-Life Battery	43	37	38
Electronic Digital Clock	61	52	53
Maximum Cooling	142	121	123
Electric Rear-Window Defroster	125	106	108
Illuminated Entry System	72	61	62
Body Sound Insulation, Salon	30	26	27
Power Seat, Left, Medallion	197	167	169
Power Seat, Left & Right, Medallion	394	335	339

Prices are accurate at time of printing; subject to manufacturer's change.

	Retail Price	Dealer Cost	Low Price
Power Windows	$235	$200	$203
Power Decklid Release	32	27	28
Conventional Spare Tire	51	43	44
Automatic Speed Control	155	132	134
Leather Steering Wheel	50	43	44
Tilt Steering Column	95	81	82
Power Glass Sunroof	982	835	844
Heavy-Duty Suspension	26	22	23
Trunk Dress-Up, Salon	50	43	44
Undercoating	39	33	34
Deluxe Wipers	47	40	41

DODGE 400

	Retail Price	Dealer Cost	Low Price
2-Door Coupe	$8043	$7179	$7679
LS 2-Door Coupe	8308	7412	7912

OPTIONAL EQUIPMENT:

	Retail Price	Dealer Cost	Low Price
2.6-liter (156-cid) 4-cyl. Engine	$171	$145	$147
3-Speed Automatic Transmission (req. w/2.6 engine)	396	337	341
Light Package (std. LS)	79	67	68
Exterior Appearance Package, Base 400			
w/Crystal Coat Paint	212	180	182
w/o Crystal Coat Paint	113	96	97
Sport Appearance Package			
w/Crystal Coat Paint	309	263	266
w/o Crystal Coat Paint	210	179	181
Air Conditioning	676	575	581
Long-Life Battery	43	37	38
Bumper Guards, Front or Rear	23	20	21
Console	100	85	86
Heavy-Duty Cooling System	142	121	123
Electric Rear-Window Defroster	125	106	108
Tinted Glass	88	75	76
Halogen Headlamps (std. LS)	15	13	14
Cornering Lights (std. LS)	57	48	49
Reading Light (std. LS)	23	20	21
Crystal Coat Paint	99	84	85
Two-Tone Paint			
LS w/Crystal Coat	212	180	182
LS w/o Crystal Coat	113	96	97
Power Trunklid Release	32	27	28
Power Seat	197	167	169
Power Windows	165	140	142
Seats/Trim			
Buckets, Vinyl w/Dual Recliners (NA LS)	93	79	80
Buckets, Cloth & Vinyl w/Armrest & Dual Recliners, LS	151	128	130
Buckets, Leather w/Armrest & Dual Recliners			
LS w/o Sport App. Pkg.	415	353	357
LS w/Sport App. Pkg.	264	224	227

Prices are accurate at time of printing; subject to manufacturer's change.

	Retail Price	Dealer Cost	Low Price
Conventional Spare Tire	$ 51	$ 43	$ 44
Speed/Cruise Control	155	132	135
Steering Wheels			
Leather Wrapped, w/o Spt. App. Pkg.	50	43	44
Leather Wrapped, w/Spt. App. Pkg.	NC	NC	NC
Sport (incl. w/Sport App. Pkg.)	50	43	44
Tilt	95	81	82
Sunroof	275	234	237
Heavy-Duty Suspension	27	23	24
Trunk Dress-up (std. LS)	50	43	44
Undercoating	39	33	34
Vinyl Protection, Lower Body	39	33	34
Deluxe Wipers	47	40	41

DODGE MIRADA

2-Door Hardtop	$8619	$7429	$8029

OPTIONAL EQUIPMENT:

	Retail Price	Dealer Cost	Low Price
Engines			
5.2-liter (318-cid) V-8 2-bbl. (NA Cal.)	$ 70	$ 60	$ 61
5.2-liter (318-cid) V-8 4-bbl. (Cal. only)	70	60	61
Light Package	159	135	137
Basic Group			
w/o CMX Package	1072	911	921
w/CMX Package	1229	1045	1056
Protection Package	137	116	118
CMX Package	935	795	803
Air Conditioning	731	621	628
500-amp. Long-Life Battery	43	37	38
Electronic Digital Clock	61	52	53
Console	124	105	107
Maximum Cooling	141	120	122
Center Front Cushion w/Folding Armrest	48	41	42
Electric Rear-Window Defroster	125	106	108
Triad Horns	25	21	22
Cornering Lights	62	53	54
Illuminated Entry System	65	55	56
Power Assists			
Left Bucket or 60/40 Split Bench Seat	197	167	169
Left & Right 60/40 Bench	394	335	339
Windows	165	140	142
Door Locks	106	90	91
Decklid Release	49	42	43
Landau Vinyl Roof	157	133	134
Seats/Trim			
Vinyl Buckets w/Armrest			
w/o CMX Package	48	41	42
w/CMX Package	NC	NC	NC
Leather Buckets w/Armrest &			
Dual Recliners			
w/o CMX Package	564	479	484
w/CMX Package	515	438	443

Prices are accurate at time of printing; subject to manufacturer's change.

	Retail Price	Dealer Cost	Low Price
60/40 Split Bench w/Armrest & Dual Recliners			
w/o CMX Package	$251	$213	$216
w/CMX Package	202	172	174
Conventional Spare Tire	51	42	43
Automatic Speed Control	155	132	134
Steering Wheels			
Sport	50	43	44
Tilt	95	81	82
Leather-Covered	50	43	44
"T" Bar Roof	790	672	679
Suspension			
Sway Bar	35	30	31
Heavy-Duty Suspension	31	26	27
Trunk Dress-up	60	51	52
Undercoating	39	33	34
Deluxe Windshield Wipers	47	40	41

DODGE OMNI/024 AND PLYMOUTH HORIZON/TC3

Miser 3-Door Coupe	$5799	$5494	$5794
Miser 5-Door Sedan	5499	5215	5515
Custom 3-Door Coupe	6421	5880	6280
Custom 5-Door Sedan	5927	5435	5735
E-Type 5-Door Sedan	6636	6073	6573
Charger 2.2/TC3 Turismo 3-Door Coupe	7115	6504	7004
Calif. only, Deduct from Above:			
Misers	55	56	56
Others	57	51	51

OPTIONAL EQUIPMENT:

2.2-liter (135-cid) 4-Cylinder 2-bbl. Engine	$112	$ 95	$ 96
3-Speed Automatic Transmission	396	337	341
Vinyl Bodyside Moldings	45	38	39
Tape Stripe, Sedan	39	33	34
Cloth & Vinyl Bucket Seats, Misers	27	23	24
Light Package	74	63	64
Sport Package, Custom Coupe	138	117	119
Air Conditioning	612	520	526
Maintenance-Free Battery	26	22	23
Bumper Guards, Custom Sedan	56	48	49
Cargo Compartment Dress-up & Sound Insulation, Custom Coupe	56	47	48
Electric Clock w/Trip Odometer	48	41	42
Shift Lever Console	41	35	36
Heavy-Duty Cooling	142	121	123
Electric Rear-Window Defroster	120	102	104
California Emission System	65	55	56
Tinted Glass, Sedan	82	70	71
Engine Block Heater	19	16	17
Rallye Instrument Cluster, Custom Models	114	97	98
Luggage Rack, Sedan	93	79	80
Power Assists			
Brakes	93	79	80
Steering	190	162	164

Prices are accurate at time of printing; subject to manufacturer's change.

	Retail Price	Dealer Cost	Low Price
Automatic Speed Control	$155	$132	$134
Rear Deck Spoiler, Custom Coupe	68	58	59
Sunroof, Coupe	275	234	237
Sport Suspension, Custom Coupe	52	44	45
Rear Tonneau Cover, Coupe	64	54	55
Undercoating	39	33	34
Rear-Window Wiper/Washer, Sedan	117	99	100
Intermittent Wipers	47	40	41

IMPERIAL

	Retail Price	Dealer Cost	Low Price
2-Door Coupe	$20988	$17733	$19733

OPTIONAL EQUIPMENT:

	Retail Price	Dealer Cost	Low Price
Frank Sinatra Edition	$1078	$906	$916

Ford Motor Company

FORD ESCORT/EXP

	Retail Price	Dealer Cost	Low Price
Escort 3-Door Sedan	$5518	$5121	$5471
Escort L 3-Door Sedan	6046	5365	5715
Escort L 5-Door Sedan	6263	5541	5941
Escort L 5-Door Wagon	6461	5711	6111
Escort GL 3-Door Sedan	6406	5664	6064
Escort GL 5-Door Sedan	6622	5850	6250
Escort GL 5-Door Wagon	6841	6039	6539
Escort GLX 3-Door Sedan	7086	6249	6749
Escort GLX 5-Door Sedan	7302	6435	6935
Escort GLX 5-Door Wagon	7475	6584	7084
Escort GT 3-Door Sedan	6706	5922	6322
EXP 3-Door Coupe	7387	6461	6961

OPTIONAL EQUIPMENT:

	Retail Price	Dealer Cost	Low Price
3-Speed Automatic Transmission	$411	$345	$349
Air Conditioning	611	513	519
Roof Air Deflector, Wagons	29	25	26
Heavy-Duty Battery	24	20	21
Deluxe Seatbelts	24	20	21
Lower Bodyside Protection	68	57	58
Power Brakes (std. EXP)	93	78	79
Bumper Guards, Front or Rear	26	22	23
Bumper Rub Strips	41	35	36
Digital Clock (std. EXP)	57	48	49
Console (std. EXP)	111	93	94
Electric Rear-Window Defroster (std. EXP)	120	100	102
Engine Block Heater	18	15	16
Tinted Glass	82	69	70
Instrumentation Group (std. EXP)	87	73	74

Prices are accurate at time of printing; subject to manufacturer's change.

	Retail Price	Dealer Cost	Low Price
Remote Liftgate Release (std. GL, GLX Sed.)	$ 30	$ 26	$ 27
Light Group (std. EXP)	43	36	37
Luggage Rack	93	78	79
Vinyl-Insert Bodyside Moldings	45	38	39
Metallic Glow Paint	51	43	44
Tu-Tone Paint/Tape	122	102	104
Protection Group	55	46	47
Reclining Front Seatbacks	65	54	55
Low-Back Reclining Front Bucket Seats			
L.................................	98	82	83
GL, GT	33	28	29
Cloth & Vinyl Seat Trim	29	25	26
Shearling & Leather Seat Trim			
GL, GT	138	116	118
GLX	109	91	92
Open-Air Flip-Up Roof			
w/Squire Option, Wagon	183	154	156
Others	276	232	235
Speed Control	151	127	129
Squire Option, Wagons	293	246	249
Power Steering	190	160	162
Handling Suspension			
L.................................	187	157	159
GL	139	117	119
GLX	41	35	36
Aluminum Wheels			
L.................................	377	317	321
GL	329	277	280
GLX, GT, EXP	232	195	197
Opening Front Vent Windows (NA EXP)	60	50	51
Remote-Control Rear Quarter Windows	109	91	92
Intermittent Wipers (std. EXP)	48	40	41
Rear-Window Wiper/Washer, Escorts	117	99	100

FORD FAIRMONT FUTURA

2-Door Sedan	$5995	$5569	$5969
4-Door Sedan...................................	6419	5693	6193
2-Door Coupe	6517	5778	6278

OPTIONAL EQUIPMENT:

3.3-liter (200-cid) 6-Cylinder Engine	$213	$179	$181
3-Speed Automatic Transmission	411	345	349
Air Conditioner	676	568	574
Traction-Lok Axle.................................	76	64	65
Heavy-Duty Battery	24	20	21
Lower Bodyside Protection	41	35	36
Bumper Rub Strips	50	42	43
Rear Bumper Guards	28	24	25
Electric Clock	32	27	28
Console	191	161	163
Remote Decklid Release	32	27	28
Interior Luxury Group	282	237	240

Prices are accurate at time of printing; subject to manufacturer's change.

	Retail Price	Dealer Cost	Low Price
Electric Rear-Window Defroster	$124	$104	$106
Extended-Range Fuel Tank	46	39	40
Floor Shift	49	41	42
Tinted Glass	88	74	75
Illuminated Entry System	68	57	58
Instrumentation Group	100	84	85
Light Group	49	41	42
Rocker Panel Moldings	33	28	29
Metallic Glow Paint	63	53	54
Tu-Tone Paint			
2-Door Sedan	144	121	123
Others	105	88	89
Appearance Protection Group	57	48	49
Full or Half Vinyl Roof	137	115	117
Open-Air Flip-up Roof	276	232	235
Power Seat	139	117	119
Speed Control	155	130	132
Power Steering	195	154	156
Tilt Steering Wheel	95	80	81
Accent Stripe	39	33	34
Handling Suspension	52	44	45
Cloth & Vinyl Bench Seat	29	25	26
Michelin P190/65R-390 BSW TRX Tires and Metric Wheels			
2-Door Sedan	583	490	495
Others	529	444	449
Power Windows			
2-Doors	165	138	140
4-Doors	235	198	200
Manual Front Vent Windows	63	53	54
Interval Wipers	48	40	41

FORD GRANADA

L 2-Door Sedan	$7126	$6187	$6687
L 4-Door Sedan	7301	6334	6834
L 5-Door Wagon	7983	6907	7407
GL 2-Door Sedan	7543	6538	7038
GL 4-Door Sedan	7718	6684	7184
GL 5-Door Wagon	8399	7257	7757
GLX 2-Door Sedan	7666	6641	7141
GLX 4-Door Sedan	7840	6787	7287

OPTIONAL EQUIPMENT:

Engines:			
3.3-liter (200-cid) 6-Cylinder	$213	$179	$181
3.8-liter (232-cid) V-6			
Wagons	70	58	59
Others	283	238	241
3-Speed Automatic Transmission	411	345	349
Manual-Control Air Conditioner	676	568	574
Optional Axle Ratio	NC	NC	NC
Traction-Lok Axle	76	54	55

Prices are accurate at time of printing; subject to manufacturer's change.

	Retail Price	Dealer Cost	Low Price
Heavy-Duty Battery	$ 24	$ 20	$ 21
Lower Bodyside Protection	41	35	36
Front License Bracket	NC	NC	NC
Bumper Rub Strips	50	42	43
Electric Clock	32	27	28
Cold Weather Group	77	65	66
Console	191	161	163
Electric Rear-Window Defroster	124	104	106
Extended-Range Fuel Tank	46	39	40
Floorshift	49	41	42
Tinted Glass	88	74	75
Illuminated Entry System	68	57	58
Cornering Lamps	59	49	50
Two-way Liftgate, Wagons	105	88	89
Light Group	51	43	44
Vinyl-Insert Bodyside Moldings	49	41	42
Metallic Glow Paint	63	53	54
Tu-Tone Paint			
L	144	121	123
GL	105	88	89
Protection Group	59	49	50
Full Vinyl Roof	140	118	120
Half Vinyl Roof	140	118	120
Open-Air Flip-up Roof	276	232	235
Power Split Bench	196	165	167
Power Bench	139	117	119
Speed Control	155	130	132
Squire Option, Wagon	282	237	240
Power Steering	195	164	166
Tilt Steering Wheel	95	80	81
Bodyside/Decklid Stripes	57	48	49
Heavy-Duty Suspension	24	20	21
Split Bench Seat	230	194	196
Vinyl Seat Trim	29	25	26
Luxury Wheel Covers, L	49	41	42
Wire Wheel Covers			
L	152	128	130
GL, GLX	104	87	88
Cast-Aluminum Wheels (4)			
L	396	334	338
GL, GLX	348	292	295
Michelin 190/65R 390 BSW Radial Tires & Metric Wheels			
L	583	488	493
GL, GLX	534	447	452
Power Windows			
2-Doors	165	138	140
4-Doors, Wagons	236	198	200
Vent Windows, Front	63	53	54
Interval Wipers	48	40	41
Liftgate Wiper/Washer, Wagon	99	83	84

FORD LTD

	Retail Price	Dealer Cost	Low Price
LTD 2-Door Sedan	$8455	$7333	$7823

Prices are accurate at time of printing; subject to manufacturer's change.

	Retail Price	Dealer Cost	Low Price
LTD 4-Door Sedan	$8574	$7433	$7933
LTD 5-Door Wagon	9073	7852	8452
Crown Victoria 2-Door Sedan	9149	7916	8516
Crown Victoria 4-Door Sedan	9294	8038	8636
Country Squire 5-Door Wagon	9580	8278	8878

OPTIONAL EQUIPMENT:

	Retail Price	Dealer Cost	Low Price
5.0-liter (302-cid) V-8 (std. wagons)	$ 59	$ 49	$ 50
Automatic Temperature Air Conditioner	761	639	646
Manual-Control Air Conditioner	695	584	590
Autolamp On/Off Delay System	73	61	62
Heavy-Duty Battery	26	22	23
Lower Bodyside Protection			
Country Squire	52	44	45
Others	39	33	34
Rear Bumper Guards	30	26	27
Bumper Rub Strips	52	44	45
Electric Clock	32	27	28
Electronic Digital Clock			
Crown Victoria, Country Squire	46	39	40
Others	78	66	67
Convenience Group			
Crown Victoria w/Interior Luxury Group	90	76	77
Country Squire w/Interior Luxury Group	98	82	83
Other Sedans	98	82	83
Other Wagons	116	97	98
Electric Rear-Window Defroster	124	104	106
Tinted Glass	102	86	87
Illuminated Entry System	68	57	58
Interior Luxury Group			
Crown Victoria 2-Door	734	617	624
Crown Victoria 4-Door	807	678	685
Country Squire	727	611	618
Cornering Lamps	55	46	47
Light Group	43	36	37
Deluxe Luggage Rack	104	87	88
Rocker Panel Molding	32	27	28
Vinyl Insert Bodyside Moldings	51	43	44
Metallic Glow Paint	77	65	66
Tu-Tone Paint/Tape Treatment			
Crown Victoria	66	55	56
Others	105	88	89
Protection Group	67	56	57
Full or Half Vinyl Roof	165	138	140
Power Seat, Single Control	198	166	168
Power Seats, Dual Control	395	332	336
Dual-Facing Rear Seats, Wagons	167	140	142
Speed Control	155	130	132
Leather-Wrapped Steering Wheel	51	43	44
Tilt Steering Wheel	95	80	81
Handling Suspension	49	41	42
Heavy-Duty Suspension	26	22	23
Conventional Spare Tire	51	43	44

Prices are accurate at time of printing; subject to manufacturer's change.

	Retail Price	Dealer Cost	Low Price
Trailer-Towing Package			
Wagons	$251	$211	$214
Sedans	200	168	170
Trim			
Leather Split Bench Seat	412	346	350
Duraweave Vinyl Seat	62	52	53
All-Vinyl Seat	28	24	25
Luxury Wheel Covers	82	67	68
Wire Wheel Covers	152	128	130
Power Windows			
2-Doors	165	138	140
Others	240	202	205
Opening Front Vent Windows	63	53	54
Interval Wipers	48	40	41

FORD MUSTANG

	Retail Price	Dealer Cost	Low Price
L 2-Door Coupe	$6345	$5892	$6292
GL 2-Door Coupe	6844	6067	6567
GL 3-Door Coupe	6979	6183	6683
GLX 2-Door Coupe	6980	6184	6684
GLX 3-Door Coupe	7101	6288	6788
GT 3-Door Coupe	8308	7326	7826

OPTIONAL EQUIPMENT:

	Retail Price	Dealer Cost	Low Price
Engines			
3.3-liter (200-cid) 6-Cylinder	$213	$179	$181
4.2-liter (255-cid) V-8			
GT (credit)	(57)	(48)	(48)
Others	283	238	241
5.0-liter (302-cid) V-8			
w/TRX Performance Package	402	338	342
Others	452	380	384
3-Speed Automatic Transmission	411	345	349
5-Speed Manual Transmission, 4-cylinder	196	165	167
Air Conditioner	676	568	574
Optional Axle Ratio	76	64	65
Traction-Lok Axle	24	20	21
Lower Bodyside Protection	41	35	36
Front License Bracket	NC	NC	NC
Power Brakes	93	78	79
Cargo Area Cover	51	43	44
Console	191	161	163
Electric Rear-Window Defroster	124	104	106
Tinted Glass	88	74	75
Hood Scoop	38	32	33
Light Group	49	41	42
Power Lock Group	139	117	119
Liftgate Louvers	165	138	140
Rocker Panel Molding	33	28	29
Metallic Glow Paint	54	45	46
Tu-Tone Paint, Lower	104	87	88
Protection Group	48	40	41
Carriage Roof	734	617	624
Open-Air Roof	276	232	235

Prices are accurate at time of printing; subject to manufacturer's change.

	Retail Price	Dealer Cost	Low Price
"T" Bar Roof	$1021	$857	$866
Vinyl Roof	137	115	117
Recaro Bucket Seats	834	701	709
Speed Control	155	130	132
Power Steering	190	160	162
Leather-Wrapped Sport Steering Wheel	55	46	47
Tilt Steering Wheel	95	80	81
Handling Suspension	50	42	43
TRX Performance Package			
L	583	490	495
GL	533	448	453
GT	105	88	89
Power Windows	165	138	140
Interval Wipers	48	40	41
Rear Window Wiper/Washer	101	85	86

FORD THUNDERBIRD

	Retail Price	Dealer Cost	Low Price
2-Door Coupe	$ 8492	$ 7364	$ 7864
Town Landau 2-Door Coupe	9703	8381	9381
Heritage 2-Door Coupe	12742	10934	11934

OPTIONAL EQUIPMENT:

	Retail Price	Dealer Cost	Low Price
Engines			
4.2-liter (255-cid) V-8 (std. Heritage)	$ 241	$ 203	$ 206
3.8-liter (232-cid) V-6			
Heritage	NC	NC	NC
Others	241	203	206
Auto-Temperature Air Conditioner			
Thunderbird, Landau	754	633	340
Heritage	78	66	67
Manual Control Air Conditioner	676	568	574
Autolamp On/Off Delay System	73	62	63
Heavy-Duty Battery	29	20	21
Lower Bodyside Protection			
Heritage	39	33	34
Others	54	45	46
Digital Clock	46	39	40
Exterior Decor Group	385	324	328
Interior Decor Group	372	312	316
Electric Rear-Window Defroster	126	106	108
Diagnostic Warning Lights	59	49	50
Tinted Glass	88	74	75
Illuminated Entry System	68	57	58
Sports Instrumentation (std. Heritage)			
2-Door w/Interior Luxury Group	321	269	272
Others	367	308	312
Keyless Entry System	139	117	119
Cornering Lamps	59	49	50
Light Group	35	30	31
Luggage Compartment Trim	48	40	41
Interior Luxury Group			
Town Landau	683	574	580
Others	1204	1011	1022

Prices are accurate at time of printing; subject to manufacturer's change.

	Retail Price	Dealer Cost	Low Price
Metallic Glow Paint	$ 80	$ 67	$ 68
Protection Group	51	43	44
Automatic Parking Brake Release	12	10	11
Half Vinyl Roof	156	131	133
Carriage Vinyl Roof			
w/Exterior Decor Group	766	643	650
Others	973	817	826
Luxury Rear-Half Vinyl Roof			
w/Exterior Decor Group	163	137	139
Others	320	268	271
Flip-up Open-Air Roof	276	232	235
Power Seat, 6-way Driver	198	166	168
Bucket Seats w/Console			
w/Interior Decor Group, Town Landau	NC	NC	NC
Others	211	177	179
Recaro Bucket Seats w/Console			
Heritage	222	186	188
Models w/Interior Luxury Group	405	340	344
Models w/Interior Decor Group	523	440	445
Speed Control	155	130	132
Tilt Steering Wheel	95	80	81
Heavy-Duty Suspension	26	22	23
Trim			
All-Vinyl Seat	30	26	27
Ultra-Soft Leather	409	343	346
Power Windows	165	139	141
Interval Wipers	48	40	41

LINCOLN CONTINENTAL

	Retail Price	Dealer Cost	Low Price
4-Door Sedan	$21302	$18089	$20089
Signature Series 4-Door Sedan	24456	20707	23207
Givenchy Series 4-Door Sedan	24803	20995	23495

OPTIONAL EQUIPMENT:

	Retail Price	Dealer Cost	Low Price
Keyless Entry System	$ 141	$ 117	$ 119
Dual Illuminated Visor Vanity Mirrors	146	121	123
Vinyl-Insert Bodyside Moldings	64	53	54
Power Glass Moonroof	1259	1045	1056
Paint			
Moondust	257	213	216
Two-Tone, Base Model	298	247	250
Delete Dual Tone, Signature (credit)	(298)	(247)	(247)
Appearance Protection Group	47	39	40
Leather-Wrapped Steering Wheel, Base Model	59	49	50
Leather Trim			
Base Model	535	444	449
Givenchy, Signature	NC	NC	NC
Aluminum Wire-Spoke Wheels, Base Model	395	328	332

LINCOLN

	Retail Price	Dealer Cost	Low Price
4-Door Sedan	$16100	$13694	$15194
Signature Series 4-Door Sedan	17394	14768	16768

Prices are accurate at time of printing; subject to manufacturer's change.

	Retail Price	Dealer Cost	Low Price
Cartier Edition 4-Door Sedan	$18415	$15615	$17615

LINCOLN MARK VI

	Retail Price	Dealer Cost	Low Price
2-Door Coupe	19452	16533	18523
4-Door Sedan	19924	16925	18925
Signature Series 2-Door Coupe	22252	18857	21357
Signature Series 4-Door Sedan	22720	19245	21745
Givenchy Edition 2-Door Coupe	22722	19247	21747
Pucci Edition 4-Door Sedan	23465	19864	22364

OPTIONAL EQUIPMENT:

	Retail Price	Dealer Cost	Low Price
Traction-Lok Limited-Slip Differential	$ 128	$ 107	$ 109
Heavy-Duty Battery	28	24	25
Defroster Group (std. Signature)	151	125	127
Dual Exhausts	83	69	70
Garage Door Opener (std. Signature)	110	91	92
Headlamp Convenience Group	175	146	147
Illuminated Entry System	77	64	65
Electronic Instrument Panel, Town Car	804	667	674
Electronic Instrument Panel Delete (credit), Mark VI	(804)	(667)	(667)
Keyless Entry System	141	117	119
Touring Lamps	78	65	66
Power Glass Moonroof	1259	1045	1056
Dual-Shade Paint	298	247	250
Moondust Paint	257	213	216
Lower Bodyside Protection	40	33	34
Vinyl Roofs			
CJC 4-Dr., Signature	368	305	309
CJC 4-Dr., Others	640	531	537
CJE 2-Dr., Signature	757	628	635
CJE 2-Dr., Others	1028	854	863
Coach Roof, Town Car	331	275	278
Twin-Comfort Power Seat w/Passenger Recliner, Town Car	288	239	242
Speed Control, Town Car	178	148	150
Tilt Steering Wheel, Town Car	96	80	81
Leather Interior Trim, Mark VI	535	444	449
Leather Interior Trim, Town Car	498	413	418
Aluminum Wheels (4), Town Car	465	386	390
Turbine-Spoke Wheels (4), Town Car	465	386	390
Interval Wipers, Town Car	53	44	45

MERCURY CAPRI

	Retail Price	Dealer Cost	Low Price
3-Door Coupe	$6711	$6226	$6626
L 3-Door Coupe	7245	6417	6917
GS 3-Door Coupe	7432	6577	7077
RS 3-Door Coupe	8107	7158	7658
Black Magic 3-Door Coupe	7946	7020	7520

OPTIONAL EQUIPMENT:

	Retail Price	Dealer Cost	Low Price
Engines			
3.3-liter (200-cid) 6-Cylinder	$ 213	$ 179	$ 181

Prices are accurate at time of printing; subject to manufacturer's change.

	Retail Price	Dealer Cost	Low Price
4.2-liter (255-cid) V-8			
RS (credit)	$ (57)	$ (48)	$ (48)
Others	283	238	241
5.0-liter (302-cid) V-8			
L, GS	452	380	384
Black Magic or w/TR Perf. Pkg.	402	338	342
3-Speed Automatic Transmission	411	345	349
5-Speed Manual Transmission (4-Cyl. Only)	196	165	167
Air Conditioning	676	568	574
Appearance Protection Group	48	40	41
Traction-Lok Axle	76	64	65
Heavy-Duty Battery	24	20	21
Electric Rear-Window Defroster	124	104	106
Tinted Glass	88	74	75
Light Group	49	41	42
Rear Window Louvers	165	138	140
Right Remote-Control Mirror (std. GS)	41	35	36
Rocker Panel Moldings	33	28	29
Glamour Paint	54	45	46
Tu-Tone Paint	66	55	56
Lower Bodyside Protection	41	35	36
Open-Air Flip-up Roof	276	232	235
"T"-Bar Roof	1021	857	866
Hood Scoop	72	60	61
Recaro Bucket Seats	834	701	709
Speed Control	155	130	132
Power Steering	190	160	162
Leather-Wrapped Steering Wheel	55	46	47
Tilt Steering Wheel	95	80	81
Handling Suspension	50	42	43
Trim			
Base Cloth w/Vinyl (NA GS)	23	20	21
Leather/Vinyl	409	343	347
TR Performance Pkg.			
RS	483	406	411
Others	533	448	453
Wire Wheel Covers	91	77	78
Aluminum Wheels (4)	348	292	295
Styled-Steel Wheels w/Trim Rings (4)	72	60	61
Power Windows	165	138	140
Rear Window Wiper/Washer	101	85	86
Interval Wipers	48	40	41

MERCURY COUGAR

	Retail Price	Dealer Cost	Low Price
GS 2-Door Sedan	$7983	$6913	$7413
GS 4-Door Sedan	8158	7060	7560
GS 5-Door Wagon	8216	7109	7609
LS 2-Door Sedan	8415	7276	7776
LS 4-Door Sedan	8587	7421	7921

OPTIONAL EQUIPMENT:

	Retail Price	Dealer Cost	Low Price
3.8-liter (232-cid) V-6 Engine	$ 70	$ 58	$ 59

Prices are accurate at time of printing; subject to manufacturer's change.

	Retail Price	Dealer Cost	Low Price
Air Conditioning	$676	$568	$574
Appearance Protection Group	59	49	50
Traction-Lok Limited-Slip Differential	76	54	55
Heavy-Duty Battery	24	20	21
Bumper Rub Strips	50	42	43
Electric Clock	32	27	28
Cold Weather Group	77	65	66
Electric Rear-Window Defroster	124	104	106
Tinted Glass	88	74	75
Illuminated Entry System	68	57	58
Cornering Lamps	59	49	50
Two-Way Liftgate, Wagon	105	88	89
Light Group	51	43	44
Protective Bodyside Moldings	49	41	42
Glamour Paint	63	53	54
Two-Tone LS Paint	82	69	70
Two-Tone GS Paint	105	88	89
Lower Bodyside Protection	41	35	36
Vinyl Roof	140	118	120
Open-Air Flip-up Roof	276	232	235
Twin-Comfort Seats	204	171	173
Power Seat			
6-Way Twin-Comfort	196	165	167
4-Way Flight Bench	139	117	119
Speed Control	155	130	132
Power Steering	195	164	166
Leather-Wrapped Steering Wheel	55	46	47
Tilt Steering Wheel	95	80	81
Trim			
Leather, LS	409	343	347
Vinyl	29	25	26
Villager Option, Wagon	282	237	240
Luxury Wheel Covers (std. GS)	49	41	42
Wire Wheel Covers (4)			
GS	152	128	130
LS	104	87	88
Aluminum Wheels (4)			
GS	396	333	337
LS	348	292	295
Power Windows			
2-Door	165	138	140
4-Door, Wagon	235	198	200
Interval Wipers	48	40	41
Liftgate Wiper/Washer, Wagon	99	83	84

MERCURY COUGAR XR-7

GS 2-Door Coupe	$9094	$7863	$8863
LS 2-Door Coupe	9606	8293	9293

OPTIONAL EQUIPMENT:

Engines:

3.8-liter (232-cid) V-6	$241	$203	$205

Prices are accurate at time of printing; subject to manufacturer's change.

	Retail Price	Dealer Cost	Low Price
4.2-liter (255-cid) V-8	$241	$203	$205
Automatic Air Conditioning	754	633	640
Manual-Control Air Conditioning	676	568	574
Appearance Protection Group	51	43	44
Autolamp On/Off Delay System	73	61	62
Automatic Parking Brake Release	12	10	11
Traction-Lok Limited-Slip Differential	76	64	65
Heavy-Duty Battery	24	20	21
Seatbelt Warning Chimes (std. LS)	27	23	24
Day/Date Clock	46	39	40
Electric Rear-Window Defroster	126	106	108
Diagnostic Warning Light System	59	49	50
Tinted Glass	88	74	75
Illuminated Entry System	68	57	58
Electronic Instrument Cluster	367	308	312
Keyless Entry System	277	233	236
Cornering Lamps	59	49	50
Light Group	35	30	31
Luggage Compartment Trim	48	40	41
Glamour Paint	80	67	68
Tu-Tone Paint	112	94	95
Lower Bodyside Protection	54	45	46
Vinyl Roof, Delete (credit)	(156)	(131)	(131)
Open-Air Flip-up Roof	276	232	235
Luxury Vinyl Roof	187	157	159
Carriage Roof	885	744	752
Recaro Bucket Seats	523	439	444
Power Seat 6-Way Twin-Comfort, Left	198	166	168
Speed Control	155	130	132
Leather-Wrapped Steering Wheel	51	43	44
Tilt Steering Wheel	95	80	81
Heavy-Duty Suspension	26	22	23
Trim			
Leather	409	343	347
Vinyl	28	24	25
Luxury Wheel Covers, GS	54	45	46
Wire Wheel Covers			
LS	99	83	84
GS	152	128	130
Manual Front Vent Windows	63	53	54
Power Windows	165	138	140
Intermittent Wipers	48	40	41
Tripminder Computer			
w/Elec. Inst. Cluster	215	180	182
Others	261	219	221

MERCURY LYNX/LN7

Lynx 3-Door Sedan	$5559	$5164	$5514
Lynx L 3-Door Sedan	6159	5458	5858
Lynx L 5-Door Sedan	6376	5644	6044
Lynx L 5-Door Wagon	6581	5820	6220
Lynx GL 3-Door Sedan	6471	5726	6126
Lynx GL 5-Door Sedan	6688	5913	6313

Prices are accurate at time of printing; subject to manufacturer's change.

	Retail Price	Dealer Cost	Low Price
Lynx GL 5-Door Wagon	$6899	$6094	$6594
Lynx GS 3-Door Sedan	7257	6402	6902
Lynx GS 5-Door Sedan	7474	6588	7088
Lynx GS 5-Door Window Defroster	7594	6692	7192
Lynx LS 3-Door Sedan	7762	6836	7336
Lynx LS 5-Door Sedan	7978	7022	7522
Lynx LS 5-Door Wagon	8099	7126	7626
Lynx RS 3-Door Sedan	6790	6001	6501
LN7 3-Door Coupe	7787	6883	7483

OPTIONAL EQUIPMENT:

3-Speed Automatic Transmission	$411	$345	$349
Air Conditioning	611	513	519
Roof Air Deflector, Wagon	29	25	26
Heavy-Duty Battery (std. LN7)	24	20	21
Deluxe Seatbelts	24	20	21
Lower Bodyside Protection	68	57	58
Power Brakes (std. LN7)	93	78	79
Bumper Guards, Front or Rear	26	22	23
Bumper Rub Strips	41	35	36
Digital Clock	57	48	49
Console	111	93	94
Electric Rear Window Defroster (std. LN7)	120	100	102
Engine Block Heater	18	15	16
Tinted Glass (std. LN7)	82	69	70
Instrumentation Group	87	73	74
Light Group	43	36	37
Luggage Rack	93	78	79
Vinyl-Insert Bodyside Moldings	45	38	39
Protection Group	55	46	47
Reclining Front Seatbacks, Lynx L	65	54	55
Low-Back Reclining Bucket Seats, Lynx L	98	82	83
Cloth and Vinyl Seat Trim	29	25	26
Open-Air Flip-up Roof			
w/Villager Option, wagon	183	154	156
Other	276	232	235
Speed Control	151	127	129
Villager Option, Wagons	259	217	220
Power Steering	190	160	162
Handling Suspension			
Lynx L, GL	139	117	119
Other Lynx	41	35	36
Leather Trim, LN7	138	116	118
Shearling & Leather Trim			
LN7, Lynx GL & RS	138	116	118
Lynx GS	109	91	92
Lynx LS	59	49	50
Opening Front Vent Windows, Lynx	60	50	51
Remote-Control Rear Quarter Windows, Lynx	109	91	92
Intermittent Wipers (std. LN7)	48	40	41
Rear Window Wiper/Washer	117	98	99

Prices are accurate at time of printing; subject to manufacturer's change.

MERCURY MARQUIS	Retail Price	Dealer Cost	Low Price
Marquis 4-Door Sedan	$ 8674	$7532	$8132
Marquis 5-Door Wagon	9198	7973	8573
Marquis Brougham 2-Door Sedan	9490	8218	8818
Marquis Brougham 4-Door Sedan	9767	8450	9050
Grand Marquis 2-Door Sedan	10188	8804	9404
Grand Marquis 4-Door Sedan	10456	9029	9629
Colony Park 5-Door Wagon	10252	8858	9458

OPTIONAL EQUIPMENT:

	Retail Price	Dealer Cost	Low Price
5.0-liter (302-cid) V-8 Engine	$ 59	$ 49	$ 50
Automatic Air Conditioning	761	639	646
Manual Air Conditioning	695	584	590
Appearance Protection Group	67	56	57
Traction-Lok Limited-Slip Differential	80	68	69
Autolamp On/Off Delay System	73	61	62
Heavy-Duty Battery	26	22	23
Front & Rear Bumper Rub Strips	52	44	45
Seatbelt Warning Chimes	27	23	24
Electric Clock, Marquis, Marquis Wagon	32	27	28
Digital Clock			
Marquis, Marquis Wagon	46	39	40
Others	78	66	67
Convenience Group			
Grand Marquis	90	76	77
Wagons	116	97	98
Others	98	82	83
Electric Rear-Window Defroster	124	104	106
Tinted Glass (std. Grand Marquis)	102	86	87
Grand Marquis Decor Option, Colony Park	555	466	471
Handling Package	49	41	42
Illuminated Entry System	68	57	58
Cornering Lamps	55	46	47
Light Group			
Grand Marquis	27	23	24
Others	43	36	37
Luggage Carrier, Wagons	104	87	88
Luggage Compartment Trim (std. Grand Marquis)	49	41	42
Protective Bodyside Moldings	51	43	44
Rocker Panel Moldings, Colony Park	32	27	28
Glamour Paint	77	65	66
Bodyside Paint Stripes	39	33	34
Hood Paint Stripes	17	14	15
Two-Tone Paint			
Grand Marquis	117	98	99
Others ex. Colony Park Wagon	156	131	133
Lower Bodyside Protection	52	44	45
Power Bench Seat (NA Grand Marquis)	198	166	168
6-Way Power Seats w/Recliners	262	220	223
Dual-Facing Rear Seats, Wagons	167	140	142
Power Twin-Comfort Seats, Marquis Brougham, Colony Park	460	386	390

Prices are accurate at time of printing; subject to manufacturer's change.

	Retail Price	Dealer Cost	Low Price
Power Twin-Comfort Seats, Marquis	$262	$220	$223
Conventional Spare Tire	51	43	44
Speed Control	155	130	132
Leather-Wrapped Steering Wheel	51	43	44
Tilt Steering Wheel	95	80	81
Heavy-Duty Suspension	26	22	23
Trailer Towing Package			
Sedans	251	211	214
Wagons	200	168	170
Trim			
Cloth-Trim Comfort Seats, Wagons	41	35	36
Leather Twin-Comfort Seats, Grand Marquis or w/Grand Marquis Option	412	346	350
Duraweave Flight Bench Seats, Wagons	62	52	53
Vinyl Flight Bench Seats, Marquis, Marquis Brougham (std. Wagons)	28	24	25
Tripminder Computer			
Marquis Sdn. & Wagon	293	246	249
Others	261	219	222
Coach Vinyl Top, Brougham	638	536	542
Full Vinyl Top, Marquis Sedan	165	138	140
Vinyl Top Delete (credit)	(71)	(59)	(59)
Luxury Wheel Covers			
Marquis, Marquis Wagon	82	69	70
Others	52	44	45
Wire Wheel Covers			
Marquis, Marquis Wagon	152	128	130
Others	132	102	105
Vent Windows	63	53	54
Power Windows, 4-Door Marquis, Marquis Wagon (std. Others)	240	202	205

MERCURY ZEPHYR

	Retail Price	Dealer Cost	Low Price
4-Door Sedan	$6411	$5689	$6089
Z-7 2-Door Coupe	6319	5609	6009
GS 4-Door Sedan	6734	5967	6367
Z-7 GS 2-Door Coupe	6670	5911	6311

OPTIONAL EQUIPMENT:

	Retail Price	Dealer Cost	Low Price
3.3-liter (200-cid) 6-Cylinder Engine	$213	$179	$181
3-Speed Automatic Transmission	411	345	349
Floor Shift (Automatic Transmission)	49	41	42
Air Conditioning	676	568	574
Appearance Protection Group	57	48	49
Traction-Lok Limited-Slip Differential	76	64	65
Heavy-Duty Battery	24	20	21
Rear Bumper Guards	28	24	25
Bumper Rub Strips	50	42	43
Electric Clock	32	27	28
Console	191	161	163
Electric Rear-Window Defroster	124	104	106
Extended-Range Fuel Tank	46	39	40

Prices are accurate at time of printing; subject to manufacturer's change.

	Retail Price	Dealer Cost	Low Price
Tinted Glass	$ 88	$ 74	$ 75
Illuminated Entry System	68	57	58
Instrumentation Group	100	84	85
Light Group	49	41	42
Deluxe Bodyside Moldings, Z-7	59	49	50
Glamour Paint	63	53	54
Two-Tone Paint	105	88	89
Lower Bodyside Protection	41	35	36
Vinyl Roof	137	115	117
Open-Air Flip-up Roof	276	232	235
Power Seat, 4-Way Bench or Flight Bench	139	117	119
Speed Control (incl. Luxury Steering Wheel)	155	130	132
Power Steering	195	164	166
Tilt Steering Wheel	95	80	81
Handling Suspension	52	44	45
Trim, Cloth & Vinyl	29	25	26
Electric Trunklid Release	32	27	28
TRX Performance Pkg.	583	490	495
Styled Wheel Covers	54	45	46
Wire Wheel Covers	134	113	115
Styled-Steel Wheels w/Trim Rings (4)	107	90	91
Opening Front Vent Windows (NA Z-7)	63	53	54
Power Windows			
2-Doors	165	138	140
4-Doors	235	198	200
Interval Wipers	48	40	41

General Motors Corporation

	Retail Price	Dealer Cost	Low Price
BUICK LESABRE			
4-Door Sedan	$ 8876	$ 7662	$ 8270
2-Door Coupe	8774	7574	8175
Limited 4-Door Sedan	9331	8054	8654
Limited 2-Door Coupe	9177	7921	8525
4-Door Estate Wagon	10669	9209	9810
BUICK ELECTRA			
Limited 4-Door Sedan	11884	10258	11258
Limited 2-Door Coupe	11713	10110	11110
Park Avenue 4-Door Sedan	13559	11704	12704
Park Avenue 2-Door Coupe	13408	11573	12573
4-Door Estate Wagon	12911	11144	12144

OPTIONAL EQUIPMENT:

	Retail Price	Dealer Cost	Low Price
Engines			
4.1-liter (252-cid) V-6 4-bbl.			
LeSabre, LeSabre Limited	$267	$227	$230
5.0-liter (307-cid) V-8 4-bbl.			
LeSabre, LeSabre Limited	242	206	209
Electras ex. Wagon	NC	NC	NC

Prices are accurate at time of printing; subject to manufacturer's change.

	Retail Price	Dealer Cost	Low Price
5.7-liter (350-cid) Diesel V-8			
LeSabre ex. Wagon	$924	$785	$793
LeSabre Wagon	752	639	646
Electras	752	639	646
Accessory Group			
Electra Limited	86	73	74
Electra Park Avenue	46	39	40
Electra Wagon	86	73	74
Air Conditioning, LeSabre	695	591	597
Touch Climate Control Air Conditioning			
LeSabres	845	718	726
Electras	150	128	130
Limited-Slip Differential	80	68	69
Heavy-Duty Battery	25	21	22
Electric Clock, LeSabre	60	51	52
Heavy-Duty Cooling			
w/o Air Conditioning	38	32	33
w/Air Conditioning	73	62	63
Cruise Master Cruise Control	155	132	134
Rear Window Defogger	125	106	108
Engine Block Heater	18	15	16
Electric Fuel Cap Lock	44	37	38
85-amp. Generator			
w/o Air Conditioning or HD Cooling	85	72	73
w/Air Conditioning or HD Cooling	35	30	31
Tinted Glass	102	87	88
Four-Note Horn	28	24	25
Halogen High-Beam Headlamps	10	8	9
Cornering Lamps	57	48	49
Door Courtesy & Warning Lights			
(std. Park Avenue)			
Coupes	44	37	38
Sedans, Wagons	70	60	61
Front Lamp Monitor, ex. Electras	37	31	32
Front & Rear Lamp Monitor, Electras	74	63	64
Luggage Rack, Wagon (std. Electras)	140	119	121
Designers' Accent Paint, LeSabre ex. Wagon	215	183	185
Special Color Paint	200	170	172
Firemist Paint	210	179	181
Astroroof (NA Wagons)			
LeSabre	1125	956	966
Electra	1125	956	966
Power Seat, Driver or Passenger			
LeSabre	197	167	169
Electra	167	142	144
Power Seat, Driver & Passenger			
LeSabre	394	335	339
Electra	364	309	313
Power Seatback Recliner, Left or Right	139	118	120
Third Seat, Wagon	215	183	185
Sport Steering Wheel, LeSabre	40	34	35
Tilt Steering Wheel (std. Electra Wagon)	95	81	82
Tilt & Telescope Steering Wheel			
LeSabre, Electra Limited	150	128	130

Prices are accurate at time of printing; subject to manufacturer's change.

	Retail Price	Dealer Cost	Low Price
Electra Park Avenue	$ 55	$ 47	$ 48
Electra Wagon	55	47	48
Automatic Level Control Suspension	165	140	142
Firm Ride & Handling Suspension	27	23	24
Gran Touring Suspension, LeSabre ex. Wag.	49	42	43
Remote-Control Tailgate Lock	49	42	43
Theft Deterrent System (NA Wagon)	159	135	137
Full Vinyl Top			
LeSabre ex. Wagon	165	140	142
Electra Limited	180	153	155
Full Vinyl Top, Heavily Padded, Electra	225	191	193
Landau Vinyl Top, LeSabre Coupe	225	191	193
Landau Vinyl Top, Heavily Padded,			
Electra Limited	225	191	193
Trailer Wiring Harness & Flasher			
5-Wire	28	24	25
7-Wire	42	36	37
Trim			
Custom, 55/45 Seat, LeSabre	125	106	108
Leather & Vinyl, Electras ex. Wagon	515	446	451
Trunk Carpeting, Electra	65	55	56
Trunk Trim, LeSabre	53	45	46
Electric Trunk Lock, Electra	72	61	62
Electric Trunk Release	32	27	28
Power Windows (std. Electra)			
Coupes	165	140	142
Sedans, Wagons	240	204	207
Controlled-Cycle Wipers	47	40	41
Woodgrain Vinyl Applique, LeSabre Wagon	320	272	275

BUICK RIVIERA

	Retail Price	Dealer Cost	Low Price
2-Door Coupe	$14272	$12318	$13318

OPTIONAL EQUIPMENT:

Engines			
5.0-liter (307-cid) V-8 4-bbl.	NC	NC	NC
5.7-liter (350-cid) V-8 Diesel	$924	$785	$793
Automatic Air Conditioning	150	128	130
Heavy-Duty Battery			
w/Gas Engine	25	21	22
w/Diesel Engine (2)	50	43	44
4-Wheel Disc Brakes	235	200	203
Heavy-Duty Cooling	38	32	33
Rear Window Defogger	125	106	108
Automatic Electric Door Locks	74	63	64
Engine Block Heater	18	15	16
Electric Fuel Cap Lock	44	37	38
Halogen Headlamps	10	9	10
Four-Note Horn	28	24	25
Low-Fuel Indicator	18	15	16
Coach Lamps	102	87	88
Courtesy/Reading Lamp	48	41	42
Fuel Usage Light	35	30	31

Prices are accurate at time of printing; subject to manufacturer's change.

	Retail Price	Dealer Cost	Low Price
Illuminated Door Lock & Interior Light Control	$ 72	$ 61	$ 62
Front & Rear Light Monitors	74	63	64
Bodyside Moldings	61	52	53
Door Guard Moldings	15	13	14
Designers' Accent Paint	235	200	203
Special Color Paint	210	179	181
Astroroof	1125	956	966
Seat Adjusters			
Power Passenger 6-Way	197	167	169
Electric Recliner, Left or Right	139	118	120
Two-Position Memory Power Seat (left)	178	151	153
Sports Steering Wheel, Riviera	40	34	35
Tilt Steering Wheel	95	81	82
Tilt & Telescope Steering Wheel	150	128	130
Bodyside Stripe	63	54	55
Firm Ride & Handling Suspension	27	23	24
Gran Touring Suspension	27	23	24
Theft Deterrent System	159	135	137
Landau Heavily Padded Vinyl Top (incl. Coach Lamps)	305	259	262
Trailer Tow Flasher & 5-Wire Harness	28	24	25
Interior Trim			
45/55 Notchback Front Seat, Leather w/Vinyl	405	344	348
Trunk Carpeting & Trim	30	26	27
Electric Trunk Release	32	27	28
Electric Trunk Lock (Electric Release required)	72	61	62
Wipers w/Low-Speed Delay	47	40	41

BUICK REGAL

4-Door Sedan	$8862	$7384	$7884
2-Door Coupe	8712	7520	8120
2-Door Sport Coupe	9738	8405	9005
Limited 4-Door Sedan	9364	8083	8683
Limited 2-Door Coupe	9266	7998	8598
4-Door Estate Wagon	9058	7819	8419

OPTIONAL EQUIPMENT:

Engines			
4.1-liter (252-cid) V-6 (NA Sport Coupe)	$ 95	$ 81	$ 82
4.3-liter V-6 Diesel (NA Sport Coupe, Wagon)	874	743	751
5.7-liter (350-cid) V-8 Diesel (NA Sport Coupe)	924	785	793
Air Conditioning	675	574	580
Automatic Air Conditioning	825	701	709
Limited-Slip Differential	80	68	69
Heavy-Duty Battery (Each)	25	21	22
Electric Clock	30	26	27
Electric Digital Clock	60	51	52

Prices are accurate at time of printing; subject to manufacturer's change.

	Retail Price	Dealer Cost	Low Price
Console, Operating	$100	$ 85	$ 86
Heavy-Duty Cooling			
w/o Air Conditioning	73	62	63
w/Air Conditioning	38	32	33
Cruise Master	155	132	134
Rear Window Defogger	125	106	108
California Emission System	TBA	TBA	TBA
Engine Block Heater	18	15	16
Tinted Glass			
All	88	75	76
Windshield Only	65	55	56
Halogen Headlamps (std. Sport Coupe)	10	9	10
Headlamps-on Indicator	16	14	15
Trip Odometer Instrumentation	16	14	15
Instrument Gauges (std. Sport Coupe)	48	41	42
Cornering Lights	57	48	49
Dome Reading Light	24	20	21
Front Light Monitor	37	31	32
Regal Decor Package (NA Sport Coupe)	428	364	368
Astroroof	895	752	760
Hatch Roof	790	672	679
Power Seat, 6-Way	197	167	169
Passenger Seat Recliner	75	64	65
Seats/Trim			
55/45 Bench (std. Limited)	133	113	115
Buckets, ex. Limited	56	48	49
"Limited" Cloth, Sport Coupe	385	327	331
Sport Coupe Decor Package, Sport Coupe	355	302	306
Sport Steering Wheel	40	34	35
Tilt Steering Wheel	95	81	82
Automatic Level Control Suspension	165	140	142
Firm Ride & Handling Suspension	27	23	24
Gran Touring Suspension (std. Sport Coupe)	49	42	43
Theft Deterrent System	159	135	137
Landau Vinyl Top			
Base	166	141	143
Heavily Padded	220	187	189
Trailer Wiring Harness & Flasher			
5-Wire	28	24	25
7-Wire	42	36	37
Electric Trunk Release	32	27	28
Trunk Trim	47	40	41
Power Windows			
2-Door	165	140	142
4-Door	235	200	203
Power Windows-Front Only, 4-Door	165	140	142
Wiper Delay Feature	47	40	41
Woodgrain Bodyside Applique, Wagon	330	281	284
BUICK SKYLARK			
2-Door Coupe	$7477	$6678	$7178
4-Door Sedan	7647	6830	7330
Limited 2-Door Coupe	7917	7071	7571
Limited 4-Door Sedan	8079	7216	7716

Prices are accurate at time of printing; subject to manufacturer's change.

	Retail Price	Dealer Cost	Low Price
Sport 2-Door Coupe	$8219	$7187	$7687
Sport 4-Door Sedan	8048	7340	7840

OPTIONAL EQUIPMENT:

	Retail Price	Dealer Cost	Low Price
Engines			
2.8-liter (173-cid) V-6	$125	$106	$108
2.8-liter (173-cid) H.O. V-6	250	213	216
3-Speed Automatic Transmission	396	337	341
Acoustic Package (std. Limited)	60	51	52
Air Conditioning	675	574	580
Heavy-Duty Battery	25	21	22
Electric Clock	30	26	27
Electric Digital Clock (NA Sport)	60	51	52
Heavy-Duty Cooling			
w/o Air Conditioning	73	62	63
w/Air Conditioning	38	32	33
Console	100	85	86
Cruise Master Cruise Control	165	140	142
Rear Window Defogger	125	106	108
Engine Block Heater	18	15	16
85-amp. Generator	85	72	73
Tinted Glass	88	75	76
Dual Horns	15	13	14
Special Instrumentation	48	41	42
Coach Lamps (Limited)	102	87	88
Designer Accent Paint (NA Sport)	210	179	181
Seat Recliner, Passenger or Driver (each)	50	43	44
Power Seat	197	167	169
Superlift Rear Shock Absorbers	68	58	59
Sport Steering Wheel (std. Sport)	50	43	44
Tilt Steering Wheel	95	81	82
Sunroof, Vista-Vent	275	234	237
Firm Ride & Handling Suspension	27	23	24
Rallye Ride & Handling Suspension, F41	206	174	176
Vinyl Top			
Landau, Padded (Coupes)	195	166	168
Long	140	119	121
Trailer Wiring	43	37	38
Electric Trunk Release	32	27	28
Power Windows			
Coupes	165	140	142
Sedans	235	200	203
Intermittent Wiper System	47	40	41

CADILLAC CIMARRON

	Retail Price	Dealer Cost	Low Price
4-Door Sedan	$12131	$10676	$11676

OPTIONAL EQUIPMENT:

	Retail Price	Dealer Cost	Low Price
3-Speed Automatic Transmission	$370	$315	$319
Heavy-Duty Battery	22	19	20
Rear Window Defroster	142	119	121

Prices are accurate at time of printing; subject to manufacturer's change.

	Retail Price	Dealer Cost	Low Price
Luggage Rack	$ 98	$ 83	$ 84
Heavy-Duty Radiator	37	31	32
6-Way Power Driver's Seat	183	156	158
Dual 6-way Power Front Seats	366	311	315
Tilt Steering Wheel	88	75	76
Sunroof	261	222	225
Power Trunklid Release	29	25	26
Power Windows	216	184	186

CADILLAC DEVILLE

	Retail Price	Dealer Cost	Low Price
Coupe DeVille 2-Door	$15249	$13009	$14009
Sedan DeVille 4-Door	15699	13393	14393

CADILLAC ELDORADO

	Retail Price	Dealer Cost	Low Price
2-Door Coupe	18716	15976	17476

CADILLAC FLEETWOOD

	Retail Price	Dealer Cost	Low Price
Brougham 2-Door Coupe	18096	15438	16938
Brougham 4-Door Sedan	18567	15840	17340
Limousine	27961	23853	25853
Formal Limousine	28941	24689	26689

CADILLAC SEVILLE

	Retail Price	Dealer Cost	Low Price
4-Door Sedan	23433	19990	21990

OPTIONAL EQUIPMENT:

Engines

	Retail Price	Dealer Cost	Low Price
4.1-liter (252-cid) V-6 (credit)	$ (165)	$ (139)	$ (139)
5.7-liter (350-cid) Diesel V-8 Engine			
w/3-speed Auto Trans.	179	150	152
w/4-speed Auto Trans.	351	295	298
Accent Striping, Fleetwood Brougham, DeVille	74	62	63
Astroroof	1195	1004	1015
d'Elegance Package, Brougham			
Cloth Upholstery	1195	1004	1015
Leather Upholstery	1730	1453	1468
Cruise Control (std. Seville)	175	147	149
Rear Window Defogger (std. Seville)	198	166	168
DeVille Cabriolet Package, Coupe	398	334	338
DeVille d'Elegance Package	1115	937	947
Limited-Slip Differential, ex. Eldorado, Seville	106	89	90
Automatic Door Locks	145	122	124
Dual-Comfort Front Seats, DeVille	413	347	351
Biarritz Package, Eldorado	3335	2801	2830
Eldorado Cabriolet Package	398	334	338
Electronic Level Control, DeVille	198	166	169
Engine Block Heater	26	22	23
Garage Door Opener	140	118	120
100-amp. Generator	48	40	41
Headlamp Control, Guidematic	93	78	79
Heavy-Duty Ride Package, DeVilles, Brougham 4-Door	310	260	263
Illuminated Entry System	76	64	65
Leather Upholstery			
Seville	680	571	577

Prices are accurate at time of printing; subject to manufacturer's change.

	Retail Price	Dealer Cost	Low Price
DeVille	$ 498	$ 418	$ 423
Others ex. Limousines	535	449	454
Memory Seat (NA Limousines)	180	151	153
Illuminated Visor Vanity Mirrors	136	114	116
Firemist Paint	229	192	194
Two-Tone Paint			
Regular Colors, ex. Limousines, Seville	335	281	284
w/Firemist Colors, ex. Limousines, Seville	450	378	382
Power Recliner			
Driver (w/Dual-Comfort Seats)	150	126	128
Passenger, Including Power Adjustment (w/Dual-Comfort Seats)	85	71	72
Passenger (w/notchback seat), DeVille	150	126	128
Padded Vinyl Roof, DeVilles	267	224	227
Elegante Package, Seville	3095	2600	2627
Tilt & Telescope Steering Wheel	169	142	144
Theft Deterrent System	179	150	152
Tire Puncture Sealing	130	109	111
Touring Suspension, Eldorado, Seville	109	92	93
Trumpet Horn (NA Seville)	35	29	30
Power Trunklid Release & Pull-Down DeVille, Limousines	112	94	95
Twilight Sentinel, DeVilles & Limousines	76	64	65
Controlled-Cycle Wipers, DeVille	53	45	46

CHEVROLET CAPRICE/IMPALA

	Retail Price	Dealer Cost	Low Price
Impala 4-Door Sedan	$7918	$6835	$7335
Impala 2-Seat Wagon	8516	7351	7851
Impala 3-Seat Wagon	8670	7484	7984
Caprice Classic 2-Door Coupe	8221	7096	7596
Caprice Classic 4-Door Sedan	8367	7222	7722
Caprice Classic 3-Seat Wagon	9051	7813	8413

OPTIONAL EQUIPMENT:

	Retail Price	Dealer Cost	Low Price
Engines			
4.4-liter (267-cid) V-8 2-bbl. (std. wagon)	$ 70	$ 60	$ 61
5.0-liter (305-cid) V-8 4-bbl.			
Coupes, Sedans	70	60	61
Wagons	NC	NC	NC
5.7-liter (350-cid) V-8 Diesel			
Coupes, Sedans	825	701	709
Wagons	653	555	561
4-speed Automatic Overdrive Transmission	172	146	148
Vinyl Bench Seat, Coupes & Sedans	28	24	25
Knit or Sport Cloth Bench Seat	28	24	25
Knit Cloth 50/50 Seat			
Coupes & Sedans	257	218	221
Wagons	285	242	245
Special Custom Cloth 50/50 Seat			
Coupes	428	364	368
Sedans	452	384	388
Four-Season Air Conditioning	695	591	597
Limited-Slip Differential	80	68	69

Prices are accurate at time of printing; subject to manufacturer's change.

	Retail Price	Dealer Cost	Low Price
Heavy-Duty Battery, Gas Engine	$ 25	$ 21	$ 22
Heavy-Duty Battery, Diesel Engine (2)	50	43	44
Bumper Guards	62	53	54
Roof Carrier, Wagons	140	119	121
Digital Electric Clock			
Impala	66	56	57
Caprice Classic	34	29	30
Electric Clock, Impala	32	27	28
Cold-Climate Package	99	84	85
Heavy-Duty Cooling			
w/o Air Conditioning	70	60	61
w/Air Conditioning	40	34	35
Rear Defogger	125	106	108
Estate Equipment, Wagons	307	261	264
Floor Carpeting			
Load Floor, Wagons	89	76	77
Deluxe Cargo Area, Wagons	129	110	112
Gauge Package	64	54	55
Tinted Glass	102	87	88
Halogen High-Beam Headlamps	10	9	10
Cornering Lamps	55	47	48
Auxiliary Lighting			
Impala Sedan, 3-Seat Wagon	52	44	45
Impala 2-Seat Wagon	64	54	55
Caprice Classic..............................	42	36	37
Deluxe Luggage Compartment (ex. wagons)	59	50	51
Two-Tone Paint	65	55	56
Custom Two-Tone Paint	141	120	122
Quiet Sound Group, Impala			
Power Seat (50/50 seat required)	197	167	169
Automatic Speed Control ....:...............	155	132	134
Comfortilt Steering Wheel	95	81	82
Superlift Rear Shock Absorbers, wagons	64	54	55
Heavy-Duty Suspension...........................	26	22	23
Sport Suspension (ex. wagons), F41	49	42	43
Power Tailgate Lock	49	42	43
Puncture-Sealant Tires			
Wagons	131	111	113
Others	106	89	90
Power Trunk Opener	32	27	28
Value Appearance Group, Impala	113	96	97
Vinyl Top (ex. wagons)	165	140	142
Power Windows			
Coupes	165	140	142
Sedans, Wagons	240	204	207
Intermittent Wiper System........................	47	40	41

CHEVROLET CAVALIER

2-Door Sedan	$6966	$6131	$6631
3-Door Coupe	7192	6336	6836
4-Door Sedan..................................	7137	6281	6781
5-Door Wagon	7354	6472	6972
CL 2-Door Sedan	7944	6991	7491

Prices are accurate at time of printing; subject to manufacturer's change.

	Retail Price	Dealer Cost	Low Price
CL 3-Door Coupe	$8281	$7288	$7788
CL 4-Door Sedan	8137	7161	7661
CL 5-Door Wagon	8452	7438	7938

OPTIONAL EQUIPMENT:

	Retail Price	Dealer Cost	Low Price
Air Conditioning	$625	$531	$537
3-Speed Automatic Transmission	370	315	319
Optional Axle Ratio	20	17	18
Heavy-Duty Battery	22	19	20
Cargo Area Cover	60	51	52
Gauge Package	46	39	40
Tinted Glass	82	70	71
Halogen Headlamps	38	32	33
Special Instrumentation			
Base Sedan, Wagon	124	105	107
Base Coupe	78	66	67
CL ex. Coupe	78	66	67
Auxiliary Lighting			
Sedans	72	61	62
Wagon	81	69	70
Heavy-Duty Radiator			
w/Air Conditioning	37	31	32
w/o Air Conditioning	65	55	56
Roof Luggage Carrier	98	83	84
Power 6-Way Driver's Seat	183	156	158
Speed Control	155	132	134
Power Steering (std. CL)	180	153	155
Tilt Steering Wheel	88	75	76
Sunroof	261	222	225
Sport Suspension			
Base	46	39	40
CL	10	9	10
Power Windows			
2-Doors	152	129	131
4-Doors	216	184	186
Rear Washer/Wiper (ex. CL Wagon, Coupe)	109	93	94
Intermittent Wipers	44	37	38

CHEVROLET CHEVETTE-41 states

	Retail Price	Dealer Cost	Low Price
Scooter 3-Door Sedan	$4997	$4597	$4897
Scooter 5-Door Sedan	5238	4819	5119
3-Door Sedan	5513	4907	5207
5-Door Sedan	5660	5038	5338
Diesel 3-Door Sedan	6579	5856	6356
Diesel 5-Door Sedan	6727	5987	6487

AK,AZ,CA,HI,ID,NV,OR,UT,WA

	Retail Price	Dealer Cost	Low Price
Scooter 3-Door Sedan	4997	4597	4897
Scooter 5-Door Sedan	5238	4819	5119
3-Door Sedan	5392	4799	5099
5-Door Sedan	5539	4930	5230
Diesel 3-Door Sedan	6458	5748	6248
Diesel 4-Door Sedan	6606	5880	6380

Prices are accurate at time of printing; subject to manufacturer's change.

OPTIONAL EQUIPMENT:

	Retail Price	Dealer Cost	Low Price
3-Speed Automatic Transmission	$380	$323	$327
Air Conditioning	595	506	512
Heavy-Duty Battery	25	21	22
Custom Interior Trim Including Custom			
Cloth Bucket Seats	160	136	138
Power Brakes	93	79	80
Roof Carrier	87	74	75
Electric Clock	32	27	28
Heavy-Duty Cooling			
w/Air Conditioning	40	34	35
w/o Air Conditioning	70	60	61
Rear Window Defogger	120	102	104
Deluxe Exterior	138	117	119
Tinted Glass	82	70	71
Halogen Headlamps	10	9	10
Lighter (Scooter)	10	9	10
Auxiliary Lighting			
Scooter	41	35	36
Others	42	36	37
Bodyside Moldings (Scooter)	45	38	39
Quiet Sound Group			
w/o Custom Interior Trim	60	51	52
w/Custom Interior Trim	48	41	42
Two-Tone Paint	133	113	115
Sport Cloth Bucket Seats			
w/o Rear Seat	16	14	15
w/Rear Seat	28	24	25
Rear Seat Delete (credit)	(50)	(43)	(43)
Power Steering	190	162	164
Comfortilt Steering Wheel	95	81	82
Sport Striping	89	76	77
Rear Wiper/Washer	117	99	100

CHEVROLET CITATION

	Retail Price	Dealer Cost	Low Price
3-Door Sedan	$6754	$6032	$6532
5-Door Sedan	6899	6162	6662

OPTIONAL EQUIPMENT:

	Retail Price	Dealer Cost	Low Price
2.8-liter (173-cid) V-6 2-bbl. Engine	$125	$106	$108
3-Speed Automatic Transmission	396	337	341
Air Conditioning	675	574	580
Heavy-Duty Battery	25	21	22
Power Brakes	93	79	80
Bumper Guards	56	48	49
Bumper Rub Strips	50	43	44
Electric Clock	32	27	28
Heavy-Duty Cooling			
w/o Air Conditioning	70	60	61
w/Air Conditioning	40	34	35
Console	100	85	86
Rear Window Defogger	125	106	108

Prices are accurate at time of printing; subject to manufacturer's change.

	Retail Price	Dealer Cost	Low Price
Deluxe Exterior			
3-Door w/o Two-Tone Paint	$ 157	$ 133	$ 135
3-Door w/Two-Tone Paint	118	100	102
5-Door w/o Two-Tone Paint	169	144	146
5-Door w/Two-Tone Paint	130	111	113
Gauge Package	104	88	89
Tinted Glass	88	75	76
Dual Horns	12	10	11
Auxiliary Lighting	50	43	44
Maximum Efficiency Package	42	36	37
Two-Tone Paint	176	150	152
Quiet Sound/Rear Compartment Decor	87	74	75
Seatback Recliner, Passenger & Driver	96	82	83
Automatic Speed Control	165	140	142
Power Steering	195	166	168
Comfortilt Steering Wheel	95	81	82
Sunroof	275	234	237
Heavy-Duty Suspension	26	22	23
Sport Suspension, F41	33	28	29
Trim/Interior			
Sport Cloth Bench Seat	28	24	25
Sport Cloth Bucket Seats			
Coupe	131	111	113
Sedan	160	136	138
Custom Interior w/Cloth Bench Seat	418	355	359
Custom Interior w/Cloth Bucket Seats			
Coupe	509	433	438
Sedan	534	454	459
Custom Interior w/Vinyl Bench Seat	418	355	359
Power Windows			
Coupe	165	140	142
Sedan	235	200	202
Remote Swing-Out Rear Side Windows, 3-Door	108	92	93
Intermittent Wiper System	47	40	41
X-11 Sport Equipment Package, 3-Door	1744	1482	1650

CHEVROLET CORVETTE

	Retail Price	Dealer Cost	Low Price
2-Door Coupe	$18290	$15421	$18000
Collector Edition 2-Door Coupe	22538	19001	22500

OPTIONAL EQUIPMENT:

	Retail Price	Dealer Cost	Low Price
Heavy-Duty Cooling	$ 57	$ 47	$ 48
Rear Window Defogger	129	107	109
Removable Glass Roof Panels	443	368	372
Roof Panel Carrier	144	120	122
Power Seat	197	164	166
Automatic Speed Control	165	137	139
Gymkhana Suspension	61	51	52
Aluminum Wheels (std. Coll. Edition)	458	380	384

CHEVROLET MALIBU

	Retail Price	Dealer Cost	Low Price
4-Door Sedan	$8137	$7023	$7523

Prices are accurate at time of printing; subject to manufacturer's change.

	Retail Price	Dealer Cost	Low Price
4-Door Wagon	$8266	$7134	$7634

CHEVROLET MONTE CARLO

2-Door Sport Coupe	8177	7058	7558

OPTIONAL EQUIPMENT:

	Retail Price	Dealer Cost	Low Price
Engines			
4.4-liter (267-cid) V-8 2-bbl.	$ 70	$ 60	$ 61
5.0-liter (305-cid) V-8 4-bbl. (wagon)	70	60	61
5.7-liter (350-cid) Diesel	825	701	709
Vinyl Bench Seat, Sedan	28	24	25
Cloth Bench Seat, Wagon	28	24	25
Vinyl 55/45 Bench Seat			
Sedan	101	137	139
Wagon	133	113	115
Cloth 55/45 Bench Seat			
Sedan	133	113	115
Wagon	161	137	139
Custom Cloth 55/45 Bench Seat, Sedan	358	304	308
Air Conditioning	675	574	580
Rear Window Air Deflector	36	31	32
Limited-Slip Differential	76	65	66
Performance Axle Ratio	21	18	19
Heavy-Duty Battery	25	21	22
Bumper Guards	56	48	49
Bumper Rub Strips	50	43	44
Load Floor Carpet, Wagon	84	71	72
Roof Carrier, Wagon	115	98	99
Electric Clock	32	27	28
Cold Climate Package	99	84	85
Heavy-Duty Cooling			
w/o Air Conditioning	70	60	61
w/Air Conditioning	40	34	35
Electro-Clear Rear Window Defroster	125	106	108
Estate Equipment, Wagon	307	261	264
Gauge Package	95	81	82
Tinted Glass	88	75	76
Halogen Headlamps	10	9	10
Auxiliary Lighting			
Sedan, Coupe	38	32	33
Wagon	45	38	39
Custom Two-Tone Paint	138	117	119
Removable Glass Roof Panels, Monte Carlo	790	672	679
Cargo Security Package, Wagons	44	37	38
Power Seat, Monte Carlo	197	167	169
Automatic Speed Control	155	132	134
Comfortilt Steering Wheel	95	81	82
Pinstripping	57	48	49
Heavy-Duty Suspension (ex. wagons)	26	22	23
Sport Suspension, Monte Carlo	49	42	43
Power Tailgate Window Release	33	28	29
Wheel Cover Locking Package	39	33	34
Power Windows			
Coupe	165	140	142

Prices are accurate at time of printing; subject to manufacturer's change.

	Retail Price	Dealer Cost	Low Price
Sedans, Wagons	$235	$200	$203
Intermittent Wiper System	47	40	41

OLDSMOBILE CUTLASS SUPREME

	Retail Price	Dealer Cost	Low Price
4-Door Sedan	$8712	$7520	$8120
Brougham 4-Door Sedan	9255	7989	8589
2-Door Coupe	8588	7413	8013
Brougham 2-Door Coupe	9160	7907	8507
Calais 2-Door Coupe	9379	8096	8696
Cruiser 4-Door Wagon	8905	7686	8286

OPTIONAL EQUIPMENT:

	Retail Price	Dealer Cost	Low Price
Engines			
4.1-liter (252-cid) V-6 2-bbl.	$ 70	$ 60	$ 61
4.3-liter (262-cid) Diesel V-6	775	659	666
5.0-liter (307-cid) V-8 4-bbl., Wagons	70	60	61
5.7-liter (350-cid) Diesel V-8	825	701	709
Four-Season Air Conditioning	675	574	580
Tempmatic Air Conditioning	730	621	628
Rear-Window Air Deflector, Wagons	37	31	32
High-Capacity Alternator	85	72	73
Astroroof, Coupes Only	875	744	752
Limited-Slip Differential	80	68	69
Heavy-Duty Battery			
w/Gasoline Engine	25	21	22
w/Diesel Engine (2)	50	43	44
Electric Clock	30	26	27
Electric Digital Clock	61	52	53
Console	100	85	86
Convenience Group (std. Brougham)			
Base Coupe, Sedan	51	43	44
Wagons	57	48	49
Calais Coupe	36	31	32
Cooling System, Engine and Transmission			
w/Air Conditioning	38	32	33
w/o Air Conditioning	83	71	72
w/Diesel Engine & Air Conditioning	30	26	27
w/Diesel Engine w/o Air Conditioning	60	51	52
High-Capacity Cooling System	24	20	21
Cruise Control	155	132	134
Electric Rear-Window Defroster	125	106	108
Engine Block Heater	19	16	17
Gauge Package (standard Calais)	142	121	123
Tinted Glass	88	75	76
Dome/Reading Lamp			
w/o Convenience Group	28	24	25
w/Convenience Group	13	11	12
Lamp Monitor	74	63	64
Locks, Tire Storage, Rear Quarter Storage,			
Wagon	55	47	48
Luggage Rack, Wagon	115	98	99
Removable Glass Roof Panel, Coupes	790	672	679
Full Vinyl Roof (NA Wagons)	140	119	121

Prices are accurate at time of printing; subject to manufacturer's change.

	Retail Price	Dealer Cost	Low Price
Full Padded Vinyl Roof, Sedans	$220	$187	$189
Landau Vinyl Roof, Coupes	220	187	189
Contour Bucket Seats	57	48	49
Power Seat, 6-Way			
Left Bucket (NA Broughams, Wagon)	197	167	169
Divided Bench (NA Calais, Cruiser)	197	167	169
Bench, ex. base Supreme	197	167	169
Manual Seatback Recliner, Brougham,			
Cruiser	75	64	65
Custom Sport Steering Wheel (NA Calais)	48	41	42
Tilt-Away Steering Wheel	95	81	82
Firm Ride & Handling Package			
Sedans, Coupes (ex. Calais)	44	37	38
Calais, Wagons	28	24	25
Power Tailgate Release, Wagon	35	30	31
Custom Leather Seating, Brougham	364	309	313
Travel In Style Value Package			
Incl. Super-Stock Wheels	340	289	292
Inc. Wire Wheel Covers	430	366	370
Power Trunklid Release (NA Wagons)	32	27	28
Deluxe Trunk Trim	60	51	52
Power Windows			
2-Doors or Front only	165	140	142
4-Doors	235	200	203
Pulse Wiper System	47	40	41
Woodgrain Applique, Wagon	264	224	227

OLDSMOBILE DELTA 88/98

	Retail Price	Dealer Cost	Low Price
Delta 88 4-Door Sedan	$ 8603	$ 7426	$ 7926
Delta 88 Royale 2-Door Coupe	8733	7538	8138
Delta 88 Royale 4-Door Sedan	8894	7677	8277
Delta 88 Royle Brougham 2-Door Coupe	9202	7943	8543
Delta 88 Royale Brougham 4-Door Sedan	9293	8022	8622
Custom Cruiser 5-Door Wagon	9614	8599	9199
Ninety-Eight 2-Door Regency Coupe	12117	10458	11458
Ninety-Eight 4-Door Regency Sedan	12294	10611	11611
Ninety-Eight Regency Brougham Sedan	13343	11517	12517

OPTIONAL EQUIPMENT:

	Retail Price	Dealer Cost	Low Price
Engines			
4.1-liter (252-cid) V-6, Delta 88			
(ex. wagon)	$ 70	$ 60	$ 61
5.0-liter (307-cid) V-8, Delta 88			
(ex. wagon)	242	206	209
5.7-liter (350-cid) V-8 Diesel (inc. 3-speed			
automatic transmission) Delta 88			
(ex. wagon)	825	701	709
Wagon, Ninety-Eight	653	555	561
Four-Season Air Conditioning (std. 98)	695	591	597
Tempmatic Air Conditioning, 98	55	47	48
Others	750	638	645
High-Capacity Alternator	85	72	73
Astroroof	1125	956	966

Prices are accurate at time of printing; subject to manufacturer's change.

	Retail Price	Dealer Cost	Low Price
Limited-Slip Differential	$ 80	$ 68	$ 69
High-Capacity Battery			
w/Gasoline Engine	25	21	22
w/Diesel Engine (2)	50	43	44
Rear Bumper Step, Wagon	22	19	20
Electric Digital Clock			
Delta 88	96	82	83
Ninety-Eight	35	30	31
Cooling System			
w/Air Conditioning	38	32	33
w/o Air Conditioning	83	71	72
w/Diesel Engine w/Air Conditioning	30	26	27
w/Diesel Engine w/o Air Conditioning	60	51	52
High-Capacity Cooling System	24	20	21
Cruise Control	155	132	134
Electric Rear-Window Defroster	125	106	108
California Emission System			
w/Gasoline Engine	46	39	40
w/Diesel Engine	182	155	157
Diesel Engine Block/Fuel Line Heater	49	42	43
Tinted Glass (std. Ninety-Eight)	102	87	88
Halogen High-Beam Headlamps	10	9	10
Illumination Package	72	61	62
Cornering Lamps	57	48	49
Dome/Reading Lamp			
Delta 88, Wagon	28	24	25
Others	13	11	12
Sail Mounted Reading Lamp, 98 Sedans	64	54	55
Lamp Monitors	74	63	64
Automatic Load-Leveling System	165	140	142
Luggage Carrier, Roof, Wagon	140	119	121
Reminder Package	30	26	27
Full Vinyl Roof			
Delta 88s	165	140	142
Ninety-Eight Sedans	180	153	155
Full Vinyl Roof, Padded (NA Delta 88s)	225	191	193
Landau Vinyl Roof	225	191	193
Power Seat, 6-Way	197	167	169
Manual Seatback Recliner	75	64	65
Divided Front Seat			
Delta 88 Royale	133	113	115
Delta 88, Wagon	174	148	150
Third Seat, Wagon	215	183	185
Tilt & Telescope Steering Wheel	150	128	130
Firm Ride Suspension			
Delta 88	44	37	38
Wagon, Ninety-Eight	28	24	25
Trailer Wiring Harness 5-Wire	28	24	25
Custom Leather Trim, Ninety-Eight	379	322	326
Trip Odometer	16	14	15
Power Trunk Release	32	27	28
Twilight Sentinel	57	48	49

Prices are accurate at time of printing; subject to manufacturer's change.

	Retail Price	Dealer Cost	Low Price
Power Windows			
Delta 88 2-Doors	$165	$140	$142
Delta 88 4-Doors, Wagon	240	204	207
Pulse Wiper System	47	40	41
Bodyside Vinyl Woodgrain Applique, Wagon	281	239	242

OLDSMOBILE OMEGA

	Retail Price	Dealer Cost	Low Price
2-Door Coupe	$7388	$6599	$7099
4-Door Sedan	7574	6765	7265
Brougham 2-Door Coupe	7722	6897	7397
Brougham 4-Door Sedan	7891	7048	7548

OPTIONAL EQUIPMENT:

	Retail Price	Dealer Cost	Low Price
2.8-liter (173-cid) V-6 Engine	$125	$106	$108
3-Speed Automatic Transmission	396	337	341
Air Conditioning	675	574	580
Heavy-Duty Battery	25	21	22
ES Package			
w/4-cylinder Engine (ES 2500)	896	761	769
w/V-6 Engine (ES 2800)	1146	973	983
Gauge Package (inc. w/ES)	120	102	104
Tinted Glass	88	75	76
Dual Horns	15	13	14
Electric Clock	30	26	27
Electric Digital Clock	61	52	53
Heavy-Duty Cooling			
w/o Air Conditioning	83	71	72
w/Air Conditioning	38	32	33
Console	100	85	86
Cruise Control	165	140	142
Electric Rear-Window Defroster	125	106	108
Dome/Reading Lamp	28	24	25
Bodyside Paint Stripes	40	34	35
Paint Scheme	194	165	167
Trip Odometer	16	13	14
Seat Recliner, Passenger or Driver (each)	80	68	69
Power Seat	197	167	169
Bucket Seats			
Omega	102	87	88
Brougham	57	48	49
Custom Sport Steering Wheel	48	41	42
Tilt Steering Wheel	95	81	82
Sunroof	275	234	237
Firm Ride & Handling Package	36	31	32
Travel In Style Value Package			
Incl. Super-Stock Wheels	262	223	226
Incl. Wire Wheel Covers	352	299	302
Power Trunklid Release	32	27	28
Full Vinyl Top, Sedans	140	119	121
Landau Vinyl Top, Coupes	195	166	168
Power Windows			
Coupes	165	140	142

Prices are accurate at time of printing; subject to manufacturer's change.

	Retail Price	Dealer Cost	Low Price
Sedans	$235	$200	$203
Intermittent Wiper System	47	40	41

OLDSMOBILE TORONADO

Brougham 2-Door Coupe	$14462	$12482	$13982

OPTIONAL EQUIPMENT:

	Retail Price	Dealer Cost	Low Price
5.7-liter (350-cid) Diesel V-8 Engine	$825	$701	$709
Tempmatic Air Conditioning	55	47	48
Astroroof	1125	956	966
Console	80	68	69
Automatic Door Locks	74	63	64
Electric Rear-Window Defroster	125	106	108
Engine Block Heater	19	16	17
Engine Block & Fuel Line Heater (Diesel)	49	42	43
Gauge Cluster	44	37	38
Power Seat, 6-Way Passenger	197	167	169
Power Seat, 6-Way Driver w/Memory	178	151	153
Power Seat Recliner, Passenger	139	118	120
Manual Seatback Recliner, L or R	75	64	65
Reminder Package	48	41	42
Leather-Wrapped Steering Wheel	52	44	45
Tilt & Telescope Steering Wheel	55	47	48
Firm Ride & Handling Suspension	44	37	38
Twilight Sentinel	57	48	49
Theft Deterrent System	159	135	137
Power Trunklid Release	32	27	28
Landau Vinyl Roof	225	191	193
Leather Seat Trim	384	326	330
Pulse Wiper System	47	40	41

PONTIAC BONNEVILLE MODEL G

4-Door Sedan	8527	7360	7860
4-Door Wagon	8694	7504	8004
Brougham 4-Door Sedan	8995	7775	8305

PONTIAC GRAND PRIX

2-Door Coupe	$8333	$7193	$7693
LJ 2-Door Coupe	8788	7586	8186
Brougham 2-Door Coupe	9209	7949	8549

OPTIONAL EQUIPMENT:

Engines			
4.1-liter (252-cid) V-6 2-bbl.	$95	$81	$82
5.7-liter (350-cid) Diesel V-8	924	785	793
Custom Air Conditioning	675	574	580
70-amp. Alternator			
w/o Rear Defroster, Air Conditioning, or			
Cold-Weather Group	51	43	44
w/Rear Defroster or Air Conditioning	NC	NC	NC
Limited-Slip Differential	76	65	66
Heavy-Duty Battery, w/o Cold-Weather Group,			
ex. Diesel	25	21	22
Heavy-Duty Battery, Diesel Engine (2)	50	43	44

Prices are accurate at time of printing; subject to manufacturer's change.

	Retail Price	Dealer Cost	Low Price
Custom Seatbelts, Base Grand Prix	$ 26	$ 22	$ 23
Brougham Landau Package, Grand Prix	810	689	696
Front or Rear Bumper Guards	26	22	23
Digital Clock	30	26	27
Cold-Weather Group Delete w/Diesel Engine (credit)	(99)	(84)	(84)
Cruise Control	155	132	134
Remote Decklid Release	32	27	28
Electric Rear-Window Defroster	125	106	108
Rallye Instrument Cluster (inc. Trip Odometer & Tachometer)	152	129	131
Tinted Glass	88	75	76
Hatch Roof, Grand Prix			
w/o Brougham Landau Pkg.	826	702	710
w/Brougham Landau Pkg.	791	672	679
Halogen High-Beam Headlamps	10	9	10
Additional Sound Insulation, Grand Prix	39	33	34
Cornering Lamps	58	49	50
Dome/Reading Lamp, Grand Prix	22	19	20
Door Courtesy Lamps	43	37	38
Roof Luggage Carrier, Wagon	112	95	96
Luggage Compartment Trim	50	43	44
Super-Cooling Radiator	40	34	35
6-Way Power Driver Seat	196	167	169
60/40 Power Driver & Passenger Seat	392	333	337
Vinyl Bench Seat (std. wagon)			
Notchback 60/40 Seat			
Ex. Broughams	133	113	115
Brougham (Leather)	475	404	409
Bucket Seats w/Console	267	244	247
Reclining Front Passenger Seat	75	65	66
Super-Lift Rear Shocks	64	54	55
Custom Sport Steering Wheel			
Bonneville, Grand Prix	93	79	80
Brougham Sedan, Grand Prix LJ	68	58	59
Luxury-Cushion Steering Wheel (std. Brougham & LJ)	25	21	22
Tilt Steering Wheel	95	81	82
Power Glass Sunroof	875	744	752
Power Steel Sunroof	595	506	511
Heavy-Duty Springs	16	14	15
Power Tailgate Release, Wagons	31	26	27
Full Vinyl Top (ex. Wagons)	140	119	121
Padded Vinyl Top (ex. Wagons)	220	187	189
Trailer Light Cable, 5-wire	27	23	24
Custom Trim Group, Wagon	211	179	181
Power Windows (std. Brougham Landau)			
Coupes	165	140	142
Sedans, Wagons	235	200	203
Controlled-Cycle Wipers	47	40	41
Wagon Bodyside Woodgrain Applique	283	241	244

PONTIAC J2000

2-Door Sedan	$6999	$6160	$6660

Prices are accurate at time of printing; subject to manufacturer's change.

	Retail Price	Dealer Cost	Low Price
4-Door Sedan	$7203	$6343	$6843
3-Door Coupe	7275	6402	6902
5-Door Wagon	7448	6555	7055
LE 2-Door Sedan	7372	6488	6988
LE 4-Door Sedan	7548	6643	7143
SE 3-Door Coupe	7654	6730	7230

OPTIONAL EQUIPMENT:

	Retail	Dealer	Low
Air Conditioning	$625	$511	$517
3-Speed Automatic Transmission	370	315	319
Heavy-Duty Battery	22	19	20
Cargo Area Cover (ex. Sedans)	60	51	52
Cruise Control	155	132	134
Electric Rear-Window Defroster	115	98	99
Custom Exterior Group (NA LE, SE)	79	67	68
Rallye Gauges (NA SE)	46	39	40
Rallye Gauges with Tachometer			
SE	78	66	67
Others	124	105	107
Tinted Glass	82	70	71
Handling Package	46	39	40
Halogen Headlamps	29	25	26
Additional Sound Insulation	36	31	32
Lamp Group	37	31	32
Roof Luggage Carrier	98	83	84
Heavy-Duty Radiator			
w/o Air Conditioning	65	55	56
w/Air Conditioning	37	31	32
Power Seat	183	156	158
Rear Spoiler, Coupe	69	59	60
Power Steering	180	153	155
Formula Steering Wheel	45	38	39
Tilt Steering Wheel	88	75	76
Sunroof	261	222	225
Cloth Interior Trim	28	24	25
Trim Group, Base Coupe	195	165	167
Power Windows			
Coupe, 2-Door Sedan	152	129	131
4-Door, Wagon	216	184	186
Controlled Cycle Wipers	44	37	38
Rear Wiper/Washer, Coupe & Wagon	109	93	94

PONTIAC PHOENIX

	Retail	Dealer	Low
2-Door Sedan	$6964	$6220	$6720
5-Door Sedan	7172	6406	6906
LJ 2-Door Sedan	7449	6653	7153
LJ 5-Door Sedan	7658	6840	7340
SJ 2-Door Sedan	8722	7790	8390
SJ 5-Door Sedan	8884	7934	8534

OPTIONAL EQUIPMENT:

	Retail	Dealer	Low
2.8-liter (173-cid) V-6 Engine (NA SJ)	$125	$106	$108

Prices are accurate at time of printing; subject to manufacturer's change.

	Retail Price	Dealer Cost	Low Price
3-Speed Automatic Transmission	$396	$337	$341
Air Conditioning	675	574	580
Heavy-Duty Battery	25	21	22
Deluxe Seatbelts (std. SJ)	26	22	23
Power Brakes	93	79	80
Bumper Guards, Front or Rear	26	22	23
Cargo Cover (std. LJ)	44	37	38
Luggage Carrier, 5-Door Sedan	105	89	90
Electric Clock	32	27	28
Console	100	85	86
Cruise Control	165	140	142
Electric Rear-Window Defroster	125	106	108
Tinted Glass	88	75	76
Dual Horns (std. LJ)	12	11	12
Additional Sound Insulation (std. LJ)	39	33	34
Dome/Reading Lamp	22	19	20
Lamp Group	45	38	39
Two-Tone Paint Package			
Base 2-Door	176	150	152
Others (std. SJ)	148	126	128
Heavy-Duty Radiator	72	61	62
Seat Recliner, Passenger or Driver			
5-Doors w/Bench Seat	48	41	42
Others	79	67	68
Power Seat	196	167	169
Bucket Seats			
Phoenix, Vinyl	104	88	89
Phoenix, Cloth	134	114	116
LJ	55	47	48
Superlift Rear Shock Absorbers	64	54	55
Rear Spoiler, SJ 2-Door	74	63	64
Power Steering (std. SJ)	195	166	168
Luxury-Cushion Steering Wheel, Base	25	21	22
Tilt Steering Wheel	95	81	82
Sunroof	275	234	237
Suspensions			
Heavy-Duty Springs	16	14	15
Handling Package			
Ex. SJ	317	269	272
SJ	88	75	76
Landau Vinyl Top, 2-Doors	195	166	168
Luxury Trim Group, 2-Doors			
w/Bucket Seats, Base	312	265	268
w/Bucket Seats, SJ	208	177	179
w/Notchback Seat, Base	257	218	221
Luxury Trim Group, 5-Doors			
w/Bucket Seats, Base	356	303	307
w/Bucket Seats, SJ	252	214	217
w/Notchback Seat, Base	301	256	259
Power Windows			
2-Doors	165	140	142
5-Doors	235	200	203
Intermittent Wipers	47	40	41

Prices are accurate at time of printing; subject to manufacturer's change.

PONTIAC T1000	Retail Price	Dealer Cost	Low Price
3-Door Sedan	$5782	$5146	$5546
5-Door Sedan	5945	5291	5691

OPTIONAL EQUIPMENT:

3-Speed Automatic Transmission	$380	$323	$327
5-Speed Manual Transmission	196	167	169
Air Conditioning	595	506	512
Heavy-Duty Battery	25	21	22
Power Brakes	93	79	80
Cargo Cover	64	54	55
Electric Clock	27	23	24
Electric Rear-Window Defroster	120	102	104
Tinted Glass	82	70	71
Deluxe Sound Insulation	46	39	40
Lamp Group	42	36	37
Luggage Carrier	87	74	75
Heavy-Duty Radiator			
w/o Air Conditioning	70	60	61
w/Air Conditioning	40	34	35
Cloth Seat Trim	28	24	25
Power Steering	190	162	164
Tilt Steering Wheel	95	81	82
Rear-Window Wiper/Washer	117	100	102
Controlled-Cycle Wipers	47	40	41

Imports

AUDI 4000 AND COUPE

2-Door Sedan, 5-speed	$ 9755	$ 8424	$ 9424
4-Door Sedan, 5-speed . . . . /	10865	9377	10577
4-Door Sedan, Automatic	11270	9732	10932
2-Door Coupe, 5-speed	12370	10676	11876
2-Door Coupe, Automatic	12775	11028	12228
4-Door Diesel Sedan , 5-speed	10515	9069	10269

AUDI 5000

4-Door Diesel Sedan, 5-speed	$12390	$10629	$12129
S 4-Door Sedan, 5-speed	13665	11123	13123
S 4-Door Sedan, Automatic	14070	12074	13574
S 4-Door Diesel Sedan, 5-speed	13990	11997	13497
4-Door Turbo Sedan, Automatic	18490	15844	17844

DATSUN MAXIMA

4-Door Sedan, 5-speed	$11049	$ 9502	$11002
5-Door Wagon, Automatic	11859	10198	11698
4-Door Diesel Sedan, 5-speed	11419	9820	11320
5-Door Diesel Wagon, Automatic	12229	10517	12017

Prices are accurate at time of printing; subject to manufacturer's change.

	Retail Price	Dealer Cost	Low Price
DATSUN 200SX			
2-Door Hardtop	$7739	$6655	$7455
3-Door Coupe	7939	6830	7630
DATSUN 210			
Standard 2-Door Sedan	$4799	$4319	$4719
MPG 2-Door Sedan	5139	4625	5025
Deluxe 2-Door Sedan	5819	5063	5563
Deluxe 4-Door Sedan	5989	5210	5710
Deluxe 3-Door Coupe	6149	5350	5850
Deluxe 5-Door Wagon	6299	5480	5980
DATSUN 280ZX			
3-Door 2-Seat Coupe	$11299	$ 9548	$11048
3-Door 2+2 Coupe	14949	12557	14557
Turbo 3-Door 2-Seat Coupe	16999	14249	16749
Turbo 3-Door 2+2 Coupe	18299	NA	NA
DATSUN 310			
3-Door Deluxe Sedan	$5689	$4892	$5392
GX 5-Door Sedan	6389	5495	5995
GX 3-Door Coupe	6689	5753	6173
HONDA ACCORD			
3-Door Coupe 5-speed	$7654	$6670	$7170
3-Door Coupe Automatic	7904	6880	7380
LX 3-Door Coupe 5-speed	8704	7552	8052
LX 3-Door Coupe Automatic	8954	7762	8362
4-Door Sedan 5-speed	8500	7380	7880
4-Door Sedan Automatic	8750	7590	8190
HONDA CIVIC			
1300 3-Door Sedan 4-speed	$5154	$4774	$5074
1300 FE 3-Door Sedan 5-speed	6254	5469	5869
1500 DX 3-Door Sedan 5-speed	6204	5426	5726
1500 DX 3-Door Sedan Automatic	6404	5596	5996
1500 GL 3-Door Sedan 5-speed	6554	5724	6124
1500 4-Door Sedan 5-speed	7104	6191	6791
1500 4-Door Sedan Automatic	7304	6361	6991
1500 5-Door Wagon 5-speed	6604	5766	6366
1500 5-Door Wagon Automatic	6804	5936	6536
HONDA PRELUDE			
2-Door Coupe, 5-speed	$8250	$7170	$8070
2-Door Coupe, Automatic	8700	7548	8448
MAZDA GLC			
3-Door Sedan 4-speed	$5295	$4862	$5262
Custom 3-Door Sedan 4-speed	5695	5050	5550
Custom L 3-Door Sedan 5-speed	6095	5402	5902
Sport 3-Door Sedan 5-speed	6545	5797	6297
Custom 5-Door Sedan 5-speed	5795	5092	5442
Custom 5-Door Wagon 4-speed	5995	5314	5814
Custom 4-Door Sedan 4-speed	6245	5533	6033
Custom L 4-Door Sedan 5-speed	6745	5973	6473

Prices are accurate at time of printing; subject to manufacturer's change.

	Retail Price	Dealer Cost	Low Price
MAZDA RX7			
S 2-Door Coupe	$ 9695	$ 8495	$ 9495
GS 2-Door Coupe	10295	8914	9914
GSL 2-Door Coupe	11895	10218	11718
MAZDA 626			
2-Door Coupe	$7545	$6601	$7301
2-Door Luxury Coupe	9345	8096	8896
4-Door Sedan	7245	6340	7040
4-Door Luxury Sedan	8845	7666	8466
SUBARU			
STD 3-Door Sedan, 4-Speed	$4549	$4341	$4541
STD 4WD 3-Door Sedan, 4-Speed	5399	5132	5232
DL 3-Door Sedan, 5-Speed	5504	4915	5215
DL 4WD 3-Door Sedan, 4-Speed	6129	5463	5763
DL 4-Door Sedan, 4-Speed	5729	5112	5412
DL 4-Door Sedan, 5-Speed	5854	5222	5522
DL 2-Door Hardtop, 4-Speed	5879	5244	5544
DL 2-Door Hardtop, 5-Speed	6004	5354	5754
DL 5-Door Wagon, 4-Speed	5979	5332	5732
DL 5-Door Wagon, 5-Speed	6104	5442	5842
DL 4WD 5-Door Wagon, 4-Speed	6729	5937	6337
GL 3-Door Sedan, 5-Speed	5929	5242	5642
GL 3-Door Sedan, Automatic	6179	5461	5861
GL 3-Door 4WD Sedan, 4-Speed	6529	5714	6114
GL 4-Door Sedan, 5-Speed	6279	5546	5946
GL 4-Door Sedan, Automatic	6529	5763	6163
GL 5-Door Wagon, 5-Speed	6529	5763	6163
GL 5-Door Wagon, Automatic	6779	5982	6382
GL 5-Door 4WD Wagon, 4-Speed	7129	6231	6731
GLF 2-Door Hardtop, 5-Speed	6529	5714	6114
GLF 2-Door Hardtop, Automatic	6779	5993	6393
TOYOTA CELICA/SUPRA			
Celica ST 2-Door Coupe, 5-Speed	$ 7159	$ 6121	$ 6621
Celica GT 2-Door Coupe, Automatic	8599	7309	7809
Celica GT 2-Door Coupe, 5-Speed	8159	6935	7435
Celica GT 3-Door Coupe, Automatic	8829	7505	8005
Supra L-Type 3-Door Coupe, 5-Speed	13598	11218	12218
Supra L-Type 3-Door Coupe, Automatic	14098	11635	12635
Supra Performance 3-Door Coupe, 5-Speed	14598	12108	13018
TOYOTA COROLLA			
Standard 2-Door Sedan, 4-Speed	$5448	$4713	$5213
Deluxe 2-Door Sedan, 5-Speed	6018	5175	5675
Deluxe 2-Door Sedan, Automatic	6318	5433	5933
Deluxe 4-Door Sedan, 5-Speed	6138	5279	5779
Deluxe 4-Door Sedan, Automatic	6438	5537	6037
Deluxe 3-Door Liftback Coupe, Automatic	6648	5717	6217
Deluxe 5-Door Wagon, 5-Speed	6508	5597	6097
Deluxe 5-Door Wagon, Automatic	6808	5855	6355
SR5 2-Door Hardtop, 5-Speed	7148	6126	6626
SR5 2-Door Hardtop, Automatic	7588	6502	7002
SR5 3-Door Sport Coupe, 5-Speed	7228	6194	6694
SR5 3-Door Liftback Coupe, 5-Speed	7128	6109	6609

Prices are accurate at time of printing; subject to manufacturer's change.

	Retail Price	Dealer Cost	Low Price
TOYOTA CORONA			
Deluxe 5-Door Wagon, 5-Speed	$7549	$6492	$6992
Deluxe 5-Door Wagon, Automatic	7989	6870	7370
Luxury Edition 4-Door Sedan, Automatic	8939	7643	8143
Luxury Edition 5-Door Sedan, Automatic	9199	7865	8365
TOYOTA CRESSIDA			
4-Door Sedan	$12249	$10105	$11105
5-Door Wagon, Automatic	12699	10477	11477
TOYOTA STARLET			
3-Door Sedan	$5578	$4797	$5297
TOYOTA TERCEL			
2-Door Sedan, 4-Speed	$4998	$4498	$4798
Deluxe 2-Door Sedan, Automatic	5678	4911	5411
Deluxe 2-Door Sedan, 5-Speed	5378	4652	5152
Deluxe 4-Door Sedan, 5-Speed	5548	4799	5299
Deluxe 4-Door Sedan, Automatic	5848	5058	5558
Deluxe 3-Door Sedan, Automatic	6018	5176	5676
SR5 3-Door Sedan, 5-Speed	6428	5509	6009
VOLKSWAGEN RABBIT			
2-Door Convertible, 5-Speed	$10100	$8767	$ 9767
2-Door Convertible, Automatic	10505	9122	10122
3-Door Sedan, 4-Speed	5990	5541	5841
L 3-Door Sedan, 4-Speed	6615	5719	6019
L 3-Door Sedan, 5-Speed	6820	5891	6291
L 3-Door Sedan, Automatic	6995	6054	6454
L Diesel 3-Door Sedan, 4-Speed	7140	6165	6565
L Diesel 3-Door Sedan, 5-Speed	7345	6337	6737
LS 3-Door Sedan, 4-Speed	7065	6035	6435
LS 3-Door Sedan, 5-Speed	7270	6207	6607
LS 3-Door Sedan, Automatic	7445	6370	6770
LS Diesel 3-Door Sedan, 4-Speed	7590	6481	6881
LS Diesel 3-Door Sedan, 5-Speed	7795	6653	7053
S 3-Door Sedan, 5-Speed	7305	6312	6712
L 5-Door Sedan, 4-Speed	6825	5900	6300
L 5-Door Sedan, 5-Speed	7030	6072	6472
L 5-Door Sedan, Automatic	7205	6235	6635
L Diesel 5-Door Sedan, 4-Speed	7350	6346	6746
L Diesel 5-Door Sedan, 5-Speed	7555	6518	6918
LS 5-Door Sedan, 4-Speed	7275	6216	6616
LS 5-Door Sedan, 5-Speed	7480	6388	6788
LS 5-Door Sedan, Automatic	7655	6551	6951
LS Diesel 5-Door Sedan, 4-Speed	7800	6662	7162
LS Diesel 5-Door Sedan, 5-Speed	6775	5857	6257
VOLKSWAGEN JETTA			
2-Door Sedan, 5-Speed	7975	6889	7389
2-Door Sedan, Automatic	8380	7244	7744
Special Edition 2-Door Sedan, 5-Speed	8425	7276	7776
4-Door Sedan, 5-Speed	8195	7076	7576
4-Door Sedan, Automatic	8600	7431	7931
Special Edition 4-Door Sedan, 5-Speed	8645	7463	7963

Prices are accurate at time of printing; subject to manufacturer's change.

	Retail Price	Dealer Cost	Low Price
2-Door Diesel Sedan	$8620	$7437	$8037
Special Edition Diesel 2-Door Sedan	8720	7523	8123
4-Door Diesel Sedan	8840	7624	8224
Special Edition Diesel 4-Door Sedan	8940	7710	8310

VOLVO

	Retail Price	Dealer Cost	Low Price
DL 2-Door Sedan, 4-Speed + OD..................	$ 9785	$ 8220	$ 8720
DL 2-Door Sedan, Automatic......................	10110	8495	8995
DL 2-Door Sedan, Manual Shift/Sunroof...........	10305	8660	9160
DL 2-Door Sedan, Automatic/Sunroof..............	10630	8930	9430
DL 4-Door Sedan, 4-Speed + OD..................	10260	8620	9120
DL 4-Door Sedan, Automatic......................	10585	8895	9395
DL 4-Door Sedan, Manual Shift/Sunroof...........	10780	9060	9560
DL 4-Door Sedan, Automatic/Sunroof..............	11105	9330	9830
DL 5-Door Wagon, 4-Speed + OD.................	10760	9040	9540
DL Diesel 4-Door Sedan, 4-Speed + OD...........	12990	10915	11915
DL Diesel 4-Door Sedan, Automatic	13180	11075	12075
DL Diesel 5-Door Wagon, 4-Speed + OD..........	13810	11605	12605
DL Diesel 5-Door Wagon, Automatic	14000	11760	12760
GL 4-Door Sedan, 4-Speed + OD.................	13630	11245	12245
GL 4-Door Sedan, Automatic.....................	13955	11515	12515
GL 5-Door Wagon, 4-Speed + OD................	14130	11660	12660
GL 5-Door Wagon, Automatic....................	14455	11930	12930
GL Diesel 4-Door Sedan, 4-Speed + OD..........	14630	12070	13070
GL Diesel 4-Door Sedan, Automatic	14820	12230	13230
GL Diesel 5-Door Wagon, 4-Speed + OD..........	15130	12485	13485
GL Diesel 5-Door Wagon, Automatic	15320	12640	13640
GLT 2-Door Sedan, 4-Speed + OD................	11945	9855	9955
GLT Turbo 2-Door Sedan, 4-Speed + OD..........	12870	10815	11815
GLT Turbo 2-Door Sedan, Automatic..............	13195	11085	12085
GLT Turbo 2-Door Sedan, 4-Speed + OD, Hi-Line	14610	12055	13055
GLT Turbo 2-Door Sedan, Automatic Hi-Line	14935	12325	13325
GLT Turbo 4-Door Sedan, 4-Speed + OD, Hi-Line	14970	12355	13355
GLT Turbo 4-Door Sedan, Automatic Hi-Line	15295	12620	13620
GLT Turbo 5-Door Wagon, 4-Speed + OD, Hi-Line	15470	12765	13765
GLT Turbo 5-Door Wagon, 4-Speed + OD, Hi-Line	15795	13035	14035
GLE 4-Door Sedan, Automatic	16390	13280	14280

Another way to get current information on car prices is to use a computerized estimating service. For a fee, you can get a printout showing what the dealer pays for a car with specific equipment. This provides you with an excellent bargaining tool you can use with the salesman. For more information, we suggest you contact:

Nationwide Auto & Truck Brokers
17517 West Ten Mile Road
Southfield, Michigan 48075
Telephone: 800-521-7257

Prices are accurate at time of printing; subject to manufacturer's change.

Used Cars

BUYING A USED car can be tricky, but done knowledgeably it's an excellent way to beat today's high new car prices and the heavy expense of depreciation during the first two years of a vehicle's life.

In general, look for the smallest, most economical car that meets most of your driving needs. You can determine those needs by making a list of the ways you plan to use the car. Then think about how long you plan to keep it. If you plan to drive it for the remainder of its useful life, look for a mechanically simple car; it will cost less to maintain in the long run. If you plan to resell in a year or two, look for a model equipped with popular options that will be attractive to the next buyer.

But most of all, buy the car you want. Buying a car based on the sort of vehicle you think you *should* own rather than the one you *want* to own will, sooner or later, lead to dissatisfaction and an earlier trade-in (with all the expense that entails).

Of course, there's no such thing as the "perfect" car, new or used. But you can look for signs that the car you're considering has been given reasonable care. Keep in mind that mileage, overall condition, and specific equipment will affect price, as will general demand for a given make and model and the seller's willingness to negotiate price with you.

Best Buys '82

CONSUMER GUIDE® magazine's automotive staff has selected the following models as the "Best Buys" among used cars readily available today. Our selections, in alphabetical order, are based on many factors, such as overall reliability and durability, frequency-of-repair record, operating economy, ride, handling, quietness, interior room and comfort, and performance.

 Used Cars

1975-81 AMC Concord and **Hornet** are mechanically and bodily the same, sharing a basic design that has been in production some 12 years now. Hornet was renamed Concord for 1978 and can be found at bargain prices. Both series have acceptable frequency-of-repair records and offer good, but not spectacular, fuel economy. Interior room and luggage space are not as generous as in more recently designed cars like the Fairmont/Zephyr, but at least late-model Hornets and most all Concords are nicely appointed and comfortable. Watch for premature rust, especially in areas of the country where roads are salted in the winter, and for electrical and suspension problems in 1975-77 Hornets. The best engine for either model is AMC's reliable and durable 258-cubic inch six, which is still in production. Avoid the Hornet's optional V-8 and the Concord's anemic four-cylinder powerplant.

1975: $1080-$1750; **1976:** $1440-$2175; **1977:** $1935-$3225; **1978:** $2565-$4000; **1979:** $3125-$4900; **1980:** $3845-$5675; **1981:** $4725-$6700.

1975-81 Buick Century and **Regal** have always seemed a cut above their corporate cousins in quality, standard features, and finish. Buick revived the Century name for its intermediates in 1973 when all GM's mid-size cars got a new bodyshell. Recommended models are the downsized 1978-81 cars with their lighter, more space-efficient body design and better fuel economy. (These are still in production as the 1982 Regal series.) Look for Buick's sturdy yet fairly thrifty V-6 engine in the 1975-'77 Century Special. For best interior room stay away from the shorter-wheelbase Century and Regal two-door coupes built before 1978. Also avoid the troublesome turbocharged engine in the sporty models from 1978 on. Buick intermediates have a fair dependability record and are among the most comfortable cars in their class.

Century 1975: $1100-$2075; **1976:** $1595-$2750; **1977:** $2115-$3250; **1978:** $2745-$4350; **1979:** $3440-$5675; **1980:** $4520-$7050; **1981:** $5735-$7676

Regal 1975: $1415-$2225; **1976:** $1845-$2800; **1977:** $2655-$3825; **1978:** $3620-$5400; **1979:** $4545-$6000; **1980:** $5490-$7050; **1981:** $6320-$8475

1975-81 Buick Electra and **LeSabre** have built an enviable reputation for durability and troublefree service over the years, and enjoy a slower-than-average depreciation rate. Today's record gas prices have hurt demand for full-size cars, so you'll probably find a few Buick bargains. The downsized 1977-80 models are preferred for their better fuel economy and interior room compared to earlier models, though they cost somewhat more. City mileage on pre-1977 Buicks was always on the wrong side of 15 miles per gallon, but economy was improved slightly by adoption of the catalytic converter in 1975. LeSabre uses a slightly smaller body than Electra, and can be found with a V-6 engine after 1975. Electras tend to be more lavishly equipped, so watch for electrical troubles with power accessories. All the big Buicks are comfortable, smooth-riding, quiet cars and seem built to last. Both series have a better-than-average repair record.

Electra 1975: $1125-$2050; **1976:** $1665-$2950; **1977:** $2855-$4275; **1978:** $3755-$5775; **1979:** $4790-$7025; **1980:** $6615-$9550; **1981:** $8075-$10675

LeSabre 1975: $945-$2775; **1976:** $1440-$2550; **1977:** $2225-$3750; **1978:** $2745-$4550; **1979:** $3690-$5950; **1980:** $4680-$7050; **1981:** $5960-$8375

1976-81 Cadillac Seville has all the comfort, luxury, and panache of the bigger DeVille and Fleetwood models, plus reasonable gas mileage for a domestic luxury car, good visibility, and that big-car ride. Through 1978, the only engine offered was a fuel-injected version of GM's 5.7-liter (350-cubic inch) V-8. But beginning in 1979, Seville offered an optional diesel engine, the Oldsmobile-built 5.7-liter (350-cid) V-8, then rated at 21 mpg. Offsetting its mileage bonus is the diesel's need for more frequent oil changes, usually at 3000-mile intervals. Also, GM claims no extra durability for its diesel V-8. Indeed, the engine has proved troublesome. Watch, too, for the expected electrical gremlins associated with cars like this equipped with many convenience gadgets. On the other hand, earlier Sevilles have held their value well. While this means second-hand models carry steep prices, it also means these cars have investment potential. Seville was redesigned for 1980 around a front-wheel-drive chassis (also used for the Eldorado coupe) with all-independent suspension. This is the current model, the one with the controversial "bustleback" trunk. The second-generation cars have a bit more room but somewhat soggier handling than their predecessors. Beware the 1981 model's "V-8-6-4" engine and its electronic fuel injection system, which has proven to be a real headache for owners and dealers alike.

1976: $4770-$6200; **1977:** $5940-$7750; **1978:** $7020-$9200; **1979:** $8730-$11600; **1980:** $11880-$14300; **1981:** $14805-$18950

1976-81 Chevrolet Chevette is a practical and sturdy little car that squeezes a lot of miles from each gallon. The simple front-engine/rear-drive layout robs the interior of needed room, but does make do-it-yourself service chores easier than in many front-wheel-drive models. The 1.6-liter (98-cubic inch) four-cylinder engine is a sturdy unit that gives fairly peppy performance in town driving, although it's noisy and rough and does not encourage fast driving. Chevette's overall durability and repair rating is average for all years. Automatic transmissions are consistently trouble-prone. Visibility is good all-around, but the cramped rear quarters make this strictly a commuter car. The hatchback rear door and fold-down back seat, however, turn it into a mini-wagon with only two persons aboard. A five-door version, added for 1978, rides on a three-inch-longer wheelbase and offers a bit more interior room. Parts and service are still readily available as the design has been basically unchanged since its debut. Rugged simplicity and attractive second-hand prices make the littlest Chevy a used-car bargain hunter's delight.

1976: $1530-$2400; **1977:** $1955-$2950; **1978:** $2520-$3650; **1979:** $3035-$4225; **1980:** $3665-$4925; **1981:** $4230-$5800

1975-81 Datsun B210 and **210** show why simplicity is a virtue in a used car. Both have rugged little four-cylinder engines with good accessibility for do-it-yourself chores. Their conventional front-engine/rear-drive layout is straightforward, which helps keep maintenance costs low. Most important, both models enjoy very low frequency-of-repair records. Economy is also a virtue these days, and the small Datsuns boast high mileage ratings. Still, these are rather basic cars in both design and finish. Neither offers as much room as other, more technically advanced economy models. But as inexpensive runabouts, the B210 and 210 are hard to beat. The price for such economy is comfort. The B210's coal-cart ride was somewhat improved over its last few years of production, but this Datsun still has the bumpiest ride of all minicars. The newer 210, introduced for the 1978 model year, is preferred for its better ride and nicer interior appointments. Watch for rust on older B210s.

1975: $1145-$2025; **1976:** $1440-$2450; **1977:** $1755-$3225; **1978:** $2205-$3800; **1979:** $2610-$4400; **1980:** $3240-$5000; **1981:** $4285-$6125

1976-80 Dodge Aspen/Plymouth Volaré had a hard time matching the good reliability record of their Dart and Valiant forerunners. These slightly larger compacts, introduced in 1976, got off to a bad start by earning a reputation for poor quality control. The cars were mostly debugged by 1978 but were never the sales winners Chrysler had hoped. Now that they've been replaced by the front-drive Aries/Reliant, their secondhand prices look quite reasonable in relation to size and passenger accommodations. We suggest used-car buyers look for the 225-cubic inch six, which has enough power for most driving needs, and a much lower frequency-of-repair rate than the bigger V-8s. Watch for signs of rust, especially on lower body panels, the trunk area, and the tops of front fenders; 1976-78 models were especially susceptible. Otherwise, Aspen and Volaré have much to recommend them; good visibility, average ride comfort, responsive handling, and quick steering. They're not quite as roomy as the Fairmont/Zephyr, but still compare favorably for spaciousness with contemporary competitors. We prefer the four-door sedan or the five-door wagon over the two-door coupes. The latter have a four-inch-shorter wheelbase that all but eliminates rear seat leg- and footroom. Fuel consumption was considered good when these cars were current, but now seems only fair in light of today's gas prices.

Aspen 1976: $1440-$2550; **1977:** $1710-$3000; **1978:** $2360-$3600; **1979:** $2835-$4200; **1980:** $3350-$4875

Volare 1976: $1440-$2550; **1977:** $1755-$3000; **1978:** $2360-$3600; **1979:** $2790-$4200; **1980:** $3260-$4775

1974-76 Dodge Dart/Plymouth Valiant can be summed up as boring bargains. Both were discontinued after 1976 to make way for the Dodge Aspen/Plymouth Volaré. Because these replacements used many Dart and Valiant mechanical pieces, getting parts and service for the older compacts is still pretty easy. Being off the market so long, they're also among the lowest priced used cars around. Both were largely un-changed over a nine-year period. Their boxy styling offers good visibility, comfortable and upright seating, and a roomy trunk. Cars with the standard 225-cubic inch slant six have a pretty good repair history, and the straightforward engineering makes most service fairly easy. Handling, steering, and directional stability are all good. The suspension is tough, the ride acceptable. Fuel economy isn't great, but it's the equal of the other early-1970s compacts. Because these cars have been out of production so long, a careful check of mileage and condition is more important in picking a used example.

Dart 1974: $750-$1600; **1975:** $1125-$2200; **1976:** $1550-$2525

Valiant 1974: $750-$1575; **1975:** $1125-$2200; **1976:** $1550-$2450

1978-81 Dodge Omni/Plymouth Horizon are domestically built front-drive subcompacts that make practical used cars today. We like the five-door hatchback body style in these identical twins because of its more spacious interior compared to the three-door 024/TC3 fastback coupe. Fuel economy is impressive: around 25 miles per gallon in the city and 30 mpg or more on the highway. Chrysler wisely chose to use a modified version of the Volkswagen Rabbit engine for Omni/Horizon. It gives decent acceleration in these fairly light cars with manual transmission. Pick-up is poor, however, with automatic. Both body types offer hatchback convenience. Ride is surprisingly smooth. The trim dimensions make easy work of maneuvering in traffic despite rather stiff, low-geared manual steering. Assembly quality seems to be better on Omni/Horizon than on other mid- to late-'70s Chrysler products. Aside from minor appearance and equipment changes, the sensible L-body design continues in production, which means parts and service are still readily available. Potential trouble spots include brakes, electrical and cooling systems, and transmissions on 1978-79 models, plus premature rust and rattles on cars not properly cared for. Paint durability seems to be much better than the norm, though. All in all, Omni and Horizon make fine used-car buys.

1978: $3260-$4125; **1979:** $3620-$4775; **1980:** $4250-$5475; **1981:** $4860-$6350

1978-81 Ford Fairmont/Mercury Zephyr are well-designed, roomy, yet lightweight family cars. The boxy body offers first-rate visibility and more passenger room and trunk space than some mid-size models. Many drivetrain components are shared with other Ford Motor Company products (including the upmarket 1981-82 Ford Granada/Mercury Cougar versions), are thoroughly proven, and are familiar to most mechanics. The conventional front-engine/rear-drive mechanical layout also simplifies servicing to some extent, which helps hold down maintenance costs. Several different engines are offered, but our choice is the 3.3-liter (200-cubic inch) six. It should also be yours. The standard 2.3-liter (140-cid) four doesn't have enough power and the optional V-8 has too much. The six gives acceptable performance and mileage that's almost as good as the four's. It's also quieter, smooth-running, and better able to handle a full load of passengers and cargo. Handling is very good and the car can be cushy and quiet when properly equipped.

Durability is pretty good except on V-8 models. Judging by their sales success, Fairmont and Zephyr still have most of what a lot of buyers want. Ford hasn't changed these cars much since their 1978 debut, which means you can save quite a bit of money in first-year depreciation by buying a used model instead of a new one. Parts and service are no problem now, nor should they be for some years to come as the basic design will live on in the Granada/Cougar through the mid-'80s at least.

Fairmont 1978: $2450-$4225; **1979:** $2925-$5250; **1980:** $3710-$6100; **1981:** $4860-$7175

Zephyr 1978: $2450-$4325; **1979:** $2990-$5250; **1980:** $3755-$6100; **1981:** $4925-$7200

1974-77 Ford Maverick/Mercury Comet are simple compacts of the old school, offering decent transportation at a bargain price. Many drivetrain components used on these twins were carried on in the Fairmont and Zephyr, the lighter and more space-efficient replacements which came along for 1978. This means most parts and service are still readily available. The main problems with Ford Motor Company's early-'70s compacts are lack of interior room and poor visibility in the two-door models. Therefore, we suggest buyers look for the four-door sedan, which has more upright rear roof pillars for better headroom, plus a wheelbase that is 6.9 inches longer for correspondingly more rear seat legroom. Handling for all models is stable and predictable, and braking is the best among the compacts. Steering, however, is slow, and ride comfort and quietness are only average. For best economy, stay with either of the rugged 200- or 250-cubic inch six-cylinder engines. Compared to more recent designs, Maverick and Comet now seem quite overstyled and outdated, but their basic sturdiness will compensate for these faults in the minds of many buyers. As with other older models, check mileage and condition carefully before you buy. Maverick/Comet seems prone to early suspension deterioration, which means a used one may need to have new springs or shocks installed to restore ride and handling to original levels. Also beware of rust along the rocker panels and other structural members.

Maverick 1974: $675-$1325; **1975:** $1125-$2125; **1976:** $1530-$2600; **1977:** $1935-$2800

Comet 1974: $700-$1250; **1975:** $1125-$2125; **1976:** $1550-$2675; **1977:** $1935-$2800

1974-80 Ford Pinto/Mercury Bobcat are simple, slightly crude economy runabouts that make good sense as used cars. Make sure, though, the car you're considering has received the all-important safety modification to the fuel tank and fuel filler neck. The huge recall of 1971-76 Pintos and 75-76 Bobcats in the wake of adverse publicity surrounding cases of fuel tank explosions in rear-end collisions has understandably made many buyers wary of these models. Simple engineering and a spacious engine compartment make it easy for do-it-yourselfers to carry out most routine service. Front seat leg- and headroom are only adequate, and the rear is strictly for children. Steering and handling are generally good, but a short wheelbase and very basic suspension give a buckboard ride on anything except glass-smooth roads. Noise is on the high side, but braking is good, especially with the recommended front discs. The interiors of Pintos without many options have about as much luxury as a taxicab, but the Bobcat has a bit more standard equipment than Pinto and is a little quieter, too. The station wagon versions offer better utility than the sedans. Trunk space in the standard Pinto is laughable. Look for the hatchback Runabout models if you plan to carry anything bigger than a breadbox. Neither car is really suited for long-distance highway travel, but makes a good, low-cost around-town commuter. For better economy and fewer service headaches, stick with the standard 2.3-liter (140-cubic inch) four-cylinder engine introduced for the 1974 model year. The optional 2.8-liter (171-cid) V-6 is less mechanically reliable, though it offers a decided performance advantage.

Pinto 1974: $700-$1275; **1975:** $1035-$2100; **1976:** $1305-$2850; **1977:** $1820-$3425; **1978:** $2270-$3925; **1979:** $2810-$4525; **1980:** $3305-$4825

Bobcat 1975: $1055-$1825; **1976:** $1575-2700; **1977:** $2070-$3500; **1978:** $2655-$4075; **1979:** $3080-$4750; **1980:** $3575-$4825

1977-81 Honda Accord struck a chord with value-conscious new-car buyers, and has been in demand since it went on sale here in 1977. As a consequence, you may have trouble finding a used one. If you do, the price will no doubt be high. The reason? Accord is a car most owners don't want to trade in. It's fairly quiet, well equipped, economical (32 mpg), and offers the traction and handling bonuses of front-wheel drive. Like most Japanese cars, the Accord will seem too small for some people, but its space utilization is excellent considering the compact external dimensions. (The rebodied 1982 model has somewhat different styling and a slightly longer wheelbase, but retains most of the mechanical components of the first-generation series covered here.) Equipped with numerous standard extras, the Accord is available as a three-door hatchback coupe or four-door sedan (beginning in 1979) with conventional trunk. The four-door is slightly longer but offers little more rear seat room, though it does provide easier rear seat access. Visibility in both body styles is excellent, and seating is upright and comfortable. Honda's attention to fit and finish has generally been slightly better than that of most Japanese car makers. An exceptionally good frequency-of-repair record tops a long list of pluses that make the Accord a gem among small cars, new or used.

1977: $2855-$3875; **1978:** $3375-$4950; **1979:** $3935-$5275; **1980:** $4545-$6175; **1981:** $5580-$7400

1974-81 Honda Civic has always been popular when new, which points up its attractions as a used car. The first-generation Civic has a fine repair record and excellent fuel economy—28 mpg or more in city driving. Interior room is on the short side, so this should be considered primarily a two-passenger car, better suited for urban driving than long trips. On the plus side, the Civic offers peppy performance, nimble handling, and a comfortable ride for its size. We suggest buyers look for the 1.5-liter four-cylinder CVCC engine which, with its larger displacement, delivers livelier performance than the standard 1.2-liter four and is even more troublefree. The two-door sedan with its separate trunk and non-folding back seat has limited cargo room. The three-door hatchback—or better yet the five-door wagon—is preferred. The first Civics were plagued by paint and engine mechanical problems, but these were eliminated on 1974 and later models. For the best economy and performance, avoid the two-speed Hondamatic semi-automatic transmission. The Civic's four- or five-speed manual gearboxes are a pleasure to use and are more reliable. These comments also apply to the current, second-generation Civic introduced for 1980. These have slightly more interior room, and decor is a bit nicer, too. Prize pick is the 1981 four-door sedan with its separate boxy trunk and refined highway performance. The newer Civics are not plentiful now as used cars, and their prices are relatively high, but they're worth searching out—or waiting for.

1974: $1000-$1750; **1975:** $1125-$2100; **1976:** $1350-$2625; **1977:** $1800-$3150; **1978:** $2250-$3700; **1979:** $2720-$4625; **1980:** $3150-$5000; **1981:** $4140-$6350

1977-80 Mazda GLC is a true economy car in several respects. It isn't loaded with frills, is rather noisy, and has a somewhat bumpy ride. But car's repair record is much better than average. Problems seldom arise, but if they should, repairs are usually easy and cheap, adding to economy of ownership. The engine runs well enough, but doesn't have much pep. In 1979, Mazda upped displacement on the original 1272cc (78-cid) inline four to 1415cc, which increased horsepower by 25 percent. The tradeoff was a small loss in mileage, which fell to an average of 35 mpg. The EPA city economy rating for the 1980 model with a five-speed manual transmission is 30 mpg. This GLC is a rear-wheel-drive design, so luggage and passenger room are not as ample as in most front-drive competitors. It does offer hatchback practicality, however, and there's a five-door wagon model (from 1979 on) with even more cargo room. In all, Mazda's mini is serviceable, cheap to run, and should last a long time given reasonable care.

1977: $1730-$2775; **1978:** $2160-$3475; **1979:** $2630-$4100; **1980:** $3215-$4775

1975-81 Oldsmobile Cutlass scores as a solid used-car choice because of its decent frequency-of-repair record and reasonable maintenance costs. Styling of pre-1978 models hampers all-around visibility and interior room, but the cars are quiet, comfortable, and plush in the Olds tradition. Economy is competitive with other mid-size models of the period but the high is only 18 miles per gallon in 1976 and '77, and considerably less in previous years. We recommend the newer downsized Cutlass, which appeared for 1978. It's lighter, more economical, and has about as much room as the earlier cars. Handling is also more responsive. The sloping "aero" fastback roofline used on two-door and four-door sedans through 1979 limits rear visibility. The personal-luxury Cutlass Supreme series parallels the sedans and wagons, and uses the same mechanical pieces in a sleeker coupe body. Prices for used Supremes will also be slightly higher. Diesel power was offered beginning with the '79 models but there's a performance drop, especially with the 4.3-liter (260-cubic inch) engine. A larger 5.7-liter (350-cid) diesel may also be found on some late-model used cars, but we don't recommend it because of its relatively high incidence of mechanical problems. Instead, look for the sturdy and fairly thrifty V-6 powerplants offered from 1977 on. With that proviso, Cutlass is highly recommended for used-car value.

1975: $1280-$1925; **1976:** $1865-$2400; **1977:** $2340-$4050; **1978:** $2925-$5225; **1979:** $3530-$6675; **1980:** $4500-$7700; **1981:** $5645-$8275

1975-81 Oldsmobile Delta 88 and **98** are good choices among full-size models for the used-car shopper. The downsized 1977 and newer cars are the choice for better fuel economy and maneuverability with little sacrifice in interior room or riding comfort compared to earlier versions. Economy-minded motorists will be interested in the availability of diesel engines in these cars starting in 1978. A used diesel Olds, however, will cost more than the same model with a gasoline engine. You may not be able to make up that extra cost in fuel and maintenance savings for a very long time. Also, the early diesel models suffered from a variety of driveability and service headaches, so think carefully before you buy. Economy in the earlier, larger models is low but typical of the class. For 1975 the figure inched up to 16 miles per gallon thanks to use of the catalytic converter, and that's why we don't recommend cars built before then. Delta 88 uses the same bodyshell as Chevy's Impala and Caprice, and the 98 is Oldsmobile's version of the Buick Electra and Cadillac DeVille. Both have a reputation for sturdiness and live up to it with an exemplary repair record. Neither series is tops in ride, handling, or steering, but both still rate better than average. Overall, the full-size Oldsmobiles get the nod as reliable used-car buys.

Delta 88 1975: $945-$2900; **1976:** $1440-$2600; **1977:** $2225-$3525; **1978:** $2720-$5125; **1979:** $3620-$6250; **1980:** $4680-$7450; **1981:** $6005-$8175

98 1975: $1100-$2025; **1976:** $1595-$2625; **1977:** $2655-$4000; **1978:** $3620-$5775; **1979:** $4545-$7325; **1980:** $5535-$9250; **1981:** $6725-$10550

1979-81 Plymouth Champ/Dodge Colt, identical except for nameplates and trim, are among the best-looking Japanese imports. They're also among the nicest used-car buys. The space-saving transverse-mounted engine and front drive give these subcompacts front seat room that borders on generous. The small overall dimensions, however, make back seat accommodations cramped. With a curb weight under 2000 pounds, the Champ/Colt offers adequate to brisk acceleration, and the well-designed suspension gives a surprisingly comfortable ride. The interior is tastefully designed and finished, and noise levels are satisfactory for the class. An unusual feature is the optional "Twin-Stick" dual-range manual transmission with eight forward speeds, four each in "economy" or "power" mode. In our tests, either mode provided a median economy figure of 35 miles per gallon. Reliability record so far is excellent; only the optional air conditioning gives trouble. Fine construction quality adds to low running costs and driving pleasure. The latest models are little changed from the ones you'll see used, so parts and service are no problem. All in all, these are practical, fun-to-drive little cars for around town use or for two people on a highway journey.

1979: $3015-$4500; **1980:** $3755-$5625; **1981:** $4475-$6275

1975-81 Toyota Celica is very appealing as economical transportation with a dash of sports-car verve. Introduced in 1971, this Japanese "ponycar" evolved through the '70s with minor mechanical and styling changes. The original 95.5-inch wheelbase was lengthened nearly three inches (to 98.3) for 1976, and the two-door hardtop coupe was joined by a three-door fastback. The inline four-cylinder engine was enlarged for 1975. In 1978, the Celica was given a completely new body, making it slightly wider, longer, and heavier than the '71-'77 series. The earlier Celicas are nice little sporty coupes. Room is good for those in front, but very cramped in back. The rather high beltline and shallow windows mean mediocre visibility and a closed-in interior. Headroom is also a shortcoming. The ride is bouncy on rough surfaces, and there's noticeable understeer in tight corners. Performance is adequate, and doesn't seem to vary much with model year. The newer '78-'81 Celica is more of a long-distance highway cruiser. Its redesigned suspension is softer, so there's more front-end plowing in corners, accompanied by noticeable body roll. Ride, however, is much better. Outward vision is better, too, a benefit of a slightly higher seating position and more glass area. Fuel economy hasn't varied much over the years. Most owners should see an overall average for either series of 20-22 mpg in mixed conditions. Like all Toyotas, Celicas come well equipped and well assembled. Workmanship is very good to excellent in all years and the car's excellent repair record shows it. Mechanical reliability is particularly good. The Celica shares many drivetrain components with the Corona, which is highly rated for reliability. All in all, the Celica stands as the best used-car buy among sporty coupes.

1975: $1620-$2650; **1976:** $2115-$3150; **1977:** $2565-$4000; **1978:** $3150-$4800; **1979:** $3710-$5525; **1980:** $4475-$6400; **1981:** $5375-$7375

1975-81 Toyota Corolla is designed to please almost everyone, so it's not particularly outstanding in any category except one: reliability. Despite the inherent flaws of its scaled-down Detroit-style design, this subcompact needs less maintenance and fewer repairs than the vast majority of small cars. The Corolla earns excellent durability ratings in almost every area: engine, transmission, suspension, and body. Nonetheless, the car has its shortcomings. Handling is a little tipsy and stability in gusty crosswinds isn't very good. Like many late-'70s Japanese cars, the Corolla has stiff springs, relatively soft shock absorbers, a short wheelbase, and simple live-axle rear suspension. The result is a jarring ride on bumpy surfaces. Another flaw is visibility due to a fairly high beltline, low seating position, and thick rear side pillars. Parking is harder than it should be considering the Corolla's small size and delightfully light steering. Otherwise, the car is easy to maneuver in tight traffic. Tight is the word for the interior. Headroom is marginal in front for taller occupants, elbow and shoulder room is restricted. Legroom is tolerable in front. Ease of entry and exit is poor on two-door models. Body styles with the separate trunk don't have much cargo room. Fuel economy is a plus. The 1977 and later models obtained an overall 33-mpg average in our tests, and earlier models did almost as well. The current Corolla design was new for 1980. It retains its predecessor's good points, and adds prettier styling, a slightly roomier interior, and more attractive appointments. Summing up, the Corolla is a simple yet well executed small car, easy to maintain and cheap to run.

1975: $1145-$2225; **1976:** $1485-$2850; **1977:** $1800-$3425; **1978:** $2205-$3950; **1979:** $2655-$4525; **1980:** $3420-$5200; **1981:** $4725-$6550

1974-81 Toyota Corona is a fine example of what used-car value is all about. It has probably the best repair record in the subcompact class, plus the usual Toyota virtues of solid workmanship, competitive economy, and an inviting list of standard convenience features. In all years, the Corona delivers fairly high mileage with better-than-average performance. Ride and handling are average to very good. Seat comfort is among the best, but suspension feels fairly harsh on rough roads. Passenger room is good in the four-door models. Headroom is below average. Trunk volume is okay. The Corona is a fairly simple car mechanically, and engine accessibility is good. With the large number of Toyota dealers, service is readily available, and replacement parts are reasonably priced. Mechanical and body durability are uniformly high, frequency of repairs much lower than average. The Corona is no longer Toyota's best-selling new-car line, but it remains one of the bright lights on the used-car lots.

1974: $1250-$1925; **1975:** $1350-$2400; **1976:** $1620-$2800; **1977:** $2180-$3475; **1978:** $2720-$4125; **1979:** $3350-$4875; **1980:** $4095-$5950; **1981:** $5580-$7150

1977-81 VW Rabbit is efficiently engineered and offers excellent room, visibility, handling, and fuel economy. The early German-made Rabbits had numerous mechanical teething troubles, most of which were solved by the time the 1977 models went on sale. That's why we don't recommend the 1975-76 cars here. Beginning with the '79 models, production for the American market was shifted to VW's U.S. factory.

Front-wheel drive gives the Rabbit safe, predictable roadholding. Braking is swift and sure with little fade, but lots of squealing from the standard front discs. A high level of mechanical noise is also a problem, and the ride on earlier cars will seem harsh to most Americans. The diesel Rabbit has near-50 mpg highway fuel economy, and gets close to 40 mpg in city driving, but this kind of economy doesn't come cheaply. In fact, with the current high demand for economy cars, a used Rabbit of any kind won't be a bargain. The earlier 1975-76 Rabbits sell for less; just make sure troubles related to brakes, electrical system, exhaust system, and carburetor have been attended to and put right if you're considering one. Keep in mind that VW service is a bit more expensive than for some other makes; the same goes for parts costs. Nevertheless, with an overall repair record that is now average to above average for both diesel and gasoline models, VW's trend-setting economy car still rates high on the list of used-car buys.

1977: $2115-$3525; **1978:** $2565-$4800; **1979:** $3015-$5425; **1980:** $3645-$8300; **1981:** $4680-$9300

1975-81 Volvo 240 can be summed up as a fairly large car with mid-size passenger room, subcompact economy, and Sherman tank sturdiness. With these qualities, the solid Swede is an appealing used-car prospect. The model's overall repair record is a little better than average since 1977, the biggest problem being early exhaust system failures. Aside from this, the car is built like a bank vault, thanks to the Swedish preoccupation with safety engineering. The roomy interior has upright, comfortable seating and good visibility. Handling is good, although there is unwanted body roll in tight low-speed turns. Disc brakes are used all-around and stop the relatively heavy Volvo quite well. Fuel economy is better than that of many American intermediates, averaging around 20 to 24 miles per gallon overall. A six-cylinder engine is also offered in the same bodyshell as the 260 series with plusher trim and more standard equipment. For most driving needs, however, the 240 models (two- or four-door sedan and five-door wagon) have more than enough power and better gas mileage than the 260 series. The four-cylinder models also cause much less trouble. For 1980, the 240 series became known as the DL and a plusher GL version was added. The 260 was renamed GLE. Volvos are expensive used as well as new. Even though their design is aging, the newer four-cylinder Volvos still seem right up to date as sensible, safe, and sturdy used-car buys.

1975: $2070-$3600; **1976:** $2610-$4250; **1977:** $3260-$5050; **1978:** $4025-$5725; **1979:** $4925-$6625; **1980:** $5715-$7850; **1981:** $7020-$9000

Television Sets

TELEVISION SETS for 1982 haven't changed much since last year; their features are basically evolutionary. However, there are some exceptions, including very good 45- and 50-inch projection television sets, five- and seven-inch black-and-white models with AM/FM radios, and the industry's first black-and-white receiver with basically a single integrated circuit (IC).

Sylvania/Magnavox—owned by North American Philips—offers the 50-inch projection set, which is an optical screen projection unit that can be viewed in full daylight. Zenith is beginning to deliver a 45-inch pop-up version, which has excellent picture resolution and definition, and Zenith also makes the small integrated-circuit black-and-white set. Because no one has ever offered an entire TV on essentially a single integrated circuit before, this advance by Zenith could decrease future prices of black-and-white receivers and lead to better quality.

Top-of-the-line 19- and 25-inch color sets from manufacturers this year feature at least 91 or 105 VHF/UHF and cable television (CATV) channels. And Zenith and RCA have extended TV tuner ranges for a total of 112 and 127 different channels, respectively. But before buying a receiver with the more expensive CATV station tuner, take a look at your local situation.

For example, you don't need a set with a cable-ready tuner if you have to lease a set-top converter to unscramble a cable signal. The same is true if you have no access to cable television, and don't expect any for some time; a set with a less expensive electronic—not mechanical—tuner will probably serve your needs. However, the top-of-the-line sets have tuners with better adjacent channel rejection and larger CATV capture ranges than cheaper models. And they can probably handle nonscrambled cable transmissions with less noise, or "snow," than sets with tuners that require a set-top converter.

TV Features to Look For

IF YOU'RE IN the market for a new TV set, you should buy one with an all-electronic, varactor-diode-controlled, solid-state tuner that uses phase-locked-loop frequency synthesis for maximum channel accuracy and minimum service requirements. The best sets offer an extra broadband-range, automatic fine-tuning (AFT) feature to pull in difficult or nonstandard CATV channels that are deliberately tuned off standard frequencies because of co-channel interference or other factors; sets with poor CATV capture characteristics can be impossible to tune. As for some "cable-ready" television advertisements, this sometimes means the set only has a simple 75-ohm coaxial cable jack input rather than an actual wideband tuner for mid-, super-, and hyperband CATV reception.

Also, set-top or receiving-dish satellite converters are certain to appear as soon as stationary and Direct Broadcast Satellite services become more common. Signals of these satellites must be reduced from the 4, 6, and 12 gigahertz (GHz) range to TV channels such as 2, 3, or 4, which operate between 54 and 72 megahertz (MHz). For the least noise and best reception, such frequency reduction must be done with very expensive space-age electronics receivers, low-noise amplifiers, and audio/video detectors—something no existing TV receiver can do.

Plug-In Modules. Only a few U.S. manufacturers, such as Zenith, General Electric, Magnavox, and Sylvania, still use independent circuit boards or plug-in modules in their receivers. All others use a "planar," or single-board, chassis with the components rigidly soldered in, except for those with ICs mounted in sockets. TV receivers with plug-in modules can usually be serviced at home, while those with planars cannot. Whatever set you choose, your new television set could operate from three to five years without needing service. So if either shop or home service is acceptable, buy either type. If you want a set that can be serviced at home, consider a TV receiver with plug-in modules.

Frequency Synthesis and Phase-Locked-Loop Tuning. More manufacturers and distributors are featuring television sets with crystal-controlled frequencies that are synthesized within the tuner compartment and compared with the incoming signal. When the synthesized and incoming signal frequency phase-match, reception is maximum, normally without the bother of either manual or automatic fine-tuning. Signals are then locked in, and often even remembered after the set is shut off until you select another channel. Many sophisticated signal-receiving systems use microprocessors and microcomputers for maximum effect, and all are reliable and easy to use.

Comb Filters. These electronic devices, which are becoming almost universally used in more expensive color sets and video recorders are relatively new and important, and are often designed as plug-in modules. They cleanly separate ordinary luminance (brightness), which is fine-detail black-and-white picture information, from the red, blue, and green primary TV colors, and all shades in between, preventing chroma/luminance interference. They also provide approximately 25 percent better horizontal resolution for a much sharper picture. For example, a well-designed comb filter can produce 4 MHz (330 lines) of horizontal resolution, as opposed to conventional methods of chroma/luminance separation of 3 MHz (240 lines).

VIR II/ColorPilot II/ColorTrak/Color Sentry. These are all names of various electronic systems designed to defeat poor broadcast TV transmissions. Hue (tint) controls color-phase while color knobs adjust color gain (amplitude). And when broadcast stations sloppily misadjust such color-phase and amplitude or black levels, your receiver has to have some means to combat purple people and green-eyed monsters. VIR II, invented by General Electric, and ColorPilot II—both now manufactured by Matsushita—are two of the basic systems that don't produce fleshtone distortion.

The other manufacturers use electronic feedback, color mixing, or fixed signal-shift circuits that move oranges and reds together for exaggerated fleshtones, add blues or subtract greens, and often broaden overall color rendition in an attempt to get truer colors. If TV broadcasters used available automated equipment, this TV receiver correction wouldn't be necessary.

Remote Controls. Remote controls have become very common. You can obtain remote controls that feature direct address (one button, one station) and/or up/down scan. And, in one instance, there's a remote control that is programmable from either the set or your easy chair. Infrared remote controls and coded commands have largely replaced remote controls using old-style ultrasonics to provide more immunity from external interference.

Picture Tubes. In the United States, picture tubes are primarily produced by Rauland (Zenith), RCA, and Sylvania (now North American Philips). Almost all now have in-line guns, slot masks, and black matrix features; they are much improved over the old tri-dot phosphor picture tubes of yesteryear. Today, 99 percent white convergence of the primary colors—red, blue, and green—which produces a clean, pure color picture, isn't unusual.

Best of all, however, is that American picture tube sales are increasing measurably since the U.S.-Japanese Orderly Marketing Agreement of 1977. Now, most Japanese manufacturers and assemblers in the United States—Toshiba in Lebanon, Tennessee; Sharp in Memphis, Tennessee; Panasonic in Chicago, Illinois; Mitsubishi in Compton, California; and Sanyo in Forrest City, Arkansas—buy at least 19- and 25-inch tubes from American sources, aiding the economy and the U.S. labor market.

Color Monitors. Color monitors, in a number of screen sizes, are beginning to appear in Japan and the United States. For 1982, these monitors for consumers are mostly wideband television sets with both video and audio plugs and jacks designed to produce high resolution/definition pictures and sound by avoiding tuner and other TV-type amplifying electronics. This produces maximum bandpass pictures with minimum noise interference from video cassette recorders, videodisc players, and home computers.

Projection TV. Indirect-view, large-screen projection television sets are coming into their own, with both Zenith and Sylvania/Magnavox entering the market. Their $3,000-to-$4,000 projection sets are expected to create quite a stir—despite their prices—and produce some demand for this kind of quality video product. At last, 45- and 50-inch flat-screen sets are now beginning to compete at least imagewise with direct-view sets whose nominal maximum diagonal diameter is 25 inches. True, Sony has both 26- and 30-inch direct-view versions, but both are also in the $1,000-to-$10,000 category.

Antennas, Satellite Dishes, and Transmission Lines

ACCEPTABLE PICTURE RECEPTION requires a good antenna and quality down-lead to the TV receiver. Usually, the better the antenna, the better your reception. In most instances, best reception is obtained by using a good-quality, dual-shielded coaxial cable with matching transformers and VHF/UHF signal splitters at the set. You will have greater noise protection, suffer less signal loss, and all but eliminate self-generated ghosts. Coaxial cable costs more but will last for years.

As for satellite-dish antennas, you should be very cautious. This is a new technology and an engineering challenge. Many distributors are buying components from varied sources to assemble an acceptable package. You must be sure the satellite dish's receiver and low-noise amplifiers do their jobs with little or no interference "trash" in the audio-visual signal. Manual aiming of the dish antenna, rather than aiming by microprocessor or other electronic means, can save about $1,000, but think of those cold winter nights when 21-channel SATCOM I doesn't have your special programs and you'll have to go outside and manually aim your dish at some other satellite. At the moment, better satellite reception is for those with $5,000 or $10,000 to spend. Later, prices could tumble, but by then program-scrambling devices may require you to pay an additional monthly fee.

Warranties

UNLESS STATED IN writing, TV receiver standardized warranties are 90-day home or carry-in service; one-year coverage on semiconductor, inductor, and capacitor parts; one-year coverage on black-and-white picture tubes, and two-year coverage on color tubes. Other suggested or implied conditions should be considered carefully to avoid partial or prorated guarantees.

Best Buys '82

OUR "BEST BUY" and "Also Recommended" television sets follow; they are listed alphabetically within each category. Remember that a "Best Buy" designation applies only to the model listed; it doesn't necessarily apply to other models made by the same manufacturer, or to an entire product line.

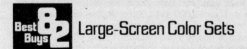

Best Buys '82 Large-Screen Color Sets

General Electric 25EM2858K is mounted in a Mediterranean-styled cabinet of tawny oak that is plain but handsome. The 25-inch set has GE's non-distorting, broadcast-controlled VIR II color lock; room light sensor; 100-degree, in-line, black matrix picture tube; red LED channel numbers; and audio output jack. Midband and superband CATV channels have been added to the all-electronic, quartz-accurate tuner. There is a one-button direct address or up/down push-to-scan remote control that's programmable from the hand-held transmitter. Other

Prices are accurate at time of printing; subject to manufacturer's change.

features include bass and treble controls, woofer and tweeter speakers, a self-regulating and line-isolating power supply, and modular chassis for easier home servicing. Due to the set's reliable EM chassis, the picture is better than some sets with broadband comb filters, which this receiver doesn't have.

Concealed controls include brightness, internal/external audio, sharpness, tint, VIR II color lock, custom picture (contrast and brightness control), on/off, volume, tone up/down, and 11 channel "enter" and two up/down buttons. The cabinet is 30⅞ inches high, 46¼ inches wide, and 21⅞ inches deep; the set weighs 160 pounds. Power consumption is 140 watts.

Ratings: brightness/sharpness—very good; **color**—very good; **signal pickup**—excellent; **control operation and location**—very good; **serviceability**—good.

Approximate Retail Price	Approximate Low Price
Not Available	$855.00

Magnavox (BB)4610 is a 25-inch table/console on legs in an appealing walnut-grained cabinet made of hardwoods and wood products. So new that it's a late listing in the 1982 Magnavox catalog, this receiver is one of the better value models in the T809 series of sets with a plug-in modular chassis. Model (BB)4610 has automatic fine tuning; automatic color leveling; manual, solid-state tuning; effective electronic voltage regulation; and a 100-degree, in-line, vertically striped picture tube. This model, however, doesn't have a comb filter. Buyers should like the receiver's picture and tone-controlled sound. There is an oval six- by four-inch speaker.

Front-panel controls include separate VHF and UHF tuners, AFT, volume, and on/off button. Concealed behind a swing-out panel are brightness, picture, tint, sharpness, color, and tone controls. Rear controls are for technician servicing. The cabinet is 29½ inches high, 32½ inches wide, and 17½ inches deep. The set weighs 120 pounds; power consumption is 96 watts.

Ratings: brightness/sharpness—very good; **color**—good; **signal pickup**—very good; **control operation and location**—very good; **serviceability**—very good (totally modular).

Approximate Retail Price	Approximate Low Price
$580.00	Not Available

RCA GFR723, at the top of RCA's line, is a contemporary-styled 25-inch console with a trapezoidal-shaped, oak-finished cabinet on a swivel base. The receiver has all the electronic trimmings. There's a comb filter, channel lock, keyboard scan control, black level clamping, automatic light sensor, automatic contrast and color, AccuFilter picture tube, fleshtone correction, quartz-crystal electronic tuning for 127 separate VHF/UHF/CATV stations, automatic sharpness, extra audio crispness and power, separate bass and treble controls, and a high-compliance speaker system with a six-inch speaker.

Front controls are on/off and volume adjustments, LED channel readout, and direct address and up/down channel and volume buttons.

Prices are accurate at time of printing; subject to manufacturer's change.

Inside a front/panel door are channel programming and tint controls, and double controls for contrast/color, brightness/sharpness, and treble/bass. People with large hands may have some trouble with these dual controls, but the overall effect in tuning is excellent. On the rear of the set, there's an on/off ColorTrak switch; otherwise, the controls are for technician servicing. The cabinet is 29¾ inches high, 37⅞ inches wide, and 20¼ inches deep. The set weighs 155 pounds. Power consumption is 102 watts.

Ratings: brightness/sharpness—very good; **color**—very good; **signal pickup**—very good; **control operation and location**—good; **serviceability**—fair (no modules).

Approximate Retail Price   Approximate Low Price
$870.00.. $789.00

Zenith N2526P is a 25-inch, classic-style console without remote control that comes in a pecan finish. Model N2526DE has a dark oak finish. The receiver's System III chassis combines eight automatic picture and color subsystems, and offer a tri-focus picture tube, comb filter, LED channel display, 112 VHF/UHF/CATV channels, quartz microprocessor-controlled tuning, excellent voltage regulation, surface wave filter input, and automatic fringe lock for distant-station picture stability. This set and the Model SN2527, which has Space Command 3000 remote control, are priced somewhat less than a more deluxe model with Space Command 4000, which has the telephone receive-and-dial system, but they have all the deluxe model's other features.

The front-panel controls of the Model N2526P include on/off, volume, channel selector, and up/down tuning. On remote-control models, however, there's up/down scanning and key number selection with channel numbers and the time displayed in white numbers on a black background on the screen. Under a long vertical front door are Color Sentry, picture, black level, color level, tint, sharpness, tone, CATV, and AFT controls. There are no rear controls. Remote-control models also have channel select programming. The cabinet is 31⅛ inches high, 39⅝ inches wide, and 19⅛ inches deep. The set weighs 153 pounds. Power consumption is 111 watts.

Ratings: brightness/sharpness—very good; **color**—very good; **signal pickup**—very good; **control operation and location**—very good; **serviceability**—excellent (totally modular).

Approximate Retail Price   Approximate Low Price
$860.00.. $746.00

Also Recommended

Panasonic CT-5162R is an expensive 25-inch console in modern dark oak styling, but it has every available TV feature possible except phone service. This receiver has a detachable, 16-button, infrared remote control for power, tuning, and volume. It also offers a 100-degree, in-line, tri-potential picture tube; quartz-accurate, frequency-synthesized 105-channel tuner; comb filter; ColorPilot II; automatic fine tuning; and light sensor.

Prices are accurate at time of printing; subject to manufacturer's change.

The front-panel controls include sharpness, Panabrite, tone, and ColorPilot II. On the rear are technician adjustments only. The cabinet is 29⅜ inches high, 34⁹/₁₆ inches wide, and 20¾ inches deep. The set weighs 132 pounds. Power consumption is 126 watts.

Ratings: brightness/sharpness—very good; **color**—good; **signal pickup**—good; **control operation and location**—very good; **serviceability**—fair (no modules).

Approximate Retail Price   Approximate Low Price
$900.00.. $775.00

Sony KV-2602 is a 26-inch console with an oak-grained finish. It features a new 30-P integrated chassis, 14-button Express Tuning, a velocity-modulation scanning system, dynamic color circuits, and better-than-average audio. This set represents a good buy in this size receiver. True, it does have variable resistor, analog channel tuning and lacks a comb filter, but power consumption is only 91 watts, and there's sufficient picture brightness for average room lighting.

Front-panel controls include 14-pushbutton variable tuning for any combination of VHF/UHF channels—no CATV—on/off, volume, and the usual color and picture controls. There are only technician adjustments on the rear. The cabinet is 30¼ inches high, 36¾ inches wide, and 22⅞ inches deep. The set weighs 184 pounds.

Ratings: brightness/sharpness—good; **color**—good; **signal pickup**—good; **control operation and location**—good; **serviceability**—fair (no modules).

Approximate Retail Price   Approximate Low Price
$1,000.00.. $825.00

Zenith SN2311W is a 23-inch table model with a vinyl-clad metal cabinet. It features remote programmable up/down channel scanning; 112 VHF/UHF/CATV channels; chromatic one-button color control; color-timed programmer; quartz-controlled, phase-locked-loop, all-electronic tuning; and on-screen channel number and time display. Also included are automatic fringe-lock high-stability circuits, all-electronic power supply voltage regulation, and picture control for varying room light conditions. There is no comb filter.

Except for programmer auto on/off buttons, all controls are behind a front panel; there are none in the rear. There's a sharpness, channel and time programming, color, picture, black level, and on/off controls. The remote transmitter controls channel and sound up/down, recall, and auto on/off. There's a five-inch speaker. The cabinet is 20¼ inches high, 29½ inches wide, and 16¼ inches deep. The set weighs 99 pounds. Power consumption is 113 watts.

Ratings: brightness/sharpness—very good; **color**—very good; **signal pickup**—very good; **control operation and location**—good; **serviceability**—excellent (totally modular).

Approximate Retail Price   Approximate Low Price
Not Available.. $627.00

Prices are accurate at time of printing; subject to manufacturer's change.

RCA FFR495 isn't one of the most stylish sets available, but it is one of the world's best 19-inch receivers. The Model FFR495—the Model FFR488R has remote control—is a deluxe 127-channel table model. It has the best RCA has to offer in design and performance—automatic color control; automatic contrast and color tracking; AccuFilter picture tube; dynamic fleshtone correction; quartz-accurate, frequency-synthesis electronic tuning; comb filter; and automatic light sensor.

Front-panel controls are on/off and volume switch and 12 up/down and direct-address buttons. There is a red LED channel readout. Behind a small panel, there are controls for add/erase channel programming, contrast, sharpness/brightness, color, tint, and treble and bass; at the bottom is a room light sensor. On the rear are an on/off ColorTrak switch, Dual-Dimension audio outputs, and technician adjustments.

The cabinet, in silver-accented walnut-grained plastic, is 17¼ inches high, 26⅛ inches wide, and 17½ inches deep. The set weighs 76 pounds. Power consumption is 102 watts.

Ratings: brightness/sharpness—excellent; **color**—very good; **signal pickup**—very good; **control operation and location**—very good; **serviceability**—fair (no modules).

Approximate Retail Price	Approximate Low Price
$580.00.. $526.00	

Zenith N1960 is a 19-inch receiver with a cabinet covered in simulated pecan. It has a gold-colored pedestal base with matching front panel and screen trim. The receiver features 112-channel, non-programmable tuning; phase-locked-loop tuner control; comb filter; advanced Color Sentry circuits; and very sharp picture detail because of its special picture circuits and tri-potential picture tube. Model N1970P, which has a cabinet of pecan veneer, is a remote-controlled, programmed version.

Front-panel controls include on/off; volume; and 10 direct-address, two up/down channels, and "enter" buttons. There's also an LED channel readout and Color Sentry light. Behind the front-panel door are Color Sentry controls, special CATV and AFC controls for cable tuning, and picture, black level, color level, tint, and sharpness controls. The set has a five-inch speaker. There are no rear controls. The cabinet is 17⅝ inches high, 26⅝ inches wide, and 17⅞ inches deep; the Model N1970P is slightly larger. The Model N1960 weighs 63 pounds. Power consumption is 102 watts.

Ratings: brightness/sharpness—very good; **color**—very good; **signal pickup**—very good; **control operation and location**—excellent; **serviceability**—excellent (totally modular).

Approximate Retail Price	Approximate Low Price
$570.00.. $494.00	

Prices are accurate at time of printing; subject to manufacturer's change.

Zenith SN1973P is a deluxe 19-inch receiver in a cabinet covered with pecan veneer; Model SN1963W has a walnut finish. This set will attract those who want all the conveniences of telephone receive-and-dial service and a remote control that offers virtually every TV feature available on the market. The receiver's SC4000 computer Space Command can tune any programmed VHF/UHF/CATV channel—by direct access or up/down scan. The set also features automatic fringe-lock circuits, and a pre-set clock timing control that turns the set on or off automatically, and an earphone jack for private listening. It also contains a comb filter, Color Sentry, and an acoustically matched and balanced five-inch oval speaker. Telephone, time, and channel numbers are displayed on-screen in white on a black background.

Controls are concealed behind a large cabinet front door. They include the usual tuning, clock-set, pre-programming, color, black level, sharpness, special cable switch, extended AFT, and volume controls. The remote unit offers complete channel tuning and volume controls, including programmer auto on/off, Space Phone, and TV mute. There are no rear controls. The cabinet is 18⅝ inches high, 27⅛ inches wide, and 18¼ inches deep; the Model SN1963W is slightly smaller. The Model SN1973P weighs 81 pounds. Power consumption is 117 watts.

Ratings: brightness/sharpness—very good; **color**—excellent; **signal pickup**—very good; **control operation and location**—excellent; **serviceability**—excellent (totally modular).

Approximate Retail Price	Approximate Low Price
$770.00 (model SN1973P)	$682.00
$750.00 (model SN1963W)	$636.00

Also Recommended

General Electric 19EC2732W is a 19-inch set with 91 quartz-synthesized VHF/UHF and midband cable channels. The receiver is pretty much a carryover from last year. Instead of VIR II, however, it has GE's Color Monitor that is reasonably effective in preserving fleshtone correction without undue distortion. The cabinet is made of high-impact plastic with a walnut-grained finish.

The set has direct-address and "enter" buttons, an on/off and volume switch, red LED channel digital readout, and Color Monitor light. Under the front apron, there are on/off Color Monitor, color, tint, brightness, and picture controls, with a sharpness control on the side. This model has much the same vertical chassis as GE's larger EM receiver, with good picture, reasonable sound, and a four-inch speaker. Rear controls are not customer-accessible. The cabinet is 17⅛ inches high, 27⅞ inches wide, and 18¾ inches deep. The set weighs 56 pounds.

Ratings: brightness/sharpness—very good; **color**—very good; **signal pickup**—very good; **control operation and location**—good; **serviceability**—good.

Approximate Retail Price	Approximate Low Price
$535.00	$429.00

Panasonic CT-9071 is a full-featured 19-inch receiver with 305-line horizontal resolution comb filter; ColorPilot II, a non-distortion broadcast

Prices are accurate at time of printing; subject to manufacturer's change.

color and tint lock; whiteness enhancer; video brightness sensor; 105-channel electronic synthesized tuner; LED channel indicator; quick-on picture tube; and Panabrite picture control. The set's slim, metal, remote control unit has volume and channel up/down, direct-address, and mute controls; it's magnetically attached to the receiver. An earphone and jack are provided for private listening.

Front-panel controls include tuning selector, on/off, brightness, tint, color, and Panabrite. The rear controls are for technician servicing. The cabinet, which is walnut-grained plastic, is 18⅛ inches high, 26½ inches wide, and 19⅜ inches deep. The set weighs 56.5 pounds. Power consumption is 104 watts.

Ratings: brightness/sharpness—very good; **color**—very good; **signal pickup**—good; **control location and operation**—good; **serviceability**—fair (no modules).

Approximate Retail Price	Approximate Low Price
$660.00	$559.00

Toshiba CB-967 is an attractive 19-inch receiver. Its cabinet is made of two-tone plastic and has silver accents. The set has a comb filter, resolving about 288 horizontal lines; automatic dark-picture intensifier and white-detail purifier; and a very thin magnetically attached remote control for 105-channel tuning, including midband and superband CATV. One four-inch speaker delivers better-than-average sound, and the set's room light sensor operates constantly to keep picture at proper contrast and brightness. The signal-seeking tuner has fast and slow up/down, direct-address, volume, and mute buttons. All integrated circuits are socket-mounted for quick removal and replacement.

Concealed front-panel controls include manual/remote, on/off, and horizontal, and vertical resolution. Rear controls are for technician servicing. Front-panel controls under the apron include picture, tint, color, and Tomatic Eye. The cabinet is 17¼ inches high, 25 inches wide, and 18½ inches deep. The set weighs 58 pounds. Power consumption is 97 watts.

Ratings: brightness/sharpness—very good; **color**—very good; **signal pickup**—good; **control operation and location**—fair; **serviceability**—good.

Approximate Retail Price	Approximate Low Price
$750.00	$699.00

 17-Inch Color Sets

RCA EFR398R is a good-looking 17-inch receiver in a walnut-grained plastic cabinet with cream-colored accents. This set has infrared remote control, which features scanning, on/off, volume on/off or mute, and up/down channel selection, including 23 CATV channels. The receiver

Prices are accurate at time of printing; subject to manufacturer's change.

has bright LED channel readouts. A 3½-inch speaker and all controls are concealed under a plastic door. There are channel programming, volume and channel up/down, brightness contrast, color, and tint controls. Rear controls consist of vertical hold and sharpness. The cabinet is 15½ inches high, 24½ inches wide, and 18¼ inches deep.

Ratings: brightness/sharpness—very good; **color**—very good; **signal pickup**—good; **control operation and location**—good; **serviceability**—fair (no modules).

Approximate Retail Price	Approximate Low Price
$570.00	$380.00

Zenith N1720W is a low-cost, reliable, easily serviced 17-inch receiver that has standard tuners but a fully transistorized tuning system with a high-gain VHF tuner for weak signal areas. The modular chassis—like Zenith's larger sets—has modules for electronic voltage regulation, automatic fine tuning, automatic color, digital sync countdown, surface wave filter input, synchronous video detection, and a ganged color-video picture control.

The cabinet is simulated American walnut with silver trim. On the front are the AFT, on/off, volume, and tuning controls, and a four-inch speaker. Tint, color, black level, sharpness, and picture controls are on the rear. The cabinet is 16⅛ inches high, 24⅛ inches wide, and 15⅝ inches deep.

Ratings: brightness/sharpness—good; **color**—very good; **signal pickup**—very good (on VHF); **control operation and location**—satisfactory; **serviceability**—very good (totally modular).

Approximate Retail Price	Approximate Low Price
Not Available	$389.00

 Small-Screen Color Sets

General Electric 13AC2542W is a remote-controlled 13-inch receiver, which is a holdover from 1981 and a very good one. The cabinet is cream-colored and walnut-grained plastic. This is a very good programmable set with up/down remote control and adequate Color Monitor.

The Model 13AC2542W has an infrared remote control that can tune 91 VHF/UHF/CATV channels, handle volume, and turn the set on or off. It features DC restoration, automatic color control, a four-inch speaker, earphone jack, and coaxial cable connector. The overall color picture is as sharp or sharper than you'll find in any small chassis on the market. Programming controls are under a small front panel. On/off and channel up/down buttons are in front alongside the LED channel readout. Under the set's apron are color, tint, brightness, contrast, and Color Monitor on/off controls. Recessed rear controls are for technician servicing. The

Prices are accurate at time of printing; subject to manufacturer's change.

set is 14 inches high, 20½ inches wide, and 15¼ inches deep. It weighs 35¼ pounds. While not strictly a portable, its size and weight do allow easy movement. Power consumption is 98 watts.

Ratings: brightness/sharpness—excellent; **color**—very good; **signal pickup**—very good; **control operation and location**—good; **serviceability**—good (no modules but printed-circuit boards can be unplugged).

Approximate Retail Price	Approximate Low Price
$500.00..	$400.00

RCA EFR333W is a modest XL-100 series 13-inch receiver with manual VHF/UHF solid-state tuners. It features automatic fine tuning, automatic color and contrast tracking, black level compensation, automatic flesh-tone correction, and a 3½-inch round speaker.

Brightness, contrast, color, and tint controls are under the set's front apron; vertical hold and peaking controls are on the rear. The cabinet, in walnut-grained plastic with light-colored accents, is 13⅛ inches high, 18 inches wide, and 16⅜ inches deep. It weighs 29 pounds.

Ratings: brightness/sharpness—good; **color**—good; **signal pickup**—good; **control operation and location**—good; **serviceability**—fair (no modules).

Approximate Retail Price	Approximate Low Price
Not Available..	$295.00

Zenith N1310A is a small, manually tuned 13-inch receiver. The cabinet is almond-colored plastic with a textured finish and nickel-gold trim. This set, one of Zenith's Slim-Line models, has a picture that's remarkably bright and clean, with good color; the controls are responsive. The receiver also has a modular chassis, an 82-channel tuning system, tri-focus EFL picture tube, voltage regulation, and digital picture-lock and fringe-lock circuit. It provides adequate sound with a three-inch speaker.

On the front are two manual tuners, AFC, and on/off volume buttons. On the left top of the cabinet are sharpness, tint, color, black level, and picture controls. The cabinet is 13¾ inches high, 20⅛ inches wide, and 14⅞ inches deep. There is a folding handle for easy portability. The set weighs 40 pounds. Power consumption is 87 watts.

Ratings: brightness/sharpness—very good; **color**—good; **signal pickup**—good; **control operation and location**—good; **serviceability**—very good (totally modular).

Approximate Retail Price	Approximate Low Price
Not Available..	$344.00

 Projection Sets

Sylvania/Magnavox SuperScreen LSA5000 was developed by Canada's Freen Screen for Sylvania, using Sylvania's D54 chassis with

Prices are accurate at time of printing; subject to manufacturer's change.

comb filter. The projection set's new 50-inch optical lens system with black striped coating that rejects high ambient light is really composed of many lenses and can be constructed in any size. Currently, this unit has 4.2 MHz horizontal resolution, which is scheduled to be expanded to 6 MHz in 1982, and improved green and red rare earth CRT phosphors, and f/1.0 U.S. Precision lenses. Horizontal viewing angle is ±45 degrees with 330 lines of TV broadcast resolution and 410 lines at baseband (standard video). Audio is rated at 16 watts TV RMS or two-channel stereo at eight watts per channel into 4-ohm loads. There are stereo and video input and output jacks.

The LSA5000 also offers a built-in crosshatch generator, a four-speaker sound system, light sensor, separate bass and treble controls, 105-channel tuning with remote control and pre-programmed stations, direct or up/down tuning, on/off, and volume up/down. Front-panel controls duplicate those on the remote, plus tone, convergence, and balance controls. Other controls are for technician servicing. The roll-around cabinet, with chestnut laminate and simulated woods with brown accents, has front shelf space for a video cassette recorder or videodisc player. It is 63 inches high, 45 inches wide, and 41 inches deep. It weighs 414 pounds.

Ratings: brightness—very good; **sharpness**—good; **color**—good; **signal pickup**—very good; **control operation and location**—good; **serviceability**—good.

Approximate Retail Price	Approximate Low Price
$3,500.00	Not Available

Zenith SN4545P is a projection set with a high price, but if you want a 45-inch projection unit with everything including a disappearing screen, this is it. Developed from Zenith's original modular X chassis, with the addition of a very new and effective chroma/luminance integrated circuit, this receiver offers 112-channel Space Command 5000 remote tuning with in/out telephone facilities and programmable on/off clock timing. Three very high resolution electron guns with slanted faceplate tubes and f/1.0 lenses provide good brightness and, with Zenith's glass delay line comb filter, offer exceptional definition and picture quality. When the receiver isn't in use, the remote control can lower the 45-inch flat screen out of sight, leaving a credenza of pecan wood and veneers. There are bass and treble sound controls, and a voice/music switch. The set also can be used as a monitor for a video cassette recorder, videodisc, or home computer. Two 8-inch woofers and two 2.5-inch tweeters deliver more-than-adequate sound. Best viewing is directly in front of the set.

Front-panel controls and the remote control handle all receiver commands such as: telephone, mute, auto on/off programming, channel "enter" numbers and time, recall, channel direct-address buttons, screen up/down, power on/off, and volume or channel up/down. There are no user-adjustable rear controls. The cabinet is 34⅜ inches high with the screen down, 57⁵/₁₆ inches high with the screen up, 44¹¹/₁₆ inches wide, and 29¹/₁₆ inches deep. It weighs about 300 pounds. Power consumption is 148 watts.

Ratings: brightness—good; **sharpness and resolution**—very good,

Prices are accurate at time of printing; subject to manufacturer's change.

color—very good; **signal pickup**—very good; **control operation and location**—good; **serviceability**—very good (totally modular).

Approximate Retail Price   **Approximate Low Price**
$3,750.00... $3,450.00

 Video Monitors

Kloss Novabeam Model One video projection monitor—without tuner—provides direct color projection on a 6.5-foot screen, although it will project onto a 10-foot screen (not available from Kloss). This is the largest of this year's monitors offered in a compact projector console and a separate, freestanding screen that is more than 80 foot-lamberts bright and capable of very good resolution and definition. The console has a comb filter, a wide-ranging loudspeaker system with equalized power amplifier, video and audio inputs and outputs, and built-in test-pattern generator. The monitor is available finished in wood-grain vinyl or genuine oak and walnut. A wired remote control is available at extra cost.

Brightness, contrast, focus, convergence, color, tint, volume, and fine-detail controls are conveniently positioned. Other controls are for technician servicing. The projector is 18.5 inches high, 27.5 inches wide, and 22 inches deep. The actual picture size on the screen is 4 by 5.5 feet. The projector weighs 118 pounds; the screen weighs 50 pounds. **Ratings: brightness/sharpness**—very good; **color**—good; **signal pickup**—not available; **control operation and location**—good; **serviceability**—very good (with modules).

Approximate Retail Price   **Approximate Low Price**
$2,495.00 .... Not Available

Panasonic CT-5511 and CT-7711 are five-inch and seven-inch portable monitors in silver-colored cabinets with black trim. They feature VHF/UHF continuous electronic tuning, ColorPilot (VIR), AC/DC operation, dipole antennas, tinted screen cover, earphone jack and earphone for private listening. The cabinets, which come with stands, are 5¼ inches high, 9½ inches wide, and 11¼ inches deep for the five-inch Model CT-5511 and 7⅜ inches high, 9⅝ inches wide, and 12⅛ inches deep for the seven-inch Model CT-7711. The sets weigh 8⅞ and 12½ pounds, respectively. The front controls include tuning, volume, picture, and power on/off. The speaker, plug-ins, and switching is on the side. **Ratings: brightness/sharpness**—good; **color**—good; **signal pickup**—good; **control operation and location**—fair; **serviceability**—fair; (no modules).

Approximate Retail Prices   **Approximate Low Prices**
$440.00 (model CT-5511)... $380.00
$450.00 (model CT-7711) $395.00

Prices are accurate at time of printing; subject to manufacturer's change.

RCA TC1110 is a nine-inch black-and-white monitor with 700 lines of horizontal resolution, fast-acting AFC for stable video cassette recorder playback, regulated power supply, and 10 kV high voltage. Front controls are on/off, brightness, contrast, and vertical and horizontal holds. Rear controls are Hi Z(300)/75 ohms, video normal/sharp, and DC restoration on/off. The cabinet is metal with a plastic front. It is 9.4 inches high, 8.7 inches wide, and 10.5 inches deep. It weighs 12.8 pounds.

Ratings: brightness/sharpness—very good; **signal pickup**—good; **control operation and location**—good; **serviceability**—fair.

Approximate Retail Price	Approximate Low Price
$205.00	Not Available

Zenith SN1975P, with a 19-inch screen, is among the fanciest and most expensive of all the receiver-monitors. It stands virtually alone in several respects. It has an ultramodern-styled cabinet in pecan-grained plastic and light gold trim. This deluxe monitor not only has the SC3000 Space Command, but also two sets of external high-performance 5-inch woofers and 2.5-inch tweeters in separate enclosures; each enclosure is 11 inches high, 7¼ inches wide, and 6⅜ inches deep.

On the cabinet's front panel are tuner program buttons, up/down channel scan, "enter," and direct-address buttons, a voice/music switch, and volume and bass/treble controls. The unit features surface wave filter input, comb filter, full-wave synchronous detector, and an audio output of 10 watts. Hidden behind a cabinet door are sharpness, color, tint, and picture controls. The set has quartz-controlled electronic tuning for 112 channels, and clock-timed on/off capability within any 24-hour period. The cabinet is 16⅜ inches high, 22¾ inches wide, and 17⅛ inches deep. Power consumption is about 110 watts.

Ratings: brightness/sharpness—very good; **color**—very good; **signal pickup**—very good; **control operation and location**—very good; **serviceability**—excellent (totally modular).

Approximate Retail Price	Approximate Low Price
$800.00	$682.00

 # Black-and-White Sets

General Electric 15XB9212W is a 15-inch holdover from last year, but a very good buy with better-than-average sound, contrast, and brightness. It has recessed handgrips on the side, and the cabinet is walnut-grained plastic. There are two manual tuners, off/on switch, volume control, three-inch speaker, and brightness and contrast controls. On the rear are vertical and horizontal hold and size controls. The set is

Prices are accurate at time of printing; subject to manufacturer's change.

13⅞ inches high, 18¾ inches wide, and 12 inches deep. It weighs 22⅜ pounds. Power consumption is 32 watts.

Ratings: brightness/sharpness—good; **signal pickup**—good; **control operation and location**—good; **serviceability**—fair.

Approximate Retail Price	Approximate Low Price
$146.00	$115.50

General Electric 19XA9312K is a 19-inch receiver that's held over from 1981, but it's a good one. The cabinet is oak-grained plastic. There are recessed handgrips on the sides and a matching roll-around stand on casters that's optional. Manual VHF/UHF tuner sensitivity and sound are relatively good for a black-and-white receiver. And there is satisfactory contrast and brightness, and good picture definition. Front controls include on/off, volume, brightness, and contrast; vertical and horizontal holds and size controls are on the rear. The set is 16¼ inches high, 22⅞ inches wide, and 14¼ inches deep. It weighs 36.5 pounds. Power consumption is 49 watts.

Ratings: brightness/sharpness—good; **signal pickup**—very good; **control operation and location**—good; **serviceability**—fair.

Approximate Retail Price	Approximate Low Price
Not Available	$154.50

Zenith N125J is Zenith's deluxe, three-way 12-inch portable, which is encased in a stitched, western-style leatherette case with handle. It has three stages of IF, DC restoration, 3.5-inch oval speaker, removable sunshield, and two manual tuners. Controls on the front are black level, contrast, and on/off volume; on the rear are horizontal and vertical holds. There's also an earphone jack. It is 11⅝ inches high, 16½ inches wide, and 12.5 inches deep. It weighs 18.5 pounds. The Model S127Y rechargeable battery pack is optional.

Ratings: brightness/sharpness—good; **signal pickup**—good; **control operation and location**—good; **serviceability**—fair.

Approximate Retail Price	Approximate Low Price
Not Available	$125.00

Zenith N162W is a 16-inch model that is basically the same as last year's "M" model except for gold front trim instead of white. The black-and-white receiver has good resolution and definition. It is DC-coupled and has a full three-stage tuned IF, Perma-Set VHF fine tuning, 70-position UHF channel selection, and Zenith's Sunshine picture tube. The set has a built-in handle.

On the front are the two VHF/UHF tuning knobs, and off/on volume switch, black level, and picture controls. On the rear are vertical and horizontal holds. The set is 14⅜ inches high, 20½ inches wide, and 13⅜ inches deep. It weighs 29 pounds.

Ratings: brightness/sharpness—good; **signal pickup**—good; **control operation and location**—good; **serviceability**—fair.

Approximate Retail Price	Approximate Low Price
Not Available	$143.50

Prices are accurate at time of printing; subject to manufacturer's change.

Video Cassette Recorders/ Videodisc Players

IN TERMS OF increased sales in 1981 compared with sales a year earlier, the video cassette recorder (VCR) is the fastest-growing consumer electronic product by far. Today, more than four million homes in the United States have a VCR connected to a television receiver.

Sony, the originator of one video recording format, calls home video recording a form of time shifting; a TV viewer who finds that a favorite program is going to be broadcast at an inconvenient time can record the program without being present and can then view it when time permits. Indeed, this is probably still the most important application of video recording for most people. But, as more and more people become involved with video recorders, other applications assume increased importance. For one thing, the number of pre-recorded videotapes available for sale or rental has grown tremendously in the past two years. Almost any reasonably successful motion picture, from early classics to films that are still being shown in theaters, is available at one of thousands of video stores that are appearing in many neighborhoods.

Sales of video cameras for use with home or portable VCR's are on the rise as well. Unlike 8mm or 16mm home movie photography, videotaping offers the advantages of instant playback, the ability to erase an unsatisfactory scene, and best of all, a cost that is just a small fraction of home movie-making.

VCR Formats

THE TWO MOST popular video cassette recorder formats are Beta and VHS. Although the term "Betamax" is sometimes applied to all VCR's, only about one third of the machines in the country use the Beta format and not all of these are Betamax machines. Only Sony Corporation, who developed the Beta format and introduced it to consumers in late 1975, makes Betamax video recorders. Other manufacturers licensed by Sony to manufacture and sell Beta-format VCR's include Sanyo, Sears, Toshiba, and Zenith.

The first Betamax machines offered by Sony were able to record and play only an hour's worth of videotape. The tape speed of approximately

1½ inches per second (ips) used on these early video cassette recorders is known as Beta I, or X-1. The need for longer record and play times was soon apparent, so Sony improved the operation of its system enough to permit a slower tape speed for longer playing time. The Beta II speed (0.79 ips) increased record/play time to three hours and, more recently, Beta III speed (0.53 ips), which is available on just about all new Beta-format VCR's, increases maximum record/play time to five hours. If you plan to purchase a new Beta-format VCR and now own some pre-recorded tapes with the Beta I speed, check to make certain that the machine you select can play those tapes at the now-obsolete Beta I speed. Several currently available machines can play tapes at Beta I, but none that we know of will record at Beta I speed.

As is true of audio tape recording, the slower the tape speed, the poorer the fidelity you can expect during playback. In the case of video, the slower the speed, the poorer the picture quality, or resolution. Nonetheless, thanks to advances in electronics, the picture quality obtained even at the slowest Beta speed—Beta III—is remarkably good and, in some cases, is indistinguishable from the picture quality obtainable at the more rapid Beta II tape speed.

In 1976, about a year after Sony introduced its first home Betamax machine, Victor Company of Japan, known as JVC in this country, introduced a competing video recording format known as VHS (Video Home System). The videotape cassette used in VHS-format machines is somewhat larger than that employed in Beta-format machines, though both formats use ½-inch-wide tape.

Like Beta-format machines, VHS machines have also undergone much the same "time-stretching" evolution. The first VHS machines had a maximum record time of two hours, using a tape speed (1.31 ips) that is known as SP (Standard Play). This was soon increased to a maximum of four hours at the LP (Long-Play) tape speed, and more recently, to SLP (Super Long Play), or ELP (Extra Long Play) speed, which yields up to six hours of recording and playback time from a cassette.

While Beta cassettes are designated by the approximate footage of tape they contain (L-125, L-250, L-370, L-500, L-750, and L-830), VHS cassettes are designated in terms of the number of minutes they will record or play, using the SP tape speed (T-30, T-60, T-90, and T-120). Thus, a T-120 VHS cassette will record for 120 minutes or two hours at the SP speed, four hours at the LP speed, and six hours at the SLP or ELP speed.

The main difference between Beta and VHS machines lies in the method in which the videotape is threaded or fed around the rapidly spinning tape drums in a VCR. The Beta system uses "U-loading"; tape is automatically threaded and comes in contact with the videotape head drum as soon as the cassette is placed in its compartment. The tape follows a U-shaped path. In VHS machines, the tape is threaded into place and extracted from the cassette only when the "play" or "record" control is activated. When the tape is in position to record or play, its path forms an "M" shape, which is why the VHS format's tape-loading system is often called "M-loading."

To date, there are many more companies licensed to manufacture

VHS machines than there are companies using the Beta format, even though, in the opinion of CONSUMER GUIDE® magazine experts, both formats are capable of providing excellent video pictures. Such differences as do exist are more likely to be the result of differences between quality control levels and manufacturing care from one maker to another, rather than fundamental differences in formats. VCR's made or sold by Akai, Curtis-Mathes, General Electric, Hitachi, JVC, Magnavox, Mitsubishi, Panasonic, Philco/GTE, Quasar, RCA, Sharp, and Sylvania are all of the VHS type.

Recognizing that both the Beta and VHS formats are likely to coexist for many years to come, leading manufacturers of blank videotape package tape for both types of machines, and distributors of pre-recorded videotape cassettes always stress the point that their video cassettes of films and other entertainment are available on both VHS and Beta cassettes. Naturally, before choosing a format or selecting one brand of VCR over another, you should carefully audition the picture quality obtainable from each format and each machine. However, one additional factor you may want to consider is whether your friends own VHS or Beta machines. Because you may very well want to trade or borrow tapes from friends, bear in mind that Beta-format cassettes cannot be played in a VHS machine, nor can VHS-format cassettes be played in a Beta machine.

New VCR Formats

IN 1980, Technicolor Audio/Visual Division of Technicolor, Inc., introduced CVC (Compact Video Cassette), a new format and a new, lightweight portable VCR that weighs less than 7 pounds. CVC cassettes are slightly larger than audio cassettes and use ¼-inch videotape.

Technicolor's intention was clearly not to compete with VHS or Beta VCR's, but rather to serve as an alternative to the relatively heavy portable machines that had to be used with video cameras when taping away from home. Technicolor has stressed the business applications of its "micro-video" system as well, suggesting that the age of the "visual memo" between offices or far-flung branches of the same company may well be with us. While CONSUMER GUIDE® magazine's experts believe that this attractive format has a place, we believe that the CVC format isn't likely to replace either VHS or Beta machines simply because, at best, the small CVC cassettes can hold only enough tape for one hour's worth of recording (at the moment, only 30- and 45-minute cassettes are available). The Technicolor CVC format would therefore be unsuitable for home video recording of TV programs, but may find favor with those who want a substitute for home movies. Since Technicolor introduced its small portable, the company has produced a matching video camera, a TV tuner/timer (which, when paired with the VCR, can be used to record TV programs), and a combination TV color monitor/VCR. Meanwhile, Canon, a well-known camera manufacturer, has introduced a video cassette recorder that is compatible with the Technicolor ¼-inch tape format.

As if to further confuse the issue, Grundig of West Germany plans to market its Video 2000 system, yet another VCR format, in the United States. Widely used in Europe, the Video 2000 system was developed jointly with Philips of the Netherlands. The Grundig-Philips system uses a cassette that isn't too different in size from Beta or VHS cassettes, but can be played on both sides much like an audio cassette. Despite the reduction in the system's tape length, playing time is increased to four hours per side, or a total of eight hours. The editors of CONSUMER GUIDE® magazine feel that, with Beta and VHS so firmly established in this country, the new Grundig format will have little chance of capturing a significant share of the market for VCR's within the foreseeable future.

Programmability

AS MAXIMUM recording time on Beta and VHS VCR's increased, the need for more elaborate programmability and special effects became apparent to manufacturers. By programmability, we mean the ability to give complex instructions to the machine regarding programs to be recorded in the future while unattended, the channels to be selected, and times of turn-on and turn-off for each recording period. A fully programmable machine can, in many cases, be "told" to record the same program on the same channel each day for a week or two—a boon to the soap opera addict on vacation. In addition, the same machine may be capable of recording as many as eight different events at randomly selected starting and ending times from as many as eight different channels over a period as long as two weeks. The only limitation in programmability on such VCR's is the length of the tape itself because, obviously, once the tape runs out, the machine will shut itself off automatically, or rewind the tape to the beginning.

Of course, all of this programmability adds nothing to basic picture or sound quality, but it does increase the cost of a VCR. So, if you don't need such elaborate programmability, you may prefer to buy a more basic machine that offers adequate recording time and good picture quality, with only the minimum 24-hour, single-event programming capability.

Special Effects

MOST LATE-MODEL VCR's have special effects capabilities such as freeze-frame (still picture), slow motion, fast-motion scanning, and the like. While these features may seem like needless frills at first, each can serve a useful purpose. For example, if you videotape a sports event like a baseball game (either off the air, or at a neighborhood game using a video camera), being able to examine a batter's swing one frame at a time, in slow motion, can help to improve a player's form. A golfer, bowler, or a tennis player may find such a feature extremely practical. With so much recording time now available at the slowest tape speeds, it can be very frustrating trying to find the beginning of a specific program or portion of a program in a five- or six-hour tape using the conventional fast-forward or fast-rewind mode of a VCR. Being able to scan the picture visually, at anywhere from 2 to 20 times the normal viewing speed, solves that problem.

Even the least expensive VCR's available are likely to have a "pause" feature. This lets you stop the recording process momentarily to eliminate a commercial or other unwanted portion of a program while recording a television broadcast. In many cases, the pause control can also be used during playback to show still-frame or freeze-frame pictures. Manufacturers all warn against keeping a VCR in the pause mode for more than a few minutes at a time. In this mode, the videotape has stopped moving from reel to reel, but is still in contact with the rapidly spinning tape head drums. This action, if continued for a long period, can wear the precision components and damage the tape. Some recorders, however, feature an automatic shut-off if the pause control is left engaged for more than a few minutes.

Portable VCR's

NOT TO BE OUTDONE by the manufacturers of portable VCR's with a new format, the companies whose machines use VHS or Beta systems have come up with full-featured, lightweight, portable VCR's, too.

Complete portable models consist of two components—a battery-powered video cassette recorder that can be used at home or outdoors, and a TV tuner/timer section that stays at home. These components can be bought separately or together. In combination, a portable VCR and tuner/timer can do all of the things that the most elaborate all-in-one home VCR can do and then some. For videotaping with a camera outdoors, all you need is the camera and the battery-powered VCR. When you want to use the portable VCR to record a television program at home, you connect it to the tuner/timer, which lets you use power from an electrical outlet so you don't discharge the batteries. If you never have a need for the tuner/timer unit—that is, you only want to videotape with the camera and play what you videotape on your television set—you can purchase an optional power adapter instead; it lets you use household power to operate the portable VCR and to recharge its batteries, too.

Early portable VCR's generally operated at one speed and were equipped only with a pause control for use with a video camera when changing from one scene to another. Modern portables, however, often feature all of the special-effects capabilities and multiple tape speeds common to home VCR's. If you plan, now or later, to own a video camera and haven't purchased your first home VCR, CONSUMER GUIDE® magazine's video experts urge you to consider buying a portable VCR and a matching tuner/timer from the same manufacturer. Often, the two units will be offered at a single combined price. You can usually buy the portable VCR alone if you want to start your video activities with a camera, and you can then purchase the tuner/timer at some later time. However, models do change quickly so you should make sure that the tuner/timer for your portable VCR isn't discontinued by the manufacturer by the time you are ready to buy it. In any event, when the two components are connected, you have all of the benefits of a home VCR plus the portability of the VCR section alone for videotaping with a camera. Of course, if your purpose in owning a video cassette recorder is simply to record TV programs and to play back pre-recorded videotapes, a home VCR may be right for you and will end up costing you less than a portable system.

Videotape

JUST ABOUT ALL of the well-known manufacturers who make audio cassette and open-reel recording tape also offer blank videotape for use on video cassette recorders. Most offer a variety of tape lengths for both Beta and VHS machines. However, not all lengths are available from every manufacturer.

While most newly purchased VCR's usually come with a blank videotape cassette labeled with the name of the manufacturer of the VCR, in all but a few cases the tape was actually made and packaged by one of the major tape companies—not the maker of the VCR.

CONSUMER GUIDE® magazine has tested and evaluated most of the better-known brands of videotape and can recommend the following brands without hesitation: BASF, Fuji, JVC (VHS only), Maxell, Memorex, Panasonic/Quasar (VHS only), RCA (VHS only), Sanyo (Beta only), Scotch, Sony (Beta only), and TDK.

CONSUMER GUIDE® magazine strongly advises against purchasing unknown brands of videotape offered at bargain prices. Some so-called bargains have been known to provide shorter-than-claimed lengths of tape, and many have used tape unsuitable for video recording; they have such defects as severe drop-outs—areas where the magnetic particle coating is missing. This leads to noisy and erratic picture and sound reproduction. Bargain videotapes may also have defective cassette shells that cause jam-ups, which can damage a video cassette recorder.

Videodisc Players

IT IS NOW more than two years since the first videodisc players were introduced by Magnavox with great fanfare in a few key cities for test marketing. The machines were quickly grabbed by those who wanted to be among the first with a brand new home entertainment item. Now, however, the "great expectations" voiced for the videodisc format have become somewhat muted.

Now that videodisc players are available and plentiful, sales haven't met manufacturers' expectations. To be sure, the videodisc idea is a promising and viable one. At a fraction of the cost of a pre-recorded videotape, you can purchase a disc containing a full-length motion picture, insert it into what looks like a record player, sit back, and watch the movie whenever and as often as you wish. What's more, the best available videodisc players can be bought for far less than a video cassette recorder. Why then have videodisc players not sold as well as their makers had hoped?

Three Competing Systems

SHORTLY AFTER Magnavox introduced its videodisc player, Pioneer announced that it, too, would begin marketing a videodisc player. Happily, the players that are sold by Pioneer are fully compatible with those sold by Magnavox; both are laser-optical machines that can play the same kind of videodisc. Unfortunately, that's as far as compatibility ever got.

In March, 1981, after many years of research and development, RCA introduced its version of a videodisc player, the so-called CED-type (Capacitance-Electronic Disc), which operates under a totally different principle than the Magnavox and Pioneer players. The Magnavox and Pioneer discs have their program content picked up by a laser beam; there is no physical contact with the surface of the disc. The RCA player uses a contacting stylus, or pickup, which rides in microgrooves on the disc somewhat similar to an ordinary phonograph record. While the basic cost of the RCA player is substantially less than that of the laser-optical videodisc player, discs for the two systems are not interchangeable. And there are other major differences as well.

The laser-optical disc, because it contains no grooves and there isn't any physical contact, is able to offer a variety of special effects. For example, you can "freeze" a single frame or picture on the television screen while playing a videodisc. This is possible because the laser, above the surface of the disc, can be instructed to stop, at which time the beam traces and retraces a single spiral line of information imbedded below the surface of the disc, over and over again, causing a single picture to appear. An RCA CED player cannot do that, because its pickup is actually riding in a groove, and to repeat-play the same groove over and over again would have the same disastrous effect on the disc as that which occurs when a phonograph needle "hops" out of a record groove and plays the same passage of music over and over again —leading to a scratch on the record.

The laser-optical videodisc player can also be instructed to play fast-forward, in reverse, and in slow motion. It can be told to find and play a specific "frame" out of the some 54,000 individual frames, or pictures, stored beneath its surface. Furthermore, because the information required to reproduce TV pictures is actually stored below the disc's surface and is protected by a plastic coating, laser-optical discs can be handled freely, dropped, and even covered with dust and damaged by slight scratches with no degradation nor loss of picture quality. Finally, the sound track accompanying the picture on a laser-optical disc has two-channel stereo capability, whereas RCA discs—for the moment at least—offer only monaural sound reproduction.

The RCA CED disc can be made to play in a fast-forward or fast-reverse mode, but still pictures aren't possible. And because the disc surface contains minute grooves that could be easily damaged or impacted with dust and dirt, this type of disc is kept in a plastic holder or "caddy" except when being played; you insert the entire caddy in a slot located at the front of the player and then pull the caddy out, leaving the disc inside the player.

It should be obvious—but from what we hear from dealers around the country, it isn't—that neither the laser-optical nor the CED type of videodisc machine is capable of recording a video program. That ability remains solely with video cassette recorders. Many prospective customers seem surprised to learn that the videodisc player cannot record. In many cases, they leave the store with a video cassette recorder instead of the videodisc player, which they thought they were going to buy.

As if the incompatibility between the two available videodisc systems were not enough, JVC, the Japanese electronics firm that developed the popular VHS videotape format, has also developed its own videodisc system. Known as the VHD (Video High Density) system, it would seem to offer the best of both worlds from its description. It doesn't require a complex laser-type pickup system, but uses a capacitance pickup somewhat like that of the RCA CED system. However, the VHD disc has no physical grooves in its surface. Instead, the "arm" with the capacitance pickup is guided across the disc's surface electronically. That being the case, random access to a given picture, still-frame effects, and all the other special effects possible with the laser-optical disc are also possible with the proposed VHD disc. Several other Japanese companies, including Panasonic, have already announced support for the VHD system, which, after several postponements, should be available by mid-1982 at the earliest.

The VHD disc, however, isn't compatible with either the laser-optical or the CED systems. It is capable of delivering a stereo sound track, a feature deemed important because, sooner or later, the Federal Communications Commission will authorize a system for broadcasting television programs with stereo sound. Even before that time, a user could connect the audio outputs of the laser-optical or a VHD player to his stereo hi-fi system to enjoy stereo sound reproduction while viewing recordings of concerts, theatrical presentations, and other entertainment.

Software Availability

INDUSTRY EXPERTS tell us that one of the reasons for the slow start of the Magnavox, Pioneer, or RCA videodisc players has been the inadequate supply of disc titles in either format. There are, to be sure, dozens and dozens of recent and classic motion pictures available on videodiscs, but experts believe that new types of programming will have to be dreamed up if videodisc players are to succeed in a big way.

All three videodisc proponents have been making deal after deal to come up with a greater variety of material over the next several months. For example, VHD Programs, Inc., the software arm of the JVC/General Electric/EMI consortium—all of whom support the VHD system—has signed an agreement with the worldwide entertainment firm of MCA, which will give VHD Programs access to MCA's library of over 10,000 classic and contemporary films. And Magnetic Video Corporation, a subsidiary of 20th Century Fox, announced that it is releasing dozens of its titles in the laser-optical disc format. Interestingly, MCA is a partner in the laser-optical disc effort, but that doesn't seem to have stopped the entertainment firm from supplying program material to the company that will be competing with it in the videodisc player war very shortly. RCA, of course, already has access to a great number of films and to a veritable storehouse of old television programs.

Aside from the questions of software availability and the competition among three totally incompatible systems, the public seems to have other reservations about videodiscs. Many have expressed an unwillingness to invest in the new home electronic entertainment device simply because video cassette recorders offer a more attractive alternative. While it is true that a pre-recorded tape of a movie may cost three to four times as much as a videodisc of the same film, a videotape, at least, can be erased and used over and over again for off-the-air recording or for video camera recording when the viewer tires of watching the same movie again and again. That isn't the case with videodiscs and, as several industry experts have said, "How many times can you watch the same movie?"

Still, in all fairness to videodiscs, the picture quality obtained from even the least expensive type of videodisc is better than that obtained from the best videotapes operated at their highest speeds. Operation of videodisc players is extremely simple, too, and the machines themselves are considerably less expensive than video cassette recorders. Typically, the suggested retail price for an RCA videodisc player is around $500; the price for laser-optical players (Magnavox or Pioneer) ranges from about $700 to $800. JVC's still-to-be-released VHD player is expected to carry a suggested retail price somewhere between the other two systems. In comparison, the least expensive video cassette recorder costs about $750 at suggested retail, and models with elaborate programmability can carry price tags as high as $1,400.

Best Buys '82

OUR "BEST BUY" video cassette recorders and videodisc players follow; they are listed alphabetically within each category. Remember that a "Best Buy" designation applies only to the model listed; it doesn't necessarily apply to other models made by the same manufacturer, or to an entire product line.

 Home (Nonportable) Beta Recorders

Sanyo VCR5000 is a basic Beta-format video cassette recorder that plays and records in Beta II and III speeds. Programming capability is limited to a single event over a 24-hour period, and the tuner section, though capable of receiving VHF and UHF stations, uses turret (non-electronic) tuning; these controls must be manually operated. The machine features Time Phase Editing, which aids in making noise-free

Prices are accurate at time of printing; subject to manufacturer's change.

edits from scene to scene. Another useful control is speed search, but this feature only works in the Beta III speed. Audio response of the Sanyo VCR5000 is decent at the Beta II speed, but only barely acceptable at the slower speed. Although programmable for only one unattended recording event, this VCR does have the capability of being programmed when to *stop* as well as when to start recording, so there'll be no wasted energy and no needless use of tape if you only want a 30-minute program to be recorded in your absence on a three-hour tape. The recorder weights about 32½ pounds.

Approximate Retail Price	Approximate Low Price
$895.00	Not Available

Sony SL-5800, the Time Commander, is Sony's best video cassette recorder. A programmable Beta-format machine, it features pre-set recording of four programs over a two-week period; Variable BetaScan, fast-viewing in forward or reverse from 5 to 20 times normal speed; fast play; slow motion at one-third normal speed; variable slow motion; freeze-frame; and frame-by-frame viewing. A hand-held remote control unit allows you to duplicate all of these special viewing effects from across the room. The Sony SL-5800 incorporates 14-channel UHF/VHF touch-tuning, logic-controlled transport functions (light-touch buttons), and the ability to put an electronic signal at the beginning of each new program on the tape for memory recall. This model records and plays at the Beta II and III speeds, but only plays at the old Beta I speed. The SL-5800 weighs nearly 36½ pounds.

Approximate Retail Price	Approximate Low Price
$1,450.00	$1,075.00

 Home (Nonportable) VHS Recorders

Akai VPS-7350 is the first video cassette recorder in this country to feature stereo audio capability. Of course, this feature will only be useful at this point if you do your own recording via camera and two external microphones, but when stereo television is finally approved in the U.S., you'll be ready for it with this machine. This model may be regarded as both a portable and a home unit, because it comes in two parts: a VCR transport and a companion TV tuner/timer that can be used to program up to six programs over a one-week period or for every day repeat recording. The unit operates at the two- and six-hour speeds, but not at the four-hour LP speed. An optional remote control accessory provides freeze-frame and playback at double speed and slow speed. The deck weighs just over 13 pounds; the tuner/timer is nearly 10½ pounds.

Approximate Retail Price	Approximate Low Price
$1,695.00	$1,245.00

Prices are accurate at time of printing; subject to manufacturer's change.

Magnavox VR8325 lacks some of the sophisticated programmability of some VHS-format recorders, but in return it has a slightly lower retail price, and is equipped with visual scanning in both forward and reverse at nine times normal speed. And during recording, when the unit is placed in the "pause" mode, a new circuit automatically edits the tape for noise-free "splices" when recording is resumed. Performance of this machine in terms of picture quality at all three operating speeds was unusually good and even audio frequency response was better than average—a feature that not too many VCR's can boast about.

Approximate Retail Price	Approximate Low Price
$1,195.00	Not Available

 Portable VHF Recorders

JVC HR-2200U, at just over 11 pounds, is the lightest portable we know of that uses the VHS format. It features edit-start control for noise-free transitions between "takes," high-speed (10 times normal speed) search in both directions for locating desired portions of a tape, variable slow motion, freeze-frame, frame-by-frame advance, and remote control. For home use, it can be teamed with JVC's TU-22U tuner/timer, which is programmable for up to 10 days in advance. The one disadvantage of this VCR is that it features only a single speed—two hours maximum recording. If you are going to combine this unit with a camera you will probably want the best picture definition you can get, and this higher tape speed will give it to you, but if you want to use it at home as well, with the TV tuner/timer, two hours of recording time may fall short of some of your off-the-air recording requirements.

Approximate Retail Price	Approximate Low Price
$1,100.00 (model HR-2200U)	$899.00
$320.00 (model TU-22U)	Not Available

Sony SL-2000 BetaPak portable VCR features one-button recording, audio-dubbing, cue function, pause control, logic-controlled tape functions, and three-way power supply (AC, DC, or battery pack). It also has BetaScan II with fast, normal, and slow speeds in both directions. This VCR records in Beta II or Beta III, but can play back in Beta I, Beta II, or Beta III. It comes with an antenna switch, earphone, shoulder strap, and necessary cables, but you'll need to purchase Sony's TT-2000 tuner/timer (with four-channel, four-program, and 14-day programmability) to record programs off the air. The VCR weighs nine pounds, four ounces. Another optional accessory is the Model RMT-311, a hand-held, wireless, full-function video remote control unit.

Approximate Retail Price	Approximate Low Price
$1,150.00 (model SL-2000)	$1,015.00
$350.00 (model TT-2000)	Not Available

Prices are accurate at time of printing; subject to manufacturer's change.

Pioneer VP-1000 laser-optical videodisc player is one of the most sophisticated home electronic devices ever created. Viewing speed can be adjusted from normal to just one frame per second. Forward or reverse viewing at three times normal speed; fast-scanning while viewing picture content; complete random access by frame number (which can be "punched in" on a calculator-like keyboard); and, of course, freeze-frame viewing are all simple to operate and operate flawlessly. Picture quality is not only superior to that obtained with CED system players, but is probably better than can be reproduced by most television sets, which will prove to be the limiting factor here. Still, you will probably marvel at the clarity of the picture achieved, compared with either the best available video cassette recorders or the best off-the-air reception that you can remember.

Approximate Retail Price   **Approximate Low Price**
$749.00 .... $699.00

Sears 57 G 5478 is Sears, Roebuck and Company's version of RCA's CED videodisc player. This model is made for Sears by Hitachi, a company that has also elected to offer this type of videodisc system under its brand name. Somewhat more elaborate in its control facilities than the videodisc player offered by RCA, this Sears unit has two speeds of fast-forward and fast-reverse search; one at about 16 times normal viewing speed; the other about 60 times normal viewing, displaying every sixtieth frame for fast access to a given portion of the program. Picture quality was very good on this unit. A remote-control option is available. The player is extremely simple to operate.

Approximate Retail Price   **Approximate Low Price**
$490.00 .... Not Available

Prices are accurate at time of printing; subject to manufacturer's change.

Video Cameras

THE FIRST consumer video cameras to appear on the market in 1976 and 1977 were rather bulky models that had to be supported on your shoulder or on a tripod. They were also limited to taping black-and-white video pictures. But it wasn't long before most of those manufacturing video cassette recorders began making cameras that taped color video pictures and, in the ensuing four or five years, these cameras have become lighter in weight and easier to handle. They are also priced at levels that former home movie buffs can afford.

The convenience of videotaping is attracting additional fans who might never have even considered owning a home movie outfit. With a video camera connected to a portable or even to a home-type video cassette recorder, you can tape indoor or outdoor events running as long as several hours for a cost that is less than that which you would formerly have had to pay for just a few minutes of processed color movie film. Furthermore, a videotaped scene can be played back immediately, and if you feel that it isn't satisfactory, you can rewind the tape and re-shoot the scene as many times as necessary. No tape is wasted and you don't have to wait for days to find out if you really captured the family picnic or that once-in-a-lifetime event for posterity.

Camera Features and Terminology

IN MANY WAYS, film cameras and video cameras are similar. Both use optical lenses that may have a fixed focal length or a zoom capability to allow you to shoot close-ups from a greater distance or to "zoom" in and out of a scene as professionally as cinematographers do.

Aperture describes the lens opening of the video camera, just as it does in the case of film cameras. For example, a video camera having an f/2 lens will need more illumination than one having an f/1.4 lens. The aperture designation tells you the maximum opening of the iris—the most amount of light that can be admitted—but of course, as with camera lenses, the iris can be closed down to other f-stops when more lighting is available.

Many video cameras now feature an automatic iris adjustment, which opens and shuts down the lens as dictated by available lighting. Normally, this feature can be defeated for manual lens adjustment; this enables you to execute professional-looking "fade-outs" and "fade-ins," and to compensate for unusually bright or dark background lighting conditions in which the automatic iris adjustment might be based on average rather than "subject" lighting.

If you are a film camera buff, you know that some film works best with indoor lighting while other film is designed to be used outdoors. With video cameras, it's possible to adjust for different lighting conditions electronically. While first-generation color video cameras supplied lens filters for compensating for different types of lighting, newer cameras do the job by means of color temperature adjustment controls and some form of meter indication located on the camera body or in the viewfinder. Color temperature is a rating system that defines the color quality of a light source. The higher the color temperature, the bluer the light; the lower the color temperature, the redder the light source.

Most new color video cameras have two controls for adjusting proper color temperature. The first is a coarse control—usually a switch—with "indoor" and "outdoor" positions. The other is a continuously variable white-balance control. Adjusting the white-balance control is simple, and involves nothing more than focusing the camera on a white object, while viewing the scene being videotaped on a TV screen, and adjusting the control until the object looks as white (without color tints) as possible.

Electronic vs. Optical Viewfinders

ANOTHER FEATURE you should know about and consider when selecting a color video camera is the viewfinder. Basic cameras are equipped with an optical viewfinder; it merely shows you the same field of view that the camera lens covers. An electronic viewfinder is much more expensive because it is a small black-and-white television monitor. When you look into the eyepiece of a video camera equipped with an electronic viewfinder, you see a small TV screen, usually 1½ inches by 2 inches or so. Except for the color, it shows you exactly what is being recorded by the video cassette recorder. It is difficult to make a mistake in videotaping when your camera is equipped with an electronic viewfinder. In addition to seeing the video picture as it is being recorded, most viewfinders of this type also have indicators that tell you if your picture has too little or too much light, and whether or not the tape in your VCR is actually moving and recording the scene. Finger triggers on the body of the camera usually allow you to start and stop the tape, so as to "cut" between scenes without having to press the VCR's pause control, which may be some distance from the camera, separated from it by an 8- or 10-foot cable.

Speaking of camera cables, it's important to make sure that the cable supplied with the video camera of your choice will plug directly into your VCR regardless of whether it is a home or portable machine. Unfortunately, there is little standardization between manufacturers with respect to interfacing cameras and recorders. Of course, one way of insuring cable compatibility between your camera and video cassette recorder is to choose both from the same manufacturer, but that may not always provide the features that you want. So, it's a good idea to tell your dealer what make and model of VCR you own when you shop for a color video camera.

It is, of course, possible to use any video camera with a home or portable VCR. And, there is no intrinsic incompatibility between VHS recorders and video cameras made by manufacturers who make Beta equipment or vice versa. However, in most instances when you use a camera with a home VCR, you may not be able to use another important feature of electronic viewfinders: the ability to play back tapes just recorded and watch the playback on the viewfinder's screen. This is especially useful when recording "in the field," but isn't all that important when you are videotaping indoors and can hook up the VCR to your color television set for instant playback.

As for the lens found on a video camera, it is very much like an ordinary high-quality photographic camera lens. In fact, many video lenses are made by the same companies who make lenses for film cameras. There is a separate focusing ring, which generally enables you to get within about three feet from your subject. If it is a zoom lens, there will be a zoom ring as well, which allows you to go from close-up to distant shots smoothly. In some cases, a zoom lens will also be equipped with a "macro" position; this enables you to shoot extreme close-ups at distances of only an inch or two from your subject. The macro lens feature is especially useful if you want to videotape still life scenes of flowers, insects, and similar small objects.

Recently, some video camera manufacturers, like Toshiba, have come up with so-called self-focusing cameras, in which a complex combination of optical lenses and mechanical devices actually rotate the focus ring automatically to properly focus on a scene being videotaped. This automatic focusing mechanism, though useful in theory, has limitations. For example, when the scene being taped has low contrast or lacks any vertical edges, the self-focusing system cannot be relied on to provide accurate focusing. Still, under ordinary circumstances it did do a good job, according to CONSUMER GUIDE® magazine's video experts, and is certainly a remarkable achievement. But, as is true of all such convenience features, it does add to the cost of the camera.

Best Buys '82

OUR "BEST BUY" video cameras follow; they are listed alphabetically. Remember that a "Best Buy" designation applies only to the model listed; it doesn't necessarily apply to other models made by the same manufacturer, or to an entire product line.

 Video Cameras

RCA CC010 color video camera is one of the lightest (5.8 pounds) models to incorporate an electronic viewfinder as well as an 8:1 f/1.8 zoom lens that can be operated manually or by automatic powered means. The lens also includes a "macro" ultra-closeup position. Manufactured for RCA by Matsushita Electric Company of Japan, who makes a similar but not identical camera under its Panasonic brand, the RCA camera features a two-position color switch, white-balance control, an auto/manual iris, and even an automatic "fade" feature for professional fade-ins and fade-outs. Requiring only about 10 footcandles of minimum illumination, the horizontal resolution (picture detail) of this camera was excellent. Because the camera is a bit on the heavy side for pistol-grip holding, it comes with a comfortable, shoulder-rest bracket. It also has a standard C-mount so you can substitute additional lenses if desired.

Approximate Retail Price **Approximate Low Price**
$1,050.00.. $859.00

Sony HVC-2200 uses that company's latest single-tube Trinicon, which delivers superb color quality and virtually no mis-registration. The camera has a detachable electronic viewfinder with a 1½-inch picture tube. When looking through the viewfinder, you can also see a tape-transport indicator, a low-illumination warning indicator, and white-balance metering system. A manual or automatic iris is featured as are color and white-balance controls. This video camera with viewfinder weighs six pounds, seven ounces, and consumes 8.3 watts of power when operating. The camera comes with a 6:1 ratio Canon f/4 power zoom lens with macro-focusing for closeup detail. Other supplied accessories include lens cap, carrying case, and earphone.

Approximate Retail Price **Approximate Low Price**
$1,300.00.. $1,020.00

Toshiba IK-1850AF, similar to Toshiba's IK-1850 video camera, has an auto-focusing feature that adds about $350 to the suggested retail price. So, if you don't feel that auto-focusing is worth that much, we suggest that you consider the lower-cost Toshiba IK-1850, which has all of the other features of the costlier version, such as an f/1.4 6:1 zoom lens with macro settings, an effective electronic viewfinder, auto/manual iris with a locking feature, and color and white-balance controls for optimum color temperature adjustment. The IK-1850 weighs just over 4½ pounds, while the most expensive IK-1850AF (auto-focus) model weighs just a bit more. The electronic viewfinder supplied with either model can be mounted on either side of the camera.

Approximate Retail Price **Approximate Low Price**
$1,395.00.. $1,065.00

Prices are accurate at time of printing; subject to manufacturer's change.

Hi-Fi Components

FOR MOST OF the 1970s, the high-fidelity component industry in the United States grew at a rate of approximately 20 percent annually. The number of audio specialty dealers proliferated, and manufacturers and distributors were convinced that this phenomenal growth rate would continue indefinitely. After all, surveys had shown that fewer than 20 percent of American homes had a component high-fidelity system, and that meant between 40 million and 50 million homes represented potential sales.

As we entered the 1980s, several factors dashed the optimism of dealers and manufacturers. The most important was the emergence of the video industry, as distinct from the well-established "television set" industry. The video cassette recorder proved to be an extremely attractive consumer item, and many experts believe the discretionary dollars that might have been spent on hi-fi components are being spent first on a video cassette recorder, and then on video software (pre-recorded films on video cassettes), and even on color video cameras, which seem destined to replace home movie cameras.

A second factor has been the failure of the industry to recognize the changing demographics of the American population. For years, audio component makers had been addressing their sales pitches to the 18- to 24-year-old male. By 1980, the number of males in this age group was beginning to decline, and it has taken some time for companies to understand that potential hi-fi component system buyers are now approaching their middle years. Nor has the industry properly addressed the female population—the millions of working, single women who have discretionary dollars to spend and who enjoy good music and good music reproduction as much as their male counterparts.

For the giant Japanese companies who manufacture *both* audio and video products, the changing buying pattern hasn't been too serious; production emphasis has been shifted to meet the new product requirements. But these companies and those who specialize only in audio have also taken important steps to cater to the "new" audio buyer—steps that will benefit the purchasers of a stereo system.

The One-Brand-System Approach

FOR NEARLY 30 years, the audio industry tried to convince everyone that no one manufacturer could offer all of the audio components for a first-rate hi-fi system. Smaller companies specialized in specific areas: electronics (tuners, amplifiers, receivers), tape decks, turntables, phono cartridges, headphones, or loudspeakers. With the participation of large, multinational electronics firms capable of designing and manufacturing every component needed for a hi-fi system, a new trend—the one-brand-system approach—is becoming popular. In a one-brand component system, a single manufacturer makes and assembles all of the components needed for the system and, in most cases, even supplies a cabinet to contain the system.

In some cases, the choice of loudspeakers—by far the most critical component in any hi-fi system—is still left up to the purchaser, while in other instances a pair of speakers is included in the one-brand system. And the entire system is offered at one price by the retailer.

An advantage of the one-brand-system approach is that it lets the manufacturer offer interesting features that would otherwise not be possible, such as complete remote control (wireless or wired) of all system components, optional timers and programmers (for unattended recording, for example), and the like. And of course, as a further inducement, the single price of most one-brand systems is usually lower than the price of comparable components made by different manufacturers and purchased separately.

Of course, even in one-brand systems you are still locked in to the component choices of the manufacturer, with no freedom to substitute one piece of equipment for another. For some, this may be the simplest way in which to choose a component system. Others who feel that they know what each component should offer may prefer to make their own selections of individual components.

One-brand systems are easy to buy—and easy to sell. That is why you are more likely to find them sold in mass-merchandising outlets such as department stores and discount chains. In such places, the salesperson who helps you isn't likely to have technical expertise about hi-fi components, and so you have to rely on the reputation of the manufacturer. Fortunately, the record so far, in terms of reliability and performance levels, has been very good, and CONSUMER GUIDE® magazine has heard of few complaints from purchasers of one-brand systems made by well-known hi-fi manufacturers. CONSUMER GUIDE® magazine's audio experts suggest that the consumer who is planning to purchase his first hi-fi component system seriously consider one of the one-brand systems offered by a leading manufacturer.

Other Component Trends

MICRO- OR MINICOMPONENTS, which were introduced in the United States about two years ago, haven't achieved as much public acceptance as anticipated. Both microcomponents *and* the one-brand systems just discussed are basically Japanese merchandising innovations. Aware that ownership of components in Japan had just about reached the saturation level (about 65 to 70 percent of all Japanese households have hi-fi component systems) and that vast population groups in the United States had still never heard of "components," leading Japanese manufacturers reasoned that smaller components would have a market and fit in nicely in the relatively small rooms of Japanese homes and into American apartments.

In Japan, the concept seems to have worked; in the U.S., microcomponent sales have been disappointing. One reason is the high cost of microcomponents. Japanese audiophiles were never introduced to the all-in-one stereo receiver, largely because their FM programming is so limited that it seemed pointless to "force" a tuner section on an amplifier purchaser who may only want to play records. But in the U.S., most people do, in fact, prefer an integrated receiver. They like its convenience and the economy involved in combining all of the needed electronics in a single component. Because receivers aren't available in microcomponent format—at least from most manufacturers of microcomponents—they have to settle for separate amplifiers, preamplifiers, and tuners. This adds up to a higher cost than would have to be spent for a basic system of standard-size components from one or even several manufacturers.

Compact Systems vs. Separate Components

THE INTRODUCTION of one-brand systems has already had a profound effect on so-called compact systems, because, in a way, the one-brand system offers a compromise between the sophisticated approach to hi-fi through separately selected components and the often not-so-hi-fi compact system that dedicated audio buffs regard as a step below true hi-fi.

In fact, a compact system contains all the elements of a component system; it usually features a receiver, a pair of speakers, a turntable system with cartridge (often mounted atop the receiver), and, in many cases, even a cassette tape recorder, which forms a part of the receiver section. Generally speaking, most compact systems sell for considerably less than one-brand systems, but that in itself should tell you something about relative performance levels.

The inexpensive compact system that promises the same fidelity as a well-designed component system or a one-brand system simply cannot live up to that claim. In a compact system, the phono cartridge, often an afterthought even by more knowledgeable consumers, may turn out to be a heavy-tracking ceramic type rather than a light-mass magnetic type. Besides the inability of such a pickup to reproduce all frequencies at their correct relative intensities, such cartridges are bound to cause increased record wear because of their heavier downward tracking forces. The tuner sections of a low-priced compact system may be able to pick up nearby FM signals, but may well sound noisy and distorted when trying to receive signals from a greater distance. Worst of all, speaker systems supplied with many compact systems often afford the manufacturer the greatest chance to skimp on quality.

Fortunately, many of the same manufacturers who make quality separate components and one-brand systems also manufacture acceptable compact systems. Among them are Fisher, Onkyo, Panasonic, Pioneer, Sanyo, and Sony. As with all consumer products, you generally get what you pay for. Don't expect any compact system selling for less than $350 to give you sound quality approaching that of a component system.

Tuner Trends

FOR A WHILE, it seemed as though the American public would continue to pay exceedingly high prices for extremely sophisticated tuners. In the last year or two, though, a good many people have begun to realize that even a modestly priced tuner—one costing $150 to $200—can reproduce FM programs with an overall fidelity that at least matches the quality of the signal most FM stations broadcast. There are, of course, exceptions, and listeners fortunate enough to live within receiving range of stations that do broadcast good program material and a technically superior signal may find it worthwhile to own an expensive tuner.

But more and more tuner manufacturers are bringing out lower-priced units that do surprisingly well with the signals being broadcast. Frequency-synthesized tuning is now a familiar feature; dual-bandwidth tuning has also become popular. The advantage of variable selectivity, another name for dual-bandwidth tuner circuitry, is that it enables the listener to obtain satisfactory reception whether in a crowded metropolitan area where stations are close together on the dial or in relatively unpopulated areas where there are only a few stations. Ideally, lower selectivity, or wider bandwidth, will provide lowest distortion. But, in areas where stations are close to each other on the dial, such wide bandwidth may result in interference from one station to an adjacent one. That's when higher selectivity, or narrower bandwidth, is desirable, even if it means a slight increase in distortion.

When shopping for a tuner, audition several in the low- to medium-price bracket, preferably with the type of antenna you are planning to use in your own home installation. If these tuners provide noise-free reception of your favorite FM stations—with good apparent stereo separation and a complete lack of interference from other FM signals or spurious unrelated transmissions—there is no reason to spend extra money for a high-priced tuner. Of course, if signals come in noisily or if music and voices seem harsh and distorted despite antenna reorientation, you may then have to seek a more expensive tuner with better sensitivity and quieting capability.

If you find it difficult to tune in an FM station properly, you should consider a tuner with frequency synthesis. Make sure, though, that a unit that looks like it has frequency synthesis actually has this circuitry. An illuminated numerical frequency readout on a tuner doesn't necessarily guarantee that it has frequency synthesis.

The AM Stereo Decision

IN APRIL OF 1980, the Federal Communications Commission—after nearly three years of deliberation—announced that it had reached a decision regarding selection of standards for stereo-AM broadcasting. The commissioners decided in favor of the Magnavox system, one of five techniques that had been proposed to the FCC and that had been field-tested on an experimental basis by selected stations throughout the United States. Proponents of competing systems, which were not chosen, then threatened to go to court to request that an injunction be issued preventing the FCC from implementing its decision. Before the threat could be carried out, the FCC rescinded its April announcement and stated that it was reconsidering the entire matter.

Even if the decision in favor of Magnavox stands, it is unlikely that any stereo-AM equipment will soon be on the market. Whenever it comes, moreover, stereo-AM gear probably won't have much impact on the high-fidelity component market. AM radio has never been regarded by audio enthusiasts as a true high-fidelity program source, and manufacturers of quality tuners and receivers have traditionally paid little attention to the AM sections of their products. AM broadcasters, in turn, have generally been guilty of not worrying much about sound quality. As a consequence, the AM radio of the future is likely to provide two channels of sound as low in fidelity as single-channel AM is now.

Receiver or Separates?

ALL-IN-ONE receivers constitute the central component in approximately 80 percent of all new systems purchased in the United States, though many sound enthusiasts believe that separate tuners, preamplifiers, and power amplifiers offer more flexibility. Ultimately, the choice depends on personal taste. If high audio power is what you want, it's more economical to acquire it in the form of an all-in-one receiver. If you care more about ultra-low distortion, you may want to select a system of separate components. Often, such a choice depends on your feeling about FM radio as a program source. If you seldom listen to radio broadcasts, you can—by selecting an integrated amplifier or even a separate preamplifier and a separate power amplifier—buy a better system than would be possible if you spent an equivalent sum on an all-in-one receiver with expensive AM/FM tuner circuits.

With the exception of the microcomponents discussed earlier, you will find that standard-size receivers offer just about every convenience, control, and switching feature found on separate preamplifier/control units. In fact, the quality line dividing well-designed receivers from comparably priced separate tuner/preamp/amplifier systems becomes finer and finer each year.

Amplifier and Preamplifier Trends

BECAUSE MANY OF the features and controls found on separate amplifiers, integrated amplifiers, and preamplifiers have also found their way into all-in-one receivers, the makers of separate components have been concentrating on performance, efficiency, and a lowering of certain subtle forms of distortion that don't lend themselves to easy measurement, but that are, nevertheless, audible to many critical experienced listeners. Static distortion levels—those measured on the laboratory test bench using single, continuous-tone test signals—have long since been brought down so low as to be insignificant. Long ago, researchers concluded that most listeners cannot hear levels of harmonic distortion that are lower than 1.0 percent. Yet, modern amplifiers boast harmonic distortion levels as low as 0.1, 0.01, and, in some cases, even 0.003

percent. That holds true for static intermodulation distortion measurements, in which a high- and a low-frequency steady-state pair of tones are fed to an amplifier and any generated sum-and-difference tones appearing at the output are measured. Thus, serious researchers have been looking for other ways to measure amplifier distortions under dynamic conditions that are equivalent to what the amplifier is asked to do when it actually reproduces and amplifies a musical signal.

In the past few years, these researchers have met with a great measure of success, identifying such subtle dynamic forms distortion as TIM (Transient Intermodulation Distortion), slew-rate distortion (in which high-frequency signals are distorted in waveshape because the amplifier cannot respond quickly enough to rapid voltage changes), and many more. And with the discovery of these more subtle forms of distortion have come more and more unique circuits to deal with them.

Whether prompted by an awareness for energy conservation or other reasons, designers have also been developing more efficient amplifiers that will dissipate less heat and, at the same time, produce little of the distortion formerly associated with higher efficiency amplifiers. Here, too, the designers have met with success, combining, in a variety of original circuits, the advantages of energy-wasteful, low-distortion "Class A" circuits with the efficiency of "Class B" amplifier designs that are somewhat distortion-prone.

To the average consumer, these fine distinctions may not be audible, but, to the experienced listener who is likely to buy a separate power amplifier, these improvements are meaningful and worth having. While it's important to audition every component in a system if you are choosing your own separates, it is especially important to listen to amplifiers of your choice as they are used to drive the actual speakers with which you plan to use them. Turn up the volume to a point that is somewhat louder than you think you will ever need and make certain that the amplifier is not adding distortion in the bass, mid-frequency, or treble regions of the audible spectrum.

If you think you'll eventually add one or more accessory devices to your system—and especially if you plan to add tape-recording facilities to your system—make certain that the amplifier or receiver you choose has an adequate number of tape monitor loops. If you are choosing a fairly powerful amplifier, make certain that it runs reasonably cool; playing it for an hour or so at reasonably loud listening levels will tell you all you need to know about this aspect of its design. And, if you plan to add extra speakers later, allow for the extra power drain when both sets of speakers operate simultaneously.

If you choose a separate preamplifier or an integrated amplifier (power amp plus preamp), make certain that the tone controls are sufficiently versatile for your needs and that the unit has enough input facilities to handle all your other components. Many of the newer separate preamplifiers now feature separate input for moving-coil cartridges, because these cartridges have been gaining in popularity in recent years. If your preamp lacks this feature and you still want to use a moving-coil cartridge, you must acquire either a special step-up transformer (usually available from the maker of the cartridge) or a pre-

138

preamplifier also known as a "head amp." Because either of these devices may add as much as $100 to the price of your system, it's a good idea to look for a preamp that already has the transformer or a pre-preamplifier incorporated into it.

Turntable Trends

WHEN MASTER RECORDS are "cut" in a record-processing plant, the arm containing the cutting stylus moves along a radius drawn from the outer perimeter of the disc to the exact center of the disc where the spindle secures it to the turntable. In other words, the cutting arm remains tangent to the groove being cut at all times. Ideally, for perfect tracking, it can be argued that the playback tonearm in which the phono cartridge is mounted should follow this same path.

Until recently, few manufacturers were able to make tonearms of this sort; the drive and friction problems were greater than the problem that was to be solved by employing tangential tracking. Earliest success in this area was achieved by the Danish firm of Bang & Olufsen, who still offer a very expensive turntable system that uses this principle. But, thanks to research and newer friction-free drive systems, several other manufacturers such as Mitsubishi, Phase Linear, Technics, and others have developed tangential tracking arms. Some of these turntables can even play a record while it is oriented "on its edge," with the turntable standing upright rather than lying with its major dimensions parallel to the floor or shelf.

Regardless of which type of tonearm is used, and regardless of whether the turntable itself stands upright or operates horizontally, the industry has, at long last, come to realize the importance of a proper match between the tonearm and the cartridge that is mounted in it. In general, the trend has been towards lower-mass tonearms and lightweight cartridges. The combination of a low-mass tonearm and a low-mass cartridge results in better tracking of the ultra-loud music passages found in the grooves of modern records; it also helps to keep the stylus firmly seated in the groove when playing warped records.

As for the drive system used in a turntable, both direct-drive and belt-drive turntables remain popular. What is important in selecting a turntable isn't the method of drive of the platter, but the performance specifications that result from a particular design. Rumble or noise should be low; it is expressed in negative dB (decibel) numbers so that a -70 dB figure means lower noise or rumble than a -65 dB figure. The speed should be accurate; some new turntables have their speed regulated by quartz-crystal reference oscillators akin to the accurate timing devices used in electronic watches. Wow-and-flutter, or cyclical variations in speed caused by various eccentricities in moving parts, is expressed as a percentage, and the lower that number the better.

Cartridge Trends

ONCE REGARDED AS the unimportant component, the importance of a good phono cartridge is now recognized by everyone concerned with assembling a good component system. Not only is it important that you listen carefully to the make and model of cartridge that you intend to buy, but it is equally important that the cartridge you choose mates properly with the tonearm of the turntable system you intend to use. Because this matching problem involves complex calculations and considerations, the maker of either the cartridge or turntable, or your dealer if he's knowledgeable in this area, should be consulted before making a final decision. Remember, records will probably be your most important program source, and your cartridge is the first important component in translating what's in those record grooves into pleasurable music. If it doesn't do its job properly, no component later in the signal path can correct distortion, resonances, or other sonic aberrations.

Although moving-magnet cartridges, or cartridges using magnetic induction principles, are still the most popular types of pickups sold, critical audio buffs continue to insist that moving-coil cartridges sound better than any moving-magnetic cartridge. Moving-coil cartridges are usually more expensive, however, and in addition to their initially higher cost, they may require a pre-preamplifier or a step-up transformer between their output and the phono inputs on your amplifier or receiver. This additional equipment isn't needed if your amp or receiver is equipped with a special moving-coil input that has the extra preamplification necessary to handle the low output of a moving-coil cartridge directly. If you do have to buy a separate transformer or a pre-preamp, a good one is likely to add up to $100 to the cost of your system.

A further point to consider is the fact that most—but not all—moving-coil cartridges must be sent back to the factory when the stylus wears out and needs replacing. With nearly all magnetic types of cartridges, this replacement task can be done by the owner.

Speaker System Trends

THE SELECTION OF a pair of speakers is perhaps the most difficult task in assembling a well-matched stereo component system. To begin with, speakers, though much improved over their predecessors of 10 years ago, are still far from perfect. Each adds its own distinct coloration or sound quality. A speaker that seems "natural-sounding" to one listener may seem to have false musical coloration to another. Add to this the fact that there are hundreds of speaker brands and thousands of models from which to choose and you can see that the job of choosing the "right" speaker can be formidable.

In the early days of hi-fi, speaker design was very often a hit-and-miss proposition. The mathematical calculations involved in designing a good speaker system were well known, but they were so lengthy and tedious that many engineers chose to design speaker enclosures and systems empirically, trusting their ears for the most part. Unfortunately, as we have said, not everyone's hearing is alike and there is no consensus as to what constitutes accurate or realistic sound.

Still, with thousands of models from which to choose, how can you begin to narrow the choices? For one thing, you need to know how much power you are going to be able to "feed" to the speakers of your choice.

Or, if you haven't selected your amplifier or receiver first, look at it the other way and decide whether you want a highly efficient speaker system—one that requires less amplifier power for a given sound level—or whether you can afford more power in your amplifier and can, therefore, consider a lower-efficiency model that may be smaller in physical size or that may be placed on a bookshelf instead of occupying a lot of floor space. Having made these initial decisions, tell the salesperson, who should then be able to lead you to several systems that fit the category you have singled out. From that point on, it's a matter of listening—and more listening.

The best way to audition speakers is by means of the so-called "A-B" test in which two brands are compared through rapid and successive back-and-forth switching while you listen to familiar recordings or another program source. Make certain that loudness levels are adjusted so that both pairs reproduce sounds at equal levels (people tend to favor the *louder* of two sounds). Listen intently for several seconds to one pair, then to the other, until you can decisively eliminate one pair. Keep the preferred pair "on line" and add another pair for comparison, repeating the process of elimination until you have zeroed in on the pair that sounds best to you.

Materials used in the manufacture of speakers have improved in recent years. Improved permanent magnets, better cone materials, and more precisely machined housings have all contributed to better sound and greater longevity. So, aside from choosing the speaker system that sounds best to you, your only other real tasks are to make certain that your chosen speaker's minimum power requirements and maximum power input limitations are compatible with your system's amplifier or receiver. Remember, too, that placement of your speakers in the listening room can have a profound effect on how they sound. Often, the complaint heard by dealers that "the speakers don't sound the same as they did in your store" can be explained by extreme differences in room size, furnishings, or speaker placement within the room.

Headphone Selection

HEADPHONE LISTENING is private listening. With a headset you can listen to what you want, when you want, and as loud as you want—without disturbing anyone. Furthermore, headphones block out most sounds that you would normally hear, although this depends on the design of the headset. Some models are made to produce a truly tight, close seal around the ears. Others don't hug the ears as snugly, and while they block out most outside noises, they permit you to hear loud or shrill sounds like the ringing of a telephone.

Headphones also highlight stereo channel separation. On the negative side, this capability makes both excessive and inadequate stereo separation far more noticeable. On the positive side, the absence of an acoustic mix (such as occurs when listening to standard loudspeakers) dramatizes whatever channel separation there is.

Like speakers, headphones are best judged according to how they sound. Criteria of good headphone performance include reasonably full bass with good tonal definition and smoothness from the midrange into the extreme highs. Within the response limits of a given headset, the sound should be natural with no false emphasis on one tonal range or another.

The sensitivity of a headset may also be of some importance. Generally, it takes relatively little signal energy to make a set of headphones respond, but a unit that is fairly inefficient might demand so much of the driving amplifier that an otherwise favorable signal-to-noise ratio would be significantly reduced.

In addition to the quality of the sound it provides, a headset must also be judged in terms of its wearing comfort. The weight, the fit, and the sense of ease with which the unit can be worn for long periods should all be considered. Adjustable headbands are quite common, but the prospective buyer should ascertain that the particular headset can be adjusted to suit personal wearing comfort.

Best Buys '82

OUR "BEST BUY" hi-fi components follow; they are listed alphabetically within each category. Remember that a "Best Buy" designation applies only to the model listed; it doesn't necessarily apply to other models made by the same manufacturer, or to an entire product line.

 One-Brand Component Systems

Fisher ACS 122A consists of a 50-watt-per-channel integrated amplifier (Model CA 660), an AM/FM stereo tuner (Model FM 440), a belt-driven turntable (Model MT 6410 C) with a magnetic cartridge, a pair of speakers (Model DS 151), and a component cabinet that is 38 inches high, 19¼ inches wide, and 16 inches deep. The speakers are the high-efficiency type, and include a 10-inch woofer, 5-inch midrange driver, and a 3-inch tweeter.

Approximate Retail Price	Approximate Low Price
$800.00	$675.00

Sansui Super Compo 6100 is made up of the following components: the A-7 45-watt-per-channel integrated DC-servo amplifier featuring a 24-LED peak power display, variable loudness, mic mixing, and front-panel tape inputs and outputs; the T-7 auto-tuning AM/FM tuner with touch up/down tuning buttons and a 10-LED signal-strength indicator; the FR-D35 direct-drive, semi-automatic turntable with up-front controls, low-mass/low-friction tonearm, and wow-and-flutter of only 0.025 percent; the D-95M metal-compatible cassette deck with a wow-and-flutter of 0.07 percent; S-47 high-efficiency acoustic suspension speaker

Prices are accurate at time of printing; subject to manufacturer's change.

systems with 10-inch woofer, 5-inch midrange, and 2-inch tweeter. A vertically oriented cabinet (GX-75) with walnut-grain vinyl finish and twin glass doors is included.

Approximate Retail Price	Approximate Low Price
$1,235.00	$950.00

 Tuners

NAD 4020A is a low-cost AM/FM tuner, which, though using conventional tuning, offers excellent sensitivity and low distortion. It features LED tuning indicators and a modern phase-locked-loop stereo-FM decoder circuit. Usable sensitivity in mono is 1.9 microvolts while the signal-to-noise ratio is a more-than-adequate -75 dB (-70 dB in stereo). We would recommend this tuner for those who already own a good stereo system and wish to add FM and AM program sources at a minimum cost, or for those who are seeking a budget component system and prefer separate components over an all-in-one receiver.

Approximate Retail Price	Approximate Low Price
$218.00	Not Available

Pioneer F-9 is an AM/FM tuner whose FM section is superb. It features wide or narrow bandwidth for the FM section. This is especially useful if you live in an area where stations are crowded together. As with most recent designs, tuning is by frequency synthesis, which assures center-of-channel tuning, and as a result, lowest possible distortion. Six AM and six FM frequencies can be stored in the unit's memory for touch-button recall. As with most such tuners, frequencies are displayed in digital form. The tuner also features signal-strength and multipath (signal reflections) indicators. A slim, sleek unit measuring only 2⅜ inches in height, the tuner weighs just under 10 pounds.

Approximate Retail Price	Approximate Low Price
$425.00	$272.50

Sony ST-J75 is, without a doubt, the finest frequency-synthesized tuner we have had an opportunity to test and use. Its noise-quieting ability (more than -90 dB) is incredible, as is its stereo separation, and its low level of distortion. Eight favorite station frequencies can be stored in the memory and instantly recalled at the touch of a button. Station frequencies are retained in memory even if a power outage occurs. Several modes of tuning besides the preset frequencies are possible, and all work flawlessly. The only possible drawback is the absence of an AM band on this tuner, which many audio buffs won't miss at all.

Approximate Retail Price	Approximate Low Price
$450.00	$290.00

Prices are accurate at time of printing; subject to manufacturer's change.

Carver M-400 power amplifier operates on an entirely new principle; it uses magnetic field circuitry that eliminates the need for oversized heat sinks, power transformers, and massive chassis. Though able to deliver an incredible 200 watts per channel, this tiny cube-shaped amplifier measures a mere 6¾ inches on each of its sides. The front face has two columns of indicating LED's that display instantaneous output power level. Now in the field for more than a year, its reliability has been established sufficiently for us to recommend this very novel power amplifier.

Approximate Retail Price	Approximate Low Price
$399.00	Not Available

Hafler DH-101 preamplifier, recommended for use with just about any high-quality power amplifier, is available either in kit form or as an assembled unit. Although not the most attractive-looking preamp, it offers excellent value, especially if you are handy at kit-building and can wire and assemble the unit yourself. Even if you purchase it in assembled form, however, its specifications are excellent, with ultra-low-noise performance in phono. It offers provisions for patching in external equipment, and has two switched and two unswitched AC convenience receptacles.

Approximate Retail Price	Approximate Low Price
Kit: $200.00	Not Available
Assembled: $300.00	Not Available

Kenwood KA-801 is a powerful integrated amplifier that delivers 110 watts per channel into 8-ohm loads with less than 0.015 percent total harmonic distortion. There are dual peak power meters on the front panel, while internally, there are completely separate power supplies for each channel. The amp has the usual array of precision tone controls, plus tape dubbing facilities and two tape monitor circuits. The power amp section features direct current, high-speed circuitry that yields a slew rate of 150 volts/microsecond and a fast rise time of only 0.8 microseconds. When a DC-coupled switch is in its "off" position, a circuit acts as a subsonic filter to deal with ultra-low-frequency DC signals, protecting the amp and your speakers from possible damage.

Approximate Retail Price	Approximate Low Price
$699.00	$448.00

Luxman X-480 integrated amplifier boasts an output power rating of 70 watts per channel into 8-ohm loads at less than 0.03 percent total harmonic distortion. This amp features dual LED power level indicators with peak indication. It is one of the few top-rated integrated amplifiers to

Prices are accurate at time of printing; subject to manufacturer's change.

include a moving-coil cartridge input in addition to the usual moving-magnet phono input pair. It also has two-way tape dubbing and two tape monitor circuits. Bass and treble tone controls have selectable turnover frequencies for more accurate control of system response. Subsonic and high-cut filter circuits are also provided. Critical listeners have given this amplifier high marks for musical sound quality.

Approximate Retail Price   **Approximate Low Price**
$500.00 .... Not Available

 Receivers

Mitsubishi DA-R25 offers excellent FM reception, an amplifier that seems capable of delivering more than its rated power of 60 watts per channel, and controls that are arranged for easy and logical use. Pressing down the "up" or "down" button permits automatic or manual tuning. The digital frequency display is an accurate and useful aid to tuning, showing frequencies on both FM and AM bands at a glance. A total of 14 stations—seven on each band—can be memorized for pushbutton recall. All sections of this receiver—tuner, preamplifier, and power amplifier—are well balanced with each other.

Approximate Retail Price   **Approximate Low Price**
$540.00 .... $480.00

NAD 7020 is one of the best-sounding receivers in its price class. Able to deliver nearly twice its rated power under music listening conditions, it has no trouble handling those frequent musical peaks that occur in well-recorded program material. FM reception is superb, and tuning indications are accurate at all points on the FM dial.

Approximate Retail Price   **Approximate Low Price**
$348.00 .... Not Available

Radio Shack Realistic STA-2250 combines a powerful 50-watt - per - channel amplifier section with a frequency-synthesized tuner section. An eight-station memory pre-set system is included, as are separate bass, treble, and midrange controls—unusual in a receiver at this price level. In addition, there are subsonic (low-cut) and high-cut filters. An extremely noise-free phono preamp circuit and a sensitive tuner section make this an unusual value-packed receiver and one that sounds good at any listening level short of overload. Don't overlook the fact that Radio Shack stores are plentiful should the receiver need servicing.

Approximate Retail Price   **Approximate Low Price**
$440.00 .... Not Available

Prices are accurate at time of printing; subject to manufacturer's change.

Dual 528 is a fully automatic, single-play turntable featuring an ultra-low-mass tonearm system suspended on a four-point gimbal. Used with the optional Ortofon ULM cartridge, total effective tonearm mass is less than 8 grams. Four adjustable isolators suppress external shock and vibration. This belt-driven unit has variable pitch control (a 6-percent speed change is possible), an illuminated strobe, and a viscous-damped cueing control. Because the hinges of the dust cover slide forward as the cover is opened, the turntable can be placed against a wall.

Approximate Retail Price	Approximate Low Price
Without Cartridge: $180.00	$113.50
With Cartridge: $290.00	$134.50

Pioneer PL-L800 is the company's top-of-the-line linear-tracking turntable system; it uses a tangential-tracking tonearm that guarantees a tracking error of no more than 0.2 degree. The direct-drive motor is accurately driven by a phase-locked-loop quartz-controlled circuit; and all operations are fully automatic and electronically controlled. The straight tonearm is made of rigid polymer graphite. The table features an auto-repeat play function and comes equipped with a moving-coil cartridge (Model PC-4MC), which means your electronics must be equipped to handle that type of cartridge output or else you will need a separate transformer or pre-preamplifier. Wow-and-flutter of this excellent turntable is only 0.012 percent and the signal-to-noise ratio is an impressive -78 dB.

Approximate Retail Price	Approximate Low Price
$450.00	$290.00

Technics SL-DL1 features a linear-tracking (tangential) tonearm that eliminates all angular tracking error and tonearm "skating." Although the drive system for the tonearm is fairly complex, operation of the unit is simple. You put a record on the platter, close the cover, and press the "start" key. An opto-electronic sensor detects record size, sets speed, moves the tonearm to the proper place, and sets it down gently in the first groove. In keeping with Technics' reputation, this system uses a direct-drive motor. All operating controls are on the front panel, outside the dust cover. A possible disadvantage is that you must buy this system with Technics' own cartridge. On the other hand, if you like the sound of that cartridge when auditioning this component, you won't have to fumble with what is considered by many to be the most difficult part of assembling your own component system—installing the delicate phono cartridge.

Approximate Retail Price	Approximate Low Price
$360.00	$224.00

Prices are accurate at time of printing; subject to manufacturer's change.

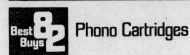

Phono Cartridges

Nagatron 165S employs the induced-magnet principle. Despite its low price, the performance specifications are similar to those of cartridges costing several times as much. Its sound is excellent in every respect. Its tracking force of nearly 2 grams is, however, a bit high for a 0.5-mil spherical stylus.

Approximate Retail Price	Approximate Low Price
$55.00	$25.00

Shure M97HE tracks very well at 1 gram and even a bit better at 1.5 grams. The dynamic stabilizer, carried over from the more expensive V-15 Type IV, allows this cartridge to play warped records that would be completely unplayable with other cartridges. A better-sounding cartridge, or one with significantly better trackability, would be hard to find.

Approximate Retail Price	Approximate Low Price
$123.00	$55.00

Shure SC39ED ranks as one of the best stereo cartridges available. Its rugged construction is a bonus for the home user. While it is certainly not unbreakable, it should be able to withstand occasional careless handling better than most cartridges. It also is one of the best-performing cartridges and is priced quite reasonably by contemporary standards.

Approximate Retail Price	Approximate Low Price
$116.00	$65.00

Shure V15 Type III-HE is a superb cartridge. The unit's hyperelliptical stylus, contoured to reduce playback distortion and record wear, can reproduce without audible distortion practically anything likely to be encountered on a commercial recording.

Approximate Retail Price	Approximate Low Price
$135.00	$70.00

Stanton 681EEE carries a relatively steep price tag, but it offers ruggedness and exceptionally accurate response (within 1 dB across the audio band). These assets, plus low harmonic and IM distortion and excellent tracking performance, make the 681EEE a top performer in its price category.

Approximate Retail Price	Approximate Low Price
$116.00	$55.00

Prices are accurate at time of printing; subject to manufacturer's change.

Allison:Four stands out among the very best of bookshelf systems in its size and price class. It has a single woofer and two tweeters. Its performance rivals that of many speaker systems that cost more or occupy more space. The Allison:Four may be placed wherever convenient, and it can be wall-mounted. It carries a five-year warranty. Each speaker is 11 inches high, 19⅜ inches wide, and 10 inches deep.

Approximate Retail Price	Approximate Low Price
$280.00/each	Not Available

Celestion Ditton 150 is a fine example of how a speaker system can be created with compact dimensions, sold at a reasonable price, and still provide first-rate performance in a quality home music system. Indeed, its overall performance certainly suggests a costlier speaker, and to be better in terms of deeper bass or high-power capacity one would probably have to spend significantly more. It has a 1-inch dome tweeter, 6-inch woofer, and 8-inch passive radiator. Each speaker is 21½ inches high, 11 inches wide, and 8½ inches deep.

Approximate Retail Price	Approximate Low Price
$250.00/each	$220.00/each

EPI 100, made by Epicure Products, is a speaker system with an air-suspension design. It has an eight-inch woofer and one-inch dome tweeter. Its sound is honest, well balanced, and uncolored. Able to fit into many hi-fi systems built around low- to medium-powered amplifiers or receivers, the EPI 100 is an accurate speaker. It is 21 inches high, 11 inches wide, and 9 inches deep.

Approximate Retail Price	Approximate Low Price
$250.00/pair	$218.00/pair

Koss CM-1010 speaker systems from the well-known maker of stereo headphones were designed with the aid of a computer and employ a two-way system in a carefully vented enclosure. The 10-inch driver isn't a driver at all, but what's called a passive radiator; it takes the place of a conventional vent or port. These speakers need a power level of 15 watts, but can handle 100 watts per channel safely. Response of these smooth-sounding speakers has been measured as flat (within 3 dB) from 35 Hz to 17,500 Hz. Few speaker manufacturers ever quote speaker response so accurately. But it's the smooth, accurate sound that you will like about this Koss model. Each speaker is 28 inches high, 15½ inches wide, and 11 inches deep.

Approximate Retail Price	Approximate Low Price
$540.00/pair	$315.00/pair

Prices are accurate at time of printing; subject to manufacturer's change.

Phase Research "Little D," sold in pairs, are made by a small, relatively new speaker company based in Dallas. For those who want big, efficient bass sound from tiny speakers, these small units, each of which is 16 inches high, 7 inches wide, and 1¾ inches deep, use a patent-pending enclosure principle that is a cross between a transmission-line enclosure and a conventional ported-bass reflex system. The units require a minimum power level of 15 watts, but can handle up to 100 watts of music power.

Approximate Retail Price   Approximate Low Price
$205.00/each $140.00/each

 Headphones

AKG K-240 stereo headphones are conventional phones that cover your entire ear when worn. They use a moving-coil transducer and six small passive radiators to achieve excellent response from 16 Hz to 20,000 Hz—more than the range of normal human hearing. Capable of delivering very loud sound levels (up to 125 dB) before overload, these phones weigh about 10 ounces, but are relatively comfortable to wear over a long listening period. Cable supplied is nearly 10 feet long.

Approximate Retail Price   Approximate Low Price
$95.00 .... $72.00

Koss KSP "Sound Partner" come from the firm that "invented" stereophone listening in 1958. These featherweight phones actually fold in half when not being worn, and fit into a denim tote bag (supplied) that, in turn, can easily fit into your pocket or purse. Yet the phones produce excellent sound and cover the range from 20 Hz to 17,000 Hz. Total weight is only 3.5 ounces, including a nine-foot cord. Phones come with accessory adaptor plugs to fit any sound system.

Approximate Retail Price   Approximate Low Price
$35.00 .... $27.50

Sony MDR-80T headphones are that firm's new top-of-the-line model. They feature 30mm drivers, one-sided cable, and superb sound quality in a nicely styled unit. The phones have a frequency response of 16 to 24,000 Hz—much more than the range of normal human hearing. They weigh 2.2 ounces. If you cannot quite afford these headphones, try the less-expensive MDR-3 model.

Approximate Retail Price   Approximate Low Price
$85.00 .... $80.00

Prices are accurate at time of printing; subject to manufacturer's change.

Bang & Olufsen Beocenter 7000 is a distinctively designed, computer-controlled audio system that combines the primary components of a complete system (stereo-FM receiver, cassette recorder, and radial-arm turntable) with a remote-control module. Its wireless remote-control module allows music from different sources to be selected from any point in a listening room. A touch of a button, for example, enables the user to listen to any of six pre-selected FM stations. Another touch activates the cassette unit or the turntable. The system's programming possibilities are limited only by your imagination. You can have it start or stop automatically—at any time. For example, you can record a radio broadcast while you sleep and have it play that broadcast when you wake. You can also program the system to play records at any time within a 24-hour period. Technically speaking, this elegant system might be defined as a "compact system," but if you call it that, you must realize that it's a far cry from the inelegant, inferior systems that were called by that name a few years ago. And the price for this unit bears no resemblance to the prices of old-fashioned cheap compacts either.

Approximate Retail Price   **Approximate Low Price**
$2,100.00 .... Not Available

JVC PC-5 Quintet is a cleverly conceived five-piece system that snaps together in a package only slightly larger than a typical portable radio-cassette recorder, making it possible to get good sound at the beach or on the road with a minimum of trouble. The units include a pair of tiny speakers (bass-reflex two-way systems measuring only 8⅝ inches high, 4¹⁵⁄₁₆ inches wide, and 8⅛ inches deep); a cassette deck with ANRS noise reduction and metal tape capability; a sensitive FM tuner that also includes a marine shortwave band; and an amplifier section rated at 14 watts per channel into 6 ohms, from 70 Hz to 15,000 Hz with less than 10 percent distortion. Obviously, this system isn't intended as a substitute for a home component system, but rather as a second system when portability is needed. The total package weighs 28½ pounds.

Approximate Retail Price   **Low Price**
$650.00 .... $429.00

Prices are accurate at time of printing; subject to manufacturer's change.

Tape Decks

CASSETTE TAPE DECKS, or recorders, have proven to be the darlings of the audio industry, at least from the point of view of the manufacturer. While high-fidelity equipment makers search for new ways to attract more consumers to their new receivers, amplifiers, tuners, turntables, and all the other staples of the audio home entertainment world, they seem to encounter no problems when it comes to selling cassette tape decks. Everyone who owns a stereo system suddenly seems interested in owning recording equipment, and of the recorder formats available, the cassette tape recorder is the clear winner.

It is highly doubtful that the giant Philips company, based in the Netherlands, foresaw such success when it introduced the cassette format in the mid-1960s. In fact, when first introduced, the cassette tape recorder was regarded by most audio buffs as nothing more than a low-fidelity "dictating machine," useful only for transcribing notes of conferences and meetings. At that time, the open-reel, or reel-to-reel, tape deck was regarded as the only true hi-fi recording instrument, and the other tape recording format, the 8-track stereo cartridge, was relegated to use primarily in automobiles.

How times have changed. Thanks to dedicated engineering and research efforts on the part of companies who appreciated the convenience of the cassette format, all of the elements involved in the cassette tape system were gradually improved to the point where this method of recording merited the appellation "hi-fi." Over the years, tape formulations were improved, and the critical tape recording heads and the tape transport mechanisms themselves were improved so that tape speeds could be accurately maintained with inaudible levels of speed fluctuation. An increasing variety of convenience features was incorporated into better cassette tape decks, including several automatic adjustment capabilities.

Types of Tape

IN CONSIDERING WHICH of the hundreds of available cassette tape decks to buy, you should clearly define your goals. Are your recording efforts going to be confined largely to capturing a baby's first words? If so, you don't need a machine capable of wide frequency response and superb signal-to-noise ratios. If you plan to record live music, or even to copy high-fidelity records onto cassette tape, you will want a machine that is capable of transcribing high frequencies accurately and one that has low speed fluctuations—known as wow-and-flutter—and excellent signal-to-noise-ratio capabilities. In that event, you will also want a machine that can handle higher-quality premium tapes properly.

At the moment, there are at least four basic types of cassette tapes available for use in cassette tape recorders. These generic tape types have been given standard numerical designations. Type I tape is generally a ferric-oxide-coated tape, requiring what has come to be known as a "standard" bias setting. Bias is a high-frequency signal that must accompany all signals being recorded on tape to achieve the lowest levels of distortion and best signal-to-noise ratios; the optimum value of bias differs from tape type to tape type and, to a lesser degree, between brands of the same tape type.

Type II tape is one that requires a higher bias level than Type I, and is generally a chromium dioxide tape or a cobalt-treated ferric-oxide equivalent.

Type III tape, sometimes referred to as ferrichrome tape, consists of a double-layer coating of magnetic particles; there is a ferric-oxide layer with a chromium dioxide layer superimposed on it. This type of tape, though popular at one time, is only made by a few tape manufacturers at the present time, and only a small number of cassette decks have appropriate settings for its use.

Type IV tape is metal or metal-particle tape. This type, introduced only three years ago, requires the highest bias voltage of all types, and only machines introduced within the last few years are able to record on this tape properly. All machines that are equipped to record and play Type II tape, however, can also play Type IV tape, because bias voltage is required only during the recording process—not during playback. Type II and Type IV tapes require the same playback settings, known as 70 microsecond equalization, whereas Type I tape requires a different playback setting, known as 120 microsecond equalization.

Because metal-particle tape promises to become increasingly important as its price decreases with increased production and usage, CONSUMER GUIDE® magazine's experts strongly advise you to purchase only a deck that is equipped for this new and better tape formulation. When metal tape was first introduced, the first available decks that could handle it were priced rather high—well above $300. Today, however, it is possible to purchase a cassette deck that will handle metal tape for less than half that price.

Noise-Reduction Systems

IN SELECTING A cassette tape recorder, you are sure to be confronted with a confusing array of features, the most predominant of which will be a noise-reduction system.

In 1970, Dr. Ray Dolby introduced an encode/decode electronic noise-reduction system that reduced tape hiss while preserving frequency response and fidelity, unlike simple high-cut filters that cut out hiss, but also cut out high-treble musical tones at the same time. His system is called "Dolby B Noise Reduction" to distinguish it from Dolby A, Dolby Laboratories' professional noise-reduction system used in recording studios. In a few short years, Dolby B literally became the standard of the world; no one would even consider purchasing a cassette deck intended for high-fidelity recording application unless it was equipped with "Dolby."

Until a few years ago, the Dolby B system reigned supreme, and it is this system that is largely credited with establishing the cassette recorder as a true hi-fi component. Dolby B cuts down tape hiss by about 10 dB (decibels). Translated to layman's terms, this means that any background hiss present on a tape recording with Dolby sounds about half as loud as it would without the Dolby process.

Now, however, there are other noise-reduction systems vying for acceptance. The best-known of these is the dbx system, developed by dbx, Inc. The dbx system provides much greater noise reduction than Dolby B. In fact, it is so effective that when dbx-encoded tapes are played back, no background tape hiss can be heard at all. Additionally, the dbx system allows you to record the full dynamic range of even the widest-range music—a feat that cannot otherwise be accomplished on even the best cassette tape decks using the best metal tape. Two objections, however, have been raised concerning the dbx noise-reduction system. One is that it is incompatible with the more universally recognized Dolby B system; a dbx-encoded tape must be played back on a cassette deck equipped with dbx decoding circuitry. The other is that with certain types of musical fare, the decoding action of the dbx circuitry can be heard in the form of rising and falling levels of background hiss, sometimes referred to as "breathing" or "pumping." In addition, it should be noted that while Dolby-encoded cassette tapes will sound reasonably good on decks not equipped with Dolby decoding circuitry, the same isn't true of dbx-encoded cassette tapes; they will be audibly unacceptable unless played back through a dbx decoder.

Cassette decks offered by JVC have still another noise-reduction system. The company calls it "ANRS" (Automatic Noise Reduction System). This system provides about the same degree of noise reduction as does the Dolby B system. For several years after its introduction, ANRS was considered similar but not identical or compatible with Dolby B. Finally realizing that it would be to its advantage to resolve minor differences between ANRS and Dolby B, JVC altered its system sufficiently so that it is now fully compatible with Dolby B.

Another noise-reduction system that gained some acceptance a few years ago, notably in cassette decks manufactured by Nakamichi, is the Hi-Com II noise-reduction system—an offshoot of a professional noise-reduction system developed by the West German firm of Telefunken. The Hi-Com II noise-reduction system is able to provide 20 dB of noise reduction—twice that of either Dolby B or ANRS—and seemed destined to gain a foothold internationally. An event that changed all that was the announcement by Dolby Laboratories last year that it had developed its own improved noise-reduction system—Dolby C. This new Dolby noise-reduction system would provide more than 20 dB of noise reduction and would be made available to all manufacturers who were already licensed to produce Dolby B circuitry in their recorders at no additional royalty fee.

Aware of the reputation and worldwide acceptance of Dolby B, most manufacturers quickly elected to go with the new Dolby C system and many of the more expensive cassette decks now available from most Japanese manufacturers now incorporate this system. It should be noted that just as Dolby B-encoded tapes provided acceptable musical reproduction when played on non-Dolby equipment, so, too, Dolby C tapes will sound reasonably good when played back through a Dolby B decoder. Of course, the full 20 dB of noise reduction will not occur, but at least a measure of compatibility between Dolby B and Dolby C is retained.

Having heard the Dolby C system under a variety of conditions, CONSUMER GUIDE® magazine's listening panel would not suggest that Dolby C tapes can satisfactorily be played with no Dolby decoding of any kind, even though Dolby Labs has suggested it as a "last resort" sort of alternative.

It is almost certain that Dolby C will assume as great an importance in cassette tape decks as Dolby B did. Furthermore, because Dolby C is a form of extension or improvement on Dolby B, all manufacturers putting Dolby C into their newer and better cassette decks will also include a switch position for Dolby B. In this way, libraries of favorite cassettes that were recorded using Dolby B will be able to be played correctly on the new generation of cassette decks. For these reasons, we would urge those planning to buy a new cassette deck to consider one that either has Dolby C or makes provision for a Dolby C adaptor.

Those who own older decks can take advantage of this new noise-reduction system by adding an "outboard" Dolby C adaptor such as the one now being offered by Nakamichi. The Nakamichi Model NR-200, however, carries a suggested retail price of $450, so you can see that Dolby C isn't considered to be suitable for use with low-cost, lower-quality cassette decks. In fact, Dolby Laboratories has recommended that the new noise-reduction technique be applied only to the better-quality decks in each licensee's product line.

Tape Speed Not Much of an Issue

FOR ALMOST THE entire life of the format to date, all cassette decks have operated at 1 7/8 inches per second (ips), the standard speed set by Philips, the inventor of the format. It was thought that the licensing agreement that all manufacturers had to sign with Philips before they could begin making cassette decks included a provision regarding standardized speed. In fact, that turned out to be a point of confusion and, a few years ago, B.I.C., a company that no longer manufactures cassette decks, decided to "test the waters" by producing several models that operated at 3 3/4 ips.

All things being equal, a faster tape speed yields better frequency response, lower noise, lower distortion, or a combination of all three improvements in performance. Of course, double tape speed also uses twice as much tape, but to a dedicated audiophile, it was argued that this would be of relatively little significance if performance could be significantly improved. In fact, with metal tape costing roughly twice as much as other premium-quality tapes at that time, it was felt that if operating at twice standard speed could produce results on conventional tape that were better than those offered by metal tape at the standard speed, then the purchaser of a dual-speed cassette deck would actually be ahead of the game.

Other manufacturers, seeing that B.I.C. was able to go ahead with its non-standard speed without any repercussions from Philips, the licensor, followed suit. Soon, there were two-speed decks from Harman-Kardon and Marantz, to name two. Nakamichi also offered two-speed cassette decks for a time, but the alternate speed wasn't 3¾ ips, but rather a half-standard speed of $^{15}/_{16}$ ips. Because not all recording work demands the ultimate in frequency response or fidelity, Nakamichi decided to try a slower speed that could offer acceptable performance while using only half as much tape. The results at the ultra-slow speed were quite impressive, yielding a frequency response that went to 15,000 hertz (Hz) at the treble extreme; it was a lot better than what most cassette decks produced only a few years earlier, even at the standard speed of 1⅞ ips.

When CONSUMER GUIDE® magazine last reviewed the "battle of the speeds" in cassette tape decks a year ago, it was in full swing. Some manufacturers were arguing for continued standardization of a single speed; others were opting for a higher alternate speed; and still others were in favor of a second, slower speed. Examining the situation now, CONSUMER GUIDE® magazine was surprised to find that the intensity of the arguments has declined considerably. At recent electronics trade shows, there were virtually no new decks featuring two speeds. And, prices for metal tape have come down considerably, negating the argument in favor of using conventional tape at twice normal speed. There is also renewed talk about a potential market for higher-quality microcassette decks for such applications where the ultimate in frequency response isn't required; the microcassette used in tiny pocket dictating recorders already has a standard speed of $^{15}/_{16}$ ips. As a consequence, manufacturers seem to have lost interest in promoting two-speed cassette tape decks, and appear to have settled back into the one-speed format that has prevailed for so many years.

Other Formats

THERE ARE TWO other tape deck formats available for consumers. These are the open-reel, or reel-to-reel, tape deck and the 8-track cartridge deck. While an open-reel deck is still capable of the best audio performance, such a machine should be considered only if you plan to engage in semi-professional or professional recording. The open-reel deck lends itself to tape editing and sophisticated multi-track recording in which individual tape "tracks" can be recorded separately and can then be mixed together for a final "master recording." Most commercial phonograph records are produced from such "master tapes" made on multi-track, open-reel tape recorders. Open-reel decks intended for consumer or semi-professional use usually have two or even three operating tape speeds. For professional applications, a tape speed of 15 ips is recommended, though excellent fidelity and frequency response can be obtained from machines whose top speed is 7½ ips. Acceptable results can even be obtained at a tape speed of 3¾ ips. While some machines of this type even offer a speed of 1⅞ ips, it would seem pointless to use such a slow speed with an open-reel machine.

The third consumer tape format is the 8-track stereo cartridge, which was actually invented before cassettes made their appearance in the 1960s. The 8-track cartridge uses a continuous "loop" of tape, on which four pairs of stereo "tracks" or programs are recorded. The loop of tape is pulled around and the first program is played, after which a bit of conductive foil on the surface of the tape engages a solenoid; it pulls the playback head downward by a fixed distance, so that the head traces and plays the second pair of tracks, and so on until all four pairs of program tracks have been played. Left unattended, the procedure can repeat itself endlessly, or, on some machines, a switch can be set to eject the cartridge after all selections have been played once. Most 8-track cartridge machines are playback devices only; they are unable to record on tape. In the 1960s, the 8-track tape format was used primarily in automobiles, because its simplicity of operation made it ideal for drivers.

The 8-track cartridge format is, however, generally quite poor in terms of frequency response and signal-to-noise ratio. When played in automobiles, the high level of tape hiss and the poor fidelity were generally unnoticed, or at least tolerated. But now, as car stereo systems approach the levels of fidelity found in home music systems, most discerning listeners find the 8-track cartridge format unacceptable. As a result, cassette players have become quite popular for use in vehicles. An advantage of the cassette player in cars is that you can record your favorite music on your home cassette deck and play it while traveling.

While audio enthusiasts had recognized the superiority of the cassette format in cars for several years, automobile manufacturers were slow to make the transition from 8-track cartridge "original equipment" to cassette decks, but now that transition has been made and just about any new car can be factory-equipped with a cassette/radio combination.

Tape Deck Specifications

SPECIFICATIONS FOR tape decks are measured in the same way for both cassette and open-reel machines. To give you some idea of how the formats have evolved in recent years, and to provide you with some basis for choosing a deck to serve your purposes, here are brief explanations of some of those specifications:

Wow-and-Flutter. This measurement of tape speed fluctuation is usually listed in percentages with the letters WRMS, like "0.1 percent WRMS." The WRMS stands for Weighted Root Mean Square, but you don't have to remember that to understand what the specification sheets say. The only thing to keep in mind is that you are looking for the smallest percentage you can get for the money you have to spend. If this measurement is quoted by a manufacturer in RMS rather than WRMS, you can expect that figure to be somewhat higher than the comparable WRMS wow-and-flutter figure for the same machine.

Not too long ago, a wow-and-flutter specification of 0.1 percent WRMS was considered a minor miracle in cassette decks because the low tape speed involved made uniformity of tape motion difficult to achieve. These days, there are decks selling for as little as $250 that rival open-reel machines with readings as low as 0.08 percent WRMS.

Frequency Response, Distortion, and Signal-to-Noise. These three important specifications are very much related to each other. Unfortunately, many manufacturers tend to emphasize frequency response because it is the specification that is most readily understood by consumers. High-fidelity equipment buyers have been conditioned over the years to believe that every hi-fi component must have so-called "flat" response from 20 Hz to 20,000 Hz.

In the case of tape decks—particularly cassette tape decks—however, frequency response extending beyond 15,000 Hz is too often achieved at the expense of other desirable capabilities. High distortion and poor signal-to-noise ratios often result. Underbiasing a given tape, for example, will result in greater output at higher frequencies, but it also increases distortion during playback. Exaggerated equalization, either during recording or playback, can also increase high-frequency output, but such modifications will result in higher tape noise. Ask a professional recordist whether he would rather have response out to 20,000 Hz and a signal-to-noise ratio of 55 dB, or response only to 15,000 Hz and signal-to-noise of better than 60 dB. The answer will always be in favor of the better signal-to-noise ratio.

While it's true that humans are supposed to hear within the range of 20 Hz and 20,000 Hz, most of us don't hear much beyond 15,000 Hz, particularly as we get older. As proof of the fact that you don't necessarily have to have flat response to 20,000 Hz in a piece of tape equipment, consider the fact that FM broadcasts transmit frequencies up to only 15,000 Hz. Because much of what you are likely to record will come from that source, it seems foolish to worry about frequency response beyond 15,000 Hz.

Signal-to-noise ratings for cassette tape decks should be a prime consideration for any purchaser. Much depends on the type of tape used as well as on the capabilities of the deck itself. A deck capable of delivering low noise won't live up to expectations if you use inferior "bargain" cassette tapes. Such tapes may be adequate for voice recording, provided they are mechanically sound and don't jam or break during a recording session. But, for serious recording work involving high-fidelity music program sources, you should select a good tape, preferably one recommended by the manufacturer of your machine. With so many different tape formulations now available, it's important, too, that your cassette machine have the necessary bias and equalization switch positions to match the characteristics of the tape you use. Generally, you don't have to be as particular about tape types used on open-reel machines; however, if you plan serious recording work, be sure to use a name-brand tape.

Open-reel tape recording offers considerably greater dynamic range and improved frequency response compared to cassette units. This is especially true if you operate at the high speed of 15 ips used by professionals, but it even applies to the slower 7½-ips speed. At 15 ips, and even at half that speed, you can expect frequency response to go way beyond 20,000 Hz on better machines. The trade-off between speed and performance is one that the user must decide.

Optimizing Cassette Deck Performance

EARLIER, WE MENTIONED that recording bias, the high-frequency signal that must accompany every program being recorded on tape, varies considerably from tape type to tape type. While most cassette decks offer fixed switch settings for the three or four types of tape available for cassette machines, there are still minor differences between brands of the same type of tape and even some differences between production batches of the same brand of tape. For this reason, a few better machines offer vernier, or fine-tuning, controls in addition to the basic settings provided by the three- or four-position tape selector switch. No such fine-tune control is needed for setting playback equalization, however, because only two standard settings are required: 120 microseconds and 70 microseconds. Sometimes, the equalization is selected by means of a separate two-position switch, while in other decks a single tape selector switch takes care of basic bias settings as well as equalization settings for the basic types of tape.

Decks having a fine-tune bias control do more than just allow you to fine-tune bias. They also permit you to choose those performance parameters that matter most within a given recording situation. For example, slightly underbiasing a deck for a given tape will result in extended high-frequency response, but at the expense of mid-frequency distortion and some decrease in output level of the tape during playback with a consequent slight degradation of signal-to-noise ratio for that tape. It is a fact of tape-recording life that the three important parameters of frequency response, distortion, and noise are all interrelated and are all dependent on tape type and bias settings. With a fine-tune bias control, you are given an opportunity to trade off one of these parameters in favor of the other two.

Going a step beyond the manually adjustable bias controls, there are now some very sophisticated cassette tape decks that, at the touch of a button and with the aid of a programmed minicomputer or microprocessor, actually "test" the tape about to be used in the deck and adjust bias, equalization, and even sensitivity (or amplification of the built-in recording and playback amplifiers), so as to provide "best" performance with that tape. Most of these automated decks tend to favor "flat" frequency response, sometimes at the expense of distortion and noise, but they are nevertheless remarkable instruments and do take a lot of the guesswork away from the non-technical recordist who would not otherwise be able to adjust the deck for optimum levels of performance.

Beyond Performance

IN ADDITION TO wow-and-flutter, frequency response, signal-to-noise ratio, and distortion, consumers should be aware of some other features and controls that are available in many cassette decks. For example, there is memory rewind. You set a tape counter to "000" at a specific point during playback. Later, if you put the tape into the fast-rewind mode, the tape transport will stop at the predetermined "000" point, enabling you to start listening from there. Some machines have a combination memory-rewind/auto-play feature, in which play is automatically resumed from the predetermined "000" setting.

Some tape decks use light indicators instead of mechanical meter movements to assist you in setting recording levels. These light-emitting diodes respond more quickly than conventional meters to fast musical transient signals. Peak-reading meters have also become quite common on cassette decks for the same reason. All of these improvements are intended to prevent accidental over-recording and distortion that can occur when sluggish meters are unable to keep pace with signal peaks. Another type of meter uses a fluorescent bar-graph that also depicts recording level electronically.

Nakamichi now makes several cassette tape decks that not only optimize important working parameters to match the tape being used in them, but also incorporate a programmable searching circuit that can recognize the pauses between selections and can therefore be instructed to play specific selections on a tape in any order—skipping some, repeating others, and so on. These features are found in both of Nakamichi's top-of-the-line decks, Model 700ZXL and Model 1000ZXL, which carry the incredible suggested retail prices of $3,000 and $3,800, respectively. Similar features can be found on top-of-the-line units from Phase Linear, Optonica, Sharp, and others. Bang & Olufsen, noted for its highly styled Scandinavian designs in audio equipment, has come up with programmable cassette decks that can be operated by remote control, programmed to play selections at given points on the tape, read out remaining time available on tape, and much more.

Many of the newer and more expensive cassette decks use three separate heads: one for erase, another for recording, and a third for playback. This arrangement provides the same monitoring capability—listening to a recording almost simultaneously with its creation—that is available on most open-reel machines. With three-head decks, there is usually some means of adjusting the angle of orientation of the record head relative to the stationary or fixed playback head; this adjustment is known as azimuth alignment. If the magnetic gap in the playback head isn't perfectly parallel to the gap in the playback head, high-frequency response suffers drastically.

Some three-head tape decks have a separate record and playback head mounted in a single housing. For those machines, azimuth alignment isn't required because the parallelism of the record and play head gaps is established and permanently sealed in when the combination record/play heads are encased at the factory.

Which Format to Buy

OPEN-REEL TAPE decks have undergone a radical change in the last few years due to the emergence of high-quality cassette units. Most open-reel tape decks sold today border on the professional level. Two types predominate: those that permit you to do multichannel recording of one channel at a time for ultimate mix-down into a stereo tape (usually supplied with four-channel, four-track capability); and a number of units that have abandoned the quarter-track format of two stereo program tracks in each direction of travel in favor of so-called half-track tape configuration. The half-track format allows for stereo recording in one direction of tape travel only because each track occupies half the tape width instead of one-quarter of that width. The advantages of half-track recording include better signal-to-noise ratio and greater dynamic range.

The Technics RS-1500US machine is an example of this breed of open-reel deck. It has a refined form of tape motion in which tape travel is unaffected by reel tension or variations in tape wind on the supply and takeup reels. The RS-1500US comes with a four-track playback head for those who already own four-track tapes, but its own record head is of the half-track variety.

Serious recording buffs now tend to purchase both a multiple-track machine plus one of the newer half-track machines, thereby equipping themselves with the basics of a total home-recording studio. Essentially, the only difference between many of these machines and the types used in recording studios lies not so much in their audio performance, but in the rugged construction of the professional studio units so that they can withstand continuous use day after day.

Clearly, however, the cassette format is the most popular. Easy to use, compact in size, and with improved electronics, the latest cassette decks can record even the most demanding of program material with near-perfect fidelity. A low-cost deck with a minimum of frills (but with proper switches for tape selection and Dolby noise reduction) connects easily to any component system, whether that system uses as its central component a receiver or separate amplifier/preamplifier. Unless you're at a near-professional recording level, therefore, your logical choice would be a quality cassette deck.

Unfortunately, there is nothing encouraging to report about recent developments or even the promise of future developments in the 8-track cartridge tape format. Indeed, it would appear that 8-track tapes and machines lag well behind the others in terms of acoustic quality and mechanical reliability. At this time, then, it is impossible to make any recommendations regarding the cartridge tape format or tape players themselves.

Tape Deck Care

NO MATTER WHAT type of deck you purchase, you must give it proper care if you expect it to live up to its performance potential. The following are simple tasks that anyone can do to keep a deck in peak condition.

Tape heads, guides, capstans, puck rollers—all the parts that come in contact with the moving tape—should be cleaned about every 20 playing hours with a cotton swab dipped in alcohol or a commercial head-cleaning solution. Even the slightest buildup of flaked-off oxide particles reduces high-frequency response considerably.

In addition, the metal surfaces that touch the tape require a second kind of cleaning—degaussing. This eliminates the gradual accumulation of magnetism to which these parts are susceptible. If allowed to build up, this magnetism permanently erases the high frequencies on your recorded tapes and simultaneously increases their hiss level. Inexpensive head demagnetizers are available at any audio dealer, and because degaussing takes only a few seconds, you should do it about as often as you clean the heads.

The proper degaussing technique is as follows:

1. Turn off your tape deck and remove all recorded tapes from the immediate vicinity.

2. If the tip(s) of the demagnetizer is exposed and hard, cover it with a layer of plastic electrical tape to prevent scratching the delicate tape heads.

3. Turn on the head degausser while holding it at arm's length from the recorder.

4. Slowly bring the head degausser up to each of the parts to be demagnetized, move it over the affected surfaces, and then slowly withdraw it to arm's length before turning it off.

Tape heads should also be inspected periodically for wear. When the passage of tape has worn a groove deep enough to catch a fingernail on, the useful life of the heads as been exhausted. Replacing heads, unfortunately, requires specialized equipment and must be handled by a competent technician.

Best Buys '82

OUR "BEST BUY" and "Also Recommended" tape decks follow; they are listed alphabetically within each category. Remember that a "Best Buy" designation applies only to the model listed; it doesn't necessarily apply to other models made by the same manufacturer, or to an entire product line.

Pioneer RT-707 is a two-speed (7½ and 3¾ ips) machine that accepts seven-inch reels and has a three-motor, four-head design. It features auto-reverse/repeat playback capability. This open-reel deck handles well and allows the dedicated recordist to become involved in reel-to-reel recording at a fraction of the cost of some of the more expensive and more elaborate models of open-reel recorders. It offers lower distortion and better frequency response—using the higher of its two speeds—than you could ever expect to get from any cassette deck, but the machine lacks the features that most professionals want in an open-reel deck, such as 15-ips tape speed and facility for 10½-inch reels.

Approximate Retail Price **Approximate Low Price**
$695.00 .... $466.00

Also Recommended

Tandberg TD 20A, a more expensive unit than our "Best Buy" selection, benefits from a new technology called Actilinear recording, which permits the three-speed unit (3¾, 7½, and 15 ips) to play metal-particle tape as well as other types of tapes. One of the finest open-reel machines we have ever tested, the four-motor Tandberg TD 20A, delivered a signal-to-noise ratio of 66 dB; distortion was lower than claimed. Recording headroom was generous, and there was extremely low wow-and-flutter.

Approximate Retail Price **Approximate Low Price**
$1,295.00 .... Not Available

Teac X-10R is a two-speed (7½ and 3¾ ips) deck that offers a generous measure of professionalism in terms of cue-monitoring, fast-buttoning, facility for 10½-inch reels, and so on. The facility for automatic recording in both directions is rather special, and the fact that it works so well is a tribute to Teac engineering. But unless you want a unit that accepts 10½-inch reels and more professional features, our "Best Buy" choice may be better suited for your purposes.

Approximate Retail Price **Approximate Low Price**
$1,200.00 .... $765.00

Technics RS-1500US, like other advanced and extremely expensive open-reel decks, is not for the casual or infrequent recordist; rather, it's a three-speed (15, 7½, and 3¾ ips) machine for the tape enthusiast who can appreciate its enviable combination of superior audio and mechanical performance and who will use its many fine attributes to full advantage. Our audio experts were especially impressed by its ruggedness of construction, high quality parts, and attention to detail—all of which should assure the owner of years of reliable, trouble-free performance.

Approximate Retail Price **Approximate Low Price**
$1,600.00 .... $1,049.00

 **Cassette Decks**

JVC DD-9 is that company's top-of-the-line cassette deck for 1982. Its pulse-servo direct-drive motor works with a quartz-crystal reference, resulting in a wow-and-flutter rating of only 0.019 percent. The deck

Prices are accurate at time of printing; subject to manufacturer's change.

incorporates three heads to permit tape monitoring, and adjusts itself for best results from any tape by setting bias, equalization, and tape sensitivity automatically. ANRS/Dolby B and the new Dolby C are incorporated, as are fluorescent display meters.

Approximate Retail Price	Approximate Low Price
$900.00	$578.00

Marantz SD 9000, called a Compudeck, is claimed to be the world's only two-speed, three-head, double-Dolby, totally programmable metal-handling cassette deck at its price. Its microprocessor programming and selection circuitry allows playback of selections in any desired sequence on a cassette tape. The machine features a digital counter, timer, and clock function, and three heads to allow tape monitoring. Two motors are used in the drive system. Mic and line inputs can be mixed with front panel controls for each channel and a master output level control. It handles all four generic types of tape and includes a bias fine-tune adjustment.

Approximate Retail Price	Approximate Low Price
$830.00	$523.00

Pioneer CT-8R is a three-head machine with full monitoring capability. Switchable Dolby B and Dolby C noise-reduction circuitry is included, and the unit's direct-drive system results in an incredibly low wow-and-flutter of only 0.035 percent. The deck automatically adjusts its own bias level and equalization to match the tape in use. A microprocessor controls blank space search, index-scanning, music-search, and music repeat capabilities. Tapes can be played in both directions (auto reverse). The signal-to-noise ratio, with Dolby C engaged, is better than 80 dB using metal tape.

Approximate Retail Price	Approximate Low Price
$575.00	$399.00

Sony TC-FX5C is one of the lowest-priced cassette decks to offer the new Dolby C noise-reduction system. Other features include optional wired or wireless remote control, synchronization with selected Sony turntables (using an optional accessory), 16-segment LED level display, and a slider-type level control. The deck can be used for unattended recording with the addition of an auxiliary timer. The deck also has rewind/auto-play and a record mute control.

Approximate Retail Price	Approximate Low Price
$350.00	$244.00

Technics RS-M218 is a low-cost deck with Dolby B noise reduction that maintains high sonic standards and handles three basic types of tape, including metal-particle tape. Fluorescent meters with a peak-hold feature help to set accurate recording levels. The controls are easy to use and have a positive feel to them. An additional feature is the rewind/auto-play facility. The Technics RS-M218 is an excellent value.

Approximate Retail Price	Approximate Low Price
$200.00	$149.00

Prices are accurate at time of printing; subject to manufacturer's change.

Cameras

CHOOSING A CAMERA is a personal matter, one that requires a well-conceived game plan. Except for a few oddball exceptions, there are no bad cameras on the market; almost every camera made today is ideal for someone. The real challenge is to determine which one is right for you.

The most important decision to make when you're looking for a camera is what format, or type, of camera you want. We present five basic camera types in this section: 35mm SLRs (single-lens reflex cameras), 35mm autofocus, 35mm compacts, 110 cartridge, and instant-print. Before you look at the cameras themselves, take a look at these five types to see which one is right for your situation. After you've narrowed down your choice to one or two types, go on to see what they have to offer.

Choosing the Best Format for You

THE BIG QUESTION IS, what kind of pictures do you want to take? For example, if you just want to take snapshots, with as little fuss as possible, you can immediately eliminate the SLRs. The next question may be, do you want instant pictures or pictures that need developing? If instant, then you've found your category: instant-print. If you want pictures that can be developed—offering a choice of slides or negatives, and smaller camera designs—then you still have three format options: 35mm autofocus, 35mm compact, and 110 cartridge.

The second question to answer is what type of film you want, 35mm or 110 cartridge. Both types offer negatives for duplicates, but there are advantages to each. 110 film is easier to load; it is also, generally, less expensive to develop. 35mm film offers a wider choice of film types; enlargements are also easier to make than with 110 film. If obtaining enlargements isn't a consideration, and you don't want to spend much for developing, then the 110 format should fit your needs. If you plan to enlarge your photos, and if you want a good film choice, then you've narrowed your search to two choices: 35mm compact and 35mm autofocus.

The final decision between these two 35mm snapshot formats concerns ease of use. Autofocus cameras are, generally, the easiest cameras to operate—compacts have to be focused and some compacts require the setting of exposure controls. Autofocus cameras cost more than compacts, though, and you may or may not think this convenience is worth the price. This, too, would be a consideration.

If your concerns lead you quickly to one of these five categories, that format is the best one for you, and you can go on to choose your camera.

But if you don't want to discard instant-print cameras so quickly, or you want a camera that will work easily in some situations yet still offer creative exposure control in others, or if you want to learn about photography as an art, there's more to it than that. The important thing is to keep your search first in terms of format—not brand name—and to go from there to the individual cameras. There are always exceptions to the format guidelines. For example, there are a few expensive 110 cameras that are *not* snapshot cameras; they demand a lot of the photographer. Yet by giving some serious thought to your needs, and by understanding which formats best suit them, a lot of unnecessary confusion will be quickly eliminated.

Cameras That Teach You About Photography

IF YOU WANT a camera that does more than record memories—if you want to learn about the art and the processes of photography—your choice is different. You can immediately eliminate two formats: auto-focus and instant-print. Neither of these offers any substantial creative control over your photographs. You must now choose among three possible formats: 110 cartridge, 35mm compact, and 35mm SLR (single-lens reflex).

Again, ask yourself first about film type. The 35mm format offers more possibilities for creative film types and developing processes, and also gives you a much larger choice of creative cameras. A 110 camera doesn't offer this versatility, but it is easier to carry around, and developing 110 film is less expensive. If camera size and cost of development are important to you, take a look at the 110s that will allow you to explore creative photography. If size isn't that important—and if you want to take advantage of 35mm film possibilities—then you still have two choices: 35mm compact and 35mm SLR.

If you're buying your first creative camera, this is the tough decision to make. Here's how to do it. The first consideration is cost: How much can you afford? If you're on a limited budget, a compact camera is the better choice; it offers some great creative potential at a much lower cost. The second consideration is the kind of photography you're interested in: Just how much creative control do you want? If you want all the creative control possible, an SLR is the best choice for you. Compacts give you the basics of exposure control and little else; with an SLR, you can monitor exactly what appears on the film, and you have access to a multitude of creative lenses, motor drives, and other accessories.

The final question to ask is how committed you are to creative photography? If you're not sure, a compact is an inexpensive way to find out. In fact, we believe the compact format is the best format to learn on. You'll kick yourself repeatedly for buying an expensive SLR to take simple snapshots.

Once you determine which format is best for your photographic interests, you must choose a camera within the format. This is the easy part. Each camera has a personality. Your only real struggle will be in matching the camera's personality to your own.

If you've read this introduction thoroughly, you've noticed that 35mm compacts are considered both snapshot and creative cameras. What that means is that *some* compacts are simple snapshot cameras and *some* are creative. The 35mm compact is certainly the most schizophrenic category, with 110s following close behind. The rest of the categories are pretty cut and dried—SLRs for creative photography, autofocus and instant-print for snapshots only.

Best Buys '82

OUR SELECTION OF "Best Buy" cameras follows. Reports are divided into the five different formats and models are listed alphabetically. Our choices are based on cost-efficiency, availability, and quality of design. Remember that a "Best Buy" designation applies only to the particular model in question; it doesn't mean that we necessarily recommend other models in the same product line or from the same manufacturer.

 35mm SLRs

SLR STANDS FOR single-lens reflex: You look through the same lens through which the camera takes the picture. Although what you see through the lens is about 92 percent of what will show on the photograph (some SLRs reveal 97 or 98 percent), the SLR represents a major advance over viewfinder cameras, in which you look through a lens that has no direct relation to the picture-taking lens. SLRs are the standard cameras of professional photographers who need to know precisely what they're shooting. The pros also want lens-changing flexibility, which only SLRs provide. In very short order you can convert an SLR for shooting telephoto, wide-angle, or other types of pictures, simply by changing lenses. The only other film formats that offer SLR capability are the 110 cartridge and instant print formats. These are oddball cameras within their format—there are only a few of them. Pros generally use the 35mm film format. And there's a large selection of 35mm SLRs to choose from.

Your first decision should concern the SLR's exposure system. How much exposure setting do you want the camera to do? A strictly manual-exposure camera requires that you set the aperture (the width of the lens opening) and the shutter speed (how fast the shutter clicks). A meter, registering the amount of available light, usually suggests an appropriate aperture and shutter speed; you then set the proper mechanism, focus the camera, and shoot the picture.

The automatic exposure systems are really semi-automatic. In an aperture-priority camera, you set the aperture, and the camera automatically sets what it senses to be the proper shutter speed. In a shutter-priority camera, you set the shutter speed, and the camera automatically sets the aperture. There are some SLRs on the market that you can switch back and forth between aperture-priority and shutter-priority. These are called multi-mode cameras.

A shutter-priority camera is better for taking action shots because it gives you greater control over stopping motion. Sports photographers would choose such a system. An aperture-priority camera is better for those who like to control depth of field. For example, if you want to focus on children walking through a forest, an aperture-priority camera makes it easier to emphasize the children and de-emphasize—perhaps blur—the trees in the background.

If you want an auto-exposure SLR, consider one with complete manual override. There may be times when you want to substitute your judgment for the camera's automatic capability, and the manual override allows you to indulge your creative urges in such instances.

Beyond exposure, SLRs offer a multitude of fascinating—and sometimes odd—features. These features either add to the versatility of the camera, or make it easier to operate. Features that add versatility include self-timers, double-exposure provisions, and depth-of-field previews that enable you to see the range of focus before you shoot. Features that simplify the picture-taking process include auto-winders that advance the film automatically, special designs that simplify the loading of the film or the cocking of the shutter, and special grips that make small cameras easier to hold. There are also numerous fail-safe features: shutter locks to prevent improperly exposed pictures, audible beeps that warn of camera shake, and battery checks that indicate dead or near-dead batteries. Some cameras even take the exposure control away from you when you've set it improperly and set the controls themselves. No camera incorporates all of these features. What every camera does include is a combination of features designed for a specific type of photographer. Whenever a camera has unusual features, we tell you how they're different—and what we think of them.

What you see through the viewfinder is going to play a large role in your photography. All of our "Best Buy" cameras have some form of metering; they will suggest the best exposure combination, and you can then use it or ignore it. There are as many different ways to provide this information as there are cameras to provide it. Look through several camera's viewfinders in the camera store. Make sure what you see is readable and helpful. In these profiles, we identify the unusual or commendable aspects of each camera's viewing system.

Finally, the judgment is going to be made in the camera store as you handle the camera and operate its controls. Make sure that the camera is comfortable—not too heavy or too light—and that you can easily operate its controls. In-hand comparison of cameras is the most important aspect of your search. All of these "Best Buys" are excellent cameras. Every SLR reviewed is supplemented by suggestions of other comparable cameras to consider and handle before you buy. In the end, it doesn't matter how good something looks on paper, it's how it feels in the hands that counts most.

Canon AE-1 Program is a brand-new Canon SLR, costing about $30 more than the popular AE-1. It's surprising that such a small boost in price accompanies such substantial changes. Like the AE-1, this Program camera offers a basic manual and a semi-automatic exposure mode. The most notable advance over the AE-1 is a programmed exposure mode, which allows the photographer to simply focus the camera and shoot the picture. This is an unusual feature in an SLR. It may make the AE-1 Program appear to be just another easy-to-use snapshot camera. It is not. While in the programmed mode photography is basic and simple, this camera has incredible—even highly professional—potentials, such as the acceptance of unusual accessories and the ability to respond to substantially different photographic situations.

The semi-automatic mode of the AE-1 Program uses a shutter-preferred exposure system. In shutter-preferred operation, the photographer sets the shutter speed—the speed with which the picture is taken (up to 1/1000 second)—and the camera automatically sets an appropriate aperture—the size of the lens opening. This is an especially good mode for stopping movement, encountered in, say, sporting situations. In the manual mode, both shutter speed and aperture are set by hand. This is how all SLRs worked just 10 years ago, and continues to be one of the best means toward creative success. These two modes—shutter-preferred and manual—plus the program mode make the AE-1 Program the most versatile camera in its price range.

The viewfinder contains several forms of blinking LEDs—colored lights—that inform you as to what mode you're in, what exposure has been set by either you or the camera, and if your shot will be under- or overexposed. There is no shutter-speed scale in the viewfinder, however. That means if you want to know what shutter speed has been set, you must take your eye from the viewfinder and check the control—a definite drawback. What *is* in the viewfinder, however, is positioned well and is easy to read.

The AE-1 Program feels exceptionally good in the hands. Controls act as natural extensions of your fingers. The camera rarely gets heavy, lenses attach quickly and easily, and the final feel is one of control and confidence. The textured finish on the camera makes it easier to grip than many other SLRs.

The AE-1 Program accepts the best in Canon's quality system of lenses and other accessories. It can accept two motor drives, one that shoots two pictures per second and a more expensive model that can shoot four pictures per second. One of the most exceptional features of the AE-1 Program is its ability to accept seven optional, interchangeable focusing screens. This is helpful in specialized shooting situations—architectural or microscopic photography, for example.

The Canon AE-1 Program is a good first SLR *if* you're sure you're interested in the creative aspects of photography. Don't buy the camera simply for its point-and-shoot capabilities; consider the programmed aspect as one of three major abilities of the camera. If you plan to stop a lot of action with your camera, if you want to dabble in creative effects, and if, at times, you want to sit back and let the camera take over, then the Canon AE-1 Program is an excellent choice. At simply $30 more than the AE-1, it is a highly justifiable "Best Buy." The Canon AE-1 Program, without lens, measures 5.6 inches wide, 3.4 inches high, and 1.9 inches deep. It weighs 20.3 ounces. Other "Best Buy" SLRs to consider with the AE-1 Program would include the Minolta XD-5, the Minolta XG-M, and the Konica FS-1.

Approximate Retail Price	Approximate Low Price
With f/1.8 lens: $481.00	$269.00-$299.00

Konica FS-1 is one of the more expensive shutter-preferred SLRs in production today. Its price appears to be justified not for what's inside the camera—although what's inside is good—but for some ingenious external styling. This is, simply, one of the most comfortable SLRs to hold and operate. Although beginning SLR photographers would find this camera easier to use than most, the list price places it out of the range of what you should pay for your first SLR. If the discount price remains as low as at this printing, however, the beginning SLR photographer should give the FS-1 a hard look. And if you're looking to upgrade your SLR capabilities, you can't go wrong with the FS-1.

Shutter-preferred operation means that the photographer sets the shutter speed—the speed at which the picture is taken (up to 1/1000 second)—and the camera selects the aperture—the size of the lens opening. This is the preferred mode for fast-action shots, such as sports. The camera also has a manual override, so that you can set both shutter speed and aperture. This gives you complete creative control over your photographs.

An unusual feature of the camera is the built-in auto-winder. With most cameras, you have to advance the film, but this camera automatically advances the film; there is no manual film advance. The auto-winder doubles as an exceptionally handy grip on the front of the camera. You feel more control over your shots because the camera can be stabilized in awkward shooting situations better than with almost any other downsized SLR. Even if you aren't considering this camera, make sure you handle one before you buy. It will give you a standard to judge your other options by.

Other benefits are an oversized shutter speed selector, making selection easy even with gloves on, and a film counter on the back—instead of the top—of the camera, with easy-to-read numbers. Konica has also devised one of the simplest film-loading methods known to 35mm photography: You take about three inches of film out of the spool, insert the film package into the camera, and close the camera. The auto-winder then zips the film to the first frame; there's no fuss and little chance of misloading.

All of the automation in this camera would make it appear to meet a beginner's needs. But while it's true that it's easier to work with than most, only those experienced with SLRs will know if such features as large grips, auto-winders, easy loading, oversized shutter speed controls, and easy-to-read film counters are worth the extra money. This is an expensive camera. We feel you should have experience—and perhaps frustrations—with a less expensive SLR before considering the

Prices are accurate at time of printing; subject to manufacturer's change.

FS-1. It's worth repeating, however: If the discount price remains as low as it is now, the FS-1 is a good buy for a first SLR.

Konica makes a quality system of lenses and accessories. It isn't the most extensive system by any means, but it has been proven reliable. If you plan on making a living with your photographs, you may want a different make with a more extensive system. If you're only shooting two or three rolls of film a week, however, Konica's accessories should suffice.

The Konica FS-1 is usually priced too high to be considered a good first SLR, but it is a great second SLR. You should learn photography on something less expensive, and perhaps less sophisticated in design. If you then really like your photography—or if you already do—and you can evaluate how these intelligent design features could enhance your enjoyment of the art, then the FS-1 is an exceptional buy. The Konica FS-1 with an f/1.8 lens is 5.7 inches long, 3.5 inches high, and 2.8 inches deep. It weighs 28.2 ounces. Other "Best Buy" cameras to consider with the FS-1 include the Canon AE-1 Program and the Minolta XD-5.

Approximate Retail Price	Approximate Low Price
With f/1.8 lens: $555.00	$260.00-$284.00

Mamiya ZE is the least expensive automatic SLR camera we've chosen as a "Best Buy." It's about as basic as an automatic camera can be, with few frills or extras. There is no manual mode on this camera; automation is your only choice. If you aren't interested in manual photography—and you want a simple-to-use SLR at a reasonable price—then the Mamiya ZE may be the model for you.

The ZE is an aperture-preferred automatic; you set the aperture—the size of the lens opening—and the camera automatically selects a shutter speed—the speed at which the picture is taken (up to 1/1000 second). All that's left to do is focus the picture and shoot.

Although the lack of a manual mode hinders complete creative control, there are some definite creative assets to this camera. Because you set the aperture, you have control over the picture's depth of field—the area that will be sharply in focus. If, for example, you'd like to blur the background of your subject, you can set a large aperture; if you want the whole picture in focus, you can set a small one. Other creative features include a memory lock—an excellent feature on any automatic SLR, and especially one at this price. The memory lock is useful because some lighting situations—such as the sun behind the subject—can fool automatic systems. With the lock, you can take a meter reading up close, and then step back and take your shot. The camera will hold the proper setting, and your picture will be correctly exposed.

Mamiya has one of the smaller systems among SLR manufacturers, but the components—lenses, electronic flash units, auto-winders (at two pictures per second), filters, and other specialized accessories, such as slide copiers and magnifiers—should satisfy most needs. The accessories are generally less expensive than those by the big-name manufacturers, such as Nikon and Canon.

Generally, we don't recommend cameras without some form of manual override—where you can set both aperture and shutter speed.

Prices are accurate at time of printing; subject to manufacturer's change.

Considering the price of the Mamiya ZE, however, and its thoughtful, basic capabilities, we think this is a sensible buy if you have no great creative desires; it is certainly more than a snapshot camera. And if you're learning, the Mamiya ZE is an exceptional buy for your first SLR. The Mamiya ZE, without lens, is 5.5 inches wide, 3.5 inches high, and 1.9 inches deep. It weighs one pound. Other "Best Buy" cameras to consider with the ZE include the Olympus OM-10 and the Pentax ME-Super.

Approximate Retail Price　　　　　　　　　　　**Approximate Low Price**
With f/2.0 lens: $285.00 ....$180.00-$205.00

Minolta XD-5 is our most expensive "Best Buy" camera—and it's also the least expensive multi-mode SLR camera available. As a multi-mode camera, it is—at the very least—three cameras in one, which certainly justifies its price tag. Although multi-mode cameras are somewhat complicated to operate, especially for those new to the SLR format—the XD-5 is a good choice if you want full exposure to all the possibilities of modern photography.

The multi-mode XD-5 offers two automatic modes: shutter-preferred and aperture-preferred. The shutter-preferred setting is best for action shots; the photographer sets the shutter speed—the speed with which the picture is taken (up to 1/1000 second)—and the camera automatically sets the aperture—the size of the lens opening. The aperture-preferred setting is best for tricky lighting situations, and for controlling depth of field, the portion of the picture that will be in focus. You choose the aperture, and the camera selects the appropriate shutter speed. Most automatic SLRs offer only one of these two settings, but with the XD-5, you can choose the setting that works best for each situation.

The XD-5 also has a manual mode. In this mode, you can set both aperture and shutter speed yourself. The camera, by means of a sensitive light meter, will suggest appropriate settings. This allows complete creative control.

One fail-safe feature is an automatic override in the shutter-preferred mode. If the camera senses that the photograph will be under- or overexposed, it takes over and sets both the shutter speed and the aperture. This means you can't get a bad picture by setting the speed too slow or too fast.

Besides giving you a wide choice of exposure possibilities, the XD-5 is easy to use, well balanced, and easy to hold. Your fingers fall naturally and comfortably on the controls. The viewfinder provides complete exposure information by means of LEDs—colored lights—so that controls can be easily monitored without moving the camera away from your eye. Focusing is quick and easy.

Minolta has an extensive system of quality lenses, flashes, and special items, such as an attachment for microscopes and aids for nearsighted photographers. Made especially for the XD-5 are an accessory motor drive that can shoot two pictures per second and two electronic flash units. We suggest that you purchase the XD-5 with the f/1.7 Rokkor lens; our experience with the f/2 Rokkor lens was disappointing. There was considerable flare, and color rendition wasn't

Prices are accurate at time of printing; subject to manufacturer's change.

as good as with comparable lenses from other manufacturers.

The Minolta XD-5 may be for you if you take plenty of creative photographs in varying situations. But consider it only if you plan to take full advantage of its versatility—it isn't a good choice if you're just learning photography, or if you're satisfied with a less extensive exposure choice. If you're well versed in the basics, however, and want to make the most of the electronic revolution in photography, the XD-5 ranks as a "Best Buy" for you. The XD-5, without lens, measures 5.3 inches wide, 3.4 inches high, and 2 inches deep. It weighs 18.5 ounces. Other cameras to consider with the Minolta XD-5 include the Canon AE-1 Program and the Konica FS-1.

Approximate Retail Price   **Approximate Low Price**
With f/1.7 lens: $610.00 .... $289.00-$319.00

Minolta XG-M is a good possibility for you if you're serious about your photography. Although it's not a revolutionary camera, it does combine good sense with contemporary electronic know-how. Much care has gone into the camera's manual operations, and while the XG-M has an easy-to-use automatic mode, this camera is designed for those who appreciate the manual mode and use it frequently.

The XG-M's automatic mode is aperture-preferred; the photographer sets the aperture—the size of the lens opening—and the camera selects an appropriate shutter speed—the speed with which the picture is taken (up to 1/1000 second). This is the best automatic mode to use when you want to control depth of field—the area of sharp focus within a picture. At times you'll want everything in focus, at times just one face—or the eyes of that face—in focus. Aperture control allows this creative flexibility.

The camera's manual mode allows complete use of the camera's exposure possibilities. There is also a separate manual metering system—the camera tells you, based on your aperture setting, what shutter speed to use for a normal exposure. You can either take the suggestion, or ignore it. Many automatic SLR cameras, especially within this price range, offer limited manual capabilities. The XG-M not only gives you the capabilities, but helps you out in determining the proper settings. This is the first Minolta XG camera to do so.

The XG-M has several fail-safe features. An under- and overexposure warning and a battery check, standard in most SLRs, are included in the XG-M. One feature not found on many SLRs is a shutter lock, an idiot-proof device that may save a few poorly exposed shots. If the camera chooses a shutter speed faster than 1/1000 second—the fastest possible speed—in the automatic mode, the camera locks, and the picture cannot be taken. You must adjust the aperture or use a flash.

Minolta manufactures one of the largest systems of lenses, flashes, motor drives, filters, and other specialized accessories. Introduced with the XG-M is a new accessory motor drive. This new product gives you a choice of three speeds: two pictures per second, 3.5 pictures per second, or single shot where the film is simply advanced. You decide when to shoot. This is intended for professional situations, where a speed choice is necessary—another indication that this camera is not intended for casual users.

Prices are accurate at time of printing; subject to manufacturer's change.

The Minolta XG-M is a good buy if you're anxious to explore the realms of both automatic and manual photography. We must stress the dual nature of this camera. It would be foolish to buy the XG-M strictly for its automatic capabilities—they're good, but they're only half the package; you're also paying for a detailed manual mode. If you're anxious and willing to face the challenge of manual photography, the XG-M is a good choice. The XG-M, without lens, is 5 inches wide, 2.1 inches high, and 3 inches deep. It weighs 17.8 ounces. Other "Best Buy" cameras to consider with the XG-M include the Konica FS-1, Canon AE-1 Program, and Nikon FM.

Approximate Retail Price	Approximate Low Price
With f/2.0 lens: $483.00	$225.00-$245.00

Nikon FM was Nikon's first small SLR. It is an easy-to-use, strictly manual camera, with no automatic exposure controls. Because it's manual, more work is required to get the picture you want from the FM, but the rewards are twofold: You get complete creative control over every photograph you take, and you learn—if you don't already know—what the art of photography is all about.

Setting the exposure is as simple as any manual method can be. You set both the aperture—the size of the lens opening—and the shutter speed—the speed at which the picture is taken (up to 1/1000 second). You then focus and shoot. But although it's completely manual, the FM is equipped with a built-in light meter—you don't have to simply guess at the settings; the FM will suggest correct apertures and shutter speeds. The camera also warns you when under- or overexposure is a possibility. At times you may want the picture to be slightly under-exposed—if, for example, you prefer a dark mysterious image. Overexposure provides an exceptionally bright image, also preferable at times. Other creative possibilities include double exposure, silhouettes, and intentional blurring. These are only a few examples of what manual photography allows.

The manual operation of the FM gives it one great advantage: It isn't dependent on batteries for proper operation. This may seem a slight advantage at first, but you'll never find yourself in a situation where the camera can't take a picture. When the battery fails, the meter goes dead—the camera will no longer suggest proper exposure. But you'll still be able to take pictures. Not many cameras give you this full mechanical range of shutter speeds.

The FM is more expensive than many manual-exposure cameras. But the FM does offer standard features not found on some less expensive manual cameras: depth-of field preview (to see before-hand the range of focus); a self-timer; a large film speed range (from ASA 12 to ASA 3200); LED—colored light—displays in the viewfinder; a shutter lock to prevent accidental exposures; and a battery check.

Nikon manufactures one of the most prestigious lines of accessories around. They're some of the best, but they're also some of the most expensive. Because we suggest that you buy accessories made for your brand of camera—in order to get full use of the camera's metering capabilities—this is a buying consideration. One accessory made

Prices are accurate at time of printing; subject to manufacturer's change.

especially for the FM is the MD-11 motor drive. If offers single-shot operation or up to 3.5 shots a second. The motor drive is a pleasure to use and helps to steady this small camera; you should leave the motor drive on the camera even when not using it.

If you aren't that interested in automatic exposure, the Nikon FM is an excellent buy. It is a great camera to learn on. It's also a camera that you really can't outgrow. The simplicity of the mechanical—as opposed to electronic—components makes it trouble-free in most situations; there's less chance of breakdown and the camera is easier to fix than most. All in all, the Nikon FM is an exceptional buy if you're sure of your photographic enthusiasm. The FM, without lens, measures 5.6 inches wide, 3.5 inches high, and 2.4 inches deep. It weighs 20 ounces. Other "Best Buy" cameras to consider with the FM include the Pentax K1000 and Yashica FX-3.

Approximate Retail Price **Approximate Low Price**
With f/1.8E lens $415.00 .... $233.50-$263.50

Olympus OM-10 is one of the smallest, most unusual cameras available. It is also the most versatile camera you can get for the money. If you want a small camera, and if you plan to let the camera do the thinking most of the time, then the OM-10 is a good buy, especially if you're a beginning photographer. If you're skilled in the art of SLR photography, be warned: The OM-10 may prove more of a frustration than a boost.

The OM-10 is primarily an aperture-preferred automatic exposure camera. The photographer sets the aperture—the size of the lens opening—and the camera automatically sets the shutter speed—the speed at which the picture is taken (up to 1/1000 second). This is the preferred mode for tricky lighting situations and for control of depth of field—the part of the picture that will be in focus. In this mode, the OM-10 is simple to use. Bright LEDs—colored lights—inside the viewfinder monitor what shutter speed the camera has chosen. They also warn of overexposure.

One unique aspect of this camera concerns its manual exposure alternative. Although the OM-10 does not have a manual mode, Olympus makes a manual adapter that you can purchase—at extra cost—to let you set both shutter speed and aperture. You get—and you pay for—the manual mode only if you want it. We applaud the manual possibilities, but the means of getting manual results can be awkward.

Although the adapter itself snaps right into place, what you see in the viewfinder is the shutter speed the camera *would* select—not the shutter speed you *have* set. There is also no monitor of aperture; you must remember this in both automatic and manual modes.

The OM-10 has two admirable features found on few other cameras. It turns off the viewfinder LEDs after 90 seconds—plenty of time to compose and shoot—reducing battery drain. And the camera gives you audible reminders, too; beeps sound when you use the self-timer and when you check the batteries.

Olympus manufactures an extensive system of lenses, filters, flash units, and other accessories. The OM-10 will accept an auto-winder, but

Prices are accurate at time of printing; subject to manufacturer's change.

not a motor drive. This means you can shoot your pictures as fast as you can press your finger on the shutter release—there's no need to wind the camera. But you can't get the speed of a motor drive, which would press the button for you, and do it faster. If you decide to upgrade your equipment later, all of your OM-10 lenses and accessories will work with other Olympus models.

This camera is obviously designed for the beginning SLR photographer—and for photographers who primarily want automation. If you plan to do a lot of manual photography, you're better off getting a camera with built-in manual capabilities. If manual shots comprise 10 percent or less of your shooting, then the adapter shouldn't pose much problem.

The Olympus OM-10 is a curious camera, yet a good one—especially for its price. If you like gadgets, and if you're looking for your first automatic SLR—it's worth a hard look. Few other cameras in its price range can compete with it. The OM-10, without lens, measures 5.3 inches wide, 3.3. inches high, and 2 inches deep. It weighs 15.9 ounces. Other "Best Buy" cameras to consider with the OM-10 include the Pentax ME Super, Mamiya ZE, and Minolta XG-M.

Approximate Retail Price   **Approximate Low Price**
With f/1.8 lens: $410.00 .... $219.50-$249.50

Pentax K1000 is a standard manual-exposure SLR camera at an exceptionally low price. There are no special gizmos on the camera; nothing is automatic. This is SLR photography in the most basic sense—you have to do more work with this camera than with most modern SLRs, but the results can be as brilliant as with the automatically functioning machines.

Manual exposure means the photographer sets both the aperture— the size of the lens opening—and the shutter speed—the speed at which the picture is taken (up to 1/1000 second). You then focus in on your subject and shoot. Many manual SLRs include a meter that suggests shutter speeds or apertures in the viewfinder. The K1000 does not. Instead, you must work the controls until a needle in the viewfinder becomes centered between two lines. If you've never worked with exposure controls before, this may sound difficult. But with some practice in different lighting situations, you will quickly determine the appropriate combination of shutter speed and aperture for a good picture.

With most cameras we single out various significant features. With the K1000, the omissions are more revealing. There's no self-timer on this camera, no depth-of-field preview (to check the blurring of focus), and no battery tester. These are features incorporated into most SLRs, but not necessarily used a great deal. Even the battery tester, important on many electronic SLRs, isn't essential for the K1000: If the batteries fail, you lose only the needle activity in the viewfinder; everything else will work. Few modern SLRs can make that claim.

One not-so-standard feature—the only frill—on this camera is a shutter-cocked warning flag. If your shutter is cocked, a red flag appears on top of the camera. If it isn't cocked, there's no flag—a feature that doesn't let you waste time focusing and then find out the shutter isn't

Prices are accurate at time of printing; subject to manufacturer's change.

cocked. It is, by the way, easy to make intentional double exposures with this camera.

Pentax manufactures a fine system of lenses and accessories. All of the accessories you buy for the K1000 will work on the more expensive Pentax models. The K1000 camera is one of the most inexpensive ways to enter the Pentax photographic system.

The Pentax K1000 is an excellent choice for people interested in learning the creative possibilities of photography—and are willing to do some work. It is by no means a snapshot camera. The price is one of the most attractive in the SLR market. You don't get any unnecessary gadgets with this camera; you do get a reliable SLR with exceptional photographic potential. The K1000 measures, with an f/2 lens, 5.6 inches wide, 3.6 inches high, and 3.6 inches deep. It weighs 29.5 ounces. Other "Best Buy" cameras to consider with the K1000 include the Yashica FX-3 and Nikon FM.

Approximate Retail Price　　　　　　　　　　　　**Approximate Low Price**
With f/2.0 lens: $224.00 .... $139.50-$169.50

Pentax ME Super proves our contention that while most cameras within a price range are comparable in quality, the operational differences are numerous. Pentax has tried hard to be different with the ME. The result is a camera strange in operation yet competitive in quality. This is an exceptionally workable camera—a good first SLR if you like unusual gadgets.

The ME Super is an automatic camera of the aperture-preferred variety. This means that the photographer sets the aperture—the size of the lens opening—and the camera automatically sets the shutter speed—the speed at which the picture is taken (up to 1/2000 second!). This is the preferred mode for tricky lighting situations, and it gives you more creative control over depth of field (the range of the picture in focus).

The ME Super also has a manual mode, and it's in this mode that the most unusual aspects of this camera come into play. When you set the shutter speed in the manual mode, you don't turn a dial, as on most cameras. Instead, you push one of two buttons. One button sets the shutter speed progressively faster from 4 seconds up to 1/2000 second (the best range offered by any of our "Best Buy" cameras). The second button sets the speed progressively slower, from 1/2000 down to 4 seconds. If you go a little too far on the fast end, you push the button that brings the speed down slower, and vice versa. All this is monitored through three colored LEDs—blinking lights—in the viewfinder: green for OK; yellow for caution (use tripod); and red for under- or overexposure. This camera is a tribute to the video age: a mini electronic game where your mission is to find the proper shutter speed and fire. We feel the shutter selection process is accurate enough, but it proved to be frustrating in fast-action situations—especially if you over- or under-shoot your shutter speed. Our advice: If you want quick shots, go automatic.

The ME Super works exceptionally well in the automatic mode. In our opinion, the film advance lever is just about the easiest single-stroke

Prices are accurate at time of printing; subject to manufacturer's change.

lever to use. That's an important fact, considering how often it's used. All the lights in the viewfinder become somewhat difficult to see in the poor lighting situations—and those are probably the situations where you need the lights most. Make sure to check the viewfinder in low lighting before buying the camera; it may or may not be bright enough for your purposes.

Pentax has a complete line of accessories—not as complete a system as the top four (Nikon, Canon, Minolta, Olympus), but you'd be hard pressed to find a situation where Pentax is insufficient. If you're buying your first SLR, give the Pentax ME Super a close look. Experienced photographers—especially Pentax owners—will no doubt be interested in this camera, too. The ME Super is best for those who rely primarily on the automatic mode, although the manual mode can produce good shots—if you're willing to take the time. Before you buy the ME, make sure you get the feel of the special shutter speed buttons, and compare the buttons to the conventional dials of others. The ME Super, without lens, measures 5.1 inches wide, 3.2 inches high, and 1.9 inches deep. Other "Best Buy" cameras to consider with the ME Super include the Olympus OM-10, Minolta XG-M, and Canon AE-1 Program.

Approximate Retail Price   **Approximate Low Price**
With f/1.7 lens: $437.00 .... $250.00-$276.00

Yashica FX-3 is one of the least expensive 35mm SLRs available today. It is a strictly manual-exposure camera, with few frills. There are no automatic functions; you're responsible for getting the proper exposure. As such, it's a camera to learn the basics of photography on—at an exceptionally low price.

Manual exposure means that the photographer must set both the aperture—the size of the lens opening—and the shutter speed—the speed with which the picture is taken (up to 1/1000 second) before you can focus in on your subject and shoot. This mode allows total creative control over your results. The principles are not as difficult to master as they may seem. With a little practice, the setting of the exposure becomes second nature.

The camera helps you determine proper exposure with three LEDs—colored lights—in the viewfinder. One of the LEDs is green, and when it appears, you're sure of a properly exposed shot. The other two are red; one is a plus (+) sign and the other a minus (-) sign for over- and underexposure warnings. You can ignore these signs if you want a special lighting effect.

The shutter is mechanical—as opposed to electronic—which means that the FX-3 will operate regardless of whether there are batteries. The only thing the batteries do is operate the LEDs. Although this is certainly important in many situations, many modern SLRs—even very expensive ones—won't operate at all without batteries—or at limited function. The FX-3 also has a few features commendable on such a low-priced camera. There's a shutter release lock, for example, that prevents you from accidentally taking a picture. There's also a self-timer.

Yashica is the parent group of three different photographic lines: Yashica cameras and accessories, Zeiss lenses, and Contax cameras.

Prices are accurate at time of printing; subject to manufacturer's change.

The company manufactures a good range of accessories—Zeiss lenses have been proved in bench tests to be among the best lenses made. There are not as many Yashica-brand models being manufactured today, but the Contax models—Yashica's top line of cameras—will be in production for a long time. If you ever upgrade to a Contax (most of which are too expensive to be considered "Best Buys"), you can still use your Yashica accessories with it.

The Yashica FX-3 is definitely for those who want to discover and control the subtleties of the photographic art. It is an excellent camera to learn on. It will not give you the easy automatic results of many other SLRs, but what it does produce should satisfy your demands. The best advantage, of course, is its remarkably low price. The FX-3, without lens, measures 5.3 inches wide, 3.3 inches high, and 2 inches deep. It weighs 15.9 ounces. Other "Best Buy" cameras to consider with the FX-3 include the Pentax K1000 and Nikon FM.

Approximate Retail Price   **Approximate Low Price**
With f/2.0 lens: $290.00 .... $150.00-$172.00

 ## 35mm Autofocus Cameras

AUTOFOCUS CAMERAS have attracted a great deal of interest because they combine ease of operation with near-professional results. All you have to do is choose your subject, aim, and shoot. There's no need to fret over apertures, shutter speeds, or even focusing.

Your choice of an autofocus camera rests primarily with the type of autofocusing system you desire. The original system, Visitronic (developed by Honeywell), is based on visual detectors that "see" the subject you want to shoot. The camera then translates this visual information into the setting for proper focusing. Most autofocus cameras use this system, but it has two problems. First, because the subject must completely fill the viewfinder in order for the camera to focus accurately, focusing on a distant object is difficult. Second, and worse, the Visitronic system won't work without adequate light.

Canon and Minolta each offer a system that uses infrared light to help determine focus. This invisible-to-the-eye light is projected from one window of the camera. A second window senses the reflected infrared light as it returns from the subject, and measures the light's intensity. The camera then translates this measurement into distance, and sets the lens focus. This system overcomes the Visitronic's problem with inadequate light; because it creates its own light instead of relying on available light, the system doesn't fail in dusk and dark situations. But it still has trouble determining the subject at far distances.

Probably the best system is Polaroid's sonar autofocus system, which uses sound instead of light as its measurement medium. Sonar has proved to be the most reliable means of autofocus for shooting distant subjects and working in the dark. There are some situations, however, in which it fails—like shooting through a window. The sonar waves simply reflect off the window glass, and the subject beyond remains out of focus. For just such occasions, Polaroid has equipped its autofocus cameras with an "autofocus-off" switch so that the camera can be focused manually. Polaroid cameras are the only ones offering the sonar system. They are reviewed in the instant-print section.

Besides the focusing system itself, autofocus cameras differ in focusing range (how close up will it focus?), ASA film speed range, shutter speed range, and convenience features (focus lock, auto rewind, self-timer, and shutter lock). They all employ roughly equivalent lenses.

The autofocus is generally a snapshot camera. It's a good choice for those who demand good photographic results yet want the simplest camera available. The autofocus camera is, in our opinion, the best snapshot camera made. It is also the most expensive.

Canon Sure Shot AF35M is the most automatic 35mm autofocus camera available. Not only does it set the proper exposure and focus the camera for you—all autofocus cameras do that—but it also advances the film automatically and rewinds the entire roll of film with one push of a button when you're through shooting. If you want this kind of automation—and you want some of the best photographs automatically possible—then the AF35M should be among the first cameras you consider.

Canon does not use the most common autofocusing method, the Visitronic system developed by Honeywell, but has its own system. The Sure Shot AF35M emits infrared light to measure the distance between the camera and what's being photographed; it then focuses in accordance with this information. Because it produces its own light, this system is seldom fooled in low-light situations—as is the Honeywell system. If low-light situations play an important role in your photography, then the Canon should be among your first autofocus choices.

Some fine additional features are a built-in pop-up electronic flash, a camera-shake warning that appears when the automatic shutter speed is too slow for a hand-held shot, a battery check, and a self-timer. The Sure Shot also includes what Canon calls a prefocus. This is what's usually called a memory lock, and it's essential to autofocus photography. If, for example, you take a picture of two people, you'll naturally center your focus between them. The autofocus will pick up what's in between the people—usually a background—and leave your subjects out of focus. With the prefocus, you point at one of the people, set the prefocus, and then return to shoot your original composition.

The Canon Sure Shot AF35M is an exceptional autofocus camera. Our only hesitation in recommending it is that Canon has introduced a new auto-focus model—the AF35ML—that will boast the best autofocusing lens so far. That too will be worth examination, when it's available. But regardless of the AF35ML, don't worry about the AF35M being outdated. It is still years ahead of its time. The Sure Shot measures 5.2 inches wide, 3 inches high, and 2.1 inches deep. It weighs 14.3 ounces.

Approximate Retail Price Approximate Low Price
$240.00 .... $148.00-$162.00

Konica C35AF II is an updated version of the first 35mm autofocus camera ever—the C35AF. This model differs from its pioneering predecessor in minor—though thoughtful—ways. The result is a fine autofocus camera, one that can remain an authoritative symbol of what autofocus photography is all about.

The essence of autofocus photography is simple operation and excellent results. Konica succeeds in both. The C35AF II uses Honeywell's Visitronic method of autofocusing. The system works well in all but one situation: dim or dark light. Using the built-in pop-up electronic flash, of course, will solve this problem.

Two advances over the original autofocus include a self-timer—for when you want to get in on your own shots—and a failsafe feature that will prevent you from taking pictures when the batteries are low. The camera doesn't have a memory lock, which can be useful in situations where the autofocus may fail.

For example, when photographing two people, you will center the focus between them. The autofocus mechanism will focus on whatever is in between the two people—perhaps a hill in the background. A memory lock allows you to focus in on one of the two people, set the lock, and then recompose as you originally planned. But while proper focusing can be a problem in theory, Konica believes that it isn't a significant problem in practice, and that the additional controls needed for a memory lock can be confusing. We generally feel that more control over the situation is desirable, but if you're relying on your camera for basic snapshots—and you aren't attempting many closeups—then the lack of a memory lock on the Konica shouldn't hamper your picture-taking.

The Konica C35AF II is a conservative update of a proven, reliable camera. For the snapshot enthusiast who doesn't want to mess with any controls whatsoever—and who still expects consistently good 35mm results—this camera is a good buy. The AF II measures 5.0 inches wide, 2.9 inches high, and 2.1 inches deep. It weighs 13.2 ounces.

Approximate Retail Price Approximate Low Price
$242.00 .... $133.00-$146.00

Minolta Hi-Matic AF2 does everything an autofocus camera is intended to do, and one thing more: It speaks to you. The AF2 has some audible fail-safe warning signals that can prevent a poor shot. It appears to have taken one step more toward making sure you get the shot you want every time.

Minolta has taken the cue from Canon and come up with its own infrared-beam autofocus system. The original Minolta AF incorporated Honeywell's Visitronic system, which has trouble focusing in dim light. The AF2 works better in such lighting situations, because the camera emits the necessary light for focusing. And if it gets too dark for the

Prices are accurate at time of printing; subject to manufacturer's change.

autofocus to perform properly, a light will start flashing and a beep will start sounding to warn you to use the built-in pop-up electronic flash.

The beeps serve three very useful functions. They warn, as above, when light is too low and flash must be used. They also warn when your subject is too close—an unusual and very useful warning. The third warning sounds when your subject is too far away for your flash to be effective. This, too, is a surprisingly thoughtful warning, and one that will no doubt save many shots.

Other good features include a self-timer, a shutter lock that prevents poorly exposed pictures when the battery is weak or the flash isn't ready, and a safe-load signal that ensures you that the film is properly loaded. One especially good feature is a memory lock, termed a "focus lock" by Minolta. This enables you to take control in situations where the camera may be fooled. If you want an object 10 feet away to be in focus—and you want it off center—you can first focus directly on that subject, lock in the focus, and then compose with the subject off center. If you tried to do this without a memory lock, the camera would focus on whatever was in the center, perhaps a hill 30 feet away, and your subject would be out of focus.

The Hi-Matic is a good choice if you're inexperienced in photography—we're especially impressed with Minolta's warning system; it will save both frustration and lost photographs. This is as easy-to-use a camera as any in existence; it deserves a hard look from demanding snapshot enthusiasts. The Hi-Matic measures 5.1 inches wide, 3 inches high, and 2.1 inches deep. It weighs 11.8 ounces.

Approximate Retail Price	Approximate Low Price
$248.00	$130.00-$155.00

 35mm Compact Cameras

THE 35MM COMPACT was the professional camera before the advent of the SLR. These cameras make good sense if you've been using a simple 110 snapshot or Instamatic camera and want to advance your techniques and equipment. The main advantage is the 35mm format itself, which offers a wide choice of film, as well as professional processing and enlarging possibilities.

The essential difference between compacts and SLRs lies in what you see before shooting the picture. In an SLR, you look through the picture-taking lens; in a compact, you look through a window that's positioned above the picture-taking lens. What appears in the compact's viewfinder isn't exactly what will appear on the film.

Some compacts are equipped with a rangefinder (they're called rangefinder cameras), which is a focusing aid attached to the focusing lens. The rangefinder lets you look through the viewfinder while you adjust the lens for proper focus. Zone-focus cameras are compacts that have no such aid. You must estimate the distance between camera and subject and then set the lens accordingly. Zone-focus cameras are usually more compact and less expensive than rangefinders.

You can find compacts with manual-exposure systems in which you set both aperture and shutter speed, with semi-automatic exposure systems of either the aperture-priority or the shutter-priority type, or with fully automatic exposure systems in which you merely focus the camera and shoot. The more automated the exposure system, in most cases, the more costly the camera.

The latest trend in these small cameras has been toward increased automation and miniaturization. More and more compact 35s include built-in electronic flash, automatic exposure settings, and even automatic film threading and advance. LEDs—colored lights—are replacing needle indicators on many compact metering systems, and most compacts now have a hot shoe (direct contact) for use with cordless flash units.

Nearly every camera in the compact 35mm group has a fixed picture-taking lens. That means there's no way to switch from, say, a wide-angle lens to a telephoto. The lens that comes with the camera is the only one you'll ever be able to use with it.

The 35mm compact is a fine camera if you want to learn about the art of photography. It's an inexpensive means toward high-quality, creative results.

Canonet GIII QL 17 is our most expensive "Best Buy" 35mm compact—and for good reason. The camera enables you to explore many unusual photographic situations. If you don't feel quite ready for an SLR—and if you want to get the most the photographic industry has to offer at a fair price—then the GIII 17 deserves your close attention.

This is a rangefinder compact. The rangefinder is a focusing device that breaks what you see through the viewfinder into two. By turning the lens, you try to get the two images to become one. Once you succeed, your picture is in focus and can be properly taken.

One remarkable aspect of this compact camera is its offering of two exposure modes: totally automatic or totally manual. In the automatic mode, you simply have to focus and shoot; the camera sets the appropriate aperture—the size of the lens opening—and the shutter speed—the speed at which the picture is taken (up to 1/500 second). In the manual mode, you are responsible for setting both shutter speed and aperture. The camera suggests, however, appropriate shutter speed/aperture combinations. This choice is an exceptional bonus in a compact camera; most offer only automatic exposure. The manual exposure gives you the chance to learn what photography is all about.

The viewfinder in the GIII 17 offers more information than most compacts. An aperture scale tells you what aperture was set in the automatic mode, or suggests an aperture in the manual mode. There are also warnings of over- and underexposure, and a frameline—a line in the viewfinder that frames the best picture-taking area—that moves to correct for parallax—the difference between what you see through the viewfinder and what the camera sees through the lens. The frameline helps avoid common problems, such as the cutting off of heads. Most compacts have some form of parallax correction lines—but few have these accurate moving lines.

Other commendable aspects of this camera include a battery check, a self-timer, a shutter lock to avoid accidentally taking a picture, a special film-loading feature (the QL is for Quick Loading), a special accessory electronic flash, and an exceptionally wide lens for low-light situations. In fact, this f/1.7 lens (the 17 in the camera name) gives you a better chance at nighttime photography than many standard SLR lenses.

The Canonet GIII QL 17 is a great first camera if you're interested in exploring the richness of photography. You would have to pay at least $100 more to find an SLR with the same capabilities. If you want to test your photographic enthusiasm, you can't beat this camera for its offerings. And, if you then want to step up to the SLR world, this camera will make a fine hand-me-down gift—one that will be appreciated by the second generation as much as the first. The GIII 17 measures 4.7 inches wide, 3 inches high, and 2.4 inches deep. It weighs 24.4 ounces.

Approximate Retail Price   **Approximate Low Price**
$204.00 .... $98.50-$112.00

Konica EFP isn't a revolutionary camera. In both styling and internal design, the camera could have been introduced years ago. What the Konica EFP does offer is an inexpensive means toward 35mm photography. It's a simple-to-use camera that should serve you well if your primary photographic aim is snapshots of people.

The camera doesn't have to be focused; images should be sharp from 5 to about 20 feet—the distance of most snapshots. Every shot is taken at 1/125 second; there is no range of shutter speeds as in more expensive compacts. The only variable you have is the choice of film.

One appealing aspect of the EFP is its pop-up built-in electronic flash unit. You press a button, and the flash pops up on top of the camera. It works well at distances of 5 to 16.4 feet. There is also a close-up button for flash at five to seven feet. A red light in the viewfinder goes on when the flash is popped up, and a ready light on top of the camera tells you when the flash is ready to be fired.

There are two commendable accessories available for this camera. One is a special close-up attachment for shooting super-close subjects; for example, documents. The camera will also accept different filters, which help in creating different color and mood effects.

The Konica EFP doesn't do anything fancy; its prime charm is 35mm photography at a low price. The camera does produce good snapshots, and you'll be able to enlarge snapshots up to display size of 8x10, if you wish. That's a definite benefit of 35mm photography, and a good reason to consider the inexpensive EFP as your snapshot machine. The EFP measures 5 inches wide, 2.9 inches high, and 2.1 inches deep. It weighs 11 ounces.

Approximate Retail Price   **Approximate Low Price**
$98.00 .... $70.00-$80.00

Prices are accurate at time of printing; subject to manufacturer's change.

Olympus XA2 is a prime example of modern 35mm compact photography. This is a strictly automatic camera—the only work the photographer does is focusing, and even in focusing there are only three options. The XA2 is also one of the most unusual-looking cameras, in a space-age way. It's a streamlined tiny black package that even hides its lens when not in use.

The most remarkable aspect of this camera is its ease of use. You set one of three focusing settings—close-up, average, or distant—and then shoot the picture. Results are better than the average for 35mm compacts because of the wide range of possible shutter speeds—the speed at which the picture is taken. The camera automatically chooses a shutter speed between 2 seconds and 1/750 second. If it's dark, a slow shutter speed will expose the film to more light. Two seconds is an incredibly slow speed—better than many SLRs offer. Bright surroundings photograph best with a fast shutter speed, and the fast 1/750-second shutter speed the XA2 offers is one of the best among compact 35mm cameras.

If your camera chooses an exceptionally slow shutter speed, a signal will go off in the viewfinder, warning of a situation where it's difficult to hold the camera steady—many photos come back from the processor blurred because of slow shutter speeds. When the warning goes off, you have the choice of placing the camera on a tripod or using the special Olympus All Electronic flash. This accessory flash is one of the smallest in existence. It attaches to the side—instead of the top—of the camera, further reinforcing the streamlined, space-age look.

The Olympus XA2 is an excellent snapshot camera for those who want superior results with a minimum of fuss. It includes many features found on few compacts, such as a self-timer. The design will lead to as much good conversation as it will to quality photographs. And you can be assured of owning one of the finest developments in 35mm photography. The XA2 measures 4 inches wide, 2.5 inches high, and 1.6 inches deep. It weighs just 7.9 ounces.

Approximate Retail Price	Approximate Low Price
$160.00	$89.00-$98.00

 # 110 Cartridge Cameras

YOUR CHOICE AMONG 110 cartridge cameras is greater than ever. Some of the cameras offer simplified operation; some come equipped with improved lenses for sharper photographs; still others are taking on the features—if not the look—of the more professional cameras. There are now, in fact, several SLR 110 cameras complete with interchangeable lenses.

Manufacturers are moving in two directions at once—producing one

Prices are accurate at time of printing; subject to manufacturer's change.

line of cartridge cameras for the amateur, another for the more advanced photographer. If you want the most basic camera, you'll have no trouble finding it. But because many of the cartridge cameras are now quite sophisticated machines, make sure the camera you buy is appropriate for the kind of picture-taking you intend to do.

Few of these cameras' lenses can be focused as accurately as 35mm cameras. Most have some form of distance scale (zone-focus) to set, although a few expensive 110s have rangefinders—a sophisticated focusing device found in most 35mm cameras. Some 110s have a fixed-focus lens; you cannot focus such lenses. If you want some control over the focus, look for a 110 camera with a zone-focus or rangefinder system. If you simply want to point and shoot, get a 110 with fixed focus. The more control you get over the focusing system, the more you'll pay for the camera.

You can get acceptably sharp prints with a 110 cartridge camera, but enlargements greater than 5 × 7 often come out fuzzy. If you want enlargements of 8 × 10 inches or larger, you should consider a 35mm camera. And, of course, you cannot use a 110 for taking slides.

Canon 110 ED 20 is one of the best 110 cameras in production today. It is also one of the most expensive, but its price is justified considering its quality results. If you enjoy the simple 110 format—and if you're willing to spend the extra money for exceptional results—then this Canon may be your "Best Buy."

The camera's best feature is its quality f/2.0 lens (the 20 in the name). Few 110s can match this lens for performance. The major advantage to such a lens is its ability to render sharp photographs in a variety of lighting situations—a great edge if you plan to enlarge your prints for display. No 110 photograph can be enlarged with the quality of 35mm or larger film, but the Canon 110 will give you more of a fighting chance.

Another advantage concerns exposure. The camera offers four different lens apertures—the sizes of the lens opening. It also offers a range of shutter speeds—the speed at which the picture is taken—from 2 seconds to 1/1000 second. You set the camera at one of the four aperture symbols (sunny, cloudy, etc.) according to light conditions and the camera automatically sets a shutter speed. This means the camera can expose the film in a variety of ways, depending on the situation. Many 110s offer only one or two apertures and one shutter speed.

The most unusual aspect of this camera is its date-imprinting function. The camera will automatically print the date on each of your photos if you wish. You must, of course, set the proper date before shooting. The mechanism can be turned off if you desire. If on, the date will appear in the viewfinder before you take the picture.

Canon offers an accessory electronic flash—the Canolite ED—made especially for the camera. Although not built-in, it slides easily in place on top of the camera.

The Canon 110 ED 20 is an exceptional 110 camera, and produces consistently good results. It works where a lot of other cameras may fail. If you're willing to spend the extra money for this quality in a 110 snapshot camera, you'll be rewarded with quality photos. The ED 20 measures 5.5 inches wide, 2.2 inches high, and 1.1 inches deep. It weighs 12 ounces.

Approximate Retail Price
$205.00 ....

Approximate Low Price
$128.00-$141.00

Kodak Ektralite 500 builds on Kodak's tradition of simple, dependable snapshot cameras. It's different in two important ways: You no longer have to think about when to use flash, and you have an easier time holding this tiny camera steady. Both improvements are in response to common 110 camera complaints. The result is an easy-to-use camera that helps lessen the possibility of fuzzy or poorly lighted shots.

The most notable aspect of the 500 is its Sensalite flash control. This feature turns the flash on or off automatically according to light conditions—you never have to think about it. A red or green light will appear in the viewfinder, confirming the readiness of the flash. If a red light appears, don't take the picture. If the light is green, go ahead and shoot—the flash will work automatically, if necessary. Blinking green means the flash will operate; solid green means there's no need for flash.

Another feature of this camera is its built-in hinged cover, which doubles as a handgrip. When open, the cover drops to a right angle from the camera body, in a kind of sideways L shape. You can firmly grasp the cover to help steady the camera while shooting—this helps eliminate fuzzy photos. It's a sensible idea that helps solve a big problem with these small cameras.

Most of the camera's functions are totally automatic. The focus on the lens is fixed—you never have to fuss with it. There are two shutter speeds (the speed at which the picture is taken), but these just have to be set when you load the film—ASA 400 cartridge film takes a shutter speed of 1/250 second; general-purpose 110 cartridge films (ASA 100, for example) are best used with the 1/125 second shutter speed.

The Kodak Ektralite 500 is a good buy if you want a dependable, inexpensive 110 cartridge camera; it has few frills, but it does offer intelligent responses to common 110 problems. Kodak offers a three-year warranty with the camera. The 500 measures 8.5 inches wide, 3.8 inches high, and 2.4 inches deep, and weighs 11 ounces.

Approximate Retail Price
$62.00..

Approximate Low Price
$45.00-$48.00

Minolta 110 Zoom SLR Mark II has enough features to justify the length of its name. If you're looking for a snapshot camera, stop reading. The Mark II is designed to impress the most learned camera connoisseur.

The camera is an honest-to-goodness SLR camera—you look through the same lens through which the picture is taken. This eliminates the problem of parallax, the difference between what you see through the viewfinder and what the lens sees. SLR capability is especially useful when operating a zoom lens. In fact, without SLR capabilities you'd have no idea what the zoom was doing unless you had a zoom viewfinder.

The most attractive feature of this camera is no doubt the zoom lens. It

Prices are accurate at time of printing; subject to manufacturer's change.

can make subjects 30 feet away look like closeups. It can also make them look 30 feet away—or 40 feet away. It's like having three or four lenses in one—a most unusual feature in a 110 camera.

The camera uses an aperture-preferred automatic exposure system; you have to set the aperture—the size of the lens opening—and the camera automatically selects a shutter speed—the speed at which the picture is taken (up to 1/1000 second). There are only a few other 110 format cameras that allow this type of control over your exposure. You must obviously be interested creatively in your photography to be interested in such an exposure system; if you don't want to be bothered with any controls at all, this camera isn't for you. Other 110 cameras in this section would better fit your needs.

The camera is packed with features found on very few 110 cameras. It has a rangefinder to help you focus—a device that splits part of your image in two. Once you bring both parts of the image into one, you can be assured of good focus. Very few 110s have such a sophisticated focusing system. Other features include a self-timer, the ability to accept filters, warnings in the viewfinder of over- and underexposure, and controls to deliberately over- or underexpose your film.

The primary charm of this camera is its size; no 35mm SLR is so compact. The Zoom SLR Mark II is ideally a traveling camera for those with more sophisticated 35mm equipment back home. It is an expensive camera—more expensive than some automatic 35mm SLRs. Don't buy it if you've never worked with exposure controls or zoom lenses; it is a "Best Buy" only if you're familiar with SLR photography and looking for a compact, easy-to-use backup. The Mark II measures 4.1 inches wide, 4 inches high, and 2.0 inches deep. It weighs 16.4 ounces.

Approximate Retail Price	Approximate Low Price
$342.00	$209.00-$238.00

Minolta Weathermatic A is the perfect photographic companion for the beach, the mountains—wherever the weather or environment plays an important role. It's an underwater camera, but more than that, it's a camera that can stand up to water, snow, wind, and sand. It is definitely a snapshot camera, producing predictable 110 snapshots. It costs more than the average 110 because of the weather-protective devices within its design, but if a lot of your snapshots are taken in varying weather conditions, it's a good buy.

The Weathermatic A isn't completely automatic, but it's easy to use. Two controls must be set before your picture is snapped. The first is an exposure control for one of three conditions: bright, cloudy, or dark (also used underwater). The second control is for focusing; you set this to the distance symbol you believe the subject is at. There are five different symbols—a mountain means distance, for example, and a head and shoulders means close-up. Both controls are oversized and easy to turn—a thoughtful design for people wearing gloves or operating underwater.

The Weathermatic A has a built-in electronic flash, which is recommended for all underwater shooting. This camera will operate up to 15 feet underwater. If it slips out of your hands, it will float to the surface.

Prices are accurate at time of printing; subject to manufacturer's change.

The Minolta Weathermatic A is a worry-free, weathertight camera that can perform well within the 110 cartridge format. It is the least expensive weatherproof camera available. If you'll be taking many pictures in or near the water, it's an excellent buy. The Weathermatic measures 7.5 inches wide, 2.8 inches high, and 2 inches deep. It weighs 12.2 ounces.

Approximate Retail Price   **Approximate Low Price**
$165.00 .... $90.00-$105.00

Vivitar 845 is for those who appreciate the simplicity of 110 operation, but also want a few frills found primarily on more expensive cameras. The two special features of this Vivitar are its automatic film advance— allowing you to take pictures up to one per second—and a special telephoto lens that, when slipped into position, renders your subject twice as large. Other aspects of this camera exhibit the good snapshot design expected from a Vivitar 110.

Most everything on this camera—except for the telephoto lens—is fixed: You simply point the camera and shoot. There's a built-in electronic flash that will work for up to 150 shots on one alkaline battery. A green light shows in the viewfinder when the flash is ready to use, and the camera automatically turns the flash off after 90 seconds if it hasn't been used; this helps prevent unintentional battery drain.

This is a good, inexpensive 110 camera for those who want simple operation and the chance to experiment with a few unusual features. Compact and reliable, the Vivitar 845 should serve as a good tool to record family occasions and vacations. The camera measures 6.3 inches wide, 2.4 inches high, and 1.2 inches deep. It weighs 6.2 ounces.

Approximate Retail Price   **Approximate Low Price**
$76.00 .... $46.00-$52.00

 Instant-Print Cameras

THE ONLY "BEST BUY" instant-print cameras carry the name Polaroid. Kodak, while producing an acceptable instant-print product, has not yet been able to compete with Polaroid technology. The magic of instant-print cameras is, of course, their instant results. It is amazing how well these cameras perform considering their in-the-camera photo development.

Polaroid offers an autofocus system in a few of its cameras. This means that you simply point the camera and shoot—the lens focuses itself. The results are exceptionally sharp photos with minimal effort. You pay more for the autofocus function, but we feel the results are worth the cost.

While selection of the focusing system is important, you should also consider the type of film the Polaroid camera accepts: pack or SX-70.

Prices are accurate at time of printing; subject to manufacturer's change.

Choosing between the pack film and the SX-70 film is largely a matter of personal photographic preference. The most notable difference between the film types concerns the ejection of the photo. An SX-70 print comes out instantly, as soon as you press the button; it then develops in front of your eyes. Pack film is pulled manually out of the camera; you then wait 60 seconds or longer and peel the covering off the developed photo. Polaroid pack films provide a wider selection of formats, a choice of color or black-and-white, and an opportunity to experiment and satisfy creative urges by varying exposure setting and/or development time. On the other hand, SX-70 film is both convenient and clean, and if you're considering one of the sonar autofocus cameras, SX-70 is your only choice. All of our instant-print "Best Buy" selections use the SX-70 film format. That's because it performs best under a cost/capability comparison. Less and less pack film cameras are being manufactured for the consumer. If you want the versatility of pack film, you'll have to pay more for it.

Polaroid's new Time-Zero film is the fastest-developing, best color instant-print film on the market. If you want to take advantage of it, you'll want an SX-70 (sonar or nonsonar) camera.

Polaroid The Button is the least expensive "Best Buy" selection. It's a magical camera at a magically low price. It's best for simple snapshots of your favorite people. Whether you own the most sophisticated camera made or simply want a simple camera to record your memories, The Button will serve your instant-print desires perfectly.

It's hard to imagine a camera easier to use; you just point The Button at your subject and push a button. The print pops automatically out of the front of your camera, and develops within a minute in front of your eyes.

The only control possible over your prints is a light/dark control. If it's extremely bright outside, you may want to darken the print slightly. You may also want to brighten it in dark situations. If it gets too dark, you can attach either a flashbar or Polaroid's Q-Light to the camera. Each flash will present you with well-lighted snapshots from four to eight feet; the Q-light has an extended range of nine feet.

Everything on this camera is fixed—from the focus to the developing. If that's exactly what you want and if you also want a magic machine at a low price, Polaroid's The Button should serve you well. The Button measures 5.5 inches wide, 4 inches high, and 3.5 inches deep. It weighs 14.5 ounces.

Approximate Retail Price	Approximate Low Price
$30.00	$23.00-$26.00

Polaroid Time-Zero OneStep Plus is an extremely popular camera—and for good reason. Part of the reason is simplicity—you *do* simply push one button to get the picture you want. Part of the reason is the Time-Zero film capability—the best instant-print color film is ejected automatically from the camera after the picture is taken. The best part of the reason, of course, is the low price.

When the OneStep was introduced, there was no question that it produced the best instant prints for the price. That's changed. Polaroid's

Prices are accurate at time of printing; subject to manufacturer's change.

The Button, also a "Best Buy," is virtually the same camera at $20 less. The OneStep alone can no longer be considered a best buy. What *is* a "Best Buy" is the OneStep Plus—and the plus is an electronic flash unit.

The electronic flash—the Q-Light B—now packaged in the OneStep Plus gives off up to 60 flashes with a set of four AA Alkaline batteries (included when you buy the camera). The flash attaches quickly to the top of the One-Step. When used, it automatically sets the proper amount of light for exposures at four to nine feet.

Everything about the camera is automatic—from the focusing to the developing. The only control is a light/dark control for, naturally, lighter or darker exposures.

The Polaroid OneStep Plus is a good buy if you plan on taking a lot of photographs with flash. Do not simply buy the OneStep with the intent to add the flash later. The Button is a less expensive camera with virtually the same capability. It will also accept a flash. If you bought an electronic flash for The Button, however, the combined price would most likely be more than the Time-Zero OneStep Plus. The camera measures 5.5 inches wide, 4 inches high, and 3.5 inches deep. It weighs 14.5 ounces.

Approximate Retail Price	Approximate Low Price
$68.00	$46.00-$49.00

Polaroid Time-Zero Pronto Autofocus Land Camera may be the best "Best Buy" of any photographic category. For under $100 you get what is possibly the best autofocus system made. You get a camera that automatically sets a wide range of exposure controls. And you get the best of Polaroid's instant print technology: Time-Zero color film ejected automatically from the front of the camera. What the Pronto offers that less expensive Polaroid's don't is better exposure in a variety of picture-taking situations.

The most notable feature is the remarkable sonar autofocus capability. The camera uses sound waves to measure the distance between you and the picture you want to take. It then focuses the lens automatically to that distance. Sound waves work in both light and dark—and can better handle distant subjects than many 35mm autofocus systems. The one situation in which the sonar system fails is when you photograph through something, like a window. The sound waves simply bounce off the window. For such situations, Polaroid has a manual focus provision; you then turn off the autofocus and focus the camera yourself.

A built-in light meter sizes up the available light and sets both the aperture, the size of the lens opening, and the shutter speed—the speed at which the picture is taken (up to 1/180 second). This means that, unlike the less expensive Polaroids, you will get sharper, better-exposed pictures in varying light conditions.

The Pronto accepts an electronic flash unit—the Polatronic 2—that snaps easily onto the top of the camera. The electronic flash is good for up to 75 flashes on a set of four AA alkaline batteries.

The Polaroid Pronto Autofocus is the least expensive autofocus camera made. It guarantees properly exposed, properly focused pictures in a variety of lighting situations. If you want a good instant-print

Prices are accurate at time of printing; subject to manufacturer's change.

CONSUMER GUIDE®

camera, you can't go wrong with the Pronto Autofocus. The Pronto measures 5.5 inches long, 4.5 inches high, and 3.5 inches deep. It weighs 19.3 ounces.

Approximate Retail Price
Approximate Low Price
$110.00..$79.00-$84.00

Polaroid Time-Zero SX-70 Autofocus is an expensive camera. It is a "Best Buy" only if you require the advanced capabilities this camera allows. It is as easy to use as any Polaroid. The differences are in the results. If you want just about the best that instant-print has to offer—and you want an easy-to-use, portable camera—the SX-70 Autofocus may be your best choice.

The camera uses the sonar method of autofocusing—as does the Pronto autofocus. This is probably the best autofocus system known to photography, using sound waves to measure the distance between you and your subject. These measurements are then used to focus the lens and the picture. All of this happens much faster than you read about it.

One of the surprising aspects of the SX-70 is its SLR—single lens reflex—design. This is the same viewing system used in the most sophisticated 35mm cameras. It means that you look through the same lens through which the picture is taken. This eliminates problems of parallax—the difference between what you see through the viewfinder and what the lens sees. Many heads have been cut off because of parallax errors. Because of these SLR capabilities, the SX-70 can accept an accessory telephoto lens that is attached directly to the built-in lens. It's an unusual way to get telephoto capabilities, but it's better than nothing.

The SX-70 also justifies its price tag with a variety of exposure controls. The shutter speeds—the speeds at which the picture is taken—range from 1/180 second to 14 seconds! Fourteen seconds is a longer shutter speed than found in most SLRs. It allows you to take more pictures in dark—although you'll have to put the camera on a tripod. Aperture ranges from f/8 to f/96. The aperture is the size of the lens opening. This range is the largest of the "Best Buy" Polaroid cameras. Both shutter speed and aperture are set automatically by the camera.

One more SX-70 bonus is its folding abilities. A big complaint about instant-print cameras is their size. They are big, bulky cameras. The SX-70, when not in use, can be folded to purse size.

The SX-70 is a lot of camera with a large price tag. It is no doubt one of the best instant-print cameras ever designed. If the above features are important to you—and if you feel the price is justified (we do)—then the SX-70 is a good buy. It measures, folded, 8¾ inches wide, 4 inches high, and 1 inch deep. It weighs 27 ounces.

Approximate Retail Price -
Approximate Low Price
$280.00 ....$195.00-$210.00

Prices are accurate at time of printing; subject to manufacturer's change.

Energy-Saving Products

MANY ENERGY-SAVING products are disappearing from retailers' showrooms, but it isn't because the American consumer is becoming apathetic about conserving energy. Instead, consumers are becoming smarter shoppers for energy-saving products that really work; the gimmicks are fading away or being reengineered to do a better job.

Some gimmicks, of course, are still around and competing for your energy dollar, but for the most part energy-savers are money-savers, and it's worth your consideration and time to shop for them.

Products designed to save energy in the home have been around for years. But it took a declared war on energy waste before these products were marketed as energy-savers. For example, caulking compound has been available for a long, long time to prevent air infiltration. Insulation is another example. But to read many manufacturers' literature, one might think that these products are something new. What *is* new is the sales emphasis on "new" and "energy-saving."

Benefit for Consumers

THERE IS, however, some benefit to this emphasis on energy-saving for consumers. For example, wood- and coal-burning stoves are now rated as to their Btu output and the square footage they're designed to heat. Never buy a stove unless this information is provided. And make sure that the appliance is certified by a recognized testing organization, like Underwriters' Laboratories.

Problems with many types of heating appliances are being overcome. For instance, old masonry chimneys cannot withstand the creosote buildup and heating and cooling effects created by such appliances as wood-burning stoves and free-standing fireplaces. This problem is being solved with metal flue liners. Smart shoppers are also discovering the efficiency of kerosene heaters; new designs and new laws are making and keeping these heaters safer. Thermostats are being redesigned, too, to show better burning settings for heating appliances, and better insulation is making such appliances more energy-efficient.

Despite new developments, some of the best energy-saving products still include insulation, storm windows and doors, caulking, and weather-stripping. These products should be your first priority. And one other important consideration: don't ignore your present heating and cooling system. Annual maintenance is an excellent energy- and money-saving step.

Life-Cycle Costing

CONSUMERS SHOULD BE aware that some very reliable energy-saving products can cost more to buy and install than the energy dollars they will save. For example, if the cost of insulating an unheated garage over a five-year period would be $100 per year, and the heat savings is only $20 per year, you wouldn't achieve any savings for at least 25 years. At that rate, the insulation probably isn't worth it.

To help you determine which product will give you the best return on the money you spend for energy conservation, you can use a method called life-cycle costing. Essentially, this is balancing the product's cost, operating expense, and normal useful life against an accurate estimate of how much it will save you annually. Some products, such as caulking, weatherstripping, and storm windows, can pay for themselves in just one year's energy savings. However, many products require a much longer period to repay your initial investment.

To help you decide if a product is worth the cost, figure what it would repay you over a five-year payback period. This is a good average for most products; some, of course, can last the life of your home.

Energy Tax Credits

SOME ENERGY PRODUCTS qualify for a tax credit on your federal income tax. They include insulation, caulking, weatherstripping, storm doors and windows, clock and automatic setback thermostats, modified flue openings, and automatic furnace ignition systems. The National Energy Act of 1978 provides tax credits of 15 percent on the first $2,000 you spend on these conservation products. Therefore, you could lower your federal income tax by $300 by investing in them.

Any money you spend for solar, wind, and other products manufactured to utilize "renewable" energy sources will allow you a tax credit of 30 percent of the first $2,000 you spend, and 20 percent of the next $8,000. This means that if you spend $5,000 on a solar energy system to heat water, you could subtract $1,200 from your federal income tax.

Items that are not deductible include draperies, exterior siding, paneling, carpeting, roofing, insulating paint, heat pumps, and wood- and coal-burning stoves. Life-cycle costing is your only consideration here.

Whenever you buy energy-saving products, make sure you save the receipts for tax purposes. You never know when the laws will change. When you file your income tax, fill out Tax Credit Form 5695 and attach it to Form 1040. It's also a good idea to check your state income tax regulations; some states give a tax credit for energy-saving products.

Best Buys '82

OUR "BEST BUY" energy-saving products follow. They are listed alphabetically within each category. We've chosen these products on the basis of their effectiveness and overall value. Remember to use life-cycle costing to determine whether a product is worth its cost to you.

BASIC INSULATION products include batt and blanket fiberglass, mineral wool, and vermiculite. The latter two are loose-fill insulation products; they are poured into place. Batts and blankets are usually rolled into place, and attached with staples. Urea formaldehyde foam insulation is also available, but it's the subject of considerable controversy. After installation, some homeowners have complained about odors, skin irritations, and other physical problems. The Consumer Product Safety Commission has proposed a ban on the sale of this insulation material.

You can install most insulation materials yourself in attics, basements, crawl spaces, and other accessible areas. The one exception is the walls of your home. The insulation material used here is usually blown between framing members, and because this requires special equipment and know-how, the job is best left to a professional. Check out the contractor with the Better Business Bureau, however, before you sign any papers.

Insulation works equally well against heat loss and heat gain. If you live in a warm climate, the insulation helps conserve air-conditioning energy. If you live in a cold climate, it helps you conserve heating energy. All insulation materials share a common characteristic: a relatively high resistance to heat flow. The measure of how much resistance a material has is called its R-value. The "R" stands for resistance to winter heat loss or summer heat gain. The higher the R-value of the insulation, the greater its resistance to heat flow.

As you shop for insulation, divide the cost per square foot by the R-value for that square foot of insulation to obtain the "cost per R." This ratio will typically vary from about three cents per R for cellulose, fiberglass, and loose-fill mineral wool to seven cents or more for foamed insulation.

When buying cellulose insulation, be sure to inquire about fire resistance. A label signifying that the insulation is UL-listed is worth looking for when buying such materials. When buying blown cellulose, mineral wool, or fiberglass, inquire about how much settling you can expect from the material; similarly, ask about maximum shrinkage if you're considering rigid foam insulation. No matter what type of insulation you're intending to buy, always ask about the effects of moisture on the material and about the warranty that covers it.

Although more expensive products may be necessary for certain applications where a higher R-value per inch or compressive strength is important, you should buy a material at the lowest cost per unit of thermal resistance whenever possible. In many cases, insulation is insulation—you may not gain anything with a more expensive material.

New insulation can also be added to existing insulation to increase the

R-value. Here are several typical situations:

• In attics between floor joists. If the existing insulation is loose-fill mineral wool, you can simply add more. Or you can level the mineral wool and install unfaced batts or blankets directly over it. If there's no moisture vapor barrier, such as aluminum foil or plastic sheeting, between the insulation and the warm side of the room (usually the ceiling below when it is between floor joists), the existing insulation should be removed. Then install a vapor barrier, the old insulation, and finally the new insulation. If the existing insulation is composed of batts or blankets, you can add additional batts or blankets to it.

• In attics between rafters. Remove the existing insulation from the rafters and insert unfaced insulation into the spaces. Then staple the existing insulation to the rafters.

• Over vapor barriers. With a razor knife or other sharp tool, slash the insulation's vapor barrier every 12 inches or so. Then set the new insulation over the existing insulation, with the new vapor barrier facing the warm part of the room.

• In crawl spaces. The vapor barrier should face the warm side of the space; that is, toward the floor in a floor installation. Secure the barrier with strips of wood, wire, or insulation hangers made for this purpose.

• In exterior walls. Have a contractor add new insulation, if needed, unless it is new construction. In new construction, you can fit the insulation between the studs with the vapor barrier facing the side of the wall that will be heated.

If you install insulation yourself, follow these tips:

• The vapor barrier (aluminum foil, kraft paper, or plastic sheet) must always face the warm side of the room.

• Wear gloves, protective clothing, a breathing mask, and safety goggles when installing fiberglass insulation. Take a fresh-air break about every 20 minutes during installation.

• Precut batt or blanket insulation to fit the space to be filled.

• Patch any vapor barrier that's accidentally ripped or torn. You can use heavy cellophane or plastic tape or duct tape for this purpose.

• Never crush or compact insulation between framing members; it should remain fluffy to be most effective.

Never install insulation over wet building components or in places where it can become wet; moisture causes insulation to lose its efficiency. Eliminate the moisture problem and let the area dry out completely; then insulate.

Tips for Buying Insulation

WHEN YOU BUY insulation, inquire about the following points:

• The R-value per inch of thickness.

• The amount of insulation recommended for your climate.

• The total cost based on the square footage you plan to insulate.

• The maximum shrinkage for rigid-foam insulation or the amount of settling for loose-fill cellulose, mineral wool, or fiberglass.

• The material's fire resistance, especially foam and cellulose insulations. UL-listed materials are best.

- The effects of moisture on the insulation.
- The warranty and guarantee on the product.

Specialty insulation products include rolls of plastic-wrapped cellulose or mineral wool for paneling; 16- by 48-inch rigid plastic foam panels for paneling and similar wallcoverings; "Blueboard," a 24- by 96-inch tongue-and-groove plastic foam panel that is sometimes used under wallcoverings and as an addition to sheathing; and four- by eight-foot sheets of insulation fiberboard, which is used in new construction as a sheathing.

Foilpleat Type C-4 Insulation is a versatile product that provides varying degrees of insulation value depending on where it's used. It has a value of R-19 when used on floors, R-10 on ceilings, and R-10 on walls. The insulation is thin; 125 square feet of material is contained in a one-cubic-foot package. The insulation, which is reflective, can be installed in walls, floors, or ceilings, with scissors and a stapler. It isn't affected by humidity, and no special protective clothing or handling is required.

Approximate Retail Price	Approximate Low Price
$40.00	Not Available

Johns Manville Fiberglass Insulation is available in 15- by 48-inch and 23- by 48-inch batts. It can be installed anywhere insulation is needed—attics, walls, basements, garages, and other locations. The batts come faced (with a kraft-paper or foil moisture vapor barrier) or unfaced. The insulation is stamped with its R-value, which ranges from R-11 to R-38.

Approximate Retail Price	Approximate Low Price
Not Available (R-19, unfaced, 15″×48″)	$32.00
Not Available (R-19, unfaced, 23″×48″)	$49.00

Owens-Corning Fiberglas Insulation is available in faced and unfaced blankets with an R-value rating for almost any application. For stud, joist, and rafter framing, you can buy it in 3½- and 6-inch thicknesses and in 15- and 23-inch widths. Retailers selling this insulation can provide free installation literature and special charts showing how much insulation is recommended for home heating/cooling efficiency in your area.

Approximate Retail Price	Approximate Low Price
Not Available	$12.00

 # Pipe and Duct Insulation

YOU CAN SAVE considerable energy and increase family comfort by covering the pipes and ducts that carry hot water or heated air through

Prices are accurate at time of printing; subject to manufacturer's change.

an unheated crawl space or basement. Several types of insulation products are made for this purpose. They include the following:

- Sleeves. These are lengths of cellular plastic that are split lengthwise like a hot dog bun. The sleeves are placed around the pipe and secured with duct tape or special clips furnished with the product.
- Tape. One side of this kind of material usually has an aluminum foil face; the other side is adhesive-covered. A protective covering is peeled off the adhesive side, and the tape is spiral-wrapped around the pipe.
- Extra-wide tape. This product is identical to foil-faced tape, but it's 12 to 15 inches wide. This type of insulation is designed for ducts.
- Fiberglass. This product looks like very thin insulation blankets, but it's only about ¼ inch thick and two inches wide. It doesn't have an attached facing. This material is spiral-wrapped around pipes and held with string, duct tape, or adhesive. Some products are furnished with a separate plastic wrap that goes over the fiberglass to protect it. The wrap is also spiraled around the fiberglass and taped in place.
- Rigid plastic foam panels. This product, used as paneling insulation, may also be used to cover rectangular ducts. The panels can be glued to the ducts or secured with wire, string, or duct tape.

Pipe insulation can be used for cold-water pipes as well as hot-water pipes. The reason for covering cold-water pipes is to prevent condensation in the summer months. This moisture can cause mildew and rot problems.

Bede 2″ Pipe Wrap can be used on hot-water pipes, to conserve energy, and on cold-water pipes, to prevent sweating. The self-adhesive vinyl foam wrap, from Bede Industries, has an aluminum facing to reflect heat, and will conform to any shape pipe or valve. The wrap comes in a 15-foot roll.

Approximate Retail Price	Approximate Low Price
Not Available	$2.50

Bede 12″ Duct Wrap is a vinyl foam insulation wrapping with an aluminum facing to reflect heat. The 12-inch-wide wrap, which conforms to any shape air duct or water heater, has a self-adhesive backing and comes in 15-foot rolls. The product is fire-retardant and waterproof.

Approximate Retail Price	Approximate Low Price
Not Available	$9.50

RSA Wrappitup Pipe Wrap is three inches wide and comes in 25-foot, 50-foot, and 100-foot rolls. The product has an R-4 insulation value. You spiral the wrap around a hot- or cold-water pipe, and secure it in place with string or duct tape.

Approximate Retail Price	Approximate Low Price
$3.00 (25-ft. roll)	Not Available
$4.00 (50-ft. roll)	Not Available
$6.00 (100-ft. roll)	Not Available

Stanley SP-1370 Pipe Insulation is a thick-wall, closed-cell, polyethylene foam sleeve made to fit around hot-water pipes to reduce heat loss. To prevent condensation and dripping, you can also use the sleeves on

Prices are accurate at time of printing; subject to manufacturer's change.

cold-water pipes. The sleeves require no closing device; you simply slip on the sleeve and press it shut. The insulation is flame-retardant, and can be cut and fitted to pipe elbows, bends, tees, and angle joints. Four sizes are available: ½ inch by 12 feet, ¾ inch by 12 feet, 1 inch by 12 feet, and 1¼ inch by 12 feet.

Approximate Retail Price
$6.50 .... **Not Available** **Approximate Low Price**

 Caulks and Sealants

FOR SMALL CRACKS and other openings in wood, masonry, and metal building components, standard caulking compounds, oakum rope, and asphalt roofing cement can be used to seal out the weather. The best caulking materials are the butyl, silicone, and acrylic products, because these compounds should last 10 to 20 years. Oakum is a fiber material that can be used as a base for caulking in deep cracks and other openings; fibered asphalt roofing cement—sold in cartridges—is designed for use around flashing, roof valleys, chimney and vent bases, gutters, and downspouts. You can also buy a cement caulk for cracks in masonry.

In addition, there are other types of caulks and sealants. One of the newest kinds of caulking comes in aerosol cans in the form of an insulating foam. When applied, the foam expands to fill cracks and gaps to prevent air infiltration. Sealants also come in the form of brushable coatings. These are generally available in quart and gallon cans, and also can be rolled or sprayed onto surfaces to be sealed.

There's no trick to using caulking and sealants, except this one: Be sure to break the seal inside the nozzle after you cut the tip off. You can use a nail, or any slim, sharp object. If the seal isn't broken, pressure from the plunger of the caulking gun can break the cartridge casing, causing a mess and wasting the entire cartridge.

Caulking compound is available in a range of standard colors; it no longer has to be touched up with paint to match adjoining surfaces. You can also buy clear compound to make a hardly visible seal.

General-Purpose Caulks

Dow Corning General Purpose Sealant is a highly versatile silicone-rubber product that can be used on aluminum siding, exhaust fans, roof vents, flashing, gutters, and chimneys. It can also be used to caulk around windows, doors, and screens, or to repair leaking pipes. It will waterproof and protect electrical outlets and connections, and seal cracks and rips in leather and vinyl. The sealant, which cures and bonds within 24 hours, will adhere to glass, non-oily woods, metal, porcelain, ceramic, painted surfaces, and many plastics and rubber. It is resistant

Prices are accurate at time of printing; subject to manufacturer's change.

to temperature extremes from -60° to 450° F. The sealant, which comes in a 10.3-fluid-ounce cartridge with resealable cap and nozzle, is available in aluminum, bronze, clear, black, and white colors. It carries a 20-year limited warranty.

Approximate Retail Price	Approximate Low Price
$5.50	Not Available

Fomo Seal All-Purpose Sealant, formulated from synthetic elastomers and resins, can be applied in a temperature range of 40° to 90° F, in areas where an inconspicuous yet effective caulking compound is needed. The clear sealant adheres to wood, metal, brick, stone, glass, ceramic, and other interior or exterior surfaces. The caulk comes in an 11-fluid-ounce cartridge.

Approximate Retail Price	Approximate Low Price
$8.00	Not Available

Franklin Clear Sealant and adhesive caulk is waterproof and won't crack, chip, peel, or pull away from any surface it is bonded to. The product is clear and doesn't turn cloudy with age; it can be painted. The sealant skins over in five minutes and dries in one hour; it requires no long curing times. The product comes in a 10-fluid-ounce cartridge.

Approximate Retail Price	Approximate Low Price
$4.30	Not Available

Geocel Caulking Sealant is an elastomeric copolymer mixture that will stick to almost any building material, including wood, brick, ceramic, metal, and concrete. It can be used over wet surfaces. The product, which stays flexible, has a life expectancy of 20 years. It can be painted in less than 24 hours without priming. Geocel sealant is available in clear, white, gray, black, or brown, in 10-fluid-ounce cartridges. It is also available in four-ounce tubes with an applicator-nozzle.

Approximate Retail Price	Approximate Low Price
$4.50 (10-fluid-ounce cartridge)	Not Available
$3.00 (4-ounce tube)	Not Available

Great Stuff Insta-Seal Foam Sealant is an insulating foam caulk that can be applied to cracks around windows and doors and to big spaces between sills, jambs, headers, lintels, rough openings, sole plates, and sheathing. The material, a moisture-cured polyurethane foam, is packaged in a pressurized container with a long flexible nozzle so you can get into hard-to-reach places. It is UL listed as a Class I material and is approved by three major building code organizations. The product adheres to almost any wet or dry surface; it sets in about 30 minutes and cures in 24 hours. Great Stuff sealant comes in a 14-ounce aerosol can and with a pair of plastic gloves.

Approximate Retail Price	Approximate Low Price
$8.00	Not Available

Polyseamseal All-Purpose Adhesive Caulk, made by Darworth, bonds to almost anything and accepts all paints. The latex caulking

Prices are accurate at time of printing; subject to manufacturer's change.

product, which will last for years, should be applied at a temperature over 40° F. It can be cleaned up with soap and water before it cures, and can be painted in one hour. Polyseamseal is also an adhesive, so you can glue materials together with it. The caulk is available in white, aluminum-gray, black, redwood, and bronze colors. It comes in an 11-fluid-ounce cartridge.

Approximate Retail Price	Approximate Low Price
Not Available	$3.75

3M Weather Sealing Caulk is a white, butyl-formulated product that can be used to fill gaps between dissimilar materials and in metal, brick, concrete, and wood joints. It dries within 24 hours to a flexible, weather-resistant seal and may be painted with oil- or latex-based paints immediately. It is available in 11-ounce cartridges.

Approximate Retail Price	Approximate Low Price
$3.00	Not Available

Touch 'n Foam, an insulating foam caulk that looks like shaving cream, is packaged in a 14-ounce aerosol container. The white urethane foam product expands to fill gaps and seal completely. It adheres to almost any building material; it is nontoxic and impervious to the effects of freezing and thawing. Touch 'n Foam cures in about eight hours.

Approximate Retail Price	Approximate Low Price
$7.00	Not Available

Special-Purpose Sealants

Dow Corning Concrete Crack Sealant, made of silicone rubber, is formulated to fill cracks in masonry. It can withstand temperatures from -80° to 300° F, and resists the effects of sunlight. The material, which comes in a neutral color, doesn't have to be mixed. It dries to the touch in 15 minutes and cures in 24 hours. The sealant can be applied to horizontal or vertical surfaces. The 10.3-fluid-ounce cartridge has a replaceable cap to avoid waste and mess. The sealant carries a 20-year limited warranty.

Approximate Retail Price	Approximate Low Price
$4.00	Not Available

Dow Corning Protective Coating is made of silicone rubber. The manufacturer says that the product will last five times longer than most asphalt and plastic coatings for sealing roofs, vents, chimneys, and gutters. The liquid material may be brushed, rolled, or sprayed on the surface. It's waterproof, weather-proof, flexible, and stays serviceable from -60° to 450° F. The coating, which is neutral gray in color, dries in one to two hours. It is available in one-quart cans that will cover from 25 to 50 square feet, depending on the surface. It is guaranteed by Dow Corning.

Approximate Retail Price	Approximate Low Price
$4.00	Not Available

Prices are accurate at time of printing; subject to manufacturer's change.

Dow Corning Window and Door Sealant, a silicone rubber caulk, resists temperature extremes by remaining serviceable from -60° to 450° F. It is formulated for sealing windows and door frames, although the product also can be used around foundations and on siding, soffits, gutters, downspouts, roof vents, flashings, and electrical outlets. Available in a brown color, the product will adhere to painted surfaces, but paint won't adhere to it. The sealant, which cures in 24 hours, comes in a 10.3-fluid-ounce cartridge that has a replaceable nozzle and cap for longer storage and less waste. It carries a 20-year limited warranty.

Approximate Retail Price   **Approximate Low Price**
$4.00 .... Not Available

 Weatherstripping

TIGHTENING UP your home with weatherstripping materials costs about $30 for the average three-bedroom house, but you should realize an energy savings of about $50 the first year. Multiply the savings by the life of the weatherstripping—perhaps 10 years—and you can save up to $500, less your initial investment.

Weatherstripping is a simple product that is easy to install yourself. There are several varieties available. They range from inexpensive adhesive-backed foam strips to longer-lasting metal and plastic types. When you go shopping, consider how frequently you will have to replace the product. For example, low-cost foam stripping on an attic access door or other seldom-used door or window may not need replacing for at least 10 years. If the same material is used on an often-used door or window, replacement may be necessary in three to five years. Good-quality weatherstripping can last up to 15 or 20 years on either type of opening.

Foam weatherstripping usually has an adhesive backing. You peel off a protective covering on the adhesive side and press the weatherstripping against the mounting surface. When a door or window is closed, it compresses the foam for an air-tight seal.

Some metal weatherstripping is in the shape of a "J" or "V." One length goes against the jamb of the door or window; a second length is secured to the door or window. When the door or window is closed, the two strips interlock to form a seal. Another type of metal weatherstripping, which is fastened to the side jambs of a door or window, is under spring tension. When the door or window is closed, the metal is compressed to seal the gap between the door or window and jambs.

Thermal thresholds for exterior doors are a form of weatherstripping. The threshold is usually made of metal, with a section of plastic inserted in the middle of the metal strip. When the door is closed, the bottom edge of the door compresses the plastic to form a seal.

Prices are accurate at time of printing; subject to manufacturer's change.

Garage doors are best sealed with special weatherstripping fastened to the bottom of the door. The weatherstripping may be ridged rubber or plastic in a tubelike configuration. When the door is closed, the weatherstripping compresses, sealing out the weather.

Sentinel Draft Guard Tape, made of closed-cell transluscent polyethylene foam, is impervious to water. The tape has an adhesive backing that makes installation easy on doors, windows, air conditioners, ducts, and pipes. The ⅛-inch-thick tape comes in 17-foot lengths that are one inch (EG-050) or two inches wide (EG-051). Installation instructions are provided on the package.

Approximate Retail Price	Approximate Low Price
$2.00 (EG-050)	Not Available
$3.50 (EG-051)	Not Available

3M V-Seal Weather Strip is made of flexible polypropylene. It comes in a ⅞-inch-wide roll that is 17 or 90 feet long. To install, you measure the length required, snip it with scissors, and fold and strip along a prescored line to form a V-shape. Then you stick the strip in place on a window or door frame. The strip is self-adhesive; you peel off a protective backing. It can be used on double-hung, casement, jalousie, and standard windows, and on standard or sliding doors. The product carries a five-year warranty.

Approximate Retail Price	Approximate Low Price
$5.50 (17-foot roll)	Not Available
$22.00 (90-foot roll)	Not Available

Wonderstrip Weatherstripping, designed for use around windows and doors, is made from Mylar polyester film. To use, you measure what's needed, and cut the material with scissors. Then you press the weatherstripping into position, forming a V-shape. It "hinges" open to form a compression seal similar to metal weatherstripping. The product, made by Manco Tape, comes in a 34-foot-long roll, and is available in clear, white, and brown colors. It carries a five-year limited warranty.

Approximate Retail Price	Approximate Low Price
$6.50	Not Available

 # Door and Window Insulation

DOUBLE-GLAZING in storm windows and doors ranks with insulation, caulking and sealants, and weatherstripping as an energy-saving device that is most effective. It also has another bonus feature; it eliminates drafts, making your home more comfortable.

Once considered just a fall-through-early-spring technique to block the cold, storm doors and windows are now commonly left in place all

Prices are accurate at time of printing; subject to manufacturer's change.

year to make central air conditioning systems more effective. The glazing is effective even if you're cooling the house with several large room air conditioners.

There are three ways to custom-tailor storm windows to fit over the windows in your house:

1. Build them from aluminum framing components available in hardware stores and home centers. The frames are gasketed for the glass; the glass can be cut to fit the aluminum frames after you assemble them.

2. Buy stock triple-track or single-glazed storm windows and install them. There are 18 standard stock sizes of such windows, available at many hardware and home center stores. Seal the edges of the storm windows with caulking and level them in the window opening to deter insects and to prevent the movable window and screen panels from racking and sticking.

3. Have a professional contractor measure, manufacture, and install the storm windows. Check with the Better Business Bureau before you assign the work, and make sure you get a total cost figure—in writing—before the job is started.

Inexpensive storm windows can also be fabricated from clear plastic and special strips that adhere to the window casing. The clear plastic comes in a wide range of sizes, and the plastic strips can be painted or stained to match the casings. You simply flip open the strips to remove the plastic. This system is especially efficient for large bow windows; the plastic will bend to conform with the curvature of the window.

Storm doors, like windows, come in a wide range of sizes and designs. Materials used are steel, aluminum, and wood. One type can't be recommended over another because all three can do an efficient job. Many storm doors are prehung in a frame; the frame is simply fastened to the side jambs and top header of the door after the door is leveled in the door opening. Latch and closing hardware is usually furnished with the units. Single frames for adding storm windows to patio doors are also available. These units glide on tracks that are fastened to the top header and bottom sill of the patio door.

Bede Translucent Window Insulation is a foam insulation material that sticks to glass with a high-tack adhesive to protect basements and other areas from heat loss. The product, from Bede Industries, can be used as a substitute for basement storm windows. An 18- by 96-inch roll of the material is enough to insulate six average-size basement windows. The product also can be used on glass bricks or windows in a bathroom, attic, or garage. It blocks about 30 percent of outside light, if this is a consideration.

Approximate Retail Price	Approximate Low Price
Not Available	$6.50

Bede Sill Insulation Pads are designed to form a waterproof barrier and prevent condensation from soaking into a window sill. This moisture can conduct heat out of a room and rot sills. The foam pads are made to form a tight seal against a closed window and help reduce drafts. The pads don't have to be refinished, although replacement may be

Prices are accurate at time of printing; subject to manufacturer's change.

necessary from time to time. Each package contains six 5½- by 36-inch self-adhesive foam sill pads.

Approximate Retail Price **Approximate Low Price**
Not Available $6.50

Eliminator Transparent Solar Control Window Film, made by Vacumet, is available in reflective or nonreflective versions. The product is designed to insulate glass and help keep rooms cooler in summer and warmer in winter. The material, which permanently bonds to glass, won't fade from the sun's rays. It can be installed easily with scissors and a tape measure. The reflective film, which comes in bronze or silver, is available in several sizes: 14 by 156 inches, 34 by 78 inches, and 48 by 78 inches. The non-reflective film is only available in a 20- by 120-inch size, in bronze or gray.

Approximate Retail Price **Approximate Low Price**
$13.00 to $23.00 .... Not Available

Feather-Lite Storm Doors are extruded aluminum; they're available in a number of designs, including combination storm/screen units. The doors are pre-hung, pre-spaced, and pre-drilled. To install a door, you simply fasten the frame to the top header and side jambs of the door opening. Feather-Lite storm doors have tempered safety glass inserts and are finished with acrylic enamel. All necessary hardware is included.

Approximate Retail Price **Approximate Low Price**
$59.00 to $190.00 .... Not Available

Plaskolite Vinyl In-Sider Storm Window kit consists of a four-mil sheet of clear, flexible plastic and a plastic frame, which is fastened to the window casing or wall by its own adhesive. By itself, an In-Sider storm window can offer substantial protection against heat/cold loss; when used with a regular storm window, the units can cut heat/cold loss up to 95 percent. The clear plastic can be removed from the mounting trim strips, which may be painted or stained to match the window casing. The plastic storm windows are available in a wide range of sizes that can be trimmed to fit.

Approximate Retail Price **Approximate Low Price**
$50.00 to $100.00 .... Not Available

Sentinel Draft Guard Door Sweeps, which are made of closed-cell polyethylene, fastens to the bottom of exterior or interior doors. The sweeps are self-adhering and available in white or brown colors. There are three sweeps in each package. Each sweep measures 1½ by 36 by ⅛ inches.

Approximate Retail Price **Approximate Low Price**
$1.50 .... Not Available

3M Scotchtint Window Film, which is available in three color tints— silver, bronze, and smoke—is reusable. The film is made of clear polyester, metalized with reflective aluminum that insulates glass and rejects from 64 to 74 percent of the sun's heat and from 84 to 90 percent

Prices are accurate at time of printing; subject to manufacturer's change.

of the sun's glare. Water activates the film's adhesive; you just spray water on it and stick it to the window glass. The film is available in four sizes: 30 by 48 inches, 36 by 78 inches, 48 by 78 inches, and 20 by 144 inches (bronze and smoke only).

Approximate Retail Price   **Approximate Low Price**
$17.00 to $29.00 .... Not Available

Window Quilt, from Appropriate Technology Corp., is an insulating thermal shade that is said to lower heating bills by as much as 50 percent. The product is composed of five layers; inner layers are made of polyester batting for insulation and the outer layers are decorative rayon-polyester that resist sunlight and weathering. The layers are ultrasonically welded into a quilt pattern; no thread is used. This eliminates needle holes through which cold air can penetrate. The shade operates on tracks and can seal all four sides of a window or sliding glass door. It comes in four colors: white, tan, dark blue, and off-white.

Approximate Retail Price   **Approximate Low Price**
Not Available (standard-size window) $65.00
Not Available (standard-size door) $260.00

Heating and Cooling Aids

BY CHANGING THE furnace filter at the start, in the middle, and at the end of the heating or cooling season, you can save energy and increase the comfort in your home. You should also have a professional clean the heating and cooling system annually. A minor adjustment or two by a professional can often pay for the cost of the service call in terms of the energy saved.

Setback thermostats automatically vary temperature levels at different times of the day or on individual days of the week. Most thermostat models can be installed with common household tools. By reducing the demand on your heating and cooling system with a temperature setback at certain times when heating or cooling isn't really needed, you can save both energy and money, and be comfortable in the bargain.

Heat-modulating controls that adjust your furnace's heat output to match your heating demand can save money, too. The controls trigger the heating unit to run in short on/off intervals rather than in longer cycles. This increases efficiency.

If your home is insulated—or you plan to insulate it this year—don't overlook the value of an automatic roof vent or gable vent fan that automatically switches on when heat builds up in the attic space. The temperature in an attic can surpass 175° F on hot days, and if this heat is trapped in the attic, it can penetrate the rooms below and put an additional load on your air-conditioning system.

Prices are accurate at time of printing; subject to manufacturer's change.

An attic fan is still an inexpensive method to cool a house during the summer—especially during the evening and late night hours. Open windows on opposite sides of the house and turn on the fan; it can pull cool air in through the opened windows and exhaust it through the attic. Newer attic fans are much quieter than older models. Both attic fans and roof vents are designed for do-it-yourself installation.

Ceiling fans are classic coolers, but they can also help distribute warm air throughout the house in winter. A ceiling fan with three, four, or even six blades is an ideal appliance if you operate a fireplace or a wood- or coal-burning stove.

Bede Filter Alert, from Bede Industries, is a plastic device that you insert into the filter in your heating and cooling system. When the filter clogs with dirt, the air flow through the small device causes it to whistle loudly. The Bede Filter Alert installs in seconds and can be reused every time you change the filter. No tools are required for installation.

Approximate Retail Price	Approximate Low Price
$1.00	Not Available

Emerson Universal Series Ceiling Fans, from Emerson Environmental Products, include four-blade, 36- and 52-inch models that feature simulated-wood paddles with brown or antique white finishes. The units have a two-speed, built-in control with pull-chain selection. Fairly easy for a homeowner to install, the fans come with a five-year warranty. You can also buy optional accessories that include a wall-mounted variable speed control, decorative swag chain, wall plug, and light kits, such as Victorian, Globe, School House, and Tiffany styles.

Approximate Retail Price	Approximate Low Price
$150.00 (36-inch)	Not Available
$190.00 (52-inch)	Not Available

Commodore Micro Electronic Thermostat works equally well with any kind of furnace—electric, oil, or gas—or air conditioning system. It is an automatic setback thermostat that you can install with only a screwdriver. A sliding switch sets the controls to the temperatures you want to maintain, and the controls can be programmed in just minutes. The thermostat is 5¼ inches wide, 3½ inches high, and 1½ inches deep. It carries a one-year limited warranty.

Approximate Retail Price	Approximate Low Price
$150.00	$105.00

Flexo-Therm Baseboard Heating Insulation Material, from the Ric-Nor Co., is inserted onto the back plate of a standard baseboard heating unit, directly behind the convection fins. Due to its reflective qualities, the material can help save energy by reducing the amount of heat loss through the back plate. The insulation is a reflective ceramic fiber material that is flameproof and non-conductive. It can be trimmed to fit with scissors. It has a self-adhesive backing.

Approximate Retail Price	Approximate Low Price
$15.00	Not Available

Prices are accurate at time of printing; subject to manufacturer's change.

Leslie-Locke Power Attic Ventilator helps rid attics of hot air to help reduce air conditioning loads. There are roof- and gable-mounted models that are sized to fit your attic, so calculate the square footage of your attic space before you go shopping. All models come with an adjustable automatic thermostat so that the fan only operates when needed. If the roof on your home isn't too steep, you can install the ventilator in less than one day with ordinary household tools. Complete do-it-yourself instructions are furnished. You should also install soffit vents with a ventilator. Ask the retailer for information on this system.

Approximate Retail Price	Approximate Low Price
$87.00 to $170.00 (roof-mounted models)	Not Available
$65.00 to $80.00 (gable-mounted models)	Not Available

Nautilus Whole House Ventilators are available in two sizes. Model N2024 is a 24-inch unit; Model N2030 is a 30-inch unit. The big feature of these ventilators is that you don't have to cut joists to install them; the motor assembly rests on top of the ceiling joists. Only ordinary household tools are required. The fan motor is heavy-duty and is thermally protected; a resilient motor mount reduces noise and vibration while a solid-state infinite-setting speed control lets you set the motor speed and air flow. The fan shutters are spring-loaded and balanced to open even when the unit is turned to its low setting. Options available with the fans include 12-hour timers, attic exhaust vents, and wall thermostats.

Approximate Retail Price	Approximate Low Price
$240.00 (Model N2024)	Not Available
$260.00 (Model N2030)	Not Available

Robertshaw T30-1043 Automatic Set-Back Thermostat controls a central heating/cooling unit to raise and lower temperatures automatically all year round. The thermostat has a set of dials that lets you select a schedule of temperature increases or decreases when you want them. The unit can be installed as a replacement for your present thermostat. You can make the changeover yourself with a few basic household tools.

Approximate Retail Price	Approximate Low Price
$98.00	$30.50

Tjernlund Duct Booster DB-2 is a small fan that can be installed in round, square, or rectangular ducts to increase the flow of warm air through existing ductwork. The fan's motor is located on the outside duct. The unit, from Tjernlund Products, can operate automatically in tandem with the heating/cooling system, or it can be installed so that you can control it independently. It can be installed with ordinary household tools on ducts as shallow as 3¼ inches. It comes with a one-year limited warranty.

Approximate Retail Price	Approximate Low Price
$40.00	Not Available

Prices are accurate at time of printing; subject to manufacturer's change.

THE HIGH COST of heating has been causing problems for many family budgets. One comfortable alternative that can provide sufficient heat yet help reduce energy and heating costs for many people is turning down the thermostat and using a supplemental heating unit in a room or area that sees active use.

There are several different types of such auxiliary heaters available, including electrical, kerosene, and solar units. Most of these supplemental home heaters are portable and can add warmth wherever it's needed, at less cost than whole-house heating.

The DeLonghi 930B, which looks much like a standard radiator, operates on electricity. It is an oil-filled and permanently sealed unit. You simply plug it in and move it wherever supplemental heating is needed. A complete control panel for temperature settings and on/off operation is located at one end of the UL-listed heater. A switch allows it to operate at 600, 900, or 1,500 watts. It's 18 inches long, 24.4 inches high, and 6.3 inches wide. The electric radiator weighs 38 pounds.

Approximate Retail Price   **Approximate Low Price**
$139.00 .... Not Available

Energy Mart EM-M222 portable kerosene heater delivers 9,350 Btu's per hour for about 15 hours before it needs refueling. The heater has a seven-pint cartridge fuel tank, and features automatic lighting and pushbutton extinguishing. The unit takes less space than a console television set; it's 18⅝ inches by 25⅝ inches by 14¾ inches. It weighs 27.5 pounds.

Approximate Retail Price   **Approximate Low Price**
$199.00 .... Not Available

Manumark 6048 Solar Heater resembles a room air conditioner. You set the unit into a window and it moves air from the room to a collector in the unit and then back into the room in the form of filtered, heated air. The device, which is portable, is capable of heating up to 700 square feet. There are two other models—for mounting in a wall or on a roof. All electrical components are UL listed. The solar heater carries a one-year limited warranty.

Approximate Retail Price   **Approximate Low Price**
$799.00 .... $699.00

Markel/NuTone 507-T Hydronic Convection Portable Heater features baseboard styling. Its hydronic heating element has a finned tube of water/antifreeze liquid that is permanently sealed. When the desired room temperature is reached, a thermostat turns off the power automat-

Prices are accurate at time of printing; subject to manufacturer's change.

ically. The exterior housing never gets hot, even after hours of use. It also features two indicator lights to show the status of power heating modes. The 1500-watt heater, which is UL listed, has an output of 5118 Btuh. The heater is 9½ inches high, 72 inches wide, and 6⁹⁄₁₆ inches deep. It weighs 24 pounds.

Approximate Retail Price   **Approximate Low Price**
$151.00 .... Not Available

Radiant King RK-220 kerosene heater, which is rated at 11,800 Btu's per hour, can heat rooms up to 425 square feet in area. One tank of fuel will provide heat for about 18 hours. The heater has a fiberglass wick, an enclosed combustion chamber, an extinguishing mechanism that instantly shuts off the heater if it's tipped or jarred, a pushbutton ignition system, and a removable fuel tank. The heater is 18 inches high, 25 inches wide, and 14 inches deep. It weighs 22 pounds.

Approximate Retail Price   **Approximate Low Price**
$270.00 .... $249.00

 ## Wood- and Coal-Burning Stoves and Accessories

THE ACTUAL ECONOMY of wood or coal heat used to supplement your present heating system can be marginal. It can also be outstanding. If you're looking for the romantic effect of a fire burning in a fireplace or an open-doored fireplace unit or stove, don't expect to save anything from a heating standpoint; most of the heat will go up the chimney. But if you're after efficiency, an airtight stove or a fireplace insert is the thing to buy. Both are designed for primary or supplemental heat. Some units also provide the romantic effect by means of glass and screen door inserts. But before you decide to buy one of these appliances, consider the cost of wood and coal in your area. If you have to buy wood, the expense could be prohibitive as compared with gas, oil, or electricity.

When shopping, you will find that quality stoves are rated as to the space they are designed to heat. The area goes from about 800 square feet up to about 2,200 square feet. The stove, to be efficient, must be matched to the area. Don't expect a stove placed in one end of the house to heat rooms at the other end. You can, however, move some of the heat into cold areas by means of ceiling fans and blower attachments connected to the heating appliance. But don't expect these air circulators to keep the heat even throughout the area. Ideally, heating appliances purchased for efficiency should be located in the exact center of a house. Because this is seldom possible, a stove should be located where it can provide the most heat to the largest area.

Stove prices cover a wide range, from inexpensive cast-iron models to expensive plate-steel stoves. An inexpensive cast-iron stove, however,

Prices are accurate at time of printing; subject to manufacturer's change.

can be just as efficient as its costly cousin. You should "cure" a new cast-iron stove by building small fires in the firebox until the metal becomes adjusted to the heat. About six small fires should be started before you load the stove for larger fires. Inexpensive stoves tend to leak smoke at the outset, but most manufacturers provide a stove cement to fill these cracks. Keep in mind, too, that cast iron is easily cracked and broken if the stove parts are dropped. This isn't the case with more expensive plate-steel units.

There are other important considerations for heating appliances, including the following:

● Doors and dampers should fit snugly. In a quality airtight appliance, you should be able to cut the combustion air to the point where the fire will be reduced to just a smolder. This is important because control of air flow into the firebox determines the stove's output of heat and, therefore, its efficiency. The gaskets on stoves should be changed at the start of every heating season; a worn gasket can cause a stove to be inefficient, and you often can't tell if the gasket is worn. You can buy and install one yourself. Directions are included in the package.

● Parts of the stove that are exposed to high temperatures, such as the door, door frame, and firebox, should be made of cast iron. In a metal stove, firebrick or fireclay liners are very important. These materials add life to the unit and help prevent warping from heat.

● The stove should be UL-listed, or should be approved by a national code group.

● The stove should have a Btu (British thermal unit) rating. The more Btu's, the greater the heat output will be. However, don't be too impressed by capacity; the stove should fit the area it will be used in. A stove that's too large won't work efficiently, because you'll have to keep it shut down most of the time. A stove that's too small will have to be loaded constantly with fuel, and even burning full-blast it still won't provide the heat you require.

● Ask about warranties. A quality stove will have a three- to five-year warranty against defective materials and workmanship. There's no such thing as a "lifetime" guarantee on stoves. Courts have ruled that appliances must have a time-period warranty.

● Ask about service. Can the stove be repaired locally? What's the repair procedure?

● Ask about local codes and the manufacturer's installation instructions. With the new fireboards for walls, some codes permit stoves to be located within 12 inches of walls and other combustible surfaces. Codes and instructions should also specify clearances for chimney installation; don't assume that you can connect the stove to an existing chimney.

● Inquire about delivery. A stove can weigh more than you and a neighbor can lift or haul in a car or station wagon—even if it would fit.

● If you plan to install the stove yourself, ask what tools and equipment will be needed. If you plan to have a professional install the unit, ask the dealer to recommend someone. If the store can't make this recommendation, be sure you check out the contractor before any work is started. Get the total cost in writing.

Fireplaces can be converted into efficient heating appliances with a fireplace insert. The cost of an insert is slightly more—usually—than a quality free-standing stove. Glass doors and heat-circulating grates can also improve the efficiency of a fireplace. Consider, too, fireplaces with fireboxes that circulate water or air through their walls to increase heat output, or that use outside combustion air. Units that have tight-sealing dampers are the best investments.

Components, Accessories, and Fuel

ANY WOOD- OR coal-burning appliance has to be vented through a chimney. This involves several special parts, and the parts are usually matched to and packaged with the appliance you buy. These components may include a stovepipe adaptor, stovepipe, insulated pipe, insulated elbows, insulated tee connections, support brackets, wall or ceiling thimbles, a pitched-roof assembly, flashing, and a chimney cap. The length of the chimney run, of course, determines the price of the system, which can be considerable.

If you're venting the appliance into an existing masonry chimney, chances are you'll have to install a chimney liner. The liners are stainless steel, and run from the appliance up through the chimney to the chimney cap. Old, leaky masonry chimneys are subject to creosote buildup from the wood burned in the appliance. This creosote build-up, if not contained in a liner that is cleaned regularly, can cause a chimney fire that could burn down your home. To avoid the hazards of creosote buildup, be sure to ask about a fire liner when you buy your stove or fireplace unit.

Chimneys should be cleaned at the start of every heating season and once a month during the season if the heating appliance is used on a regular basis. You can buy cleaning brushes for this job, or you can hire a professional. Chemicals added to the fire can also help prevent creosote buildup and keep the chimney clean. Regular brush cleaning, however, is recommended.

Tips About Firewood

SOME STORES THAT sell heating appliances also sell wood. Knowing how wood is "measured" for sale can save you plenty. Here are the guidelines:

Most wood is sold by the *cord.* A full cord of wood is a stack eight feet long by four feet high by the length of the wood—usually about four feet wide.

A *face cord* of wood is eight feet long by four feet high by the length of the wood—usually about 16 inches wide. The length often varies.

A *stack* of wood is about the same amount as a face cord.

A *truckload* depends on the size of the truck. If the seller says his standard pickup truck holds a cord of wood, make him prove it by stacking wood and measuring it; a standard pickup truck holds only about ⅓ cord of wood.

A *ton* (weight) of wood equals about ½ cord if the wood has been air-dried.

The amount of heat produced by wood depends on what type it is. Oak, hickory, and beech produce more heat than cedar, pine, and other softwoods on a "burn time" comparison. If possible, buy seasoned, or dry, wood. Green, or wet, wood is cheaper, but has a high moisture content, is difficult to ignite and keep burning, and produces more creosote buildup. Seasoned wood is wood that has been cut for at least six months. Split wood always costs more than unsplit wood because of the labor involved in splitting it.

Wood- and Coal-Burning Stoves

Colony Hearth Fireplace Stove, made by The Earth Stove, Inc., is a fireplace insert that projects out onto the hearth of a fireplace. The unit can also be used for cooking; it has a 141-square-inch cooking surface. The insert features an adjustable top, a forced-air heat flow unit, and a thermostat-controlled draft. A blower is optional. If you prefer, you can replace the fire door with a metal mesh or glass screen; the glass screen is an accessory. The insert has a five-cubic-foot firebox that holds 24-inch-long wood. It is available in traditional or contemporary styling.

Approximate Retail Price	Approximate Low Price
$929.00	$850.00

Country Comfort CC800 Stove, from Orville Products, burns wood or coal and features a removable ash drawer and a double vent system for flexibility in installation. Other features include an automatic draft control that provides constant stove temperature and maximum fuel economy; heat exchange tubes to move heated air throughout a room; a cast-iron gate for bottom draft and easy cleaning; and a firebrick lining. The stove carries a five-year warranty.

Approximate Retail Price	Approximate Low Price
Not Available	$880.00

Fisher Coal Bear Stove is designed to burn coal, which is usually less costly to burn and easier to stock than wood. The Coal Bear stove has a two-step design that eliminates smoking. Its doors, which are virtually airtight, are made of cast iron finished in black or nickel plate. The stove has $\frac{1}{4}$- and $\frac{5}{16}$-inch-thick steel construction, a firebrick lining, a cast-iron shaker grate, a removable ash drawer, and primary and secondary air inlets. You can burn up to 40 pounds of coal at one time.

Approximate Retail Price	Approximate Low Price
$799.00	$750.00

United States Stove Legacy 3000 Wonderwood is a stove with plenty of features, including a lift-up top for the auxiliary cooking surface, a full-size ash pan, and a firebrick lining. A two-speed blower is optional. The stove generates 3,300 Btu's and is UL listed. It has a leather-grain embossed steel cabinet and an 18-gauge aluminized steel firebox.

Approximate Retail Price	Approximate Low Price
Not Available (wood model)	$652.50
Not Available (coal model)	$732.50

Prices are accurate at time of printing; subject to manufacturer's change.

Accessories

American Stove Products' Stove-to-Ceiling Stovepipe Kit has all the 24-gauge pipe and fittings you need for installation, from the stove to Class A pipe at the ceiling. The kit is designed for both wood- and coal-burning heating appliances where required clearance from combustible walls allows the use of single-wall pipe. Included in all four kit models are a trim collar, a 12-inch slip joint, 12-inch pipe section, and two 24-inch pipe sections. You can get a kit with six- or eight-inch stovepipe. Two kits also have an adjustable elbow, if one is required.

Approximate Retail Price	Approximate Low Price
Not Available (6″ Kit A)	$21.00
Not Available (8″ Kit A)	$27.00
Not Available (6″ Kit B, with elbow)	$24.00
Not Available (8″ Kit B, with elbow)	$30.00

Champ Coal Grate and Basket turns a wood-burning stove into a coal-burning stove. The device is available in three sizes. The smallest unit is 10⅜ inches wide, 14½ inches deep, and 6½ inches high. The medium-size unit is 15 inches wide, 14½ inches deep, and 6½ inches high. The largest model is 19½ inches wide, 14½ inches deep, and 6½ inches high. The grate holds the fuel so a proper draft can flow under the grate and fuel; because it's also low enough for wood, you can burn wood for a visual effect and add coal for all-night heat without reloading the firebox. Optional side and back shields are available to increase basket capacity.

Approximate Retail Price	Approximate Low Price
$104.00 (small)	Not Available
$120.00 (medium)	Not Available
$136.00 (large)	Not Available

Dura-Chimney System, from the Dura-Vent Corp., is designed for gas-, oil-, coal-, or wood-burning appliances. The UL-listed, air-insulated chimney system, made of galvanized steel, is triple-walled for safety and has a stainless steel lining. Kits are available, with inside diameters of six, seven, or eight inches. Chimney sections come in 24-inch and 36-inch lengths. All parts are available, too, from wall strap to thimbles. The manufacturer packages complete installation instructions, including a chimney pipe length selector chart and required chimney clearances.

Approximate Retail Price	Approximate Low Price
$160.00 (kit 6-1)	Not Available
$192.00 (kit 7-1)	Not Available
$231.50 (kit 8-1)	Not Available

KemStone Stove Boards are designed to protect combustible materials from the heat of wood- and coal-burning stoves. The UL-listed boards can be fastened to a wall or used on the floor. They are made of lightweight concrete-reinforced steel and strengthened with fiberglass. Three patterns are available—stone, flagstone, and brick—in brown, gray, or red colors. Using the boards, established clearances of listed

Prices are accurate at time of printing; subject to manufacturer's change.

units can be reduced by as much as two-thirds; for example, if the required clearance is 36 inches, you can reduce it to 12 inches. This can be important when positioning a stove in a room. The stove boards are available in the following sizes: 36 by 48 inches, 48 by 48 inches, 48 by 54 inches, and 54 by 54 inches. An insert model is 18 by 48 inches.

Approximate Retail Price	Approximate Low Price
$54.00 to $84.00	Not Available

Log-A-Long Wood and Coal Carrier—the Weekender model—is built to hold logs up to 30 inches in length and up to 16 inches in diameter. There's also an optional insert that fits inside the carrier's log retainers if you want to haul coal. The cart, from CJM Enterprises, can also be used for other tasks, such as hauling trash, fertilizer, and lawn and garden tools. The carrier is made of welded steel with a rustic black finish. It has two 10½-inch diameter tires. A rubber tie strap is included to stabilize full loads. There are two larger models available, too.

Approximate Retail Price	Approximate Low Price
$90.00 (carrier)	Not Available
$90.00 (coal insert)	Not Available

Magnetic Chimgard Thermometer, made by the Condar Co., monitors both wood- and coal-burning stove operating ranges; when the temperature on the thermometer drops, it's time to refuel. The device is calibrated in degrees to show the best operating temperatures for the stove and fuel. It indicates "soot and creosoting," "best operation," and "overheating." The unit can be attached easily with a magnet and a length of wire to a stovepipe, stovetop, furnace, or heating duct.

Approximate Retail Price	Approximate Low Price
$12.00	Not Available

Thor All-Fuel Chimney features a double-wall construction with a special spacer to keep the heavy-gauge steel round and properly separated. The inner layer of pipe is made of stainless steel; this helps provide quick warm-up and a strong draft. The pipe units are available in 18-inch and 30-inch lengths, and outside diameters of 10, 11, 12, 14, and 16 inches.

Approximate Retail Price	Approximate Low Price
$20.50 to $95.00	Not Available

Worcester PB-102 Round Chimney Brush, which has a four-wire, 7-gauge spindle twisted on ⅜-inch pipe, makes it easier to clean soot and creosote from chimneys used for both wood and coal fires. The brush filament is 22-gauge-diameter, oil-tempered, black wire. The brush is offered in a variety of sizes, and square and rectangular brushes are also available. All brushes are sold either separately or in a kit with accessories.

Approximate Retail Price	Approximate Low Price
$12.50 to $20.50 (brush only)	Not Available
$43.50 to $45.50 (kit)	Not Available

Prices are accurate at time of printing; subject to manufacturer's change.

Portable Power Tools

QUALITY PORTABLE POWER tools for the consumer—drills, circular and saber saws, sanders, and so on—can vary in price considerably. The reason lies in the competition among power tool manufacturers and among retailers. Fortunately for the consumer, many stores use power tools as "loss leaders" to build customer traffic and volume sales, and you can count on 1982 to be a buyer's market for almost any type of power tool.

If the price of an item is important to you—and it should be—comparison shopping can help you find the bargains. Store ads in your local newspaper can alert you to power tool sales.

Safety Is Important

IT'S DIFFICULT TO judge how safe a product is just by looking at it. A quick way to make a reasonable decision on its worthiness as far as safety is concerned is to look for the Underwriters' Laboratories seal. This organization tests products for safety and the seal indicates that the product has met minimum standards. All of our "Best Buy" portable power tools are UL listed.

One important safety feature you should consider when purchasing power tools is double insulation. A double-insulated power tool has all of its electrical parts covered with two layers of insulation, making electrical shock virtually impossible; the double-insulated tool requires no grounding. If you're considering a tool that isn't double-insulated, make certain it is equipped with a three-wire grounding circuit. This will effectively ground the tool and protect you against electrical shock hazards—provided your home or workshop is equipped with a properly grounded electrical system. Double-insulated tools don't have—or need—a three-wire circuit.

Choose Tools by the Work You Do

SOME "BEST BUY" models in various categories are more versatile than others, and some are designed for heavier work. You must determine whether a light-duty or a heavy-duty model is best for your needs. For example, do you need a light, general-purpose portable drill, or will a heavy-duty model be worth its higher price?

Best Buys '82

THE PORTABLE POWER tools selected as "Best Buys" were chosen on the basis of their performance, ease of operation, and overall value;

they are listed alphabetically by manufacturer. Remember that a "Best Buy" designation only applies to the model listed; it doesn't necessarily apply to other models by the same manufacturer, or to an entire product line.

 **Drills**

A PORTABLE ELECTRIC drill is a basic power tool for any well-stocked household tool kit because it can do so many jobs better, easier, and faster than a hand-operated drill. The most basic models usually run in the $10-to-$20 range; heavy-duty, professional-quality drills are more expensive.

Drill prices often are based on power and capacity. The more capacity—opening of the drill chuck and the amperage of the motor—the more the drill will cost. The chuck size—¼-, ⅜-, and ½-inch—refers to the maximum diameter drill bit or accessory that will fit into the chuck. For example, you can lock a ¼-inch diameter drill into a ⅜- or ½-inch drill chuck, but you can't lock a ⅜- or ½-inch drill bit into a ¼-inch chuck.

For light, utility work, a ¼-inch drill may be suitable for your needs, but it won't handle heavy-duty work for long without serious damage. For general household and workshop use, a good choice is a drill with a ⅜-inch capacity. This tool with accessories, such as wire brushes, paint mixers, hole saws, and grinding stones, should have enough power to handle almost any job you will want it to do.

Drill motors are not usually rated by horsepower; they're rated by amps. To avoid complex conversions, you can assume that the more amps a motor has, the more powerful it is. On quality drills, chuck capacity is matched to motor power.

Drill speed is something to consider carefully. Basic drills have only one speed when you pull the trigger. Other models may have two speeds, controlled by a thumb switch to give you a choice when drilling into soft or hard materials. Finally, there are drills, usually higher-priced models, that have a variable-speed control. For example, you can start a variable-speed drill very slowly for better control. Then, after the bit has penetrated the material and is seated properly, squeezing the trigger farther increases the motor's speed so you can quickly bore the rest of the way into the material. This feature is very important on reversing drills—models that can reverse the direction of drilling—where torque, or turning power, is needed more than speed. Virtually all variable-speed drills have the reversing feature so that, with a special screwdriver accessory, you can withdraw screws as well as drive them.

For drilling situations where there's no available outlet nearby, a cordless electric drill is handy. This type of drill operates from rechargeable batteries. The batteries can be recharged by means of a transformer that is plugged into an ordinary electrical outlet. Cordless drills, however, are somewhat limited in capacity, and the batteries furnish only a short supply of power before they must be recharged.

Black & Decker 1940 is a ⅜-inch cordless drill that can recharge its batteries in one hour. The battery pack is removable from the drill itself for recharging. This drill has a reversing switch for backing out screws and jammed drill bits. A big feature is the motor's shunted brush system that guards against brush failure due to short-term overloading. The 3⅝-pound drill carries a one-year warranty.

Approximate Retail Price	Approximate Low Price
Not Available	$160.00

Black & Decker 7166 VSR electronic speed-controlled drill, which has a ⅜-inch chuck capacity, can drill ¾-inch holes in wood and ⅜-inch holes in metal. An electronic feedback switch automatically increases power to compensate for varying drilling loads. This 3.5-amp variable-speed drill has a reversing switch, and a trigger switch that maintains preselected speeds. It also has a detachable 10-foot power cord that stays flexible in cold weather, and double insulation. It weighs 3.75 pounds and carries a one-year warranty.

Approximate Retail Price	Approximate Low Price
Not Available	$65.00

Sears Craftsman 1142 single-speed drill has a ⅜-inch chuck capacity and a ½-horsepower, 2.2-amp, double-insulated motor. This basic, light-duty tool for drilling small holes is a good-quality household tool that should provide adequate service for most jobs. It weighs 3 pounds, 10 ounces, and carries a one-year warranty.

Approximate Retail Price	Approximate Low Price
$17.00	Not Available

Skil 597 is a 3.2-amp, ⅜-inch, variable-speed drill for heavy-duty jobs. It has a reversing lever and a button to lock a preselected speed. This double-insulated drill is so accurate that you can start holes in metal without first center-punching the material for the drill point. It can bore a ⅜-inch hole in steel; a ¾-inch hole in wood. This tool, which weighs 3¾ pounds, carries a one-year warranty.

Approximate Retail Price	Approximate Low Price
$78.00	$75.00

Wen 2320 is a light-duty ¼-inch drill that operates from a 12-volt battery pack, a car battery (via a cigarette lighter adapter), or 120-volt AC electrical outlet. It has a removable grip so it can be used for precision work in close quarters, double reduction gears, and a self-lubricating motor. The drill comes with chuck key, key holder, battery holder, and cigarette lighter adapter. It weighs about 1¾ pounds and carries a one-year warranty.

Approximate Retail Price	Approximate Low Price
$33.00	$23.00

Prices are accurate at time of printing; subject to manufacturer's change.

Wen PR82 is a 2.6-amp, ⅜-inch, variable-speed drill. You flip a lever to reverse drill rotation. Drill speeds may be preselected and maintained by a lock. Other features include ball thrust and needle bearings and double reduction gears. The drill weighs about three pounds and carries a one-year warranty.

Approximate Retail Price	Approximate Low Price
$38.50	$29.00

 Circular Saws

THROUGH THE USE of high-impact, super-tough plastics, portable electric saw manufacturers have reduced the weight of these power tools considerably, making it easier for the average homeowner to use them accurately.

Like portable electric drills, circular saws should be selected according to the job you plan to do. For example, a 5½-inch saw (the blade is 5½ inches in diameter), will cut through two-inch-thick lumber, but a 7½-inch model can do it easier. For all-around maintenance and home improvement work, your best choice is a 7½-inch circular saw; it lets you cut dimension lumber (2X4s, 2X6s, and so on) in rip, cross, and angle configurations with relative ease and speed. If you're planning a room addition or are going to build a garage, deck, or storage shed, the larger blade is recommended, and so is a higher motor amp rating.

Make sure any portable circular saw you're thinking of buying is equipped with safety blade guards to prevent injury, and either double insulation or a three-wire grounding system. The saw's motor should draw enough amps to handle the blade capacity, or size, and you can determine this by the amp rating on the motor; the more amps, the more powerful the motor. Quality saws are usually designed with the proper amp-to-blade ratio.

Black & Decker 7392 is a 7¼-inch circular saw with a 10-amp, two-horsepower motor; this is enough power to cut through almost any standard building material. The saw has double insulation, metal upper and lower blade guards, two handle surfaces for better control, and an ejection chute that keeps sawdust away from the cutting line. This saw is exceptionally well-balanced for ease of operation. It weighs 10 pounds and carries a one-year warranty.

Approximate Retail Price	Approximate Low Price
Not Available	$70.00

Skil 559 is a heavy-duty 7¼-inch circular saw that will cut 2⅜-inch-thick materials—1⅞ inches at a 45-degree angle. The 10-amp, 2¼-horse-

power saw has double insulation, a sawdust blower to keep the cutting line visible, safety blade guard, and a safety switch to help prevent accidental starts. A special clutch lets the saw blade slip if the blade binds in materials while cutting them; this protects you and the saw. The Model 559 weighs 9⅛ pounds and carries a one-year warranty.

Approximate Retail Price	Approximate Low Price
$75.00	$70.00

Saber Saws

SWITCH ON A saber saw and you'll have a handful of power that can rip, crosscut, miter, bevel, and cut holes in almost any material. Saber saws, also called jigsaws, rank with portable electric drills in usefulness and with circular saws in efficiency.

Possibly the biggest feature of a saber saw is its ability to cut holes—square, rectangular, round, and irregular—without the need for a pilot hole in the material for the blade. After starting the tool, you just ease the blade into the material to start cutting. With a standard blade in its reciprocating mounting, a saber saw can cut through ¾-inch material.

There is a wide variety of saber saw models from which to choose; like drills, they include single-speed, two-speed, and variable-speed saws. Your best choice, however, is a variable-speed saw because it can be started at a slow speed for control on most cuts and then switched into high speed to complete the cuts quickly. Single-speed and two-speed models are fine for most straight-line cutting and miter cuts but aren't as versatile as variable-speed machines.

Quality saber saws have double insulation. As with other power tools, the more amps the motor draws, the more powerful it is.

Black & Decker 7566 is a five-amp, ½-horsepower saber saw whose blade can pivot automatically for intricate cuts and scroll work, or be locked for straight cuts. The reciprocating blade has one-inch stroke for faster cutting and longer blade life with minimum vibration. A sawdust blower keeps the cutting line visible. The variable-speed motor offers speed settings from 1300 to 2800 strokes per minute. A combination rip fence and circle-cutting blade, a scroller, a wood-and-plastic cutting blade, and a chip deflector are included with this double-insulated tool. It weighs 5¾ pounds and carries a one-year warranty.

Approximate Retail Price	Approximate Low Price
Not Available	$115.00

Rockwell 4372 variable-speed saber saw has a motor that develops 4.25 horsepower and draws 3.75 amps. The tool's variable-speed range is 0 to 3800 strokes per minute; it has a ⅝-inch stroke length and a two-inch cutting capacity. This heavy-duty tool can cut accurately through

Prices are accurate at time of printing; subject to manufacturer's change.

plywood and veneered material; a calibrated tilting base permits intricate bevel cutting. The saw also has a scrolling feature that can be locked into four positions. This allows you to run the blade into special designs without moving the base of the saw. The double-insulated saw also has a special shut-off system that provides protection against motor damage that can be caused by worn brushes. The saber saw weighs less than 4.5 pounds and carries a one-year warranty.

Approximate Retail Price	**Approximate Low Price**
$89.50	$74.00

Wen 531 is a variable-speed, four-amp saber saw. Because you can turn the blade instead of the saw to change the direction of the cut, it's ideal for scroll work. The blade locks in four positions so you can make difficult cuts. An extra-large shoe (base) plate adjusts to left or right angles, and moves forward for plunge cuts. The saw comes with two blades, a rip guide, and a circle cutter. This model weighs 5½ pounds and has a one-year warranty.

Approximate Retail Price	**Approximate Low Price**
$55.00	$42.00

 Routers

AMATEUR CABINETMAKERS consider the router a "must" tool for all kinds of wood shaping and joinery. It allows you to make rabbets, dadoes, and dovetails; and you can groove, bevel, cove, chamfer, and make other molding cuts with this tool. It is also the tool to use for trimming plastic laminate on countertops.

The various router and cutting bits are locked in a chucking device called a collet, which is similar to the chuck on a portable electric drill. A ¼-inch collet is standard on routers, but there also are models with ⅜-inch collets. Industrial-type routers may have ½-inch collets.

Router power is almost always measured in amps. The more amps, the more powerful the motor; and the more power it has, the more versatile it will be. In a router, motor speed is important, so try to select a router with a high amp rating. This power is especially important if you plan to work with hardwoods.

The router you select should have a depth adjustment feature that is easily set by twisting the collar on top of the tool or by means of an adjustable collet. Nice to have, but usually extra in cost, is a vacuum attachment to collect flying wood chips. Another worthwhile feature is a router guide attachment, which will pay for itself later by helping you avoid miscuts in costly lumber and cabinet woods.

Router bits can vary widely in price, and the price is based on the pattern of the bit. Your initial choice should include spiral, combination panel, V-groove, straight, single flute, veining, cove, and beading bits.

Prices are accurate at time of printing; subject to manufacturer's change.

Black & Decker 7600 is a lightweight, general-purpose router with a 4.5-amp, ⅝-horsepower motor. It's a good tool for someone just getting started in woodworking and who doesn't require a heavy-duty tool; it's efficient for cutting grooves in wood and trimming plastics. It has a depth gauge that adjusts in ¹⁄₆₄-inch increments; the collet accepts standard ¼-inch bits. The double-insulated router weighs 3⅜ pounds and carries a one-year warranty.

Approximate Retail Price   **Approximate Low Price**
Not Available $33.50

Sears Craftsman 1743 is Sears' top router model. It has a 1½-horsepower motor that is ideal for most routing projects. The tool has a standard ¼-inch collet chuck, a built-in dust collector bag, a work light, and two chip-deflector shields. Depth settings are ¹⁄₆₄-inch increments; a locking trigger switch is in the handle to allow continuous two-hand control. The router weighs about nine pounds and carries a one-year warranty.

Approximate Retail Price   **Approximate Low Price**
$110.00.. Not Available

Wen 1700 router has a four-amp motor and a built-in spindle lock for quick bit changing. The tool uses standard ¼-inch bits. The double-insulated router features a micrometer-type depth adjustment with a calibrated dial in ¹⁄₁₆-inch increments and zeroing adjustment for easy reading. Accessories are optional; they include an edge- and circle-cutting attachment and an assortment of bits. The router weighs less than six pounds and carries a one-year warranty.

Approximate Retail Price   **Approximate Low Price**
$55.50 .... $47.00

Belt and Pad Sanders

SANDING BY HAND is, at best, tedious, and power sanders can save plenty of work as long as you match the sander to the job. Too much power can create more problems than the tool is worth.

Belt sanders use a continuous abrasive belt that turns on rollers around the bottom or bed of the sander. In-line pad sanders move a single sheet of abrasive, attached to the bed of the sander in a straight line back and forth. Orbital pad sanders also have a single sheet of abrasive attached to their bottom, but they move the abrasive in a series of small circles.

Belt sanders are designed to quickly take off large amounts of wood or other material from flat surfaces. Pad sanders—orbital and in-line—are made for fast removal of small amounts of wood or other material from both flat and irregular surfaces. Pad sanders are usually better for

Prices are accurate at time of printing, subject to manufacturer's change.

general wood finishing, furniture refinishing, and household sanding, while belt sanders are better for floor refinishing and rough wood shaping projects.

Of the two types of pad sanders, in-line sanders are better for general sanding work, such as smoothing woodwork during interior decorating, initial sanding of furniture, and auto body sanding. Orbital sanders are "finish" tools, providing a smooth final sanding; you'll need an orbital sander, for example, to prepare the wood before you apply a clear finish.

You can buy sanders that, with a flick of a switch, can be adjusted for either orbital or in-line action. These units cost more than their single-purpose counterparts, but the investment can be worthwhile if you find yourself with a great many different sanding chores to do.

You can frequently substitute a power drill equipped with a sanding disc, wire wheel, or other smoothing and shaping accessories for a belt sander when you have to remove lots of material quickly. But the specially equipped drill cannot match the performance of an orbital sander for final sanding or smoothing.

Compared to other power tools, sanders have few extra features to offer. Exceptions include a vacuum attachment to suck up sawdust and an adjustment switch that can change an in-line sander into an orbital sander. Both features add to the cost of a sander.

If your budget doesn't permit both a belt and a pad sander, your best choice for general sanding projects is an in-line and/or orbital pad sander.

Black & Decker 74-495 Sharp 'n Sand is a drill-powered belt sander that can be driven by most ¼- or ⅜-inch portable electric drills (not supplied). Unlike most "do-all" tools, this device really works and provides satisfactory results. It not only sands, but can also sharpen knives, chisels, and other tools. The sander can be attached to a board for portability or directly to a workbench. There is an optional base (Model 74-496) that also holds a portable drill firmly. The Sharp 'n Sand uses 3- by 24-inch sanding belts. A hose connection for a vacuum cleaner helps keep sawdust under control. The device comes with drill bracket, sharpening guide attachment, and sanding belt. It carries a one-year warranty.

Approximate Retail Price	Approximate Low Price
Not Available	$33.00

Ryobi SU-6200 orbital sander, which has a 2.9-amp motor, features a special cover to protect the tool when it is being used for wet sanding. The sander is double-insulated and well balanced. You can sand flush on three sides of the tools, which also has a lock on the trigger with a quick-release control. The orbital sander uses 4½- by 11-inch sanding paper. It weighs eight pounds and carries a one-year warranty.

Approximate Retail Price	Approximate Low Price
$124.00	Not Available

Skil 593 Sandcat is a lightweight belt sander that operates with the ease of an in-line or orbital sander. The sanding belt rotates at 550 feet per

Prices are accurate at time of printing; subject to manufacturer's change.

minute, which gives you better control than with most belt sanders, but you have to be careful; this tool removes materials very fast. The double-insulated sander, which weighs 4½ pounds, features a locking lever for easy belt removal. The sander, which has a 2.8-amp motor, comes with five 2½- by 16-inch assorted sanding belts.

Approximate Retail Price   **Approximate Low Price**
$60.00 .... $45.00

Wen 310 is an in-line pad sander with a one-amp motor. It can produce a smooth finish quickly. The sander's housing is made of lightweight aluminum. The machine, which uses 3⅝- by 9-inch sandpaper, weighs less than four pounds and has a three-wire grounding plug. It carries a one-year warranty.

Approximate Retail Price   **Approximate Low Price**
$28.50 .... Not Available

 **Planes**

PROFESSIONAL IN CONCEPT and design, the power plane can nonetheless be a valuable asset to a home workshop, especially if you're involved in extensive home remodeling and building projects. With a flick of a switch, you can use a power plane to remove small to large amounts of material quickly and easily from the edges of doors, windows, countertops, paneling, steps, flooring, shutters, and other parts of your home. It is also excellent for trimming plastics and soft aluminum.

For general work, a plane with a blade about two inches wide is a good choice. The length of the sole, or bed, can vary; but the longer the sole the more accurate the cut. A shorter sole, however, lets you operate the tool in tight quarters. If you will be doing lots of heavy cutting and smoothing, a jack plane with its longer sole is recommended. For general-purpose work, a block plane is suitable. The block plane performs well when planing either with or across the grain of wood, and because of its smaller size, it does a good job smoothing rabbet cuts.

Power is an important feature in a power plane; make sure the model you choose has a motor that will generate enough revolutions per minute so the tool won't bind in soft- or hardwoods. Usually, amps are matched to rpms in quality planes, but it doesn't hurt to check this aspect before you make a purchase.

Rockwell 167 professional block plane, which has a 2.5-amp motor, can perform a variety of jobs. The tool has a straight-side design and can plane two-inch dressed stock, and do rabbet cutting or step cuts flush to a 90-degree surface. The double-insulated block plane will handle most cabinetmaking jobs because it offers 1¹³⁄₁₆-inch width of cut at ¹⁄₁₆-inch

Prices are accurate at time of printing; subject to manufacturer's change.

depth increments. It weighs about five pounds and carries a one-year warranty.

Approximate Retail Price
$124.50 .... $103.00

Approximate Low Price

Skil 98 is a 10-amp, three-inch power plane that can handle most home maintenance and improvement projects. Features include center-line balance to help alleviate gouging and uneven cutting; a reversible chip deflector; removable rabbeting guide; a combination edge-and-miter guide that's adjustable from 0 to 45 degrees; and a depth-adjustment guide from 0 to 3/32 inch. The 13½-inch-long plane's replaceable carbide blades are driven by a nonslip cog belt drive that requires no lubrication. It weighs 9½ pounds and comes with a one-year warranty.

Approximate Retail Price
$229.00 .... $198.00

Approximate Low Price

 Nailers

IF YOU FREQUENTLY drive large quantities of small nails, a portable electric nailer can be a real worksaver.

Nailers accept cartridges of panel-type and other nails for light building materials. To operate a nailer, you pull a trigger, and the tool drives the fastener flush or slightly below the surface of the material.

Black & Decker 9720 electric brad nailer can drive 1- and 1¼-inch brad nails accurately. Its V-shaped base lets you get close for nailing in corners and other tight spots. The tool, which has a 10-amp motor, features a quick-release front-end design so you can remove jammed nails quickly without using tools. It loads from the back so that brads may be loaded from any positiion. It has a three-wire grounding cord. The nailer weighs three pounds and carries a one-year warranty.

Approximate Retail Price
Not Available $28.50

Approximate Low Price

Swingline 32001 is an electric nailer that drives and countersinks 18-gauge, 1½32-inch nails, and it's powerful enough to drive nails flush into ¾-inch oak. This 15-amp tool can handle many chores, including hanging paneling, installing weatherstripping and insulation, and assembling building components. The nailer has open-channel loading and an on/off trigger lock; these features let you load the gun quickly without having the tool firing a nail accidentally. It weighs 3 pounds, 2½ ounces and carries a one-year warranty.

Approximate Retail Price
$50.00 .... $40.00

Approximate Low Price

Prices are accurate at time of printing; subject to manufacturer's change.

Lawn and Garden Equipment

FOR MOST AMERICANS, lawn and garden care is strictly a do-it-yourself proposition. Where homeowners may be reluctant to tackle a room addition or a new roofing job, they readily go about cutting the grass or trimming back the weeds.

Expect higher prices during the 1982 lawn and garden season. Inflation is no doubt responsible for part of the price boost, yet a more telling—and commendable—aspect of the increase is a dedication to quality merchandise. Consumers are tiring of one-season throw-away lawn and garden tools. Manufacturers are responding with better—and more expensive—equipment.

Fall or early winter is the best time to purchase power lawn equipment, while retailers are clearing inventory. Be sure to shop several different stores; you may find an unadvertised bargain. And don't be frightened to talk a store manager down on a price. You could be a winner.

Buy Brand-Name Equipment

THE COST FOR quality brand-name equipment is just slightly above that of the no-name brands. Unless you're on a severely restrictive budget, we strongly recommend the brand-name equipment—the only "Best Buys" in this chapter. Our reasons are:

● A full warranty against parts and labor is usually offered. The manufacturer will honor that warranty as long as it's valid—usually a year.

● Replacement parts are readily available even if the warranty has expired.

● Repair shops prefer to work on brand-name equipment because manufacturers standardize their parts. A wider selection of repair shops is also available.

● Expendable components (such as lawnmower blades, nylon string for trimmers, special lubricants for mixing with fuels) are readily available at most home center and hardware stores. Some supermarkets and drug stores even stock them.

● Comparison shopping is possible from store to store. Most stores carry similar brand-name products. Off-brand products are usually available at one store only, making price comparison difficult.

Pay the Price for Power

MAKE SURE YOU get a first-rate engine or motor on the power equipment you buy. This should be your primary buying consideration.

The best of the gasoline-powered lawn equipment engines carry the names Briggs & Stratton, Tecumseh, Clinton, or Kohler. These engines, if properly maintained, will usually outlast the mechanical components they power.

Electric motors seldom carry recognizable name tags. Compare them, consequently, on the basis of their horsepower or amp rating. The more amps, the more power. A 12-amp motor is the equivalent of a 1½- to 2-hp engine. As a rule of thumb, go with more amps. More power, when applied to lawn equipment, usually means better.

Once you've identified the quality engines, you must make a decision between the power sources: electric or gas.

The big advantage of electric lawn equipment is easy starting—in any weather. Electric motors run quieter than their gasoline cousins, and they don't need as much maintenance; just hose and dry the housing after hard use.

Gas engines are more portable, more flexible, and usually more powerful than electric engines. They are more troublesome, however, mechanically—especially if you have to mix your gas with oil. Plan to put your engines on a regular maintenance schedule:

- Change the spark plug every year.
- Before starting the engine, make sure the spark plug wire is clean and tight on the plug.
- Change the points and condenser every two years—or more frequently if the engine is having ignition troubles. These parts are inexpensive and easy to replace. Most are sold in a package, which contains complete installation instructions.
- Change the oil at the start and about half-way through the lawn and garden season. If your lawn area is extremely dusty, change the oil after 10 to 15 hours of use. This averages about once a month.
- Check the oil level before each use.
- Hose down all metal components when used on fertilized soil. Fertilizer causes rust.
- Keep the air filter clean. Most filters are washable in mild household detergent and water. Lightly oil the filter before it is replaced in the machine.
- After the lawn and garden season, change the oil, pour out the gasoline in the tank, and hose down the housing. Wrap the engine with a sheet of plastic while in storage.

Best Buys '82

OUR "BEST BUY" lawn and garden equipment is listed below, alphabetically within each category. These products have been selected on the basis of durability, efficiency, and overall value. Remember that a "Best Buy" designation applies only to the model listed; it doesn't apply to a full product line or to other models made by the same manufacturer.

THERE ARE TWO basic types of power lawn mowers: reel and rotary. It's your job to determine which type best suits your needs. The power mowers recommended in this section are push mowers. Your other choice, of course, is a riding mower, which is covered later in this chapter.

Power reel mowers are simply a powered version of the old-fashioned, dependable, nonpowered push mower. Reel mowers are more complicated mechanically than rotary mowers—they also cost more. Quality reel mowers have five or seven cutting blades. These blades snip the grass like scissors, giving your lawn a "manicured" appearance. You've seen this look on golf courses.

The reel mower is best suited for flat lawn areas with a thin grass, such as Bermuda. If your lawn is hilly or uneven, a reel mower may scalp the ridges. To correct this problem, the cutting height must be adjusted; this can produce an uneven look. The reel mower is, therefore, not a good choice for a rugged terrain.

Besides fine cutting, reel mowers have two big advantages: They generally outlast rotary mowers, and they are safer to use; the blades stop instantly when they hit a hard object. Many modern rotary mowers, however, have built-in safety features, making them as safe as reel mowers.

Rotary mowers are workhorses. If properly powered, they can cut heavy grass and light weed stalks with ease. Prices range from under $100 up to $300 for the push- and self-propelled models.

Rotary mowers are excellent for cutting thick grass, tall grass, high weeds, and even wet grass. For the most part, you can manhandle rotary mowers without damaging them the way you might a reel mower.

If your lawn is about 5,000 square feet, an 18-inch blade is adequate. A 21- or 22-inch blade works efficiently with lawns over 10,000 sq. ft. For small, flat lawns, a 3-hp engine is adequate. For larger areas, choose a 3.5- or 4-hp engine. This engine is suggested for both reel and rotary mowers.

There's a wide selection of features with which you will be confronted when buying a new lawn mower. The most important considerations—the type of mower, the blade size, and the engine size—are listed above. And don't forget considerations of power source (electric or gasoline) and motor quality involved in every lawn and garden tool. Other features that may play a role in your buying decision are:

Mower deck. These are the housings that cover the blades of the mower. They should be narrow enough to be pushed flush against or under obstructions, such as rock borders, fences, edging strips, bushes, shrubs, and retaining walls. Aluminum and magnesium decks, although more costly and fragile than steel decks, are rust-resistant. Steel decks can rust, but they won't crack or break like cast aluminum or magnesium decks.

Blade adjustment. Some expensive mowers have levers that are flipped to raise and lower the blade height. The blades on less expensive mowers may be adjusted by removing the wheels and rebolting them to the desired height.

Exhaust. The engine may be exhausted from the top or bottom of the deck. We suggest purchasing a mower with a top exhaust. A mower exhausted on the bottom, if left running in one spot, could damage the lawn. Reel mowers don't have decks and, therefore, don't present this potential problem.

Mulching feature. A mulching mower is usually a rotary mower with crossed blades. The blades chop the cut grass twice into small particles. A grass catcher isn't needed. The grass must be cut very often, however—usually twice or three times weekly—and the mulchers are difficult to use on thick, high, and wet grass.

Grass catchers. These are available in side or rear mounts. The rear mounts are best because they don't interfere with side obstructions. Fine grass particles may be blown toward you with a rear mount, however. Also important is the material of the catcher. Plastic catchers do not become soggy and sag like fabric bags.

Safety features. Discharge chutes and rear deflectors are standard on most mowers. The chute should be designed so that it deflects downward any objects thrown by the blade; the chute should also have a guard used in conjunction with a grass-catching bag. The rear deflector—usually metal or heavy rubber or plastic—blocks any object thrown backward by the blade.

Although its effect will not be felt until the 1983 season, a federal requirement could add from $10 to $80 (or more) to the price of a mower. The requirement states that lawnmower blades stop within three seconds after the mower operator releases a "deadman's" switch handle. Mower manufacturers are attempting to keep the cost no higher than an additional $20.

Self-propelling capability. You don't have to push these mowers; they push themselves. Self-propelled mowers may have front- or rear-wheel drive. Front-wheel drive is better for flat lawn surfaces; a rear-wheel unit is better for hilly terrains. The model you buy should have an instant-stop clutch device called a "deadman's clutch" in case you slip under the cutting blades. Self-propelled mowers should have at least a 3-hp engine; this both drives the wheels and whirls the cutting blades. Any less power could cause problems, especially over large lawns. A small engine becomes overworked.

Seals of approval. Quality mowers—and other power lawn equipment—usually carry the seal of the Outdoor Power Equipment Institute (OPEI). This assures you that the equipment has been independently tested and that it has met the safety standards set forth by the American National Standards Institute. Quality equipment is also decibel (sound) rated. Be sure to fill out any warranty cards attached to the equipment. Keep your purchase receipts in a safe place for warranty purposes.

Master Cut, Aircap 5578 gasoline-powered rotary mower is self-propelled with seven forward speeds. The 4-hp engine powers a rotary blade that cuts a 22-inch swath through heavy grass and high weeds. Valuable safety features include a hand-held "deadman's" clutch that stops the mower instantly when you let go of it, and a grass chute that closes itself when the clipping bag is removed. Other features are an aluminum deck; a rear grass bagger; and a blade that can be adjusted easily to nine different heights.

Approximate Retail Price	Approximate Low Price
$300.00	Not Available

Sunbeam 3009B electric rotary lawnmower has a powerful 10-amp motor (equivalent in torque to about a 3-hp gas engine) and a 20-inch cutting swath. This makes it a best buy for medium to small lawns. The lightweight mower also features a power-cutoff switch that stops the blade in 2.5 seconds, and a side discharge with a bolt-on chute guard. The fabric catcher bag is an optional buy. The bag, however, is fairly well supported, so wet and heavy grass rides without too much sagging. The mower's deck is made of steel. Cutting height is adjustable only through the wheels; there are no levers on the handle.

Approximate Retail Price	Approximate Low Price
Not Available	$105.00

Yard-Man 15585E is a gas-powered reel mower with six tempered steel blades. The blades cut a neat 18-inch path in lawns seeded with thin-bladed grass. A rear grass catcher is optional. A safety drive clutch on the handle of this self-propelled mower activates its 3-hp engine; a belt chain drive turns the wheels. Outstanding features include a five-position height adjustment, which is operated by a lever on the handle. The handle folds so the mower can be easily stored.

Approximate Retail Price	Approximate Low Price
$415.00	Not Available

Best Buys '82 Riding Mowers

RIDING MOWERS ARE simply vehicles with rotary mowers below the chassis. As a rule of thumb, don't consider a riding mower unless your lawn measures more than 15,000 square feet. Any area less than that would probably be better served by a much less expensive self-propelled reel or rotary mower. Remember, too, that with a riding mower you must almost always have a reel or rotary mower handy to trim the areas where the riding mower can't go.

The biggest mistake many homeowners make is buying a riding mower without ample power. Under average-to-hard use, an under-powered riding mower will be in the repair shop by the end of the season. A small engine simply won't stand up to the weight of the mower, its rider, and its accessories.

A riding mower can be powered by either a gasoline or a diesel engine; horsepower ratings go up to—and at times exceed—30. If you have more than one acre of lawn to cut, buy a rider with a minimum 11-hp engine. A 16-hp unit should be seriously considered. Important features to consider are:

Mower height. If your property is loaded with fences, trees, and other obstructions, buy a riding mower with a low profile; it will make it easier to move around or under these obstructions. The blade height adjustment should be controlled by a lever that can operate quickly according to the grass height. Otherwise, you'll spend lots of time double-cutting and mulching.

Parts changing. You should have convenient access to sparkplugs, batteries, oil dipsticks, air cleaners, grease fittings, and equipment mounting bars.

Flexibility. A good riding mower should do more than cut grass. It should drive optional equipment, such as snow plows, dirt plows, cultivators, and other tools.

Transmission. The mower's transmission should have enough torque (turning power) for the jobs you want the mower to do: cut grass, cultivate, and so on. As a rule of thumb, a low-range transmission will provide maximum torque. A medium-range transmission will provide less torque but more speed. A high-range transmission has some torque but lots of speed. The more high grass and weed stalks you have to contend with, the lower speed you should buy. Many models have four-speed transmissions: three speeds forward plus reverse. Some models have "hydrostatic" drive—a single lever speed control similar to the automatic transmission on cars.

Turning radius. If you have a lot of obstructions, a short turning radius will be important. Make sure the steering wheel is responsive to your touch.

Stability. A riding mower must have good stability on hills and slopes. Wide tires enhance stability—and protect your lawn from the weight of the equipment.

Service contract. These are offered through dealers, not manufacturers. They are hard to find, but they're worth every cent. Most contracts provide for tune-ups and parts replacement at the onset of every mowing season—or twice annually. They also specify repair work for breakdowns. Many contract for a mechanic to work at your home; you don't have to haul the mower to the mechanic.

Niceties. Bonus features (some optional) include a large fuel tank, noise reduction devices, a very slow-speed "creeper" drive, seat safety switch, ampere gauge, maintenance minder, headlights, and hydraulic lift. None of these features affect the functioning of your mower as a mower. Whether they're worth the additional cost is up to you.

Jacobsen RMX 1130 riding mower is powered by an 11-hp gas engine with an electric key start. It has a rear grass catcher attachment that supports a standard trash can. The clippings go directly into this container for easy disposal. Although a bit lightweight for a large lawn (three acres or more), the RMX 1130 cuts a 30½-inch patch with a turning radius of about 30 inches. The cutting height of the blade may be adjusted from 1½ to four inches.

Approximate Retail Price   **Approximate Low Price**
$1,389.00 .... $1,042.00

Jacobsen LTX 11 11-hp rider mower has a dual-speed transmission and a high/low selector that provides three forward speeds and one reverse. This gives you a ground speed selection to meet different cutting requirements. A pivoting front axle levels the mower over uneven terrain. The width of the cut is 42 inches. Other features include a clutch/brake pedal, a flip-up hood for easy access to the engine, a safety seat that stops the mower when you get off the seat, and a low profile for cutting maneuverability. The mower can be easily converted into a snowblower or bulldozer.

Approximate Retail Price   **Approximate Low Price**
$1,999.00 .... $1,499.00

MTD Model 132-628 riding mower uses a twin-blade to provide a 38-inch cut. An 11-hp gas engine operates at three different speeds. Other features worth consideration are a telescoping steering column that adjusts to your height, a hill-holder brake for smooth up hill starts, a five-position cutting height adjustment lever with a memory setting, a reverse-gear cutout switch to prevent operation in reverse with the blades engaged, segment-and-pinion steering, and a short turning radius for easy maneuverability and close-in trimming. The 132-628 carries a one-year warranty.

Approximate Retail Price   **Approximate Low Price**
$1,490.00 .... Not Available

 Garden Tillers

THE MODERN garden tiller takes the work out of turning over the soil. You just steer as the engine powers the blades that turn, chop, and pulverize the ground—usually on the first pass. Some tillers are even convertible into cultivators, log splitters, graders, and snowblowers!

Engine size is crucial. The tiller engine should be at least four horsepower (at least five horsepower if used with an attachment like a log splitter). Generally, the price difference between a model with just adequate power and a tiller with the extra power needed to handle unexpected situations is small enough to make spending a bit more worthwhile.

Look for at least eight tines, a 20-inch tilling width, and fingertip

Prices are accurate at time of printing; subject to manufacturer's change.

controls. The weight of the unit, moreover, should be balanced over the tines for optimum performance. Other niceties, which usually cost extra, include self-sharpening tines, electric start, handles with vertical and horizontal adjustment, and a chain-drive transmission for added power.

Yard-Man 21700 is a front tine gas-powered rotary tiller for the serious gardener. It has a 5-hp engine that will turn over a 26-inch width of soil from six to nine inches deep. The 13-inch-diameter tines are easy to maneuver near walkways, walls, and other vertical obstructions. For balance and ease of operation, the engine is located directly over the working area. A plow, a cultivator, a bulldozer blade (for dirt or snow), and a rake are optional accessories.

Approximate Retail Price
$450.00 ....

Approximate Low Price
Not Available

 Trimmers

TRIMMERS ARE extremely competitive in price; almost any model could be termed a "best buy." The trimmers are either electric, gasoline, or battery (cordless) powered. The power plant drives a spool of nylon line at high speed. This nylon line clips grass and weeds to the desired height.

If your lawn has a lot of overhead projections, choose a trimmer with a low profile so you can get under them. Low-profile models will also trim flush along vertical surfaces, such as fence posts, edging, retaining walls, curbs, etc.

Electric trimmers provide plenty of power for most lawns. The extension cord can get in the way, however. Cordless battery-powered trimmers must be charged. They are efficient, but tend to run low on power quickly. For big jobs—heavy grass and weed areas—a gasoline-powered trimmer is the best buy. More preliminary work is required than with electric motors; the fuel must usually be mixed with oil.

Width-of-cut ranges are from about seven to 16 inches. Weight on most models is evenly balanced; the units are easy to control. Gas units and cordless models, however, are heavier than the straight electric tools. This may be a buymanship consideration.

Trimmers require little maintenance. The gas-powered and cordless models often come with a one-year warranty. The small electric models are so inexpensive that it is easier and cheaper to replace the tool than have it repaired. The nylon line for all models is plentiful, and usually available at drug stores, department stores, gas stations, hardware outlets, and home centers.

Black & Decker 8255 Command Feed electric grass/weed trimmer operates from a 4.3-amp motor and cuts a 12-inch swath. Its big feature

Prices are accurate at time of printing; subject to manufacturer's change.

is a line regulator that keeps the line at a maximum length for better cutting efficiency. You advance the line with your thumb. The tool is ideal for large lawns where high grass and weeds dominate.

Approximate Retail Price	Approximate Low Price
Not Available	$70.00

Homelite ST-120 String Trimmer has a 20-inch cutting swath on an engine that's located next to the ground, not your head, when in use. The unit has an automatic string advance system; a comfort strap is also included to help you balance the trimmer. It features a vibration isolater to help reduce vibration. The ST-120 can also be used as a blower. In this mode, the tool delivers up to a 100-mph wind velocity. It carries a one-year warranty.

Approximate Retail Price	Approximate Low Price
$170.00	$127.50

Homelite ST-20 String Trimmer is powered by a 2.2-amp electric motor that spins 10-inches of monofilament line at one time. The trimmer has an automatic string advancing system; the unit weighs just 3½ pounds. It's a good lightweight tool for small jobs. You can use it for edging as well as trimming. It carries a one-year warranty.

Approximate Retail Price	Approximate Low Price
$35.00	Not Available

Weed Eater 307 electric trimmer is an inexpensive electric tool with a 1.6-amp motor that gives enough power for light lawn trimming. It has a manual line advance, and the line can be changed or rewound with little effort. The line cuts an eight-inch path; the cutting head can be turned so you can use the trimmer as an edger around walkways and shrubs.

Approximate Retail Price	Approximate Low Price
$20.00	Not Available

Weed Eater XR-50 is a gas-powered, two-cycle trimmer for large lawns. The tool makes a 17-inch cut, and you advance the trim line by tapping the bottom of the spool on the ground. A big feature is the XR-50's solid-state ignition that provides quick and easy starts. The XR-50 accepts attachments for conversion to power hoe, bladed edger, and power snow shovel.

Approximate Retail Price	Approximate Low Price
$150.00	Not Available

 Powered Lawn Edgers

THERE ARE TWO types of lawn edgers: electric- and gasoline-powered. The electric models are less expensive than the gas units.

Prices are accurate at time of printing; subject to manufacturer's change.

However, the gas units are more flexible—you are not restricted by a power cord.

Buy plenty of power. The difference in price between a lightweight unit and a large-capacity unit is just a few dollars. The deeper the cut, the more powerful the engine or motor should be. For comparison, a nine-inch cutting blade should have a 12-amp engine/motor capacity. If the blade is six inches or less, a 4-amp electric motor is sufficient.

Some grass trimmers may be converted into edgers. However, the trimmers do not cut out the roots of the grass, so the edging process must be repeated every time you cut the lawn.

Other quality features include fingertip controls, an adjustable front wheel, and blades that can be easily removed for sharpening. If you go for a trimmer/edger, make sure the wheel attachments turn properly so the conversion to an edger from a trimmer is easy.

Black & Decker 8215 is a true edging tool. It has a 4.3-amp electric motor, which is enough power to drive the 6½-inch cutting blade. The blade makes a ⅝-inch-wide trench along walks, driveways, patios, etc. The 8215 has a friction clutch that stops the power if the blades hit a hard obstruction. The blade is easy to clean and change, and replacement blades are readily available.

Approximate Retail Price	Approximate Low Price
Not Available	$60.00

Weed Eater 509 is really a trimmer, but it can also be used as an edger. The tool is powered by a 4-amp motor; the cutting line advances when the spool is tapped against the ground. As a trimmer, it has a 16-inch cutting capacity.

Approximate Retail Price	Approximate Low Price
$60.00	Not Available

Best Buys 82 Powered Hedge Clippers

THESE LAWN TOOLS—like edgers—are electric- or gas-powered. The emphasis is on power, since the clipper must have the capacity to handle both thick and thin weed stalks, limbs, and branches.

Clipper's blades should be at least 13-inches long. Quality features include double insulation against electrical shock, a friction clutch for motor and blade protection, and double-edged blades.

Include with your purchase a pair of gloves and safety glasses. You'll need both when trimming overhead and pulling cut twigs and branches from trees, bushes, and shrubs.

Black & Decker Model 8118 is an electric clipper designed for light to medium cutting. It has a 2.2-amp motor. The 13-inch cutting blades

Prices are accurate at time of printing; subject to manufacturer's change.

travel at 3000 strokes per minute and cut in any direction the tool is turned. A friction clutch protects the blades and motor against burnout. The tool weighs 4½ pounds.

Approximate Retail Price   **Approximate Low Price**
Not Available $45.00

Echo HC-200 hedge clipper has a 30-inch cutting blade powered by a gasoline engine. If you have lots of hedge to trim, the HC-200 will handle the job with ease. The unit weighs less than 12 pounds, and is well-balanced. The engine has electronic ignition and an automatic rewind starter.

Approximate Retail Price   **Approximate Low Price**
$220.00 ....Not Available

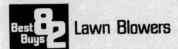 Lawn Blowers

CAPABLE OF GENERATING wind velocities up to more than 100 mph, lawn blowers can clear an area of leaves, grass, snow, dirt, and other debris very quickly.

The units are powered by gasoline or electricity and have an adjustable "wind tube" through which the wind is channeled. Both types of blowers are well-balanced, although the gas models weigh slightly more than the electrics. The gas models will go in places the electric power cord can't reach, and this flexibility may be a consideration. Other than flexibility, both models do an efficient job according to their individual power ratings. The more power, the more wind.

Black & Decker 8420 Super Sweep electric air blower handles leaves, grass, dust, and debris. Its six-amp motor generates air flow of more than 200 cubic feet per minute. Other features include a trigger lock-on switch, variable speed control, and double-insulation. The Super Sweep's weight is a balanced eight pounds.

Approximate Retail Price   **Approximate Low Price**
Not Available $49.50

Homelite Model HB-280 blower can generate up to 200 miles per hour (245 cubic feet per minute) of wind velocity. This gas-powered blower has fingertip controls and weighs only 11 pounds. It will easily handle most leaf, grass, and dust removal projects. It carries a one-year warranty.

Approximate Retail Price   **Approximate Low Price**
$190.00 ....Not Available

Prices are accurate at time of printing; subject to manufacturer's change.

MTD Multi-Vac Model 242-685 is a self-propelled, five-horsepower tool that combines a vacuum, blower, hose vacuum, and shredder in one tool. You can use it for clearing lawns and pavement, cleaning out gutters and between shrubs, and as a blower for quick yard cleanup. Other features include a safety-grip drive clutch lever, dual-pinion rear-wheel drive, 12-inch rear wheels, a five-inch front caster for maneuverability, and a six-position adjustable nozzle height. The unit clears a 30-inch-wide swath across almost any surface. The unit carries a one-year warranty.

Approximate Retail Price   Approximate Low Price
$589.00 .... Not Available

 Chain Saws

THE BEST ALL-AROUND chain saw has a 12- to 16-inch chain bar. Smaller units are satisfactory for light cutting—especially tree trimming, heavy shrubs, and small diameter logs.

Besides capacity, you also have a choice of power: an electric- or gas-powered motor. An extension cord limits the electric saw's travel; the gas model may be taken anywhere. If you have a small amount of wood to cut and distance is not a problem, the electric saw is a good buy. It is powerful enough to chew through most hard and soft woods. Electric motors are also quiet. If you have a large amount of wood to cut and you have to travel to the wood source, the gas saw is the better buy. An engine in the two-horsepower range (maximum developed) or the 3.3-cubic-inch range will give you plenty of wood-cutting authority; an electric motor in the 12-amp range matches this engine rating.

With either saw, remember that the wood must be supported off the ground for cutting. If it isn't off the ground, the chain bar will dig into the earth and immediately cause serious operating problems—often requiring the replacement of the entire cutting bar.

Quality features to consider include an automatic oiling and chain sharpening device built into the saw. Also make sure the saw has safety features, such as double insulation (electric), a nose guard on the chain's leading edge, and a chain break bar to protect your hands. The chainbreak prevents kickback by instantly stopping the chain movement when the saw hits a hard knot or other obstruction. Solid-state ignition and vibration isolation are two more features worth the price. Also consider the weight of the saw; a weight under 10 pounds is a plus feature for most homeowner lumberjacks.

Accessories to buy with the saw are a chain sharpening kit, even though the saw may have an automatic sharpener; a carrying case to protect the saw (usually included with quality saws); an extra chain; chain lubricant; an extra sparkplug for gas saws; a sawhorse or similar device to position logs for cutting. It's also nice to have a cutting wedge.

Prices are accurate at time of printing; subject to manufacturer's change.

Homelite 240 chain saw has a 2.4-cubic-inch engine, automatic chain oiling, and solid-state ignition. There is a choice of three chain bar sizes: 14, 16, or 18 inches. This chain saw, with handguard and an anti-kickback device to protect the operator and the tool, can handle most log-cutting jobs with ease, because the guide bars are designed to reduce friction and increase cutting speed and power. The Model 240 has a tank that holds 14.7 ounces of fuel; the saw weighs 9.7 pounds and carries a one-year warranty.

Approximate Retail Price	Approximate Low Price
$240.00 (14")	Not Available
$250.00 (16")	Not Available
$270.00 (18")	Not Available

Homelite 330 is a heavy-duty chain saw that has a 3.3-cubic-inch engine that drives a ⅜-inch pitch chain. The saw can accept gas-weld or sprocket-nose guidebars 16 to 24 inches long. Other features include an antikickback device to protect the operator and the tool; a chain catcher; automatic chain oiling; solid-state ignition; and vibration isolation. The fuel capacity of the Model 330 is 16 ounces. The saw weighs 12.5 pounds and carries a one-year warranty.

Approximate Retail Price	Approximate Low Price
$345.00	$330.00

McCulloch 110 chain saw has a 10-inch bar driven by a 2.0-cubic-inch engine. It can handle logs up to 20 inches in diameter, which is ample for most cutting jobs. Features include automatic and manual chain bar oiling, a throttle latch, and an all-position carburetor that permits the saw to operate in any cutting position. An antikickback system includes a low kickback chain, a chain catcher, and a chain brake/handguard that stops a moving chain in milliseconds. The Model MAC 110 also has a muffler shield and a safety trigger. It weighs 10.1 pounds.

Approximate Retail Price	Approximate Low Price
$90.00	$77.50

Wen 2600 is an electric chain saw that compares well in almost every feature with quality gasoline-powered units. The Model 2600 Wasp has a 12-amp motor that delivers 5600 rpm's on 120 volts AC; this is more than enough power to cut most fireplace and stove logs. Other features include a 16-inch reversible bar; an automatic oiler with manual override; oil-level indicator; chrome chain that minimizes kickback; in-line grip arrangement; adjustable clutch; and double-insulation. It weighs less than 10 pounds.

Approximate Retail Price	Approximate Low Price
$98.00	$80.00

Prices are accurate at time of printing; subject to manufacturer's change.

Snow Removal Equipment

T HE WEATHER DURING the past two winters hasn't been favorable for manufacturers of snow removal equipment. Therefore, consumers should be able to find some bargains this winter, especially in heavier, large-capacity machines.

How to Select Snow Removal Equipment

THE SELECTION OF snow removal equipment—like lawnmowers—begins with determining the area you want to clear of snow and the type of snow that is typical in your area. For example, if you live in a townhouse or garden apartment and must do your own snow removal, a small power snow shovel may be all you need. If you own an average-size home, a walk-behind snow thrower may be the answer, especially if the walks and driveway are of average length and width, and the snowfall is generally light and powdery. If snow is often extremely wet and dense, more powerful snow removal equipment will be required.

For small jobs such as snow removal from porches, decks, steps, and short walkways, light-duty power snow shovels or brooms are adequate. This kind of equipment works best when the snow is light and fluffy. It starts to bog down when the snow is wet and heavy, although such machines can remove heavier snow if you have the time to spend working the equipment. Usually, snow brooms and shovels are powered by an electric motor; the more amps the motor draws, the more powerful the motor is. However, you should regard this type of equipment as suitable for light-duty work.

One-stage snow throwers have an auger that directly throws or pushes snow to one side. They have the capacity to clean a 20-inch-wide path with one or two passes on the average. Usually, these machines have a 3- or 3.5-horsepower gasoline engine.

Two-stage snow throwers have an auger that drives the snow into an impeller, which then throws it out. They have the capacity to handle 24- to 28-inch-wide paths on the average. The gasoline engines for these machines vary in size from 5 to 10 horsepower—or more. As a rule, the engine is matched to the machine's capacity. It's best to buy a machine with enough power to handle the snow that's typical for your area.

Features on snow removal equipment that you should look for include an electric starter to get the machine running on cold days; a rotating discharge chute, or spout; a slow vehicle speed (too much speed can cause snow to jam in the throwing mechanism); a belt-driven power train that can withstand the shock of ice and other obstructions; reverse gears; and adjustable skid shoes. The skid shoes should be adjustable from ground level to about 1½ inches for clearing over unpaved areas.

For large-model snow throwers that can clean a 32-inch or wider path, buy one with at least a 10-horsepower engine. A model with less power just won't handle the capacity. Larger snow throwers should also have a limited slip differential and a two-stage auger system that can remove packed as well as loose snow. Many of the larger models have five forward speeds, a reverse gear, and augers that provide a shearing action when they come in contact with a hard obstruction.

If you own a riding lawnmower or lawn tractor, chances are you can purchase snow removal accessories for it. Don't overlook an electric starter for the machine if it doesn't already have one. This investment can save you hours of time and plenty of grief.

Other accessories for riding mowers or tractors include snow removal blades and rotary brushes. Blades are recommended when prevailing snows are generally light, fall infrequently, and melt rapidly. Brush attachments are limited to light, powdery snow that can be whisked away. In fact, a regular lawn blower may be adequate to handle such light snow, especially if you can team it with a snow shovel.

No matter what kind of power snow removal equipment you buy, service is extremely important. Most quality products have at least a one-year warranty. Before purchasing any equipment, find out where it can be serviced in your area—especially after the warranty expires.

When you go shopping for snow removal equipment, keep in mind that brand-name merchandise usually carries a warranty and can usually be serviced locally. It is also more likely that replacement parts for the equipment will be available at a variety of service centers.

Best Buys '82

OUR "BEST BUY" snow removal equipment follows; products are listed alphabetically. Remember that a "Best Buy" designation applies only to the model listed; it doesn't necessarily apply to other models made by the same manufacturer, or to an entire product line.

 Snow Removal Equipment

Atlas 15-3220 snow thrower, which can clear a 22-inch path, is a sensible buy if the snow in your area is generally light. Its three-horsepower gasoline engine, however, is under-powered for heavy snow. Outstanding features are this one-stage machine's lift handle and light weight; you can get on top of drifts and into hard-to-reach spots without difficulty. The push-type machine has a 180-degree swiveling snow chute and an adjustable top deflector. It has semi-pneumatic tires and a 1½-quart fuel capacity. An electric starter is optional. It comes with a one-year warranty.

Approximate Retail Price **Approximate Low Price**
$245.00 .... $200.00

Jacobsen Imperial 626 is among the best in Jacobsen's line of two-stage snow throwers. It has all the features needed for heavy snow removal. The collector/impeller is driven by a heavy-duty worm gear with a six-horsepower gasoline engine. The machine has four forward speeds and reverse. The controls are in-line for easy operation; the traction and collector/impeller operate independently. Other features include a one-gallon fuel capacity; primer; hand-crank discharge chute that moves 200 degrees; adjustable skids; and large pneumatic tires. An electric starter and tire chains are optional. The machine comes with a one-year warranty.

Approximate Retail Price **Approximate Low Price**
$800.00 .... $669.00

Sunbeam 2240 Snow Champ is an electric snow thrower that can clear an 18-inch-wide path. This machine features a weatherproof motor that exceeds the high load torque of a three-horsepower gasoline engine, a 180-degree swivel chute, flanged metal front wheels, and six-inch solid-rubber rear tires. There is a quick safety release bar that automatically stops the auger. The UL-listed snow thrower weighs 53 pounds. A 100-foot, three-wire, marine-type extension cord (Model 2003) is an extra-cost option. The Model 2240 carries a one-year warranty.

Approximate Retail Price **Approximate Low Price**
Not Available $225.00

Toro Power Shovel is designed for removing light snow along decks, steps, porches, and narrow walks. The electrically powered machine is limited to 12-inch-wide passes; you can use it for fairly heavy snow loads if you work slowly. The shovel's rotor, powered by a 6.6 amp motor, throws snow about 10 feet. The Toro Power Shovel, which weighs less than 12 pounds, is double-insulated and has a key lock. A gear drive provides positive - power transmission. It comes with a one-year warranty.

Approximate Retail Price **Approximate Low Price**
$100.00 .... $89.00

Weed Eater 6000 power snow shovel, which has a 28cc two-cycle gasoline engine, can clean a 12-inch path of snow quickly and easily. The machine even works satisfactorily on wet and heavy snow, provided you don't force it. The Weed Eater Model 6000 is lightweight, compact, and well-balanced. This unit, with a recoil starter, consists of a "power head" and snow shovel accessory. Other optional attachments include a string grass trimmer, power edger, and power hoe. The unit comes with a 90-day warranty.

Approximate Retail Price **Approximate Low Price**
$245.00 .... $200.00

Prices are accurate at time of printing; subject to manufacturer's change.

Personal Care Appliances

AMERICAN CONSUMERS spend a lot of time and money making themselves look good. No matter what the need, the chances are very good that there's a personal care product designed to make the task easier and faster. At least that's what the manufacturers of these products would like you to believe.

In most cases, personal care appliances do make a given job easier. Long hairstyles on men probably never would have become popular if blow dryers weren't available, and many of today's popular hair styles for women would not be easy to care for—or even possible—without the array of products aimed at saving time and effort.

The difficulty many consumers encounter in selecting personal care products stems from their very nature; they are personal and have been designed and packaged to play on this fact. Before you buy any personal care item, think carefully. Don't buy it on impulse. There may be another product that can serve your needs better or do more than one task.

Performance Is Your First Consideration

IF A PRODUCT doesn't perform, it's not worth having no matter how it looks. Performance should be your first consideration, and performance varies from brand to brand.

If possible, try the product in the store before you buy it; many stores have demonstration models. At the very least, insist on holding the product. If it seems awkward or difficult to handle, chances are you won't get the use and performance you expect.

If the appliance is one you must lift and hold high to use, such as a hair dryer or curling iron, be sure it isn't too heavy for you. Check the product to see if it has a solid handle and sturdy construction. If it's flimsy when new, it won't stand up to everyday use. Will the appliance be easy to store in your bathroom or bedroom? If you travel, can the product be easily packed in your luggage? Is it compact? Does it fold?

Virtually every product comes with a warranty, usually lasting a one-year period. Check the warranty for any variations.

Safety Is Important

ALMOST ANY PRODUCT sold today is safe when used as intended. Start your buying on the right foot by making sure any electrical appliance you purchase has the Underwriters' Laboratories seal. This independent organization tests products to see that they meet minimum standards.

Occasionally, a defect in a product is discovered after it has been on the market. For this reason, it's important for you to register your product purchase with the manufacturer by sending in the card that comes with the appliance. This card enables the manufacturer to notify you in case of a product recall and it also establishes a purchase date for warranty purposes.

Of course, no product is safe unless it is used with care and common sense. Never operate an electric appliance while you are in the tub, and keep them out of reach of small children. If you find it necessary to use an extension cord with your appliance, use a heavy-duty one; a light-duty cord could heat up and become dangerous if used with an appliance that draws a great deal of current.

Most importantly, read the instructions before you operate your new appliance. No matter how much you believe you know about how the device is supposed to work, it never hurts to review the instructions for every appliance you buy.

Shop for the Lowest Price

WHEN BUYING a personal care appliance, it's always smart to comparison-shop even when you think you know what you want. Discount and drug stores usually have the lowest prices. If you can postpone your purchase, watch for advertised specials. Manufacturers often sponsor sales or offer special rebates that can save you money. Department stores usually have a larger selection, but they generally ask more money because they can offer more service, including advice on which product will specifically suit your needs.

Best Buys '82

OUR "BEST BUY" and "Also Recommended" personal care appliances follow; they are listed alphabetically within each category. These products have been chosen on the basis of their usefulness, construction, and overall value. Remember that a "Best Buy" designation applies only to the model listed; it doesn't necessarily apply to others made by the same manufacturer, or to an entire product line.

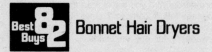

Bonnet Hair Dryers

BONNET HAIR DRYERS come in two basic types: hood and cap. The cap-type bonnet dryer has a soft bonnet that resembles a shower cap with an adjustable band. A flexible hose connects the motor unit to the cap. The advantage of this type of hair dryer is that you can set your hair and dry it, as in a beauty parlor, but you don't have to sit in one position while your hair dries; you can move around to do other tasks with such portable units, and you're only restricted by the length of power cord. Soft-bonnet dryers are also portable enough to take along on trips.

A hood-type hair dryer also allows you to dry your hair after it's set, but you must remain sitting in one place under the dryer. However, this type of dryer usually dries your hair more efficiently and quickly than a cap-type dryer. Air is circulated throughout the hood, which is more efficient than having it reach your hair through just the small connecting hose of a cap-type dryer. Hood units are more expensive than the cap dryers, but do a more professional job.

General Electric HD-21 is a portable cap-type hair dryer that is extremely quiet in operation. The 400-watt dryer has three heat settings, and a cool setting for drying hair on hot days. The flexible bonnet will fit over even jumbo rollers. The Model HD-21, which has a luggage-style round travel case, comes in a beige color with white trim; the case is white. It carries a one-year warranty.

Approximate Retail Price	Approximate Low Price
$38.00	$26.50

Sunbeam 51-28 is a hood-type hair dryer with a built-in heat control. Five heat settings and up to 1400 watts of drying power give you enough flexibility to handle almost any hairstyle. The oversized hood lets you use the dryer with a full head of large rollers. The height of the hood's drying arm is adjustable. The beige-and-white hood covers the brown base to form a compact case. It carries a one-year warranty.

Approximate Retail Price	Approximate Low Price
$65.50	$40.00

 Blow Dryers

---

BLOW DRYERS ARE extremely popular, and so many of them are on the market that it's difficult to select the better values.

When shopping for a blow dryer, you should consider its balance, its size, and its wattage. Most pistol-type blow dryers draw from 900 to 1500 watts. High-wattage dryers may not necessarily be better, depending on what type of hair you have and how you use your blow dryer. Those who prefer to take more time styling their hair with a brush while drying usually don't want a great deal of high-wattage heat.

The dryer should have at least two speeds to allow you to control the air flow over the hot coils of the appliance. And because how you dry

Prices are accurate at time of printing; subject to manufacturer's change.

your hair depends not just on the amount of heat, but on how much air is blown, two speeds give you more versatility.

The trend has been toward smaller, more compact models with high power. But there are also big units that can do small jobs, such as large-area soft drying or concentrated spot drying.

Clairol MD-1 "1 for the Road" is a mini pistol-type dryer that delivers up to 1200 watts of drying power. It folds for travel and has dual-voltage capability (120/240 volts) for overseas use. It has a folding handle that can be adjusted so it can be used as a stand, allowing two-handed styling and drying. You can set this dryer for full power, for styling at 650 watts, or for shaping at 300 watts. A snap-on concentrator for the nozzle works well. The dryer weighs 12 ounces, making it easy to handle and pack in luggage. It carries a one-year warranty.

Approximate Retail Price	Approximate Low Price
$31.00	$18.00

Clairol MPD-1 Shoot the Breeze is compact and lightweight, but powerful. This 1200-watt pistol-grip unit has four settings—low (200 watts), medium (400 watts), medium-hot (600 watts), and hot (1200 watts). We found the medium setting best for drying and the low setting best for careful styling. Control switches are located on the side of a comfortably contoured handle. You can adjust the dryer for high or low air flow. This easy-to-use model comes with a hang-up hook and a concentrator for the nozzle. It carries a one-year warranty.

Approximate Retail Price	Approximate Low Price
$22.00	$16.50

Conair 083 Pro 1200 is a professional-type pistol-grip dryer with enough power—1200 watts—to do a quick drying job. Its two temperatures and two speed settings give you some flexibility. The switches for on/off and temperature (600 or 1200 watts) are conveniently located on the left side of the handle. A unit designed and constructed to last, the Pro 1200 is well-balanced and not too heavy for convenient use. It comes with a hanger clip and nozzle. It carries a one-year warranty.

Approximate Retail Price	Approximate Low Price
$18.00	$12.00

Conair 125F Vagabond is a compact folding hair dryer with 1250 watts of power. It has dual voltage (120/240 volts) so it can be used overseas. This appliance is a top performer that's tough and reliable. Controls are on the front of the handle. There are three heat and three speed settings. The handle can be adjusted to serve as a stand, allowing two-handed styling. A concentrator nozzle is included. The dryer carries a one-year warranty.

Approximate Retail Price	Approximate Low Price
$20.00	$12.00

General Electric PRO5 Power Pro is a 1200-watt pistol-grip dryer with four heat positions and two speeds for six settings. The controls are mounted in the handle. The Power Pro comes with a concentrator nozzle for spot-drying. There is also a hang-up ring on the handle. A nice touch is a separate stand that allows hands-free drying and styling. The dryer carries a one-year warranty.

Approximate Retail Price	Approximate Low Price
$21.00	$14.50

General Electric PRO12 Compact 1200 Go pistol-grip dryer is more than compact—it's lightweight and powerful. This 1200-watt dryer folds into a hand-sized package for storage or travel. You can adjust either heat or air flow to a high or low setting; controls are in the handle. This 12½-ounce dryer performs well and can be used effectively. Although the handle may be a bit uncomfortable for some users, the blow dryer's foldability makes up for it. It comes with a nozzle concentrator and a one-year warranty.

Approximate Retail Price	Approximate Low Price
$24.00	$17.00

Gillette Promax 1500 is a large dryer that packs 1500 watts of power to do a tough drying job. It has independent heat and speed controls; there are four heat settings and two speeds for flexibility. This is an especially good model for styling and drying because its 6- by 6½-inch size makes it easy to handle. It has a nozzle concentrator for spot drying and a hang-up ring. The dryer carries a one-year warranty.

Approximate Retail Price	Approximate Low Price
$21.00	$15.00

Norelco Pistol Gotcha Gun 1200 is a compact model that delivers 1200 watts of drying power. You can set it on high for drying and low for styling. It measures only five inches in length and 2⅛ inches in width. The dryer weighs 11 ounces, making it easy to use; it also has good balance. This dryer carries a one-year warranty.

Approximate Retail Price	Approximate Low Price
$15.00	Not Available

Also Recommended

Clairol IR-1 Kindness is a 500-watt quartz dryer designed for curly hair. The product provides gentle heat and air flow to dry hair without disturbing curls. It has two heat settings and a good grip design. It's both compact and lightweight, and carries a one-year warranty.

Approximate Retail Price	Approximate Low Price
$37.00	$21.50

Sunbeam 52-421 Reversible 1200 is a 1200-watt blow dryer that's designed to handle some of today's special drying needs. One side of the dryer concentrates on drying. The other, with the heated air flowing the other way, delivers more generalized, softer drying for, say, curly hair; it's not as good at this, though, as Clairol's new quartz dryer. This Sunbeam has two heat settings and two air speeds. A selector switch

Prices are accurate at time of printing; subject to manufacturer's change.

adapts the dryer to 120 volts for domestic use or 240 volts for overseas travel. It's a combination product that gives up a little performance on each count to be able to do both jobs. It carries a one-year warranty.

Approximate Retail Price　　　　　　　**Approximate Low Price**
$33.00 .... $23.00

 Brush/Comb Styling Dryers

BRUSH/COMB STYLING dryers work like pistol-type hair dryers, but have comb and brush attachments so that you can style your hair while you're drying. Like blow dryers, styling dryers are available in a range of wattages, and dryers with higher wattages may not necessarily be advantageous.

When shopping, you should consider the design of the styling dryer. Some have smaller handles than others, and some have a rectangular shape—about the size of a paperback book—and are bulkier. Hold one of each kind and see which style suits you.

Styling dryers have various types of attachments. Check to see just what is included with the model you're considering; one unit may have a particular attachment that would be more useful to you.

Clairol Dry Guy CH-1 dryer lets you put 1000 watts to work styling or drying. A slide switch on the yellow and black unit lets you dry at full power, style at 600 watts, or shape at 250 watts. The dryer features dual voltage (120/240 volts), so you can use it overseas. It comes with a hang-up loop in the handle, which is one of the most comfortable ones around. Snap-in accessories include a fine comb, a coarse comb, and a curved styling brush. It carries a one-year warranty.

Approximate Retail Price　　　　　　　**Approximate Low Price**
$30.00 .... $18.00

General Electric SD10 Compact 1100 styling dryer comes with two attachments—a wide-tooth comb and a styling brush. This 1100-watt model has three settings—one for full-powered drying and two for styling and grooming. The appliance is comfortable to hold and easy to maneuver. The best part about it is its compact size, which makes it ideal for travel. It carries a one-year warranty.

Approximate Retail Price　　　　　　　**Approximate Low Price**
$22.00 .... $15.00

Gillette Supermax Styler 1200 gives you three drying choices—1200 watts for speed drying, 650 watts for good drying/styling, and 300 watts for excellent styling control. This dryer, which weighs just over 12 ounces, is well-balanced, making it easy to hold. It comes with brush and

Prices are accurate at time of printing; subject to manufacturer's change.

comb attachments, which are easily put on and removed. This dryer features dual-voltage capabilities (120/240 volts) for domestic and overseas use. It has a one-year warranty.

Approximate Retail Price   **Approximate Low Price**
$28.00 .... $19.00

 Heated Styling Brushes

ONE OF THE most useful of the recently developed personal care appliances is the heated styling brush. It's a cross between a curling iron and a hand brush, and it works on much the same principle as a curling iron. The difference is that the brush makes it easier for you to style your hair.

When you choose a styling brush, look for a model that features a tip that doesn't get hot. On some models, there is a curl release mechanism that allows the brush to rotate freely; this helps prevent hair from getting tangled, and eventually torn. Most heated styling brushes feature a power cord that swivels as you turn the appliance; this prevents the cord from getting twisted.

Clairol CB-4 Steam Crazy brush comes with two interchangeable sets of soft bristles—one for short hair and one for long. This appliance's gentle steam mist is designed to give you long-lasting curls. A release button allows the brush to rotate freely. It has a cool tip for safe, comfortable handling, and it comes with a swivel cord and ready-light. It has dual-voltage (120/240 volts) capability and can be used overseas. It carries a one-year warranty.

Approximate Retail Price   **Approximate Low Price**
$26.00 .... $14.00

Conair CB50 Hair Handler is a half-round heated brush for men or women. It shapes, smooths, and helps straighten hair. It has a ready-light, an on/off light, a swivel cord, and an on/off switch in the handle, and is as easy to use as a normal hairbrush. There's no release button to rotate the brush, but this product has dual voltage (120/240 volts) for domestic and overseas use. The Hair Handler carries a one-year warranty.

Approximate Retail Price   **Approximate Low Price**
$13.00 .... $9.00

General Electric HCB2 Style 'n Go II comes with two barrels to let you shape and curl in two different ways—a ¾-inch barrel is designed for a soft and wavy curl; a ½-inch barrel is made for tight curls. This allows family members with different hairstyles to use the same styling brush.

Prices are accurate at time of printing; subject to manufacturer's change.

The Style 'n Go II has a ready-light, a cool tip, and a comfortable handle, but doesn't have a rotating brush feature. It comes with a one-year warranty.

Approximate Retail Price   **Approximate Low Price**
$18.00 .... $11.00

Norelco HB-1640 Curly Plus styling brush will curl, wave, and straighten hair. It's one of the easiest heated styling brushes to use, because it has a swivel cord and a release button to allow the brush to rotate freely; it has a cool tip and a comfortable handle. The Curly Plus can also be used for mist-styling. Its dual voltage (120/240 volts) lets you use it overseas. It weighs eight ounces and carries a one-year warranty.

Approximate Retail Price   **Approximate Low Price**
$15.00 .... $10.50

Norelco HB-1650 Hot Brush + Comb hairstyler is unusual because it has a half-round design and removable bristles to let you custom-style your hair. It comes with a comb/pick accessory for finishing touches. Like the Conair CB50, this appliance has no rotating brush. It also has a ready-light and dual voltage (120/240 volts) for use overseas. The HB-1650 weighs 6½ ounces and carries a one-year warranty.

Approximate Retail Price   **Approximate Low Price**
$15.00 .... $10.50

 # Electric Setters/Rollers

MANY PEOPLE WHO curl their hair prefer electric rollers, because rollers can create a more lasting set than a curling iron. There are a number of factors to consider before buying a set of electric rollers.

First, how many rollers of each size do you need? If you wear tight curls, you'll want a set of electric rollers with as many small rollers as possible. A good set should meet your current needs and handle future ones, too. Look at the type of clips included for securing the hair to the rollers. Some are easier to remove than others, depending on your hair length.

Finally, examine the shape of the roller teeth. The size and shape of the roller "bristles" largely determine how well the roller holds your hair—and how easily your hair can get tangled on the roller. Taking some time to study a personal care appliance before you buy it will keep you from being disappointed.

Clairol K-400S Kindness is the best hairsetter available—and the most versatile. You can mist-set with conditioner, mist-set with water, or dry-set. The Kindness comes with 20 tangle-free rollers that are sized for

Prices are accurate at time of printing; subject to manufacturer's change.

flexibility—six jumbo, 10 large, and four small. The hairsetter has a built-in compartment for storing cord, clips, and accessories, plus a convenient ready-light and an on-off switch. The K-400S is clearly the easiest hairsetter to use, the most convenient, and best all-around unit for in-the-home hairsetting. The 350-watt appliance, which comes with a six-ounce bottle of conditioner, carries a one-year warranty.

Approximate Retail Price   **Approximate Low Price**
$52.00 .... $30.00

Clairol KT-8 Set-A-Way is a small unit designed for on-the-go use and ideal for traveling. It will go anywhere, even overseas, because it has dual voltage (120/240 volts). It comes in a storage case that's small enough to pack easily. This 350-watt appliance can heat rollers in about 1½ minutes on four roller posts; ready-light indicates when rollers are fully heated. This model comes with four medium and four large rollers, and a set of easy-to-use plastic clips. It carries a one-year warranty.

Approximate Retail Price   **Approximate Low Price**
$40.00 .... $24.00

General Electric HCD-4 hairsetter is a compact 400-watt unit that's large enough to do most setting jobs. It has a good assortment of rollers; there are six large, 10 medium, and four small ones, and any of the sizes will fit on any of the heat posts. You can buy extra rollers to fit your styling needs. You can set your hair dry or with a conditioner, and you can control the hairsetter's heat to suit your needs. While this model's performance is better than most, it falls a little short of the "Best Buy" Clairol K-400S. This GE model has a one-year warranty.

Approximate Retail Price   **Approximate Low Price**
$32.00 .... $23.00

 Electric Curling Irons

CURLING IRONS COME in two basic types: steam and dry. Some people feel that steam helps keep the curl firm, while others prefer to use a dry iron. Whichever type you choose, the end of the curling iron should be heat-resistant in case the appliance brushes against something it could burn. For maximum safety, look for a curling iron with a stand or rest, either separate or built-in. A swivel cord is useful, too; it prevents tangles in the cord that can reduce maneuverability when setting, and allows the curling iron to rest on a flat surface without spinning.

    Another kind of curling iron doesn't have a cord. Instead, it plugs directly into the wall. This type of iron usually needs to be reheated more often than one with a cord, so if you need more than a little curling, this type may not be too practical.

Prices are accurate at time of printing; subject to manufacturer's change.

Clairol 200Z Crazy Curl produces curls almost as fast as you handle the unit. In about 10 seconds—with or without steam—you can get a curl. A nonstick barrel coating and a cool tip make this 40-watt styling iron easy to use. It features a see-through water reservoir cap, a built-in heel rest, a ready-light, and an on/off light. It also has a swivel cord and dual voltage (120/240 volts) for domestic and overseas use. The appliance carries a one-year warranty.

Approximate Retail Price   **Approximate Low Price**
$16.50 .... $11.00

Clairol C-100Z Crazy Baby is a compact, 40-watt styling curler that's only nine inches long. You can use it with or without steam. Dual voltage (120/240 volts) lets you take it overseas. We liked its heel rest, swivel cord, nonstick barrel, ready-light, and on/off light. The Crazy Baby has a cool tip and a clear plastic heat shield that allows you to store it while it's still warm. Its handle design and light weight make it easy to use. This appliance carries a one-year warranty.

Approximate Retail Price   **Approximate Low Price**
$22.00 .... $14.00

General Electric CS-1 Touch 'n Curl comes with a waving comb attachment. You can set a high or low temperature by means of a switch on the handle. A mist activator is combined with the curl release button. This 40-watt appliance also has a swivel cord, a nonstick barrel and clamp, heel rest, and an indicator light. It's a handy, easy-to-maneuver unit that comes with a one-year warranty.

Approximate Retail Price   **Approximate Low Price**
$14.00 .... $10.00

Sunbeam 54-199 Pro-Stick III curler and styler is versatile because it comes with two different size chrome-plated barrels (⅝ inch and ½ inch) and a brush. It has two heat settings, a ready-light, a swivel cord, and a heel rest, and stores neatly in a vinyl storage case. This is the "best of the best" for the real home beauty expert. It will cost you more, but it does more and does it very well. The appliance carries a one-year warranty.

Approximate Retail Price   **Approximate Low Price**
$23.00 .... $15.00

 **Shavers**

ELECTRIC SHAVERS ARE in a period of redesign, which comes every four or five years. Currently, shavers using new rotary technology and those designed for special facial needs are popular.

Prices are accurate at time of printing; subject to manufacturer's change.

Shavers are available in both cord and cordless styles, and some work both ways. Be sure to check the voltage range on the shaver you buy. If you travel to foreign countries, you'll want a model that has a converter.

There is a difference between men's and women's electric shavers, because shaving a face is different than shaving a leg. A face is softer and needs to be treated with gentler action; legs require closeness without razor burn. Virtually all shavers come with either replaceable heads or blades.

A recent development is the electric shaver designed for the beards of black men. These have a comb or brush to lift whiskers before cutting, and then blunt-cut the whiskers to avoid ingrown hair problems, a chronic problem for black males; conventional shavers cut whiskers at an angle.

The shape of your face or legs, and how much you shave, determine what type of shaving head is most suitable for you. Shavers come with flat, curved, or rotary heads. All types work well, and you should select the type that works and feels best for you.

Norelco HP-1141 Black Pro Rotary Razor is a well-designed shaver for black men. It should shave close without creating razor bumps. It's a three-head unit with a special "Bump Brush" covering its head. This special head has hundreds of hair-raising loops to brush up whiskers, lifting them out of ingrown pockets for cutting. Its 36 blades are self-sharpening. This model has dual-voltage capability (120/240 volts), a pop-out trimmer, a coil cord, and a travel case. It carries a one-year warranty.

Approximate Retail Price	Approximate Low Price
Not Available	$39.00

Norelco HP-1601 Rotatract, a cord model, has proven itself an even better unit than Norelco's successful Tripleheader razor. Four years of development went into this new Twin Action Shaving System razor. It has 45 retractable "lifters" and 45 self-sharpening steel cutters that work together to provide close, comfortable shaves. The Rotatract has nine closeness settings, a pop-out sideburn and moustache trimmer, and a thumb-controlled on/off switch. This shaver has a sleek, streamlined shape that makes it easier to handle than previous Norelco designs. It comes in a travel case. A rechargeable version is available, Model HP-1318. The HP-1601 carries a one-year warranty.

Approximate Retail Price	Approximate Low Price
Not Available	$43.50

Norelco HP-2127 Ladybug, which is light enough to use with comfort and ease, gives a close shave. This model has a break-resistant housing and a pop-off dual-action shaving head for easy cleaning. It lives up to the Norelco tradition of a quality shaver. The Ladybug, in white and blue, comes in a travel case and carries a one-year warranty.

Approximate Retail Price	Approximate Low Price
Not Available	$21.50

Prices are accurate at time of printing; subject to manufacturer's change.

Remington PM-850 Triplehead cord shaver is a top-quality unit at an excellent price. It has a triple straight head. This model is a great starter shaver for a young man, but also handles tough beards well. Replacement heads are available. The rechargeable version is Model PM-950. The PM-850 carries a one-year warranty on parts.

Approximate Retail Price	Approximate Low Price
Not Available	$18.50

Sunbeam 75-449 SRX has 12 self-sharpening stainless steel blades in two six-blade clusters in a thin shaving head. The pop-up trimmer for sideburns and moustaches is more efficient than most. The compact size of this cord model makes it easy to handle and use. It comes in a travel case and carries a one-year warranty. The rechargeable version is Model 75-469.

Approximate Retail Prices	Approximate Low Prices
$64.00 (75-449)	$39.00
$80.00 (75-469)	$62.00

Sunbeam 76-123 Rascal is a long-handled electric razor with a built-in light and a five-position adjustable cutting head. This slimline unit shaves close and has an open-edge chrome clipper for longer hair. The cord and shaver store in a vanity case with a see-through cover. The shaver has a pushbutton head release for easy cleaning. This model comes in gold; Model 76-122 comes in lime green. Both carry a one-year warranty.

Approximate Retail Price	Approximate Low Price
$32.00	$20.00

 **Irons**

VIRTUALLY EVERY HOME in the United States that has electricity has an iron—proof that permanent-press fabrics have not yet done away with the need for all ironing. More of today's ironing, however, is for touch-up purposes. Irons are available in a wide range of prices; all heat, but some do more.

All irons have a range of temperatures for different types of fabrics, but make sure you can read the range easily on the iron you plan to buy.

A steam feature is standard on most models. An extra shot of steam is available on some irons, although the usefulness of that feature depends on the type of clothes you iron. A self-cleaning system is recommended if the iron you choose uses tap water for steam. The self-cleaning system clears the steam passages and prevents lint and mineral deposits from clogging the steam vents.

Before choosing a new iron, hold it in your hand; get a feel for it. Weight and size can make an important difference in how fast and how

Prices are accurate at time of printing; subject to manufacturer's change.

comfortably you can take care of your ironing chores. However, most irons sold today are light in weight and do quite well on modern fabrics. Weight doesn't necessarily affect performance.

Finally, for safety's sake, check to see that the iron has a wide heel rest or extended bar for stability. A spring or some other device for keeping the cord away from the iron is another good feature.

General Electric F201WH Light 'N Easy Compact is a lightweight 700-watt iron; it weighs 1.6 pounds. It is also one of the easiest units to hold and use, due to its well-designed contoured handle. It has a good heel rest, a spray feature, a water window, a polished aluminum soleplate, and good steam distribution. The heat control setting is on the side. This model, which comes in textured white, carries a one-year warranty.

Approximate Retail Price	Approximate Low Price
$28.00	$19.00

General Electric F340AL Light 'N Easy Self-Clean II iron has all you need for clothing care, including an extra shot of steam (surge) to remove stubborn wrinkles. You get instant spray, steam surge, steam, or dry ironing performance in one of the easiest-to-handle irons on the market. This 1100-watt GE model comes in a beige color and has a polished aluminum soleplate. There is a heel bar for stability and cord storage. The iron weighs 2.6 pounds and carries a one-year warranty.

Approximate Retail Price	Approximate Low Price
$43.00	$30.00

Proctor-Silex I400W Lady Light is a spray, steam, and dry iron with a pulsing self-cleaning action to clean steam vents. The controls are efficient for today's fabrics. It has a plastic easy-fill water reservoir with a water-level indicator; the soleplate has a polished aluminum finish. The heel rest is another good feature. There also is a reversible power cord; it can be connected to either side of the iron for convenience. This 1200-watt model comes in white with brown trim. It weighs 2 pounds, 14 ounces. Model I401W is a version with a nonstick coated soleplate. The I400W carries a one-year warranty.

Approximate Retail Price	Approximate Low Price
$55.00	$34.00

Sunbeam 710-46 Vista X-Iron is a compact 950-watt model for easy ironing; it's good for both home use and traveling. You can get a shot of steam at the touch of a button, so the iron can also be used as a hand steamer. This iron is self-cleaning, with controls on top and a fabric guide. It comes in beige with brown trim, and carries a one-year warranty. The iron weighs 2.5 pounds.

Approximate Retail Price	Approximate Low Price
$28.00	$20.00

Prices are accurate at time of printing; subject to manufacturer's change.

Floor Care Appliances

KEEPING A HOME or apartment clean doesn't have to be the back-breaking or hands-and-knees drudgery it used to be. The variety of vacuum cleaners and other floor care products available can't eliminate all the work, but these products can go a long way to take the break out of your back and keep you on your feet.

Today's consumer has a wide choice of vacuum cleaners designed to handle almost any cleaning problem in the home. Unfortunately, no single machine excels at all cleaning chores or performs effectively on every kind of floor covering or situation.

The variety of floor care appliances available can be confusing. However, they can be arranged into two basic types and one crossover, or combination, type. The two basics are upright and canister vacuum cleaners. The combination is a power-head canister machine.

The upright is the more popular type of machine and better for general rug cleaning because its beater bar/brush gets up embedded dirt and grit from the highest pile carpet. Due to its lower suction, it doesn't perform as well as a canister on non-carpeted floors, and its track record is mediocre at best for above-the-floor tasks, such as dusting draperies, upholstered furniture, or lamp shades.

The canister was developed to compensate for the shortcomings of uprights. With a streamlined body that can resemble anything from a flying saucer to a fat cigar, the canister is quieter than an upright and does a fine job of cleaning bare floors and low-pile carpeting. The nozzle's low profile permits access under furniture, into tight corners, and on stair treads where the cumbersome upright cannot go or else will go only with difficulty. With its easy-to-change attachment nozzles, the canister can be used effectively to remove dust from walls and lamp shades. Because it lacks the beat bar/brush of the upright, however, the canister can't remove dirt that sifts down into carpet pile.

The combination power-head canister vacuum cleaner combines the best features of upright and standard canister types. It has a tank, hose, and nozzle like a canister, but the nozzle has its own motor that drives a beater bar/brush much as an upright does. The power-head nozzle deep-cleans carpets as well as a standard upright does, while the canister aspects of the machine allow thorough cleaning of bare floors and above-the-floor materials. The drawback of the combination is price. These units carry high price tags. In addition, many power-head models have as much difficulty getting under low furniture as do standard upright vacuum cleaners.

Match Type to Needs

EVALUATE YOUR CLEANING problems before going out to buy a vacuum cleaner. Do you have more bare floors than carpeting? Do you have rugs with different pile heights? Do you have carpeted stairs? Do you have many curtains and draperies that need to be vacuumed regularly? Do you have pets who shed frequently and abundantly? Is your home large? Do you have plenty of storage space? Your answers to these questions—plus a careful look at your budget—should help you decide which type of vacuum cleaner will be the best for your home.

Other varieties of floor-cleaning products, such as shop vacs or stick/broom vacs, can fulfill special needs. Sometimes your best answer may be to buy two or more products, matching the most efficient product to a specific chore. For example, if your home is carpeted throughout, an upright vacuum cleaner would be a good choice. But if you also have a lot of above-the-floor cleaning, a lighter, more portable vacuum might be a good addition.

What About Power?

WHEN YOU LOOK at vacuum cleaners and specialty floor care products, you'll find horsepower ratings, water lift ratings, air power ratings, and revolutions per minute. You may even see phrases like "working suction power." While these things can mean something to technically qualified people, they can also be misleading. On the surface, a lot of technical terms can lead the consumer to believe that more power and bigger numbers are always better.

The best way to decide about a product's performance is through observation. And the best observation takes place in your home. If that isn't practical, a store demonstration is next best as long as you try to match your home situation as closely as possible.

Product Demonstrations Can Be Misleading

DEMONSTRATIONS CAN be somewhat akin to carnival come-ons. In general, product demonstrations are geared to show a product's best points—not necessarily its overall performance.

Have your ever seen a demonstration in which a salesperson used a vacuum to pick up a heavy item, like an iron, to show how powerful its suction was? This is impressive, but it's not very practical or meaningful. Working suction against the rug or carpeting is what measures true cleaning efficiency. Similarly, picking up a mess of filmy cotton fiber or fine powder can also be impressive, but not much suction is required to pick up these materials.

Another favorite demonstration tactic is to use the new vacuum cleaner after you've run your old machine over an area. The bag of the new cleaner is then emptied to show you how much more it picked up. Usually what has been done is that the new machine was run over the area a lot longer; perhaps conversation was used to conceal the extra time factor.

You can get the best idea of a vacuum cleaner's efficiency by testing it on gritty granular materials like sand or salt; these are tough substances to pick up. After running the machine over this material, examine the rug pile and see if the substance was actually picked up or simply pushed into the carpet.

Other Points to Ponder

THE FOLLOWING ARE some additional points to consider when considering various vacuum cleaners:

- On vacuum cleaners, the dust bag should be large enough to avoid frequent changes. Changing the bag should also be easy. Check bag costs, which can be considerable, especially for smaller sizes.
- Noise is a consideration, but one that's difficult to judge without a home demonstration. Also, quiet machines haven't sold too well in the past because noise is associated with power; most good machines have a fairly high, but tolerable, noise level.
- Operation should be convenient. The machine should be easy to move and light enough to handle. Switches and controls should be easy to use and easy to reach.

Other features can add value, but they also add cost. Many of these features don't really add to the performance of a machine. Some that deserve special note include bag-full indicators that can help you avoid declining performance as the bag gets full. Automatic cord reels are nice, but they can malfunction if not treated gently, and they add substantial cost. Settings for high or low suction can be a plus if you need your cleaner for items like draperies; carpet-height adjustments are also a good feature. An edge-cleaning feature on an upright model is a valuable extra, but it's less critical on power-head canister machines because you can accomplish this task with a hose attachment.

Warranty coverage varies, from a year on labor and parts to up to five years on some parts. Because most floor care products are carry-in items, you should check on where you can get the machine serviced; usually there's a listing of service centers in the instruction manual.

Safety is important with any electrical product. Products tested by Underwriters' Laboratories assure you that the items meet minimum safety standards. All "Best Buy" and "Also Recommended" products in this book are UL listed.

Best Buys '82

OUR "BEST BUY" selections follow. They are arranged alphabetically into the following categories: uprights, canisters, power-head canisters, multipurpose/system vacs, shampooers/polishers/buffers, stick/broom vacs, wet/dry and shop vacs, carpet sweepers. All of these appliances have been selected on the basis of convenience, performance, and overall value. Remember that a "Best Buy" designation refers only to the model listed, and doesn't necessarily apply to other models by the same manufacturer, or to an entire product line.

AN UPRIGHT VACUUM cleaner is your best choice if your floors are mostly covered by carpeting. A good upright combines suction with the agitating action of a beater bar/brush to pick up embedded gritty dirt and dust, which goes into a bag—usually disposable—attached to the handle. The dust bag should be roomy and easy to remove. The unit should remain stable no matter what position its handle is in.

An upright cleans through a cleaning head, which is part of the frame covering the motor, fan, and beater bar. The cleaning head, or nozzle, should be at least 11 inches wide and adjust to different types of carpet pile, either manually or automatically. Thick brushes should extend to both ends of the rotating beater bar; some models have replaceable brush strips.

Design features on uprights that will improve convenience are wide wheels, a contoured hand grip, a handle that's at a convenient height and isn't too heavy, and an on/off switch located within easy reach. Other features you'll find include wide furniture guards around the cleaning head—a good idea—and a headlight, which is nice, but not necessary; because of vibration and shock, lights tend to last only a short time. An automatic cord reel can be a nice feature.

Some uprights are self-propelled, which is an expensive option. But it also makes for a great deal of ease during cleaning.

Electrolux 1451E is a big, powerful machine that's backed by a two-year parts and labor warranty. It has a very large dust bag that will keep you from emptying it frequently. The machine's housing is made of high-impact plastic, and it has built-in carrying handles because it's somewhat heavy. For a large, non-self-propelled machine, it moves easily on large rollers. This model has a 25-foot cord, a convenient cord wrap recess, seven manual carpet-height settings, and a signal to tell you when the bag needs changing. The top-loading bag compartment allows you to change bags without any mess. The pushbutton controls at the top of the bag compartment are fairly well located. If the beater brush jams, the machine stops; and if you forget to install a bag, the machine won't start. This model has adequate bumper protection, but its real strength is performance. Optional accessories are available.

Approximate Retail Price   **Approximate Low Price**
$295.00 .... Not Available

Eureka 1458 is a powerful vacuum cleaner that has a special all-steel, 12½-inch beater bar that pulses to loosen dirt through vibration. It has a four-amp motor, and there is a six-position pile control, which adjusts height for regular pile—low, normal, high—or shag—low, medium, deep. This machine offers edge-cleaning on both sides, and handles

Prices are accurate at time of printing; subject to manufacturer's change.

easily. Its profile is low enough so it can get under most furniture, and the bag is large enough to last for some time without frequent changing. A six-piece set of cleaning tools is an extra-cost option.

Approximate Retail Price   **Approximate Low Price**
$130.00 .... $89.00

Eureka 5060 is a one-speed, self-propelled vacuum cleaner with plenty of suction power. This is a deep-cleaning machine with a nickel-chrome-plated beater bar and a variable sliding-scale pile adjustment that ranges from a low setting to deep shag. The nozzle is 12½ inches wide. This model also has a 30-foot cord, a headlight, about a 10-quart bag, and a heavy-duty 6.7-amp motor. The three-position handle has a comfortable grip. This machine, which has a wide vinyl furniture guard around the motor hood, offers edge-cleaning capability on both sides. The self-propelling switch locks in a manual position so you can easily move the machine from one room to another. A nine-piece set of cleaning tools (Model 2677) is an extra-cost option. This Eureka weighs 18 pounds, and carries a five-year warranty on the base.

Approximate Retail Price   **Approximate Low Price**
$290.00 .... $200.00

Hoover U3101 Concept One is the best—and the most expensive—model in the Hoover line. It's a full-featured vacuum cleaner with self-propelled power; it can also be used manually. The machine's nozzle automatically adjusts to the height of most carpets, and it has special settings for plushes and deep shags. This 21.6-pound machine moves effortlessly on big wheels, a nice feature if you choose to use it without the self-propelling action. This model has a two-speed switch, a three-position handle, an 11½-inch-wide beater brush, a 16-quart bag, twin headlights, and an automatic cord reel. The cleaner comes with a nine-piece set of cleaning tools. (U3901). This is a powerful 5.6-amp unit.

Approximate Retail Price   **Approximate Low Price**
$330.00.. $220.00

Hoover U4203 Concept One is similar to the "Best Buy" Hoover Model U3101, but this model doesn't have the higher-priced machine's extra features and frills. The Model U4203 has a 4.1-amp motor, which is slightly less powerful than the Model U3101. It has the same pile adjustment system and 16-quart bag capacity, but lacks a headlight, automatic cord reel, and self-propelling action. In addition, a set of cleaning tools is an extra-cost option. Model U4203 weighs 18 pounds.

Approximate Retail Price   **Approximate Low Price**
$190.00 .... $140.00

Panasonic MC-662 is a powerful, lightweight upright cleaner with a 600-watt motor and a nine-quart bag. The 12-inch-wide nozzle automatically adjusts itself to the proper height for the best cleaning. This model comes equipped with a headlight, a three-position handle, a 23-foot cord, a rigid bag housing that won't split or tear, and a bag-full indicator. It is one of the easiest machines to maneuver; it weighs only 13.2

Prices are accurate at time of printing; subject to manufacturer's change.

pounds. A five- or eight-piece set of cleaning tools is an extra-cost option.

Approximate Retail Price **Approximate Low Price**
$160.00.. Not Available

Sears Kenmore 20G3174C is a moderately priced vacuum cleaner that has two speeds, a 12½-inch-wide nozzle, eight pile settings, and edge-cleaning on both sides. This well-built and reliable model also has a headlight, a 17-quart bag, a vinyl bag-holder, and a 25-foot cord. The three-position handle has an easy-to-use on/off switch. The machine weighs less than 15 pounds. A set of cleaning tools is an extra-cost option.

Approximate Retail Price **Approximate Low Price**
$128.00.. Not Available

 Canister Vacuum Cleaners

A CANISTER VACUUM cleaner is a versatile, highly maneuverable machine. It operates through suction and a variety of attachments. Both the bag and the motor are contained in a housing, or canister, that can be square, round, or in the form of a long, tubelike tank. These machines work best on general bare-floor cleaning and on above-the-floor cleaning such as draperies and upholstery. They work well on lighter surface dirt, dust, and cobwebs. Because canister machines offer flexibility, they are a popular choice for consumers who want just one cleaning appliance.

Canisters come with a hose and a variety of attachments. The hose should be rugged, yet flexible. Attachments may include a rug tool (a swivel head with a brush or comb); a bare-floor tool (it usually has a swivel head and fixed brush); an upholstery tool (it may have a plate or trim to keep fabric from being sucked in); a dusting brush (it is often round with long, soft bristles); and a crevice tool (a long, narrow tool for cracks, edges, and similar difficult-to-reach places). The wands that connect to the hose should connect easily and tightly; those made of plated metal are best.

The canister itself should be easy to move and have a wide bumper, or furniture guard, where it may hit walls or furniture. Because canisters are often used for above-the-floor cleaning, a unit with two levels of suction is a good idea. Another good feature is a foot-operated on/off switch. Other features to consider include a bag-full indicator, a re-movable tool caddy, and an automatic cord reel.

Electrolux 1453 is a good-quality vacuum cleaner that should perform well for years. It doesn't have a lot of frills, but the features it does have are among the best. This tank-type canister model has a rocker-type

Prices are accurate at time of printing; subject to manufacturer's change.

on/off switch and a built-in carrying handle. The attachments are also among the best available; they include an upholstery/dust brush, a combination rug-and-floor brush, a crevice tool, and a hose with suction control. The wands fit together tightly without air loss. This machine also has a triple-lined, large-capacity bag. An automatic cord winder is an extra-cost option.

Approximate Retail Price
$379.00 .... Not Available
Approximate Low Price

Eureka 3330 is an all-steel canister machine with an on/off toe switch. Its motor develops a maximum of two horsepower, and it has an edge-and-corner cleaner on both sides of its carpet nozzle. Other attachments include a crevice tool, a dust brush, an upholstery nozzle, and a floor-and-wall brush. The wands are made of plated metal. This powerful unit rolls well on its front swivel wheel and large rear wheels. It has a large bag, a vinyl wrap-around furniture guard, and a 20-foot cord.

Approximate Retail Price
$110.00 .... $77.00
Approximate Low Price

Hoover S3187 Celebrity QS is a round canister cleaner with a 9.3-amp motor, a 14-quart bag, and selective suction—you can dial for right, left, or full-width nozzle suction. There is an automatic cord rewinder and a pedal-operated on/off switch. The machine also has a lift-off tool holder that stores a full set of attachments. The floor nozzle has two wheels, which makes it one of the easiest nozzles to use. This vacuum cleaner is also one of the easiest machines to pull around, and it's among the quietest available that offers plenty of power for tough jobs.

Approximate Retail Price
$155.00 .... $105.00
Approximate Low Price

Sears Kenmore 20G2942C is a well-built economy machine that will do a basic cleaning job well. It has a rocker-type on/off switch, a six-quart disposable filter bag, and 20-foot cord. This machine has a two-horsepower motor. Attachments include a rug-and-floor nozzle, an upholstery brush, a dust brush, and a crevice tool. Because it's an economy unit, it has polyethylene hose and wands. The attachments store on the top of the vacuum cleaner, which weighs 15 pounds.

Approximate Retail Price
$68.00 .... Not Available
Approximate Low Price

 Power-Head Canister Vacuum Cleaners

IN RECENT YEARS, manufacturers have brought part of the ability of the upright vacuum cleaner to the canister machine. This has been

Prices are accurate at time of printing; subject to manufacturer's change.

accomplished by adding a power head—a second motor and a beater assembly—that attaches to the canister's hose. This combination gives you considerable flexibility. The power head adds deep-cleaning capability to the basic canister suction cleaning. You also have the same above-the-floor capability. This added capability, however, doesn't come cheap; power-head canister cleaners are expensive machines.

This type of vacuum cleaner uses the same basic attachments as a standard canister; it also has the same type of feature options. However, there is one area that you should pay special attention to on power-head canister vacuum cleaners—the hose-to-wand connection. Running inside the wand and hose is a power cord to bring electricity to the power head's motor. To operate trouble-free, the wand and hose must fit together tightly.

Eureka 1743 is a two-motor canister machine that offers a complete home-cleaning system. It has a headlight, edge-cleaning on both sides of the power head, and the largest bag Eureka makes. Attachments, which store on the canister, include an upholstery brush, a dust brush, a crevice tool, and a floor-and-wall brush. The power head, which is four inches high, can get under almost any piece of furniture. The machine is constructed of steel and designed for long life; the attachments are made of plastic. It handles easily and has a foot-pedal on/off switch.

Approximate Retail Price   **Approximate Low Price**
$240.00 .... $170.00

Panasonic MC-881 has a 12-inch-wide power-head nozzle that automatically adjusts to any carpet pile height; it also offers efficient edge-cleaning. There are pushbutton controls to select any of four suction power levels. This model has a 750-watt motor, a nine-quart bag, an automatic cord reel, and a bag-full indicator. We like the fact that the eight-piece set of cleaning tools stores inside the canister. Large wheels make this machine easy to maneuver. It weighs 11.7 pounds without the power head.

Approximate Retail Price   **Approximate Low Price**
$200.00 .... Not Available

Sears Kenmore 20G2198L is one of the better power-head models available from Sears. The power head has a 12⅝-inch-wide beater-bar/brush that features brush-edge cleaning. There is a 6.6-quart bag, a two-speed 3.5-horsepower motor, a 20-foot auto-rewind cord, and a wide on/off pedal that we found to be among the most convenient we've seen. The unit weighs approximately 33 pounds. A suction control gives you the right power setting for drapes and upholstery, and a toe-adjustable height setting lets you select one of four settings for carpet pile. The two locking wands are made of chrome-plated steel. A set of cleaning tools stores on top of the canister.

Approximate Retail Price   **Approximate Low Price**
$270.00 .... Not Available

Prices are accurate at time of printing; subject to manufacturer's change.

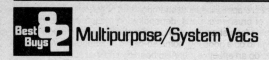

IF YOU'RE LOOKING for one cleaning machine that does just about everything—normal vacuuming, shampooing or steam-cleaning, wet or dry pickup, and above-the-floor cleaning—you want a multipurpose , or system, vacuum cleaner.

There seems to be a trend toward such cleaning machines, which are available in upright and canister versions, but system vacs can be very expensive. Generally, they do a pretty good overall job, but like most combination types of cleaning machines, they usually give up some performance on some jobs.

If you think your needs are best served by one machine that does virtually everything, investigate a multipurpose, or system, vacuum cleaner very carefully to see if its usefulness is worth the high cost.

Douglas 8001 Hydro-Flow Home Cleaning Center can handle most cleaning needs in your home. It's a wet/dry vac with a three-gallon wet capacity. This canister-type cleaner comes with a power-head attachment to give you upright capability. It has a steam-cleaning action that allows you to clean deep, but dry fast. This model's big feature is its steam-type extraction cleaning system, which works on a principle similar to commercial and rental-type units; it's exceptionally efficient at recovering the dirty cleaning liquid. This multipurpose machine gives up a little performance on standard vacuuming, but not enough to detract from its overall performance. It comes with a variety of attachments, including four 1¼-inch wands, a six-foot hose, and a seven-piece set of cleaning tools; there is an 18-foot cord. This machine weighs less than 35 pounds.

Approximate Retail Price	Approximate Low Price
$330.00	Not Available

 Shampooers/Polishers/Buffers

THIS CATEGORY CONTAINS floor care appliances that shampoo or polish and buff—or do both of these jobs. Most do both.

Grouped here are units whose basic purpose is shampooing or polishing. There also are multipurpose units available that include these functions as a feature. For such appliances, however, refer to the "Multipurpose/System Vacs" category.

Prices are accurate at time of printing; subject to manufacturer's change.

Most floor care appliances that shampoo and polish will accept one of several sets of brushes or pads, depending on the job you want to do. When shopping for a shampooer and/or polisher, look for a model that's sturdy enough to do a good job; some so-called shampooers are just too lightweight to do an effective job. Also bear in mind that such appliances generally don't see frequent use, so you should weigh the cost-against-use factor carefully before making a purchase.

Bissell 3054-0 is a shampooer-only machine that relies on a back-and-forth brush action rather than a circular motion to shampoo carpets. It's designed to lift, comb, and fluff the carpet nap. It foam-cleans carpets, which it does effectively. There is a 72-ounce shampoo tank that is removable for easy filling. The shampooer weighs 17 pounds.

Approximate Retail Price   **Approximate Low Price**
$105.00 .... Not Available

Hoover F4143 is a good-quality shampooer and polisher with a 1.7-amp motor. It scrubs, waxes, polishes, and buffs floors, and shampoos carpets—all well. The accessory package includes shampoo brushes, multipurpose brushes, buffing pads, and cleaning-and-waxing pads. It has a trigger control in the handle that is easy to use. There is a four-quart tank.

Approximate Retail Price   **Approximate Low Price**
$80.00 .... $55.00

 Stick/Broom Vacs

---

STICK/BROOM VACS are slim upright vacuum cleaners designed for quick, light-duty cleaning chores. Because they have limited suction power, they generally pick up only surface dirt, but they're ideal for cleaning hard-to-get-at areas like stairs.

Some models offer two-speed operation, which allows them to be used for additional cleaning tasks like upholstery. Some models also come with different head attachments for a variety of chores. In recent years, a few models with powered nozzles have appeared. These are supposed to be more capable of handling standard household cleaning jobs, but we have found them to be somewhat borderline for this role.

Stick/broom vacs can be ideal "pantry partners," because they require little storage space; usually they can be stored on a closet hook. This keeps them handy for cleaning entranceways or kitchens, where surface dirt and other debris collect regularly.

Bissell 3045-7 Dyna-Clean is a two-speed, lightweight unit with a brush that either locks in place for bare floors or floats to adjust automatically

Prices are accurate at time of printing; subject to manufacturer's change.

for carpets. It has a cord wrap, a swivel head, and rollers that won't mark floors. It also has straight-through suction, which means that dirt and dust don't pass through the fan; this increases motor life and keeps bag-changing to a minimum. The machine weighs 8½ pounds. A seven-piece set of cleaning tools (Model 3046-6) is an extra-cost option.

Approximate Retail Price   **Approximate Low Price**
$62.50 .... Not Available

Hoover S2041 Quik-Broom is a single-speed model with a three-amp motor. It features edge-cleaning and a nozzle with a three-position brush—one for hard surfaces and two for carpets. This machine has a cord wrap, a motor muffler to reduce noise, and a check-bag indicator. A five-piece set of cleaning tools (S2901) is an extra-cost option.

Approximate Retail Price   **Approximate Low Price**
$60.00 .... $50.00

Regina B6628 is a two-speed electric broom that has a number of good features in a lightweight, time-saving cleaner. It offers edge-cleaning, a rug pile dial that adjusts for pile height or bare floors, and a swiveling nozzle. The machine also has a dirt cup; it needs to be cleaned fairly often, but it eliminates the need for bags.

Approximate Retail Price   **Approximate Low Price**
$45.00 .... $37.00

 Wet/Dry and Shop Vacs

THE MAIN DIFFERENCE between wet/dry canister units and standard canisters is that the former have the ability to handle liquids. A wet/dry vac is electrically insulated to prevent shock when it comes into normal contact with liquids. *Caution: Never use standard vacuum cleaners on a wet or damp surface.*

Wet/dry and shop vacs are heavy-duty machines that are ideal for garage, workshop, or basement cleaning chores. Many models are made from sturdy plastic materials so they won't suffer from corrosion problems.

Wet/dry and shop vacs offer attachments that are similar to ones that come with standard canister units. Most of these machines have a permanent-type filter that must be cleaned, especially after each wet use. Some shop vacs, however, are not wet/dry vacs; they are not designed to handle wet materials. Be sure to check a unit's capabilities carefully before buying or using it. All models listed here are wet/dry vacs.

Prices are accurate at time of printing; subject to manufacturer's change.

If you have frequent need for this type of heavy-duty vacuum cleaner, consider the better models. Many cheaper units just don't perform well or last long enough unless your need is extremely infrequent.

Douglas A-7000 is a good-quality, versatile wet/dry machine. It comes with 1¼-inch and 2½-inch wands, a squeegee tool, a dusting brush, an upholstery tool, a 10-inch-wide rug tool, a crevice tool for the 1¼-inch wand, and a utility tool for the 2½-inch wand. This vac uses a foam filter for wet-pickup chores and disposable bags for dry vacuuming. It has a five-gallon dry capacity and a three-gallon wet capacity. The canister moves easily on a swiveling caster dolly.

Approximate Retail Price	Approximate Low Price
$84.00	$60.00

Shelton C820 Jet Vac is a wet/dry model with a non-metallic, eight-gallon tank that won't chip or corrode. It rides on integral casters and has a washable cartridge filter, which is one of the better reuseable ones available. This machine's low center of gravity virtually eliminates the possibility of tipping. Accessories include a six-foot, 1¼-inch hose with two wands, and a floor-and-carpet nozzle that has shag rug and squeegee attachments. This machine weighs 19 pounds and carries a one-year warranty.

Approximate Retail Price	Approximate Low Price
$110.50	Not Available

Shop-Vac 700-03 is a wet/dry vac that has an eight-gallon wet capacity and an 8½-gallon dry capacity. This machine has a six-amp motor and variable air-flow control on the hose end. The right-angle input/output openings on the canister prevent tipping when the hose is pulled. During wet pickup, this machine will shut off automatically when full to prevent overflowing. The canister is an epoxy-coated steel drum. This high-quality unit, which can handle tough jobs, comes with a six-foot, 1½-inch hose; two wands; an 18-foot cord; and a 10-inch wet/dry nozzle. It rides easily on a four-wheel dolly. The machine weighs about 19 pounds. It carries a one-year warranty.

Approximate Retail Price	Approximate Low Price
$96.00	$60.00

Shop-Vac 800-03 is a top-of-the-line wet/dry vac whose only drawback—if you can call it that—is its price, which may put it out of reach for many consumers. This machine has a 16-gallon drum with a 14-gallon wet capacity and a 14½-gallon dry capacity. This model, which is strong enough to handle even broken glass, has all the same features as "Best Buy" Shop-Vac Model 700-03, but has a bigger motor. It weighs 29¾ pounds and carries a one-year warranty.

Approximate Retail Price	Approximate Low Price
$145.00	$99.00

Prices are accurate at time of printing; subject to manufacturer's change.

Best Buys 82 | Carpet Sweepers

THERE'S A WAY to clean carpet and floors that doesn't require expensive machines or electricity—mechanical carpet sweepers. Once carpet sweepers were the only tools available for cleaning carpets; now these devices, in a new, improved version, are making a comeback. We think they make a good cleaning companion to a powered vacuum cleaner, allowing you to deep-clean with the powered cleaner on a regular basis and touch-up high-traffic areas with the mechanical sweeper.

Sweepers come in many types. Some will clean only carpets; others can clean almost any type of floor. When shopping for a carpet sweeper, look for one that's light in weight and doesn't require a lot of storage space. A model with a corner brush can be a good idea if you plan to use the sweeper for more than touch-up jobs.

Bissell 1240-A Apollo is a floor-and-carpet sweeper with a special-surface setting selector; you can raise or lower the brush for deep shag, plush pile, tight-twist fibers, indoor/outdoor carpeting, or bare floors. Its twin dust pans are kept from spilling over by metal combs that also help to keep the brush clean. This Bissell sweeper has a wide swing-over handle for two-direction sweeping. It weighs about 5½ pounds.

Approximate Retail Price	Approximate Low Price
$40.50	Not Available

Bissell 2334 Zoom Broom carpet sweeper has a removable dust pan with a built-in comb that continuously cleans the roller brush. This model has an easy action and good bumper protection for furniture. It's a good-quality sweeper for most carpet needs. It weighs 2½ pounds.

Approximate Retail Price	Approximate Low Price
$24.50	Not Available

Hoky 23T is a compact floor-and-carpet sweeper; it only weighs 2½ pounds. This model has a main boar bristle rotor brush and a boar bristle brush at each corner to let you get close to the wall. The sweeper also has an adjustable handle that you can shorten for cleaning stairs. It moves well on easy-rolling rubber wheels.

Approximate Retail Price	Approximate Low Price
$33.00	$30.00

Rolli-Sweep 500F is a floor-and-carpet sweeper. It has a rotating split boar brush that's completely covered with bristles. It also has four horsehair corner brushes that channel dirt into the rotor path. This 2½-pound model carries a five-year warranty.

Approximate Retail Price	Approximate Low Price
$25.00	$20.00

Prices are accurate at time of printing; subject to manufacturer's change.

CONSUMER GUIDE®

Food Preparation Appliances

FOOD PREPARATION appliances can make life in the kitchen a lot easier, because they make fast work of many time-consuming tasks or allow you to prepare a special dish exactly the way it should be prepared. There are small electrical kitchen appliances to do just about any job you might imagine. Many of these specialty devices have been fads that have come and gone rather quickly, leaving little impact on the way we prepare or cook food. The hamburger cooker is one example; initially millions were sold, but then the demand virtually disappeared. Other specialty appliances, like the wok, fulfill a real need for some consumers. And, of course, there are the more common electrical appliances, such as the fry pan, the mixer, the toaster, the blender, and the coffee maker—appliances that can be found in most homes. For those who do considerable cooking, there are versatile food processors and heavy-duty multipurpose machines that can chop, mix, slice, shred, grate, puree, knead, emulsify, and do many other kitchen tasks.

Because the variety of food preparation appliances is so great, many consumers don't always consider how much they will actually use a certain appliance; they often buy a novel item on impulse and then discover that after a brief period they really don't have that much use for it or have no place to store it. Unless there's plenty of room available, a less useful appliance often ends up in a basement storeroom or in a garage, virtually a guarantee that it won't see much use again. Before you buy any item, decide just how often you'll use it and where you'll keep it.

Getting the Most Value

SOME BASIC SHOPPING tips on buying food preparation appliances can help you select the best value. The appliance you choose should be made of durable materials and well assembled. It should also have a functional design. If the appliance has handles, they should be strong and attached securely. Pick up the appliance in the store as if you were going to use it. Does it feel sturdy enough to withstand plenty of use? Is it easy to handle? Will it be easy to clean? Is it immersible? No appliance is completely dishwasher-safe, but you should choose appliances that don't demand much special handling.

Most appliances have a one-year warranty, but always check the product you're considering for any variations. There'll often be a registration card and warranty information with the instruction manual.

By returning the card to the manufacturer, you establish the purchase date, and registering the product helps you make sure that you'll be notified by the manufacturer of any defect or potential hazard. Check the manual or warranty for servicing information. Unlike large appliances, most small appliances must be returned to the manufacturer or to a factory service center for servicing. Make sure you know where to go for any repairs.

The best way to get top value for your money is by comparison-shopping—comparing prices of comparable products. CONSUMER GUIDE® magazine strongly recommends this approach. It is also a good way to compare features of similar products. Is one model more expensive because of additional features, better construction, or non-functional trim?

Discount stores usually offer the lowest price, but often their selections are limited. In addition, sales people at discount stores probably won't be qualified to answer questions about an item's features or performance, or make knowledgeable recommendations.

And never assume you're getting something for nothing. If a product has extra features, they are included in the price. If the price is very low—lower than usual—it could mean the product is a discontinued model or a fad appliance that has lost its popularity.

Judging Safety

IT'S DIFFICULT to judge how safe a product is just by looking at it on a store shelf. A quick way to make a reasonable decision on its worthiness as far as safety goes is to look for the Underwriters' Laboratories seal. This organization tests products for safety, and the seal indicates that the product has met minimum standards. All "Best Buy" and "Also Recommended" food preparation appliances are UL listed.

The real safety of an appliance, however, goes beyond a seal or other endorsement. It's determined by the way you use the product. Electrical appliances in your kitchen have a high potential for danger in the wrong hands—like those of youngsters. Before operating a new appliance, read the instruction manual carefully, no matter how much you think you know about the product. Pay particular attention to warnings. And if you have a product that heats up, keep it out of reach of children and don't leave it unattended, unless this is a feature of its performance.

Never overload your kitchen outlets with electrical cords from appliances. If you're using one appliance, especially one that heats up, it's a good idea to disconnect other items on that circuit. Be especially cautious whenever you use an electrical kitchen appliance. Make sure that kitchen countertops and hands are dry when working with electrical appliances; electricity and liquids are a dangerous combination. Common sense and care should eliminate any risk of electrical shocks.

Best Buys '82

THE FOLLOWING FOOD preparation appliances, which are listed alphabetically, have been selected on the basis of their usefulness, construction, and overall value. Remember that a "Best Buy" designation applies only to the model listed; it doesn't necessarily apply to other models by the same manufacturer, or to an entire product line.

Electric Mixers

ELECTRIC MIXERS save energy and time; they quickly mix and beat foods that once had to be mixed with a strong arm, a sturdy spoon or fork, and plenty of time.

There are two basic types of electric mixers—stand and portable hand models. Some stand mixers feature a detachable head that separates from the base; these can be used as portable mixers—a good compromise. But because a stand mixer is made to be used primarily with a stationary stand and mixing bowl, these combination types are usually heavier—and harder to hold—than a truly portable mixer.

The kind of electric mixer that's best suited for your needs is a matter of personal preference. Stand mixers require considerable counter or cabinet space, but they're easier to operate than handheld models because no lifting and holding is necessary. Portable mixers, though, can be carried all over the kitchen and are more convenient for mixing small quantities of foods.

Mixers come with a wide range of speeds. If you need a machine that performs more elaborate functions, such as grinding grain or mixing bread dough, you may want to step up to the more powerful and more expensive multipurpose mixing machines. Otherwise, a more economical stand mixer or even a portable model may be what you need. A feature of some portable mixers is a button that provides extra power when you have trouble working with very thick ingredients.

When buying a mixer—either portable or stand—consider not only what you'll use it for, but how easy it will be to clean. For example, a stainless steel body will show smudges and fingerprints more than a plastic mixer body. Look for controls that are easy to operate, a low setting for stirring, and an easy-to-use beater ejector.

Portable Hand Mixers

General Electric M74CA is a portable hand mixer that has a button for extra power at any speed to deal with heavy batters and other tough jobs. The machine is well-balanced, weighs under three pounds, and is one of the more stable units when stood on its heel. The Model M74CA, which comes in a beige color, has variable speeds and markings to 10 indicated settings, and a blade ejector that works easily.

Approximate Retail Price   Approximate Low Price

$31.00 .... $22.00

Prices are accurate at time of printing; subject to manufacturer's change.

Hamilton Beach 113 is a rugged, three-speed portable mixer with nonsplash chrome-plated beaters that can stand up to hard use. It has a special power-surge feature for each speed that you can trigger by a button in the handle when working with extra-thick ingredients. The open-handle design gives the appliance excellent balance for good control. It weighs 2.3 pounds. The beater ejector works easily. This mixer, which has a detachable cord, comes in a beige color.

Approximate Retail Price   **Approximate Low Price**
$31.00 .... $18.00

Stand Mixers

Sunbeam 1-71 Deluxe Mixmaster is one of the best stand mixers around. It offers a smooth-acting speed dial that you can adjust easily to any of 12 speed/function indications while you're using the machine. The automatic bowl rotation feature works well even when the bowl is heavily loaded. With the mixer body lifted up, you have easy access to either of the two heat-resistant glass bowls—a four-quart and a 1½-quart bowl—that come with the unit. Model 1-71 is white, Model 1-73 is gold, and Model 1-76 is beige; if you prefer stainless steel bowls and a chrome mixer body, you can choose Model 1-80. All models come with dough hooks for kneading bread. The cord is detachable. Optional attachments include a food slicer/shredder, a food grinder, and a juicer.

Approximate Retail Price   **Approximate Low Price**
$116.00 (colors) $75.00
$147.00 (stainless steel) $92.00

 Toaster Oven/Broilers

TOASTER OVENS ARE most useful as a supplement to the kitchen range, but they can come in handy as a range substitute.

Toaster ovens are available in a variety of sizes and prices. Some are designed only for toasting and baking. Others also broil; they have an additional heating element for this purpose. Toaster ovens can do a good job baking potatoes, heating frozen dinners, and toasting sandwiches. Because they have a smaller capacity than a range, they can be energy-savers for preparing small quantities of food.

When buying a toaster oven/broiler, look for a model with a sturdy door that will withstand plenty of use and will be easy to clean. Is it easy to remove crumbs and baked-on foods? Some models now feature continuous-clean interiors and convenient electronic controls.

General Electric T26 is a leader among toaster oven/broilers. There are good reasons for this—and performance is the top one. This 1500-watt

Prices are accurate at time of printing; subject to manufacturer's change.

appliance does a good job on regular bread (up to four slices), thick bread, muffins, bagels, and on baking and broiling. We like the top-brown setting, which browns, crisps, or melts tops of foods, as an alternative to a full-size broiler. The appliance also has a separate "broil" setting. The eight-inch broiler pan is removable and adjustable. A signal bell rings at the end of automatic toasting and the top-brown cycle, and a hinged crumb tray swings out for cleaning convenience. The appliance has a chrome finish with simulated woodgrain side panels.

Approximate Retail Price **Approximate Low Price**
$69.00 .... $43.00

General Electric CT02000 Versatron is a big, 1600-watt countertop oven that toasts, broils, and bakes. It's large enough to accept a 13- by 9-inch cake pan, and can broil up to 11 hamburgers, 18 hot dogs, or 12 lamb chops. This appliance, which has a two-position rack and chrome-plated multipurpose pan, can toast up to six slices of bread. It also has a built-in 90-minute timer and audible end-of-toasting signal. The interior sidewalls, glass door, and backwall are removable for cleaning and are dishwasher-safe to make cleaning easy. It has a simulated woodgrain top and black side panels.

Approximate Retail Price **Approximate Low Price**
$128.00 .... $85.50

Toastmaster 320 is a 1500-watt, four-slice toaster oven broiler. It holds a 1½-quart casserole. It has a setting selector for two or four slices of bread, and a dial for toast color control. There's also an end-of-cooking-cycle signal. Double-wall construction keeps the top and back of the appliance cooler. It has a top-browning feature and bakes or broils very well. This model has a chrome top, black molded end panels, and orange trim.

Approximate Retail Price **Approximate Low Price**
$67.00 .... $43.00

 **Toasters**

ALMOST EVERY KITCHEN has a toaster. Although there are a variety of foods such as frozen waffles and pastries that you can cook in a toaster, the appliance's basic function is to toast bread—white bread, French bread, pita, a muffin, or a bagel.

Toaster technology hasn't changed much over the years. Two years ago, however, Salton introduced a convection toaster. In this unusual design—bread slices are placed lengthwise instead of side by side—the bread is toasted with convection heat, similar to that used in convection

Prices are accurate at time of printing; subject to manufacturer's change.

ovens. This method moves heated air around for more efficient toasting.

Your basic toaster choices are in design and in the number of slices that can be toasted at one time—either two or four slices. One important feature you should look for is the width of the toaster's slots; be sure it will accept what you plan to toast. Some toasters have an energy-saving feature. For example, a four-slice toaster may have two separate controls, one for each pair of slots. So if you only want to toast one or two slices of bread, there's no need to have the appliance draw its full amount of wattage.

Salton CT-2 Convection Toaster is a 900-watt appliance that uses radiant and convection heat to provide a hot-air updraft that speeds toasting. It can toast everything from French bread to English muffins in its single long, wide slot. And because there's one long slot, you can toast two regular slices of bread or one long piece of, say, French bread. It's a quality toaster that features fast performance and good construction. The toaster is white with brown trim.

Approximate Retail Price	Approximate Low Price
$45.00	Not Available

Sunbeam 20-140 is a 1425-watt, four-slice toaster with a chrome body and an energy-saving feature; it can be set for either two or four slices of bread. When adjusted for two slices (995 watts), the toaster automatically shuts off some of the power to the elements; if you inadvertently put in four slices and leave the unit set for two, half the toast will come out only partially toasted. The toaster has wide slots, and special settings for pastries, muffins, and frozen waffles. There's a convenient snap-down crumb tray for easier cleaning.

Approximate Retail Price	Approximate Low Price
$49.00	$34.00

Toastmaster B720 is an 800-watt, two-slice unit that has a popular feature—an adjustable slot. This solves problems with items that jam most toasters—bagels, muffins, or homemade bread. The unit has a wattage-reduction feature that maintains normal toasting temperature on inside elements while slightly reducing the temperature on outside elements; this helps toast frosted pastries and other specialty foods without burning. The chrome toaster has brown and woodgrain trim.

Approximate Retail Price	Approximate Low Price
$33.50	$22.00

Also Recommended

Proctor-Silex T230AL is a 1050-watt two-slice toaster with a textured body—a surface that doesn't show the fingerprints and smears so obvious on chrome toasters. The end panels are simulated butcher block. This toaster is a fairly good performer that has slots wide enough for bagels and thickly sliced bread. It also handles pastry items quite well.

Approximate Retail Price	Approximate Low Price
$29.00	$17.00

Prices are accurate at time of printing; subject to manufacturer's change.

Blenders

IN MANY HOMES, blenders get little use. Often, this appliance is bought for use in a kitchen or wet bar, then ignored. Blenders are popular as a gift item, but whether you plan to buy one for yourself or someone else, consider how useful it will really be.

Blenders perform a variety of functions; they can mix, beat, chop, grate, crush, and more. These functions, however, are just fancy names for different motor speeds, and you should consider what kinds of tasks you plan to do with the blender. Manufacturers are fond of adding speeds to blenders, and some models even have electronic controls to switch from one speed to another. While these features make a product look impressive, they don't really add much to performance; they just raise the price.

All blenders have a cylindrical container to hold the food being blended. When you shop for a blender, make sure the cap fits tightly, but isn't too difficult to remove. A pulse feature—an extra surge of power—is a benefit that helps get tough items—food that gets caught under the spinning blades and stays at the bottom of the container—mixed well without straining the unit or over-blending. Also check to be sure the blade assembly of the blender is removable for thorough separate cleaning.

Oster 890 is a versatile 10-speed blender that has some of the best control features of any blender we've seen. It has seven continuous speeds and three pulse operations. We especially like the touch-and-release, instant start-and-stop control. The unit has a five-cup plastic container and a blade assembly that removes for easy cleaning; the two-ounce measuring cap in the cover is removable for adding ingredients while processing. The blender does its job with a minimum of splattering and requires little extra handling—like scraping the sides—to blend food properly. Model 890-14 comes in two-tone gold; Model 890-16 is two-tone beige.

Approximate Retail Price	Approximate Low Price
$39.00	$26.00

Waring Titan 8 is a seven-speed blender that has a five-cup shatter-proof pitcher with removable base for easy cleaning. The lid has a removable two-ounce measuring cup. Measurements on the pitcher are graduated in ounces and metric. Cord storage in the rear of the appliance will keep the cord off a counter and tangle-free. Model BL208-1 is white, Model BL208-2 is avocado, and Model BL208-3 is gold. The blender comes with a one-year warranty.

Approximate Retail Price	Approximate Low Price
$34.00	$20.50

Prices are accurate at time of printing; subject to manufacturer's change.

MAKING A GOOD cup of coffee used to be a kind of secret process that only some people had mastered. This need not be the case today; with the right coffee maker, anyone can produce a good brew.

The most popular coffee maker on the market is the automatic drip coffee maker. This appliance comes in a wide variety of capacities and styles, but all perform basically the same function. Water poured into the holding tank heats up and passes through the top of the unit into a filter assembly that contains the coffee. The coffee then drips down into the pot, or carafe, at the base of the unit, and stays hot on a warming plate.

Coffee makers can be noisy. Models that heat all the water before allowing it to drip are quieter than models that use a percolator tube to bring hot water to the filter basket. The latter type, however, is quicker, so you don't have to contend with the gurgling sounds for long.

In a drip coffee maker, coffee grounds are not boiled or perked, so most sediment is strained out. If you let coffee sit for a long time before using the whole pot, drip coffee will probably retain its flavor better than perked coffee.

Of course, how you make coffee is a matter of personal preference. Electric percolators do the job effectively, and many people prefer them. When shopping for an electric percolator, it's a good idea to look for a model that's immersible for easy cleaning. A pot with water capacity markings on its exterior or an indicator in the handle is a good idea too.

A nice feature on some new coffee makers is an electronic or electric clock timer. It allows you to get everything ready up to 12 hours or more before the coffee maker automatically starts the brewing action. It's a boon to people who can't seem to get started without the first cup of coffee in the morning.

A special type of coffee maker is one for making espresso and capuccino. Some models make regular drip coffee too, to give you a complete, but expensive, coffee-making center.

Automatic Drip Coffee Makers

General Electric DCM15 is a good performer by the standard that counts—it makes good coffee! The coffee maker brews from 2 to 10 cups of coffee. We like its convenient see-through water reservoir because it has clear capacity markings, and the brew-starter feature is great because you can program the next morning's coffee with the built-in electric clock timer. After coffee is brewed, the 1100-watt appliance automatically shifts from brewing to a keep-warm mode. The carafe is well designed; it has a large, sturdy handle.

Approximate Retail Price	Approximate Low Price
$56.00..	$37.00

Prices are accurate at time of printing; subject to manufacturer's change.

Norelco HB5185 makes excellent coffee. This 10-cup automatic drip coffee maker, a Dial-A-Brew II model, is well-constructed. The 1225-watt appliance has a double heating element to maintain precise brewing time and temperature, and it has a strength selector on top—for weak, medium, or strong coffee—which is much better than the former basket-setting system with markings that wore off after a time. This model has an on/off switch, an indicator light, and a glass carafe with safety serving lid. It comes in a beige color with brown trim.

Approximate Retail Price	Approximate Low Price
$40.00..	$23.00

West Bend 56102 automatic drip coffee maker makes from 4 to 12 cups of coffee, without paper filters; it features a built-in, permanent polyester filter. However, you might consider using paper filters to capture oils. One of the fastest brewers available, this 1440-watt coffee maker manages to make consistently fine coffee, even when used to brew several pots in rapid succession. There is an on/off switch, and the built-in temperature control brews and keeps coffee at just the right temperature. This model comes in two-tone almond and brown.

Approximate Retail Price	Approximate Low Price
$55.00	Not Available

General Electric DCM4 Mini-Brew is not for those who drink a lot of coffee; it's a compact 580-watt unit that brews two to four cups of excellent coffee in short order. To operate, all you do is plug in the unit; unlike other GE models, it doesn't have an on/off switch. There is, however, an indicator light to tell you when it's on. After brewing, the appliance keeps coffee warm. Another benefit is that this coffee maker doesn't take much counter space. It's a good choice for dorm room or office use.

Approximate Retail Price	Approximate Low Price
$26.00..	$18.00

Electric Percolators

General Electric P15BK makes up to nine cups of coffee. The brew selector lets you adjust the strength of the coffee, and a clear tube in the handle lets you see how much water or coffee is in the percolator at a glance. This appliance is a sturdy, steadfast performer that's totally immersible once the cord is removed. This 660-watt model has an anodized aluminum body with black trim; Model P15HR has gold trim.

Approximate Retail Price	Approximate Low Price
$39.00..	$27.00

West Bend 9449 is a 600-watt automatic percolator that adds some color to your kitchen; this model comes in a beige color with decoration. The sturdy acrylic finish on an aluminum body is also available in gold with decoration (Model 9448) or beige with brown stripes (Model 54119). The appliance, which makes from five to nine cups of coffee, is well

Prices are accurate at time of printing; subject to manufacturer's change.

constructed and a practical performer at a good price. A lock-on cover helps prevent accidental spills.

Approximate Retail Price   **Approximate Low Price**
$26.00.. Not Available

Regal K7591 brews 4 to 10 cups of coffee automatically. This 650-watt appliance has a stainless steel body and black plastic cover and coffee basket that stay comfortable enough to touch for safe, easy removal. A see-through coffee level indicator in the handle, an adjustable flavor selector, and a signal light to tell you when the coffee is ready are some of its features. Although it's not the best percolator available, this unit is fairly well built and brews a pretty good cup of coffee.

Approximate Retail Price   **Approximate Low Price**
$63.50... $37.00

 Electric Fry Pans

THE ELECTRIC FRY PAN, or skillet, is one of the earliest food preparation appliances on the market, and it still has a useful place in millions of homes. It can be used for more than just frying—you also can bake, roast, thaw, and do even more with some models. Some fry pans even have a slow-cook setting.

Fry pans are available in many sizes, shapes, and colors; there are fry pans of different sizes in this section. When shopping for a fry pan, look for a model with detachable heat controls and cord, so the pan can be immersed in water for cleaning. The temperature range on an electric fry pan should extend to at least 400° F for adequate cooking; all "Best Buy" fry pans in this section have an adequate temperature range. Finally, a pan with a nonstick interior coating will ease cleanup, and a domed lid will give you extra space to bake, braise, or roast foods.

General Electric SK47CAS is a 1200-watt, 12-inch buffet skillet with a SilverStone nonstick interior coating on a cast-aluminum pan. This model has a brown pan and a beige cover. The leg-and-handle assembly detaches to make cleaning easier, and one leg tilts down for basting or draining oils. The cover, which is vented, has three positions. There's a cooking guide on a cover handle, and the removable temperature control is easy to read. The appliance carries a one-year warranty. Model SK47CGS has a gold cover.

Approximate Retail Price   **Approximate Low Price**
$49.00... $35.00

Sunbeam 7-296 is a 1250-watt, 11½-inch fry pan with a SilverStone nonstick interior. Sunbeam has established a first-rate reputation as a

Prices are accurate at time of printing; subject to manufacturer's change.

producer of durable, quality fry pans; this model, in beige, cooks beautifully and cleans up easily. The vented, multiposition cover tilts so that the unit will hold large roasts and still contain most splatter, and the leg-handle assembly makes the unit an attractive serving piece. The hand control detaches to make the porcelain-on-aluminum skillet body totally immersible. Model 7-293 comes in a gold color.

Approximate Retail Price   **Approximate Low Price**
$53.00.. $35.00

West Bend 72102 Convection Plus is a skillet, broiler, and oven. This appliance is 14½ inches long, 10½ inches wide, and 2½ inches deep. It cooks by circulating hot air around food to broil, roast, fry, bake, and steam. The aluminum base has a porcelain exterior finish and a nonstick SilverStone interior surface. The vented cover is made of aluminum. As a skillet, it draws 1300 watts; as a broiler, 1450 watts. The fan draws 17 watts. The appliance is immersible and dishwasher-safe with the heat control, fan, and broiler unit removed. The base is brown; the cover is beige.

Approximate Retail Price   **Approximate Low Price**
$90.00 .... $80.00

West Bend 72106 is an oblong-shaped skillet that's 14½ inches long, 10½ inches wide, and 2½ inches deep. It has a vented cover, a Rockcote nonstick interior, and a detachable heat control. The 1300-watt skillet is made of heavy-gauge aluminum; the legs and handles are phenolic plastic. The skillet comes in a beige and brown color.

Approximate Retail Price   **Approximate Low Price**
$40.00 .... Not Available

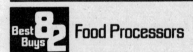 **Food Processors**

A FOOD PROCESSOR is truly a many-talented machine. Depending on brand and model, it can chop, mix, slice, shred, grate, julienne, cream, puree, knead, emulsify, and—with a few exceptions—perform almost any task those old-fashioned kitchen utensils called hands can manage.

Although the exterior designs may vary slightly, most of the processors are patterned after the Cuisinart. They consist of a motor housed in a plastic or metal base, a plastic bowl that fits onto the base, and a plastic lid with a food chute that fits over the bowl.

Two design features of the newest food processors are Cuisinart's exclusive expanded feed tube and several manufacturers' continuous-feed chutes. Cuisinart's expanded tube lets you feed whole small tomatoes, oranges, apples, and potatoes into the machine. The

Prices are accurate at time of printing; subject to manufacturer's change.

continuous-feed feature allows you to process food in quantity without emptying the bowl; the processed food is fed through a chute into any bowl set next to the machine. Both of these are convenience features; whether they're valuable convenience features depends on your cooking habits.

Most processors come with two cutting/chopping blades (one steel and one plastic), a shredding disc, and a slicing disc as standard equipment. These motor-driven blades and discs are what earn the machine its name "food processor," because that's exactly what the blades do—process food.

The metal blade will chop meat, knead dough, mix pastry, cream batters, crumb bread or crackers, liquefy fruits or vegetables, puree soups, and even make peanut butter. The plastic blade will mix softer foods. The shredding disc will handle cheese, cabbage, carrots, and other vegetables. The slicing disc will tackle partially frozen meat, cheese, vegetables, and fruits.

Food processor blades are designed to fit in different ways. Before you buy, make sure you know how the blades attach, and that you're comfortable with its method.

Many machines also have optional (and fairly expensive) accessories, such as a french-fry cutter, thick and thin slicing discs, a fine shredding (or grating) disc, a funnel for adding flour to the feed tube, a whip, and even a potato peeler. Whether you want, or need, all these accessories depends on what you cook. With one exception—the whip—all of the accessories do a fine job. The whip is supposed to whip cream, egg whites, and make butter, but it doesn't do a satisfactory job on the first two, and you can make butter with the steel or plastic blade. The food processor (and the blender) are just too fast to form the proper foam in egg whites and cream. A good rotary beater or electric mixer does that best.

Do you need a food processor? If you cook a considerable amount; if you want to cook easier, faster, or gourmet; or even if you just want to eliminate much of the manual work in the kitchen, then consider one of these handy machines.

Since features vary from brand to brand, it's a good idea to familiarize yourself with the options before you start shopping for your processor. Consider these features:

Direct or belt drive is a mechanical matter. The spindle that operates the blades or discs is either connected directly to the motor or turned by a belt. On a belt-driven machine, the motor loses a little efficiency, and the belt may require occasional changing, but that's not a big deal. One advantage to some of the belt-drive machines is that they have a lower profile and may fit better on your counter underneath a cabinet. Because the belt-driven machines are bigger side to side, however, they may take up more counter space. The strength of the motor (usually measured in horsepower) will determine how fast your food is processed. If you prepare large meals or if seconds count to you, look for a processor with a powerful motor.

Braking action is an important feature. The action helps stop the movement of the blades, making the machine safer to operate. On machines without braking, the blades will continue to move for several seconds after the processor is turned off. An impatient cook who doesn't wait for the blades to stop could be cut badly.

Cover lock mechanism is a feature on all machines. With this feature, the machine cannot be started until the cover is firmly in place. Machines with on/off switches can also be started and stopped by moving the cover in and out of locked position (when the switch is on). This can be a double safety, but it can also be a problem, because you have two ways for the machine to turn on.

Pulsing action or a pulse switch is helpful, but not an essential feature. You can get the same action by rapidly turning the motor on and off. The automatic pulse action does let you leave the processor alone instead of having to turn it on, off, and on manually, but the time involved is so short that the distinction is dubious. The simplest switchery and the models with top (lid)-operated on/off controls are usually most satisfactory.

Automatic cutoff is an important feature that can save the life of your processor. This thermostatic control will shut off an overheated motor. If this does happen, it's extremely important to remember to turn off the machine manually. Otherwise, once the motor is cool, the machine will turn on again. If you're not right at hand, that could be a problem.

Your food processing needs and budget should determine which machine you choose. Here's where the old maxim, "You get what you pay for," seems to hold true. And comparing processors is a lot like shopping for a car. You'll find Cadillacs, Chevys, and Pintos, and any one of them might be the best buy for you.

The Cuisinart is the Cadillac, unquestionably. But there are several other solid, sturdy, and good-performing processors for half the price that do almost as well—the Sunbeam Le Chef, for example. The least expensive machines, such as the GE FP1, can do an acceptable job, too, although with more noise and movement. Generally, the more money you pay, the more power you get. If you plan to knead a lot of dough and a lot of meat, plan to spend a lot of money. If your needs are general—slicing, pureeing, shredding, and grating—any of these "Best Buy" selections could do an adequate job for you.

Cuisinart DLC8E is the middle-of-the line Cuisinart. It is a powerful processor that succeeds where most food processors fail: kneading dough and chopping meat. The DLC8E has a metal motor base with a single drive shaft. The powerful and efficient motor is direct drive. As with all Cuisinart models, the DLC8E is a single-speed machine with a two-button control: one for "on," and the other for "off" and "pulse." The heavy motor rests on rubber buttons that help prevent the machine from moving on the counter. The capacity of the DLC8E is good—it can process three pounds of dough (six cups of flour) and chop 1½ pounds of meat at a time, about 20 percent more than our "Also Recommended" selection Cuisinart Model DLC10E. The bowl can hold six cups of dry ingredients, or two cups of liquid. The big feature of this and every Cuisinart is the exclusive expanded feed tube, which will accept food as big as small whole tomatoes, oranges, beets, and even small potatoes—much less preparation is needed than with the standard feed tube. You aren't limited to this expanded feed tube; a small tube and a pusher are built in for processing long and thin foods, such as carrots and pepperoni. All of the above features are standard. Additional standard features include the metal chopping blade, plastic dough blade, slicing disc, shredding disc, spatula, and cleaning tool.

The Cuisinart DLC8E is among the best new food processors; all of the usual processing tasks are performed better than the average. A quality improvement over past Cuisinart models is the improved slicing and shredding discs. The new slicer allows food slices to fall free without touching the disc; the new shredding disc prevents the teeth from cutting into the bottom of the plastic cover when hard pressure is exerted on one edge of the disc. For bread and pastry bakers, the dough blade will be appreciated. This standard Cuisinart blade outperforms all other dough-mixing blades.

The Cuisinart DLC8E is an excellent processor that continues to prove the quality of the Cuisinart name. It's available in white. Accessory blades include the french fry disc, the julienne disc, the ultra-thin (1mm), thin (2mm), medium (4mm), and thick (6mm) slicing discs. The DLC8E has a two-year warranty and a 30-year warranty on motor parts.

Approximate Retail Price	Approximate Low Price
Not Available	$150.00

Sunbeam Le Chef 14-11 is a heavy-duty, sturdy food processor at an attractive price. The strong direct-drive motor is controlled by a single on-off/pulse switch; a signal light indicates when the motor is on. The large work bowl has a limit of about two cups of firm material, but it's possible to puree soup for six people without leakage and shred almost a pound of vegetables. The steel blade chops uniformly and has an extended handle for ease in removal. The Le Chef includes a steel blade, an insert-blade holder, a medium shredding insert-blade, and a 3mm slicing insert-blade.

Overall, the Le Chef performs very well. With the large bowl, we tried to beat and whip with the steel blade. Results were surprisingly good; the cream was firm enough to hold soft peaks and the egg whites were stiff enough to use when folding into cake batters and souffles. The feed tube pusher is marked as a measuring cup, but the markings are almost invisible when the pusher is in the tube. A new design in the blades allows for interchanging individual blades on a common shaft/base. On the positive side, these insert-blades are easy to install in the holder disc, work as well as the conventional slicing and shredding blades, and are much more convenient to store. On the negative side, they allow more food to accumulate underneath, and they're difficult and time-consuming to remove. In order to change blades, you must remove the entire holder disc and then push upward on the underside of the blade. If the blade is slippery from food residue, the process can be at best awkward and at worst dangerous. Make sure you try changing the blades in the store—and compare them to conventional blades.

On the whole, the Le Chef is among the best processors for its fine performance in all tasks. It's a good choice for a busy kitchen with an

Prices are accurate at time of printing; subject to manufacturer's change.

accent on baking. Accessory blades include a thin (1mm) slicer, three thick slicers (4mm, 5mm, and 6mm), a fine shredder, a coarse julienne shredder, and a french-fry cutter. You can also buy a continuous-feed container that constantly transfers the food from the processor to a bowl. The Le Chef has a one-year warranty on parts and labor.

Approximate Retail Price   **Approximate Low Price**
$139.00 .... $86.00

Also Recommended

Cuisinart DLC10E is the newest and least expensive model from this manufacturer. The DLC10E closely resembles the other Cuisinart food processors, in looks as well as in high quality. It has a direct-drive motor housed in a metal base; two switches—one for "on," the other for "off" and "pulse"—control the one-speed motor. The DLC10E can process two pounds (four cups) of bread dough, 2½ cups of liquid, or chop ¾ pound of meat at a time. Although its capacity is not as large as that of more expensive processors, its basic capacity of four cups dry and 2½ cups liquid is adequate.

This lightweight Cuisinart comes equipped with the best of Cuisinart's features—notably the expanded feed tube, which makes it possible to slice small whole tomatoes, apples, oranges, and potatoes. This feed tube can be removed, revealing a small inner feed tube for slicing carrots and other long, thin foods. Processing blades included with the DLC10E are an efficient dough-kneading blade, off-center slicing and shredding discs, and a steel chopping blade. The heavy-duty plastic bowl and interlocking lid are of the same material as on other Cuisinart processors. This inexpensive Cuisinart comes very close to the performance of the larger models. We found that the slicing and shredding were handled as well or better as with other machines in its size and price range. The new steel blade chopped all material uniformly without slowing down; veal was easily and quickly reduced to paste; emulsifying and pureeing were both satisfactory. On the negative side, chopping hard cheese was noisy, and the machine's base moved slightly on the counter.

If you don't require heavy production in your kitchen, and you don't need a large bowl capacity, the Cuisinart DLC10E is an excellent choice. You'll get your money's worth in convenience, durability, and quality of workmanship. Blade accessories for the DLC10E include the french fry disc, the julienne disc, and the ultra-thin (1mm), thin (2mm), medium (4mm), and thick (5mm) slicing discs. The DLC10E has a two-year warranty and a 30-year warranty on motor parts.

Approximate Retail Price   **Approximate Low Price**
Not Available $100.00

General Electric FP1 is a budget food processor that can easily handle all lightweight chores. Don't buy it for kneading lots of dough or chopping lots of meat; it will only disappoint you—but for other tasks, it's quite adequate. The FP1 has these features: an extra-tall feed tube, a hollow food pusher, a double-duty reversible slicer/shredder disc, and a stainless steel blade for in-bowl processing. The durable plastic bowl

Prices are accurate at time of printing; subject to manufacturer's change.

has a safety interlock cover that assures correct assembly before the food processor can operate. The machine is belt-driven from a powerful motor that sits behind the work bowl. It's controlled by a pulse and on/off buttons on the front panel.

In testing the FP1, we found that its reversible shredder/slicer blade, which has a stem for easy lifting from the bowl, is convenient and practical. The other standard steel blade does the work of both the steel and plastic blades in most other machines. These blades are easily stored in the work bowl. The bowl lacks a handle—not a serious disadvantage, but we missed it; most other processors have this feature.

The FP1 has one of the best safety mechanisms: a button must be pushed before the lid is released. This lightweight General Electric can handle yeast dough, although no more than a three-cup flour dough (one-loaf size). All the breads in the very detailed booklet are designed with those amounts. The usual tasks tested were accomplished with good results, although there was slight vibrating at times. We found the noise level higher than most when the pulser was used. For an inexpensive food processor, we find the General Electric FP1 a good kitchen worker. Accessory french fry, thick slicer, thin ripple, and coarse shredding blades are available.

Approximate Retail Price	Approximate Low Price
$72.00	$45.00

General Electric FP6 is G.E.'s top-of-the-line food processor. With its food chute in place it resembles a futuristic space machine. It is one of the largest and heaviest processors we tested. The FP6's continuous-flow food chute, which gives you unlimited capacity when slicing and shredding, is the major feature. There is no need to fill and empty the machine when processing large quantities; the output goes into your own bowl set in place under the chute. The FP6 has a direct-drive motor that can handle the heaviest jobs. It's equipped with three blade attachments to slice, shred, chop, grate, mix, puree, and more.

The FP6 performed all the usual chores with satisfactory results. The measuring cup pusher is a handy feature, as is the stemmed slicer/shredder disc for easy removal. Although performance is above average, the FP6 does have a few faults. The cumbersome chute lid is difficult to wash, and the little tool used to reverse the slicer/shredder blade is easily misplaced. But, all in all, the General Electric FP6 is a good machine for a busy kitchen with quantity output. For the price, it stands in the top group of processors tested. An accessory kit is available, including a thick-slice disc, a french-fry disc, a reversible thin-slice/shred disc, and a food funnel for adding loose material.

Approximate Retail Price	Approximate Low Price
$136.00	$90.00

Moulinex La Machine II has a large amber six-cup bowl, and a feed tube with a measuring cup pusher. It's controlled by a convenient "Pulse and Continuous On" control switch on the base. Slicing and shredding discs are reversible, and all accessories can be stored in the bowl and all are dishwasher-safe.

Prices are accurate at time of printing; subject to manufacturer's change.

We feel that the finger holes on the La Machine II's slicing and shredding discs aid in the safe and easy removal of the blades. We also like the special safety button, which must be pushed to unlock the lid. On the debit side, there is considerable vibration when processing bread dough and chopping chunks of meat.

In all, this is a very inexpensive machine that does an adequate job on most of the tasks tested. Don't expect it to handle heavy jobs; it's recommended primarily for its low price. Optional discs are the french-fry, thin-slicing, and julienne-shredding discs. There's also an attachment for whipping egg whites, cream, and other foods. La Machine II has a one-year warranty.

Approximate Retail Price   **Approximate Low Price**
$76.00 .... $50.00

 Multipurpose Machines

MULTIPURPOSE MACHINES are based on the principle of the stand mixer, but they do many more kitchen jobs, and feature sturdier construction. They are designed for heavy-duty work, and they come with various attachments to do different jobs.

Essentially, a multipurpose machine consists of a power base, which contains the motor and its controls, and several attachments that connect to the base—a mixer, a food processor-type unit, usually a blender, and sometimes other attachments. The advantage of this is that one motor provides the power for all these functions.

But while they can be real time-savers, multipurpose machines are not for everyone. They require—in addition to a considerable outlay of capital—considerable counter or storage space, and a real commitment to cooking. If you bake bread regularly, put up your own fruits and vegetables, make your own sausage, grind your own grain, and so on, then by all means look these machines over carefully. If you're a casual cook who occasionally stirs up a cake mix or a batch of brownies, look to a portable or stand mixer.

KitchenAid K45SS—made by Hobart Corporation—is not the biggest KitchenAid multipurpose machine, but it's big enough to meet almost every need. It has a heavy-duty 250-watt motor, with a solid-state 10-setting speed control. It comes with a 4½-quart stainless steel mixing bowl, and has a nylon-coated metal flat beater, a stainless steel wire whip, and a nylon-coated metal dough hook. The beater turns in one direction while moving around the stationary bowl in the other direction, mixing quickly and thoroughly. The machine can handle both small and large jobs, whipping a cup of cream or mixing eight cups of dough equally well. Several attachments are available to make the KitchenAid

Prices are accurate at time of printing; subject to manufacturer's change.

a truly multipurpose machine—you can get (at extra cost) a food grinder (and pasta-making attachments), a vegetable slicer/shredder, a colander/sieve to make purees, a sausage stuffer, a coffee mill, a grain mill, a juicer, a can opener, and even a silver buffer. The only attachment the KitchenAid does not offer is a blender. The K45SS equals or surpasses the performance of every other mixer on the market, both the multipurpose and the standing varieties. Its new solid-state control should provide even better performance than it's always given. The K45SS carries a one-year warranty. It's available in white, almond, and gold.

Approximate Retail Price   **Approximate Low Price**
$261.00 .... $180.00

Oster Kitchen Center 980-16 is a versatile kitchen machine with a 450-watt motor, an infinite-setting speed control and on/off and pulse control. It comes with two stainless steel mixing bowls, with 1⅝-quart and 4-quart capacity, and has both beaters and dough hooks. It can be used as a mixer, a blender, a slicer/shredder/salad-maker, and a grinder; accessories are available (at extra cost) to let you puree, crush ice, open cans, make juice, and stuff sausage. The Kitchen Center gives you almost all the kitchen help you could want, with good overall performance—but like many combination units, it could do each job better. The Kitchen Center carries a warranty of one year. It comes in almond.

Approximate Retail Price   **Approximate Low Price**
$225.00 .... $145.00

Sunbeam Food Preparation Center 36-11 is a do-it-all kitchen work saver. It has a heavy-duty 450-watt motor, with an easy-to-use, 16-speed slide-action control. It comes with two stainless steel mixing bowls, with two-quart and four-quart capacity, and has both beaters and dough hooks. It blends, processes, and mixes, and does all three things well—as a mixer, it's powerful enough to knead bread; the bowl rotates automatically. As a blender, it works continuously or in touch-control pulses; as a food processor, it can process everything from rough grating to clean slicing. The Food Preparation Center is white; its sleek design makes it both attractive and easy to keep clean. Several accessories, including a continuous-feed container, a dust cover, and additional blades, are available at extra cost. The Food Preparation Center carries a warranty of one year.

Approximate Retail Price   **Approximate Low Price**
$299.00 .... $200.00

 Specialty Appliances

THERE ARE A vast number of handy and fun-to-use food preparation appliances on the market—everything from hot dog cookers to rice

Prices are accurate at time of printing; subject to manufacturer's change.

steamers, from crepe makers to bacon fryers. Many of these products are frills in the kitchen, but they can serve useful purposes, too.

CONSUMER GUIDE® magazine has selected a few of the more practical specialty appliances that perform functions not so easily managed with common kitchen appliances.

The juicer, or juice extractor, for example, is a far cry from the old-fashioned juicer that gave you a glass full of pulp. A good juice extractor can squeeze juice out of almost any fruit or vegetable and leave the pulp behind. The hot-air corn popper can give you the flavor of popcorn without the calories that oil adds; such units also work better on inexpensive popcorn.

This section includes such specialized appliances as the juice extractor, the hot-air corn popper, and others, as well as such multifunction appliances as a combination can opener, knife sharpener, and plastic-bag opener.

Hamilton Beach 300 is a switchable electric knife with a blade that rotates 90 degrees for horizontal or vertical slicing. This is a cord model with stainless steel blades, a good blade release, and a safety switch. The electric knife is white with charcoal trim.

Approximate Retail Price	Approximate Low Price
$32.00	$20.00

Rival 7442 is a combination can opener and knife sharpener with an extra feature—it has a bag opener. A cutter wheel opens foil and plastic packages easily and cleanly at the push of a button. The knife sharpener is a handy addition to the can opener, which handles tall cans efficiently. The appliance comes in white.

Approximate Retail Price	Approximate Low Price
$31.50	$18.00

Waring JE503 Juice Extractor can handle fruits and vegetables of any type, but does especially well on noncitrus fruits. It has a deep intake chute and stainless steel filter and grater/shredder. An automatic pulp ejector allows you to save the pulp, if desired, for other recipes such as for carrot cake. The chute/grater/shredder assembly is easily removed for cleaning. There is only one control—an on/off switch. The Juice Extractor comes with a cleaning brush, a glass marked in liters and ounces, and a recipe book. It carries a one-year warranty.

Approximate Retail Price	Approximate Low Price
$72.00	$45.00

Regal K6705 grill is a portable and versatile appliance; it grills, fries, toasts, and heats for indoor smokeless grilling. It cooks everything from steaks to pancakes, and you can also toast on it or grill hamburgers. The 1175-watt appliance is stainless steel; the cord and heating element detach for easy cleaning, and the fry pan/drip tray has a nonstick coating. The 9¾- by 6⅛-inch wire grill has two positions.

Approximate Retail Price	Approximate Low Price
$41.00	$30.00

Prices are accurate at time of printing; subject to manufacturer's change.

Rival 3154 Crock-Pot is a four-quart buffet-style slow cooker/server in beige and brown. It's an ideal size for roasts, meat loaf, or casseroles; the removable stoneware bowl is 8⅜ inches in diameter and has a glass cover. The appliance's case is made of steel. The Crock-Pot is a quality 160/250-watt unit that has a heat control; switch positions are "on," "low," and "high." It comes with an excellent cookbook on slow cooking.

Approximate Retail Price   **Approximate Low Price**
$40.50 .... $32.00

West Bend 5459—The Poppery—is a hot-air corn popper that pops up to four quarts of fluffy popcorn in about four minutes. Its automatic temperature control works well, and it handles all types of corn—gourmet or economy—equally well. Due to its deep popping chamber, there are very few unpopped kernels, as compared to many other units. The 1500-watt appliance has an on/off switch, a see-through cover, and a heat-resistant base; it also features a removable butter cup.

Approximate Retail Price   **Approximate Low Price**
$55.00 .... $23.00

Farberware 303 electric wok is stainless steel; the 1000-watt appliance has an aluminum-clad bottom that works with a heat control to create the traditional "heat center" that's a key to Oriental cooking. You can stir-fry, deep-fry, stew, or steam with the unit; you can also make popcorn. The wok has a temperature cooking range from 100° to 425° F. It comes with a stainless steel cover and a tempura rack.

Approximate Retail Price   **Approximate Low Price**
$70.00 .... $49.00

Simac 700 Pastamatic can make up to 1½ pounds of fresh pasta in about 10 minutes. It's a full cycle unit, which means that you just put the flour and eggs into the mixing bowl and push a button; the machine does the rest. It mixes, kneads, and extrudes the pasta through one of eight supplied discs. Ten other discs—six for pasta and four for making special items such as pizza, breadsticks, cookies, and gnocchi—are optional accessories. The PastaMatic machine is 10¾ inches high, 10½ inches wide, and 10½ inches deep; it weighs 17 pounds. This Italian-made machine is covered by a one-year warranty.

Approximate Retail Price   **Approximate Low Price**
$225.00 .... $180.00

Oster 755-04 is a continuous-roll bag sealer that lets you make air-tight, boilable cooking bags of any length; it holds up to 25 feet of Oster continuous-roll boilable freezer bag material. This appliance is an ideal companion to a microwave oven. You can seal one item or an entire meal by sealing items in sections. You can also seal other types of plastic bags (except nylon). No preheating is required. A slicing knife is included for customizing bag size. The appliance, which comes in a gold color, can be placed on a counter or mounted to the wall.

Approximate Retail Price   **Approximate Low Price**
$31.95 .... $25.00

Prices are accurate at time of printing; subject to manufacturer's change.

Microwave Ovens

THE MICROWAVE OVEN is an appliance that's perfect for our age. At a time when consumers want speed and ease, it's fast and clean. At a time when eating habits are shifting away from preparation of big family meals to accommodation of individual eating schedules, the microwave oven provides the flexibility for small-portion cooking—this also simplifies meal preparation for people who live alone. Food is cooked and served in a single container, which keeps kitchen cleanup to a minimum. And microwaving is energy-efficient, an added recommendation at a time when conservation is a major consumer concern.

Cooking for Speed and Energy Savings

COOKING IN A MICROWAVE OVEN saves energy because the oven doesn't have to be preheated, and because all microwave ovens cook much faster than conventional ranges—one-fourth of regular oven baking times and up to half of range-top cooking times. The kitchen stays cool because the only heat generated is in the food.

How Do Microwaves Work?

IN A MICROWAVE OVEN, a magnetron vacuum tube converts ordinary electricity into microwaves. The waves travel into the oven cavity, where they are circulated by a fan (called a "stirrer" in microwave jargon). As the circulating microwaves bounce off the metal surfaces of the oven interior and are absorbed by the food, they cause the molecules in the food to vibrate rapidly, creating the heat that cooks the food. Microwaves pass right through materials like glass, paper, pottery, and most forms of plastic, which stay unheated while the food in or on them gets cooked. But because microwaves bounce off metal, metal, metal-trimmed, or foil containers can't be used in a microwave oven.

It sounds great, but the microwave oven isn't infallible. For example, you must contend with what's called the multiplier effect: It takes longer to cook four strips of bacon in a microwave oven than it does to cook one strip. Why does cooking time increase with an increase of food in the oven? So far, no one knows the answer.

Another factor is that since there's no dry heat in the oven cavity, food cooked in a microwave oven doesn't brown or crisp. To some users this is a disadvantage, although food tastes much the same whether it is browned or not. A unit that combines microwave energy with convection cooking, which forces heated air over food, gives the option of browning and crisping; in the process, however, it sacrifices two of the microwave's pleasing features—speed, and dishes cool enough to handle.

Microwave/Convection Combinations

SEVEN MICROWAVE OVEN manufacturers now offer combination microwave/convection ovens. The big difference is a heat source and fans to circulate the hot air inside the oven. Added to a microwave, convection provides browning and other benefits—crisping, baking, and dehydration. A combination oven can be used solely as a microwave oven, solely as a convection oven, or as a dual-purpose oven in which food is cooked by microwaves and forced heated air simultaneously. The way the microwave and convection actions work together, the convection temperature range, the interior oven finish, and the accessories available vary from one manufacturer to another. The complexities of programming the oven and the need for accurate cookbook directions make the combination oven an appliance for second-microwave owners.

It's also possible to buy a regular gas or electric range that allows microwave or convection cooking as well as conventional cooking, either in the same oven or—in the case of some two-oven units—in a separate oven. These are discussed in our chapter on ranges.

What Do You Want From Your Microwave Oven?

ASK YOURSELF WHAT KIND of a cook you really are before shopping for a microwave oven. There are hundreds of models to choose from, and it's not easy to select one that will match your cooking interests and skills, fit into the available space, and perform well over a period of years. A microwave oven can be a simple unit that you just turn on and off. This is ideal for heating up your lunch at the office or recycling leftovers for a quick meal at home. The most sophisticated microwaves have as many numbers on the front as a calculator and can be quite intimidating to the newcomer. If you plan to use your microwave oven as your primary cooking unit, a model that has five variable power settings, a temperature probe, and two memory levels should be straightforward to use and will probably give you all the versatility you need. You can get a unit that fits on your counter, or if counter space is at a premium, an over-the-range model designed to fit into exhaust hood space. Over-the-range models are equipped with a vent to exhaust range-top heat and cooking odors.

Plan Your Microwave Purchase

BEFORE BUYING, ask current owners what they do and don't like about their microwave ovens. Once you've made your own selection, find out what repair service is available in your area for the model you favor. Look in the phone book for factory-authorized service in your area; ask if repairs are made in your home or at the service center, and who provides the transportation. Ask the dealer when the model was introduced, and don't buy one of the first off the assembly line of a brand-new model with a new feature. Design flaws and machine malfunctions may occur in these first models, and it takes a few months for the manufacturer to correct mistakes. Also before buying, see if you can figure out how to enter the cooking time and power level and start the microwave oven without having to look it up.

The Safety Question

WHILE IT SEEMS clear—as the manufacturers frequently point out—that microwaves cannot produce harmful radiation, the long-range cumulative effects are as yet unknown. Microwave technology is, after all, relatively new.

The truth is that no one knows for sure whether microwaves pose a potential health hazard. No such hazard has yet been documented, but the federal government has put a limit on the amount of microwave energy manufacturers can allow to leak from an oven. To meet that limit, manufacturers have developed special safety devices to keep the energy where it belongs—in the oven. Interlocks and automatic shutoff switches prevent the ovens from operating with the door open, and special door seals are designed to minimize microwave leakage.

Perhaps the best safety feature that comes with a microwave oven, though, is the owner's manual. Read it carefully to learn what you can and cannot do with the oven; then adhere to the guidelines. Keep the interior of the oven clean; food spills and spatters can attract microwave energy and lower cooking efficiency. Don't set anything over or in front of the air vents; this causes heat to build up inside the oven. The door should close tightly and not show any signs of being loose or needing an extra push to make the oven go on. If you're concerned about possible microwave leakage from your oven, check with your local Public Health Department to see if they will test microwave ovens for leakage. Or, for your own peace of mind, have the manufacturer's repair service test your unit for leakage every few years.

It is worth noting two considerations that make the microwave oven a practical safety choice for handicapped or visually impaired people: The unit won't work unless the door is locked, and the danger of accidental burns is minimal because the only hot surface is that of the food itself.

Microwave Oven Features

HERE ARE SOME of the features to consider when you're buying a microwave oven:

Memory Levels. Memory levels allow you to tell the oven the time and the power setting needed for cooking. You can get up to four memory levels. It's necessary to have two; four is getting into the luxury stakes. If you have a microwave oven with two memory levels you can, for instance, set a dish to cook on high power for five minutes and then on medium power for 15.

Controls. Electronic controls, found on the high- and medium-priced units, can be programmed to remember multiple cooking times, power levels, temperatures, and other useful information. Mechanical controls are used on lower-priced models.

Oven Capacity. A 1.2-cubic-foot oven is large enough to hold a variety of containers. An 8 x 12-inch rectangular dish is standard for microwave cooking, compared to the 9 x 13-inch size used for conventional oven recipes.

Cooking Power. Microwave recipes, cookbooks, and directions on food packages are tested for use in 625 to 700 watt microwave ovens. Microwave ovens with 600 watts or lower output may cook as well, but they don't cook as quickly. Very low-priced models generally have less wattage; they're designed for quick convenience cooking.

Variable Power Settings. For full cooking capability, you need a minimum of five power levels: high (100 percent), medium high (70 percent), medium (50 percent), medium low (30 percent), and low (10 percent). Electronic controls offer up to 10 power settings; mechanical models may offer the minimum of five.

Defrost Setting. All microwave ovens have a defrost setting. Most defrost at one steady power level. Some units have an automatic defrost feature that uses a combination of power levels, starting at high and decreasing to low. This method defrosts evenly, with no risk that the food will start to cook while it's defrosting.

Temperature Probe. Although it boosts the price of the unit, a temperature probe can be useful. You put it in the food—rather like a meat thermometer—and it's activated by the oven's electronic controls. You select the temperature to which the food should be cooked and the probe signals the controls when the food reaches that temperature; the controls then either turn the oven off, or hold the food at the required temperature. The temperature probe is especially helpful when cooking dense, solid foods. If you're using a temperature probe you don't have to program a cooking time.

Timer. Since time is so important in microwave cooking, make sure the unit you plan to buy has a timer that offers a wide range of precise time settings. Even inexpensive ovens with dial settings for minutes and seconds should have at least the first three or four minutes divided into 15-second intervals. The more expensive units have solid-state timers that can be set for up to 99 minutes. Stay away from timers that can't be set for at least 30 minutes: They often must be set and then reset just to cook a normal meal. Some ovens have count-down digital displays that function as regular digital clocks when the oven is not in use.

Humidity Sensor. This is a device to determine correct cooking time and power level. It eliminates guesswork when you're reheating leftovers or adapting conventional recipes to microwave cooking times.

Turntable. Some manufacturers use a turntable to move the food through the microwave energy, instead of stirrer fans to distribute the energy. Turntables limit the selection of containers you can use, and some have a "cold spot" in the center.

Talking Ovens. A computer-like voice asks questions and leads you through the programming. This is a good feature for the visually impaired user.

Door Opening. Microwave oven doors open from right to left or pull straight down. Consider which will be easier to work with in your kitchen.

Shelves. A built-in oven floor or a removable glass tray are the options. Both are efficient and easy to clean, and they're about equally durable.

Oven Racks. In some ovens, metal or plastic racks allow you to cook a number of small items at the same time. The racks can be removed to accommodate a single larger item. Both metal and plastic racks are satisfactory.

Interior Finish. Stainless steel and acrylic-coated steel are the two finishes used. Stainless steel is slightly more efficient but does not let you see the food cooking as easily as the white acrylic finish does.

Exterior Finish. Woodgrain-vinyl-clad steel is used on most ovens. Embossed or textured steel is also available. Most microwave ovens can be built in, and trim kits are available.

Best Buys '82

OUR SELECTION of "Best Buy" microwave ovens follows, chosen according to our criteria of efficiency, durability, and convenience. The models are listed alphabetically within each category. It's important to remember that a "Best Buy" label on a product applies only to that particular model. It doesn't imply that we endorse a whole product line, or that other models by the same manufacturer are also satisfactory.

Best Buys '82 Microwave Ovens

Amana Model RRL-9TB (oven capacity, over 1 cubic foot) has a two-level memory and 10 power settings. This model also has a clock, an automatic-hold cycle, a temperature probe, and a memory-recall feature. The controls are electronic, and the oven delivers 700 watts of cooking power. The quality construction, stainless steel interior, and removable glass tray are features to be appreciated. The pull-down door has a brown glass front.

Specifications: Overall Dimensions: Height, 15¼"; **Width,** 22¾"; **Depth,** 18." **Oven Capacity,** over 1 cu. ft. **Oven Dimensions: Height,** 9¾"; **Width,** 14⅝"; **Depth,** 13⅜." **Cooking Power,** 700 watts; **Controls,** electronic; **Warranty,** parts and labor, 1 year; electronic timer (parts only), second year; magnetron tube and stainless steel cavity (parts and labor), 5 years.

Approximate Retail Price	Approximate Low Price
$520.00	$450.00

General Electric JET 108 (1.3 cubic feet oven capacity) has three memory levels, 10 power settings, a temperature probe, and a digital clock/timer. The controls are electronic, and the oven delivers 625 watts of cooking power. You can cook by time as well as by temperature. The unit can be programmed for slow cooking, and there's an automatic feature for use with roasts—you add a code, like "medium," to the selected cooking temperature and the unit shifts power to cook the meat

Prices are accurate at time of printing; subject to manufacturer's change.

more evenly. There's also a defrost feature. The unit comes with a cookbook, and an optional installation kit is available.

Specifications: Overall Dimensions: Height, 15½ inches; **Width,** 22 inches; **Depth,** 20 inches; **Oven Capacity,** 1.3 cu. ft. **Oven Dimensions: Height,** 10½"; **Width,** 13¾"; **Depth,** 15¾". **Cooking Power,** 625 watts; **Controls:** electronic; **Warranty,** parts and labor, 1 year; magnetron tube (parts only), 5 years.

Approximate Retail Price	Approximate Low Price
Not Available	$445.00

General Electric Spacemaker JVM 62 (oven capacity, 0.8 cubic feet) is a cabinet-mounted microwave oven designed to fit above the range where the range hood usually goes. The oven has electronic controls, 10 power settings, and a defrost setting. You can cook by time or with a temperature probe. The oven delivers 625 watts of cooking power. An automatic cooking control is preprogrammed for frequently cooked foods—you don't have to set time, temperature, or power level. The unit has a digital readout panel and clock, a timer, a built-in vent to exhaust heat and smoke from range-top cooking, and a cooktop light. This GE design is wider and lower than most microwave ovens. A cookbook comes with the oven.

Specifications: Overall Dimensions: Height, 16"; **Width,** 30"; **Depth,** 13." **Oven Capacity,** 0.8 cu. ft. **Oven Dimensions: Height,** 7¾"; **Width,** 16"; **Depth,** 10¹³⁄₁₆". **Cooking Power,** 625 watts; **Controls,** electronic; **Warranty,** parts and labor, 1 year; magnetron tube, 5 years.

Approximate Retail Price	Approximate Low Price
Not Available	$619.00

Litton 1571 (oven capacity, 1.5 cubic feet) has side-feed energy distribution—the microwave energy is distributed from right and left instead of only from the top of the oven; we like this feature, which is exclusive to Litton units. The side-feed distribution of power makes it possible to microwave three food items at one time using the oven rack. A "delay-start" turns on automatically to start cooking at the selected time. This unit has four memory levels, 10 power settings, a temperature probe, an automatic shut-off, a defrost setting, a clock/timer, and an oven light. The controls are electronic, and the oven delivers 700 watts of cooking power. A cookbook comes with the oven.

Specifications: Overall Dimensions: Height, 15¾"; **Width,** 27"; **Depth,** 18¼". **Oven Capacity,** 1.5 cu. ft. **Oven Dimensions: Height,** 10"; **Width,** 16"; **Depth,** 16¼. **Cooking Power,** 700 watts; **Controls,** electronic; **Warranty,** parts, 1 year; magnetron tube, 5 years.

Approximate Retail Price	Approximate Low Price
Not Available	$449.00

Litton-Aire (oven capacity, 1.1 cubic feet) is a microwave oven that fits easily over your range. Like the Litton 1571, this unit has side-feed energy distribution, which lets you cook several items simultaneously using the oven rack. This unit has a four-level memory, 10 power levels, a temperature probe, a defrost setting, and a clock/timer. A delay-start feature automatically starts the cooking program at a preset time. The

Prices are accurate at time of printing; subject to manufacturer's change.

controls are electronic, and the oven delivers 600 watts of cooking power. An exhaust vent and range-top light are built in. A guide on the panel lists cooking combinations of frequently prepared foods.

Specifications: Overall dimensions: Height, 17″ (rear), 15″ (front); **Width,** 29¹⁵/₁₆″; **Depth,** 14¼″. **Oven Capacity,** 1.1 cu. ft. **Oven Dimensions: Height,** 10″; **Width,** 16″; **Depth,** 12″. **Cooking Power,** 600 watts; **Controls,** electronic; **Warranty,** parts, 1 year; magnetron tube, 5 years.

Approximate Retail Price	Approximate Low Price
Not Available	$549.00

Magic Chef M31A-5P (oven capacity, 1.1 cubic feet) gives 650 watts of cooking power. This model has 10 power levels, a temperature probe, a digital timer that can be set for up to 99 minutes, an automatic keep-warm setting, and a signal light that tells you when the oven is operating. A bell signals the end of timed cooking. The controls on this unit are mechanical, and a cookbook comes with the oven.

Specifications: Overall Dimensions: Height, 15″; **Width,** 25″; **Depth,** 16⅛″. **Oven Capacity,** 1.1 cu. ft. **Oven Dimensions: Height,** 9½″; **Width,** 14½″; **Depth,** 13½″. **Cooking Power,** 650 watts; **Controls,** mechanical; **Warranty,** parts and labor, 1 year; magnetron tube, 5 years.

Approximate Retail Price	Approximate Low Price
$369.00	$299.00

Montgomery Ward 8241 (oven capacity, 1.5 cubic feet) has electronic controls, three memory levels, five power levels, a temperature probe, and a defrost setting. It delivers 650 watts of cooking power. There's a delay-start feature that turns on the oven at a preset time. A memory-recall feature can store three programs. The unit has a rack, a removable glass cooking tray, a clock, and a timer. A cookbook is included with the oven. An optional installation kit is available.

Specifications: Overall Dimensions: Height, 15¾″; **Width,** 24⅝″; **Depth,** 18″. **Oven Capacity,** 1.5 cu. ft. **Oven Dimensions: Height,** 10⅛″; **Width,** 15½″; **Depth,** 16⅝″. **Cooking Power,** 650 watts; **Controls,** electronic; **Warranty,** parts and labor, 1 year; transformer, 2 years; magnetron tube, 5 years.

Approximate Retail Price	Approximate Low Price
$525.00	Not Available

Quasar MO5520 (oven capacity, 1.35 cubic feet) has an automatic multi-stage defrost system that uses a combination of power levels to defrost food quickly and evenly. The oven has electronic controls and delivers 700 watts of cooking power. It has three memory levels, six power settings, a temperature probe, and a temperature probe guide on the control panel that tells you the recommended temperature settings for certain foods. An automatic-hold feature will hold food at the selected temperature for up to 90 minutes. This unit has a relay-start feature, and a digital clock/timer and temperature display.

Specifications: Overall Dimensions: Height, 15″; **Width,** 24¾″; **Depth,** 17⅛″. **Oven Capacity,** 1.35 cu. ft. **Oven Dimensions: Height,**

Prices are accurate at time of printing; subject to manufacturer's change.

9½"; **Width,** 15½"; **Depth,** 15½". **Cooking Power,** 700 watts; **Controls,** electronic; **Warranty,** parts (including magnetron tube) and labor, 5 years.

Toshiba ER-781BT-1 (oven capacity, 1.6 cubic feet) uses a rotating disc to distribute microwaves evenly. You can cook by time or with the temperature probe. The unit has four memory levels and nine power settings. There's a 100-minute digital timer and a heat-and-hold setting. Controls are electronic, and the oven delivers 650 watts of cooking power. An automatic defrost setting uses a combination of power levels for quick and even defrosting. The oven interior is the largest available, but the oven remains compact in overall dimensions.
Specifications: Overall Dimensions: Height, 15"; **Width,** 24⁹/₁₆"; **Depth,** 18¹/₁₆". **Oven Capacity,** 1.6 cu ft. **Oven Dimensions: Height,** 10⅛"; **Width,** 16⅛"; **Depth,** 16". **Cooking Power,** 650 watts; **Controls,** electronic; **Warranty,** parts and labor, 2 years; magnetron tube (parts only), 5 years.

Whirlpool RJM 7700 (oven capacity, 1.3 cubic feet) is a straightforward microwave oven that offers two memory levels, a temperature probe, 10 power settings, and a defrost feature. The controls are electronic, and the oven delivers 650 watts of cooking power. This unit also has a clock/timer and a removable rack. This is a simple unit and is efficient and easy to use.
Specifications: Overall Dimensions: Height, 15½"; **Width,** 25½"; **Depth,** 18¹⁵/₁₆". **Oven capacity,** 1.3 cu. ft. **Oven Dimensions: Height,** 9¹¹/₁₆"; **Width,** 15"; **Depth,** 15¹³/₃₂". **Cooking Power,** 650 watts; **Controls,** electronic; **Warranty,** parts and labor, 1 year; magnetron tube, 5 years.

 Best Buys 82 Microwave/Convection Ovens

Amana RMC-30 (oven capacity, 1.3 cubic feet) is a microwave/ convection oven. Microwave energy is fed into the oven from the bottom of the unit, and convection heat from the top; this means correct food placement is very important for good results. The microwave oven has two memory levels, 10 power levels, a timer, and a temperature probe, and delivers 700 watts of cooking power. The controls are electronic. The convection oven temperature is preset to one temperature—275°F.

Prices are accurate at time of printing; subject to manufacturer's change.

The unit has an adjustable oven rack and an optional dehydration shelf. A cookbook comes with the unit; an installation kit is optional. **Specifications: Overall Dimensions: Height,** 17"; **Width,** 24¾"; **Depth,** 22". **Oven Capacity,** 1.3 cu. ft. **Oven Dimensions: Height,** 10½"; **Width,** 16"; **Depth,** 13¼". **Cooking Power,** 700 watts; **Controls,** electronic; **Warranty,** parts and labor, 1 year; magnetron tube, 5 years.

Approximate Retail Price	Approximate Low Price
$850.00	$733.00

Sharp Model R-8320 (oven capacity, 1.53 cubic feet) combines convection heat with microwave energy—in the microwave mode a turntable rotates the food. We like this unit because it's easy to understand and the electronic program controls are straightforward. The microwave oven has four memory levels, four power settings (including medium low/or defrosting); and delivers 650 watts of cooking power. The convection temperature range is from 100° to 450°, and the convection temperature control has an automatic preheat feature. Two settings automatically combine convection and microwave cooking—low mix for baking, and high mix for roasting. Other settings include broil and slow-cook settings, and a cycle for raising yeast dough. The unit has a timer, a clock, and a memory-recall feature; this model comes with a two-level baking rack, a broiling trivet, and a cookbook.
Specifications: Overall Dimensions: Height, 15¾"; **Width,** 24⅝"; **Depth,** 18". **Oven Capacity,** 1.53 cu. ft. **Oven Dimensions: Height,** 10¼"; **Width,** 15½"; **Depth,** 16⅝". **Cooking Power,** 650 watts; **Controls,** electronic; **Warranty,** parts and labor, 2 years; tube, 7 years.

Approximate Retail Price	Approximate Low Price
$740.00	$619.00

Also Recommended

Quasar MQ8800SW (oven capacity, 1.35 cubic feet), is a combination oven that delivers convection heat from the back of the oven and microwave energy from a rotating wand at the top. The microwave mode has electronic controls, three memory levels, six power settings, a temperature probe that can be used for both microwave and convection cooking, a delay-start feature, and a multi-stage defrost system that uses a combination of power levels to defrost evenly; it delivers 700 watts of cooking power. The convection temperature range is from 200° to 450°F. The unit has a digital clock/timer and temperature display. Standard accessories are two oven racks with a drip guard, a ceramic oven tray, and two cookbooks. Because this unit is not as energy efficient as we would like, we do not give it a "Best Buy" recommendation.
Specifications: Overall Dimensions: Height, 15⅛"; **Width,** 24¾"; **Depth,** 22"; **Oven Capacity,** 1.35 cu. ft. **Oven Dimensions: Height,** 9½"; **Width** 15½"; **Depth** 15½". **Cooking Power,** 700 watts; **Controls,** electronic; **Warranty,** in-home labor, 1 year; parts (including magnetron tube), 5 years.

Approximate Retail Price	Approximate Low Price
Not Available	$779.00

Prices are accurate at time of printing; subject to manufacturer's change.

Ranges

ITS A LONG WAY from a cooking pot over the fire to microwave energy that cooks without any perceptible heat at all. A plain old range is fast becoming a period piece, and choosing a new range from the selection now available can be a thoroughly confusing business. To cut through the confusion, it helps to go back to the basics.

Basically, a range is a box-shaped appliance with an oven inside and hot spots on top. Usually there's a broiler under the oven. Even in this progressive age, the main difference between one box and another is the kind of energy that provides the heat for cooking, and the huge majority of ranges still employ one of two heat sources—gas or electricity. Each has its supporters, and they tend to be very single-minded about their preferences.

The Basic Choice: Gas or Electricity

WITH AN ELECTRIC RANGE, heat is delivered to electrical elements on the top of the range—there are usually four of them, six or eight inches in diameter; there is no naked flame. On a gas range the elements are replaced by burners, which ignite at the turn of a knob. Most ranges have four burners the same size. Gas ranges used to be made with a standing pilot light that remained lit all the time and used a lot of energy. Many ranges now have automatic electric ignition instead of a standing pilot. A word, though, about automatic ignition. Early automatic-ignition models had troubles with the ignition systems, especially with delicate and touchy oven ignitors. Many manufacturers believe that they have solved the problem, but the word from service personnel is that failures are still frequent. There does, however, tend to be a lag effect before such an improvement becomes established.

Electric ranges outsell gas models. The trend towards electric units really took hold when consumers were threatened with a shortage of natural gas. Now that there is no shortage on the horizon, gas ranges are selling briskly again. In general, you pay a little more for a gas range than for a comparable electric model, but you also pay less to operate it. Over the long run, both cost about the same. Gas surface burners give you instant on and off and more precise heat adjustment than electric elements; elements take time to heat up or cool down. And gas is easier to monitor visibly—the flame is there, and you can see just how high it is.

From Conventional to Convection

UNTIL RECENTLY, the gas vs. electric question was about the only major issue you had to decide when choosing a range. Today, however, new cooking techniques are moving the consumer away from that conventional "either-or" decision.

The convection oven, a comparative newcomer to the cooking scene, uses a conventional heat source (gas or electricity), but a new technique—it forces air over the heat source. A convection gas oven is more energy-efficient than a conventional gas unit—tests have shown energy savings up to 50 percent in a convection gas unit equipped with electric ignition. But the convection technique does not significantly alter the energy consumption of an electric oven. The convection feature (which is essentially just a fan) raises the price of a unit by some $50.

Harnessing New Technology

THE MICROWAVE OVEN doesn't use heat at all—microwaves are a form of invisible radiant energy, like radio waves. In a microwave oven, a magnetron vacuum tube converts ordinary energy into microwaves. The waves travel into the oven cavity, where they are circulated by a fan (called a "stirrer" in microwave jargon). As the circulating microwaves bounce off metal surfaces and are absorbed by the food, they cause the molecules in the food to vibrate rapidly, creating the heat that cooks the food. Microwaves pass right through materials like glass, paper, pottery, and most forms of plastic, which stay unheated while the food in or on them gets cooked. Microwave ovens are so unlike ranges that use conventional energy sources that we are including in this discussion only units that use both microwave and other cooking techniques. You'll find full information and "Best Buy" selections for standard microwaves in the separate section on microwave ovens.

Another unconventional cooking technique is induction, or magnetic cooking. It has been tried before and is now being reintroduced, but it is still in the experimental stage. Chambers, Roper, and several Japanese manufacturers offer induction units that create a magnetic field in cooking utensils that, in turn, creates heat. This unique method creates heat only in the pot or pan, while the smooth range surface stays cool to the touch. One of the initial drawbacks to induction cooking was that it called for high-quality and expensive special utensils. Manufacturers claim to have solved this problem, but it may, as with all new techniques, take a few years for induction cooking to catch on, and for the performance of these magnetic ranges to become stable.

Easing the Energy Load

IN RECENT YEARS range manufacturers have been making changes to bring their products in line with anticipated federal energy requirements. Although those expected standards may not now be enforced, customers reap the benefits of the manufacturers' labor in the shape of energy-efficient features already incorporated into some new ranges. As we've mentioned, automatic ignition has replaced standing pilots on most gas ranges (and adds $30 or $40 to the purchase price), and some gas and electric ranges now feature thicker and better insulation and improved door seals.

Energy-efficiency is an important consideration when you're choosing a range. Another major factor is style and suitability for your work space and your way of life.

Today's changes in living and cooking styles have created a market for kitchen equipment to meet a broad range of needs. Many people have little time, or little inclination, for elaborate meal preparation and want their kitchens geared to speed and efficiency. On the other hand, the rise in popularity of gourmet cooking and home entertaining presents a demand for sophisticated equipment.

Even assuming that you're staying with a straightforward gas or electric range, making your choice is probably going to be less straightforward than you anticipate. That original square box design now shares the market with a number of sophisticated cousins that perform all kinds of specialized cooking operations.

Choose for Your Lifestyle, Work Space

BASICALLY, HERE ARE the types you can choose from. The following styles come in gas or electric versions, and can be free-standing (with the oven enclosed in a metal cabinet below the cooking surface) or built or set into a wall or an island:

• Single-oven ranges are the simplest "square box" designs. They have one oven below the cooktop and no frills.

• Over-and-under ranges have two ovens, one above and one below the cooking surface. They're also called eye-level or double-decker ranges.

• Combination units use two different cooking techniques in one unit. For example, several manufacturers now offer an over-and-under range with a microwave oven on top and a conventional oven below. Others offer combination units that can provide both microwave power and conventional gas or electric heat in the same oven.

• Set-in or drop-in ranges are also available and are popular with some kitchen designers. If you want a built-in oven with a separate cooktop, you can get it. If you want a drop-in designed for a sidewall, island, or peninsula installation, you can get it. If you want to install a range between two cabinets, you can select a slide-in model with unfinished sides and back. The slide-in range fits snugly, looks built-in, and usually has a top that overlaps the counter on either side. If you're looking for a built-in unit, be sure to check out your work space carefully and match its measurements to those of the range. This may sound elementary, but appliances tend to look a lot smaller in the showroom than they do in your own kitchen.

Other types of ranges don't give you the option of choosing a gas model. The two that follow are available only in electric versions:

• Most manufacturers offer grill range models—a field that was opened up by Jenn-Air. Grill ranges feature interchangeable surface accessories that you can lift out and replace as you please—regular surface elements, a griddle, a charcoal grill, and a deep-fat fryer are among the accessories available for use with some models. The range oven may feature convection cooking.

• Smoothtop ranges have a ceramic surface that hides the heating elements. This is less energy-efficient than a standard electric unit because the heat must travel through the surface before it reaches the pan.

Details Help You Decide

BEYOND THE BASIC CHOICES—gas or electric, combination or conventional—shopping for a new range involves making decisions on many important features. Here are some of them:

Burners and Elements: Gas ranges have four same-size burners, usually with pilotless ignition (either a glow or a spark ignition), although some gas models still have standing pilots. We recommend that you avoid thermostatically controlled automatic burners; they cost extra and break down frequently. Electric ranges usually have two six-inch and two eight-inch elements. A fast-heating element and infinite-position heat controls—two convenience features on electric ranges—are worth having.

Broilers. Broilers are positioned under the oven in a separate compartment, or built into the top of the cavity itself. The latter type, known as a waist-high broiler, is a little more convenient simply because you don't have to bend down to use it. Unless otherwise specified, the broilers on the ranges we discuss are positioned under the oven.

Cooktops. Look for a top that lifts and locks so that you can clean under the burners easily. Removable reflector pans or bowls under the burners or elements are both energy-efficient and helpful during cleanup.

Range Hood. An unvented range hood traps and holds grease and odors. Whenever possible, opt for a vented range hood because it removes both grease and odors. Remember that a range hood is not a standard feature on all ranges.

Range-Top Accessories. Interchangeable surface accessories for grill ranges are available, including a rotisserie, a deep fryer, a griddle, a smoothtop, a cutting board, and a conventional electric element set.

Programmed Ovens. Although convenient, the fully programmed oven is too expensive to be worthwhile for many homemakers. "Delay-cook-and-hold" is the most useful program. It delays the start of cooking to a preset time, cooks for a set period, and then drops the oven to keep-warm temperature until you shut the range off. Next best is a cook-and-hold program, followed by the delay-and-cook system that turns the oven on at a preset time, cooks, and then turns the oven off. You can also get a start-and-stop program. There are now more ranges with electronic control systems—mostly of the "touch" types.

Other Features. Clocks, timers, and cooktop lighting are useful to most cooks. Removable griddles, meat thermometers, and rotisseries are also available on many ranges; they are practical features only if you will use them often enough to justify paying extra for them.

Removable Oven Door. A lift-off oven door makes cleaning easier, especially on ranges that don't have a self-cleaning system.

Warming Shelf. Some ranges have a shelf above the cooktop for keeping cooked foods warm. Most people find this an unnecessary feature.

Window and Oven Lights. A window and an interior oven light allow you to check cooking progress without opening the oven door.

Oven-Cleaning Systems. Your choice is between self-cleaning and continuous cleaning. The self-cleaning oven uses high heat (up to 1000°F) to incinerate oven grime to a powdery ash that you can wipe up with a damp cloth. The cycle takes from two to four hours, depending on brand and model. Although expensive to buy and to operate, it makes oven cleaning a breeze. If you bake a great deal, you'll love a self-cleaning oven. Continuous cleaning isn't a mechanical system; it relies on a special porous finish on the oven interior to absorb and spread soil in such a way that the residue will oxidize at normal oven temperatures. Continuous cleaning is often described as a "clean-look" feature; it does a "cosmetic" job, but cannot duplicate the thorough cleaning job of a self-cleaning oven. You must wipe up large spills yourself, and you must never use abrasive cleaners. The cost efficiency of a self-cleaning oven depends—not surprisingly—on how often you use the self-clean operation. Moreover, some customers consider the convenience well worth any extra cost.

Best Buys '82

OUR "BEST BUY" and "Also Recommended" selections represent the best of available products according to our criteria of quality, efficiency, energy use, and value. The individual product profiles, listed alphabetically within each category, detail reasons for each rating. As we said earlier, an enormous variety of ranges is available, and we have tried to offer selections to suit all cooking styles and all pocketbooks. We've also kept in mind that some units, though glamorous, are not appropriate for all users. A 40-inch range, for instance, won't be the choice of a casual cook; it's also too large for many kitchens. And a built-in unit presupposes that you've got somewhere to install it. Remember, too, that a "Best Buy" or "Also Recommended" label applies only to one particular unit. It doesn't mean that we endorse a whole product line, or that other models by the same manufacturer also meet our selection criteria.

 Free-Standing Gas Ranges

Caloric RMR 364 is a 30-inch gas unit with a continuous-cleaning oven and automatic pilotless ignition. A separate broiler drawer slides out for easy use. The unit has an automatic-timed oven system, surface and oven lights, a tilt-top cooktop, a black glass oven window, and a lift-off door. This model has extra insulation for better energy efficiency.

Specifications: Overall Dimensions: Height, 45"; **Width,** 30"; **Depth,** 26½". **Oven Dimensions: Height,** 13¾"; **Width,** 24"; **Depth,** 19". **Warranty,** parts and labor, 1 year.

Approximate Retail Price	Approximate Low Price
Not Available..	$499.00

Magic Chef 33B-4KLW is a 30-inch gas model with pilotless ignition and extra insulation for energy savings. It has a continuous-cleaning oven, a digital clock, a spill-catching top, a one-hour timer, an oven door window, and a worktop light. The cooktop lifts up and off for easy cleaning. The same model with a black glass oven door and black lower panel is Model 33B-4KLX.
Specifications: Overall Dimensions: Height, 45⅞"; **Width,** 30"; **Depth,** 25⅝". **Oven Dimensions:** Not Available. **Warranty,** parts and labor, 1 year.

Approximate Retail Price	Approximate Low Price
$539.00..	$459.00

Tappan 30-3871 is a 30-inch model with a self-cleaning convection oven and pilotless ignition on the burners. It has two adjustable double-nickel oven racks, a lift-off oven door, lift-up/lock top, a digital clock/timer, a cooktop light, chrome burner bowls, and a recessed top that keeps spills from running over. This model is expensive, but it offers value commensurate with the price and should appeal to cooks who want the convection capability.
Specifications: Overall Dimensions: Height, 46⅝"; **Width,** 30¹/₁₆"; **Depth,** 27⅝". **Oven Dimensions: Height,** 14¼"; **Width,** 23"; **Depth,** 16⅞". **Warranty,** parts and labor, 1 year.

Approximate Retail Price	Approximate Low Price
$1,030.00	$799.00

Also Recommended

Roper 1648 is a big 36-inch range with pilotless surface burners and oven/broiler. It has a continuous-cleaning oven, a lift-up/off cooktop, a roll-out broiler, a removable oven door with window, removable oven racks and rack supports, an oven light, and a four-hour clock-timer. This model has good storage space to the left of the oven. The size of this unit, however, makes it unsuitable for many kitchens, which is why we don't give it a "Best Buy" rating.
Specifications: Overall Dimensions: Height, 47"; **Width,** 36"; **Depth,** 24". **Oven Dimensions:** Not Available. **Warranty,** parts and labor, 1 year.

Approximate Retail Price	Approximate Low Price
$650.00...	$499.00

Tappan 30-3457 is a 30-inch range with pilotless ignition. It has many good features: a continuous-clean oven, a lock top, a black glass door, two adjustable chrome oven racks, a glide-out broiler, and an oven light. This unit, however, is less well built than our "Best Buy" selections in this category.

Prices are accurate at time of printing; subject to manufacturer's change.

Specifications: Overall Dimensions: Height, 46⅝"; **Width,** 29¹⁵/₁₆", **Depth,** 25¹/₃₂". **Oven Dimensions:** Not Available. **Warranty,** parts and labor, 1 year.

Approximate Retail Price
$680.00...

Approximate Low Price
.... $535.00

 Best Buys 82 Combination Gas Ranges

Caloric RKR396 is an over-and-under combination range with a lower gas oven and an upper microwave oven (1.1-cubic-foot interior capacity), both with black glass doors. The lower oven is self-cleaning, with automatic oven controls, a cooktop light, and a lift-up-and-lock top for easy cleaning. The pilotless gas surface burners offer excellent flame control. The upper microwave oven offers variable power up to 675 watts, and has touch controls, a digital clock, a rotating antenna to beam microwaves directly at food, and an interior light. An optional venting hood is available.
Specifications: Overall Dimensions: Height, 66"; **Width,** 30"; **Depth,** 26½". **Oven Dimensions: Height,** 13¾"; **Width,** 22"; **Depth,** 19". **Microwave Oven Capacity:** 1.1 cu. ft. **Microwave Oven Dimensions: Height,** 9⅛"; **Width,** 14⅝"; **Depth,** 13⅜". **Warranty,** parts and labor, 1 year; magnetron tube (parts only) 5 years.

Approximate Retail Price
Not Available..

Approximate Low Price
.... $1,195.00

Caloric RRR383 is a 30-inch combination gas range with microwave and convection capabilities all in the same self-cleaning oven. The unit has automatic pilotless ignition in the oven and on the cooktop, digital clock, timed oven, a microwave timer, variable power for the microwave action, two oven racks with five positions, and a forced convection system. The combination means faster cooking, energy savings, and efficient cooking at lower temperatures.
Specifications: Overall Dimensions: Height 47¾"; **Width,** 30"; **Depth,** 25¼". **Oven Dimensions: Height,** 16"; **Width,** 23"; **Depth,** 15¾". **Warranty,** parts and labor, 1 year; magnetron tube (parts only), 5 years.

Approximate Retail Price
Not Available..

Approximate Low Price
.... $1,159.00

Also Recommended

Hardwick CK8442-K*-910A is an over-and-under combination of an upper microwave oven and a lower gas oven. The lower continuous-cleaning oven has a drop-down broiler, a removable lift-up top, and a lift-

Prices are accurate at time of printing; subject to manufacturer's change.

off door with window. The adjustable oven rack, lighted back panel, and programmed cook-and-hold controls, delay-start program (up to 12 hours), three levels of memory programming, and variable power for its 625 watts of total cooking power. An automatic probe is available. Model CK8441-K*-910A is the same unit with a full-width black glass door and window in the lower oven.

Specifications: Overall Dimensions: Height, 64⅝"; **Width,** 30"; **Depth,** 24¾". **Oven Dimensions: Height,** 13⅝"; **Width,** 24"; **Depth,** 19¼". **Microwave Oven Capacity:** 1.3 cu. ft. **Microwave Oven Dimensions:** Not Available. **Warranty,** parts and labor, 1 year; magnetron tube (parts only), 4 years.

Approximate Retail Price	Approximate Low Price
$1,449.50	$1,000.00

Over-And-Under Gas Ranges

Sears Kenmore 22G78501N is an over-and-under gas range with two continuous-cleaning ovens (both with black glass doors). The unit has a programmable lower oven with a roll-out broiler beneath it, oven lights, dial clock-timer, and removable lower oven door. Pilotless ignition throughout saves energy. A range hood with a vent is optional.

Specifications: Overall Dimensions: Height, 66"; **Width,** 29⅞"; **Depth,** 28". **Upper Oven Dimensions: Height,** 13⅝"; **Width,** 20¹³⁄₁₆"; **Depth,** 13¹¹⁄₁₆". **Lower Oven Dimensions: Height,** 17"; **Width,** 24"; **Depth,** 18½". **Warranty,** parts and labor (except glass parts), 1 year; glass parts; 30 days.

Approximate Retail Price	Approximate Low Price
$760.00 (white)	Not Available
$770.00 (other colors)	Not Available

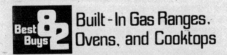

Built-In Gas Ranges, Ovens, and Cooktops

Hardwick CK7142*-800R, in a choice of colors, is a continuous-cleaning, built-in, single-oven model with pilotless ignition, a clock-timer, four oven rack positions, non-tilt oven racks, an oven window, and oven light. The companion Hardwick Model C423 gas cooktop, also in a

Prices are accurate at time of printing; subject to manufacturer's change.

choice of colors, has four burners with pilotless ignition.
Specifications: Overall Dimensions: Height, 38¹³/₃₂″ (oven), 2⅞″ (cooktop); **Width,** 23⅝″ (oven), 30″ (cooktop); **Depth,** 23″ (oven), 21¹³/₁₆″ (cooktop). **Oven Dimensions: Height,** 14″; **Width,** 18″; **Depth,** 19¼″. **Warranty,** parts and labor, (oven and cooktop), 1 year.

Approximate Retail Price	Approximate Low Price
$419.00 (oven model CK7142*-800R)	$350.00
$159.00 (cooktop model C423)	$139.00

Roper 1088 is among the best of the double-oven gas ranges. Both ovens have lights and black glass doors; the upper oven is equipped with a broiler and a digital clock-timer. Pilotless ignition in both continuous-cleaning ovens saves gas. The companion cooktop is Roper Model 1178, a pilotless four-burner gas cooktop with chrome spill trays and lift-up top.
Specifications: Overall Dimensions: Height, 50⁷/₁₆″ (oven), 3″ (cooktop); **Width,** 23¾″ (oven), 28½″ (cooktop); **Depth,** 23¾″ (oven), 20¾″ (cooktop). **Oven Dimensions:** Not Available. **Warranty,** parts and labor, (oven and cooktop), 1 year.

Approximate Retail Price	Approximate Low Price
$880.00 (oven model 1088)	$689.00
$190.00 (cooktop model 1178)	$145.00

Roper 1560 is a 30-inch drop-in gas unit with a continuous-cleaning oven and energy-efficient pilotless ignition. It has a lift-up steel top surfaced with brushed chrome, a black glass door with a window, a digital clock-timer, and an oven light.
Specifications: Overall Dimensions: Height, 28″; **Width,** 29¼″; **Depth,** 22⅞″. **Oven Dimensions:** Not Available. **Warranty,** parts and labor, 1 year.

Approximate Retail Price	Approximate Low Price
$680.00	$519.00

Also Recommended

Tappan 12-1467 is a pilotless, continuous-cleaning gas oven with a digital clock-timer, an oven light, and chrome oven racks with four-position glides. Both the oven and the separate broiler have black lift-off glass doors. The companion Tappan Model Z14-2629 four-burner gas cooktop has removable burner bowls and lifts up for cleaning. The large-capacity burners are preadjusted for precise control. This is a good unit, but not quite up to our "Best Buy" standard in overall value.
Specifications: Overall Dimensions: Height, 42⅜″ (oven), 3½″ (cooktop); **Width,** 22⁵/₁₆″ (oven), 25¾″ (cooktop); **Depth,** 21″ (oven), 21⁹/₁₆″ (cooktop). **Oven Dimensions:** Not Available. **Warranty,** parts and labor (oven and cooktop), 1 year.

Approximate Retail Price	Approximate Low Price
$580.00 (oven model 12-1467)	$395.00
$160.00 (cooktop model Z14-2629)	$135.00

Prices are accurate at time of printing; subject to manufacturer's change.

Free-Standing Electric Ranges

General Electric JBP26W is a 30-inch self-cleaning unit with two six-inch and two eight-inch plug in elements. It has infinite-setting controls on the burner elements, and an interior light. This model also has a recessed, no-drip porcelain top; an oven window; an automatic oven timer; a clock and a one-hour timer; and a full-width lower storage drawer. Chrome-plated side trim makes the unit look "built-in" when it's slipped into a 30-inch cabinet opening.
Specifications: Overall Dimensions: Height, 44¾"; **Width,** 29⅞"; **Depth,** 27". **Oven Dimensions:** Not Available. **Warranty,** parts and labor, 1 year.

Approximate Retail Price   **Approximate Low Price**
Not Available.. $500.00

Magic Chef 38B-4CXW is a 30-inch self-cleaning range with a black glass door (with window) and a black lower storage drawer. It has two six-inch and two eight-inch plug-in elements. The removable reflector bowls and lift-up spill-catching top make for easy cleaning. The unit has chromed self-lock oven racks, an automatic oven timer, a fluorescent backguard light, a digital clock, and an oven light.
Specifications: Overall Dimensions: Height, 45⅞"; **Width,** 30"; **Depth,** 26". **Oven Dimensions: Height,** 15"; **Width,** 22"; **Depth,** 18". **Warranty,** parts and labor, 1 year.

Approximate Retail Price   **Approximate Low Price**
$629.00.. $535.00

Whirlpool RJE3300, a 30-inch range with a continuous-cleaning oven, is judged best among economy-priced ranges. It has two six-inch and two eight-inch plug-in elements with infinite-setting heat controls, a clock, two adjustable oven racks, and an oven light. The oven door has a window and can be removed for cleaning, and the lift-up cooktop has raised edges to contain spills. The full-width lower storage compartment is another good feature.
Specifications: Overall Dimensions: Height, 46⅛"; **Width,** 30"; **Depth,** 27⁵/₁₆". **Oven Dimensions:** Not Available. **Warranty,** parts and labor, 1 year.

Approximate Retail Price   **Approximate Low Price**
$453.00.. $409.00

White-Westinghouse KF330D is a 30-inch continuous-cleaning oven with three six-inch and one eight-inch elements. This model has oven and surface "on" signal lights, and automatic and interior oven lights; the oven door lifts off. The unit also has a clock-timer, two adjustable, plated oven racks, and a full-width storage drawer.

Prices are accurate at time of printing; subject to manufacturer's change.

Specifications: Overall Dimensions: Height, 45⅞"; **Width, 30";
Depth,** 25¹³/₁₆". **Oven Dimensions: Height,** 15⅞"; **Width,** 23¾"; **Depth,**
18". **Warranty,** parts and labor, 1 year.

Approximate Retail Price	Approximate Low Price
$360.00	$345.00

White-Westinghouse KF735D has a special broiling system—one
element above and another element below—to cook faster and eliminate turning. This 30-inch self-cleaning range was judged best in overall
value among the higher-priced models. Two six-inch and two eight-inch
plug-in elements on the cooktop have infinite-position heat controls.
Features include two adjustable, plated oven racks; a full-width lower
storage drawer; an oven light; a surface light; a digital clock; a recessed
top to contain spills; and a lift-off, black glass oven door with a window.
Specifications: Overall Dimensions: Height, 47⅛"; **Width, 30";
Depth,** 25½". **Oven Dimensions:** Not Available. **Warranty,** parts and
labor, 1 year.

Approximate Retail price	Approximate Low Price
$730.00	$629.00

Also Recommended

Admiral 653WA-CLW is a 30-inch model with a continuous-cleaning
oven; it has two six-inch and two eight-inch elements with removable
chrome drip bowls. It has two self-lock oven racks, a clock with a one-
hour timer, a window in the oven door, and an oven light. The removable
oven door and lift-up spill-catching cooktop assist cleanup. There's a big
storage drawer below the oven, and increased insulation and a new
venting design improve energy efficiency. We like this unit, but found
better ones in its price range.
Specifications: Overall Dimensions: Height, 45⅞"; **Width, 30";
Depth,** 25⅛". **Oven Dimensions:** Not Available. **Warranty,** parts and
labor, 1 year.

Approximate Retail Price	Approximate Low Price
$530.00	$349.00

Hotpoint RC548W, a 40-inch unit with a standard oven, is a no-frills
basic range for cooks who need an especially large unit. It has a lift-off
door, plenty of storage and work space, automatic controls, a clock-
timer, oven and cooktop lights, and two six-inch and two eight-inch
elements. The trim rings remove for easy cleaning. The size of this unit,
however, may make it unsuitable for many users.
Specifications: Overall Dimensions: Height, 45¾"; **Width, 40";
Depth,** 27½". **Oven Dimensions:** Not Available. **Warranty,** parts and
labor, 1 year.

Approximate Retail Price	Approximate Low Price
Not Available	$335.00

Prices are accurate at time of printing; subject to manufacturer's change.

Over-And-Under Electric Ranges

General Electric JHP56V is an over-and-under electric range with eye-level controls that feature automatic timers for both ovens. The lower oven has a window; the upper oven has a full-width black glass door. A cooktop light is over two six-inch and two eight-inch plug-in elements. The unit has a two-level exhaust system at the top, and storage drawer at the bottom. You can remove the upper oven panels and clean them in the lower self-cleaning oven.
Specifications: Overall Dimensions: Height, 71¾"; **Width,** 30"; **Depth,** 27½". **Oven Dimensions:** Not Available. **Warranty,** parts and labor, 1 year.

Approximate Retail Price	Approximate Low Price
Not Available	$929.00

 Combination Electric Ranges

Litton 773 is a combination free-standing range with both microwave and conventional electric power in the same self-cleaning oven. In addition to first-rate performance, this unit has many features, including closed-door broiling, automatic oven controls, two six-inch and two eight-inch elements, and a defrost setting in the microwave mode. A ceramic shelf insert in the oven shows you where to position small items correctly for microwaving.
Specifications: Overall Dimensions: Height, 47¾"; **Width,** 29⅞"; **Depth,** 28¼". **Oven Dimensions: Height,** 15½"; **Width,** 22¾"; **Depth,** 18". **Warranty,** parts and labor, 1 year; magnetron tube (parts only), 5 years.

Approximate Retail Price	Approximate Low Price
Not Available	$799.00

Magic Chef 28B-6CXWM7 is an over-and-under combination micro-wave and electric range. The upper microwave oven has a 1.51-cubic-foot interior, touch-control panel, four-level memory including "slow cook" and "keep warm" settings, and a 12-hour delay-start feature. It can also be used with a temperature probe. The lower electric oven is self-cleaning, and has front controls and a clock with a one-hour timer. The range has two six-inch and two eight-inch elements, and a cooktop light.

Prices are accurate at time of printing; subject to manufacturer's change.

Specifications: Overall Dimensions: Height, 67½"; **Width,** 30"; **Depth,** 25½". **Oven Dimensions:** Not Available. **Microwave Oven Capacity:** 1.51 cu. ft. **Microwave Oven Dimensions:** Not Available. **Warranty,** parts and labor, 1 year.

Approximate Retail Price   Approximate Low Price

$1,295.00.. $1,095.00

Whirlpool RHM973PP is an over-and-under combination with an upper microwave oven (1.3 cubic feet interior capacity) and a self-cleaning electric lower oven. The microwave oven features variable power and digital control for up to one hour of continuous cooking; it also has a defrost setting and a temperature probe. There are two six-inch and two eight-inch surface elements with infinite-position heat controls. The chrome lift-up cooktop and backsplash make for easy cleaning.
Specifications: Overall Dimensions: Height, 66³/₁₆"; **Width,** 30"; **Depth,** 27⁵/₁₆". **Oven Dimensions:** Not Available. **Microwave Oven Capacity:** 1.3 cu. ft. **Microwave Oven Dimensions:** Not Available. **Warranty,** parts and labor, 1 year.

Approximate Retail Price   Approximate Low Price

$1,356.00.. $1,170.00

Also Recommended

Tappan 77-4971 is a combination over-and-under range. A self-cleaning lower electric oven, topped by two six-inch and two eight-inch infinite-setting elements, is equipped with two removable oven racks with five positions, a digital clock-timer, a black glass lift-off door, a lift-and-lock top, and a waist-high broiler. There is also a spacious lower storage drawer. The upper microwave oven puts out 615 watts of cooking power. It has a touch-control panel and a temperature probe. The microwave oven has a black glass door, a lighted digital display, and an interior light. The microwave oven is a little smaller and less powerful than our "Best Buy" choice in this category.
Specifications: Overall Dimensions: Height, 66⁵/₁₆"; **Width,** 29¹⁵/₁₆"; **Depth,** 25". **Oven Dimensions: Height,** 16¾"; **Width,** 23"; **Depth,** 14¾". **Microwave Oven Capacity:** Not Available. **Microwave Oven Dimensions: Height,** 8"; **Width,** 15½"; **Depth,** 14". **Warranty,** parts and labor, 1 year; microwave (parts only), 2 years; magnetron tube, 5 years.

Approximate Retail Price   Approximate Low Price

$1,330.00.. $1,199.00

 Built-In Ranges, Ovens, and Cooktops

General Electric JKP16G is a self-cleaning electric oven with a black glass door and an automatic rotisserie. It has programmed oven control,

Prices are accurate at time of printing; subject to manufacturer's change.

an electronic meat thermometer, a digital clock-timer, two oven shelves, and an oven light. GE's companion Model JP661V electric cooktop provides two six-inch and two eight-inch elements in a sturdy unit. **Specifications: Overall Dimensions: Height,** 28⅛″ (oven), 1³/₁₄″ (cooktop, but 6 inches free area required underneath); **Width,** 24¾″ (oven), 29¹³/₁₆″ (cooktop); **Depth,** 24″ (oven), 20⁷/₁₆″ (cooktop). **Oven Dimensions:** Not Available. **Warranty,** parts and labor (oven and cooktop), 1 year.

Approximate Retail Price	Approximate Low Price
Not Available (oven model JKP16G)	$705.00
Not Available (cooktop model JP661V)	$233.00

Gibson OH27C4NJ is a continuous-cleaning, electric wall unit with a double oven. It has black glass doors, digital clock, two chrome oven racks, and programmed oven controls. Companion Model BE34B2BJ is a built-in cooktop with two six-inch and two eight-inch plug-in elements. The cooktop has a brushed-chrome surface for easy cleaning. **Specifications: Overall Dimensions: Height,** 45⅛″ (oven), 3″ (cooktop); **Width,** 25″ (oven), 33⅝″ (cooktop); **Depth,** 23¾″ (oven), 20⅝″ (cooktop). **Oven Dimensions:** Not Available. **Warranty,** parts and labor (oven and cooktop), 1 year.

Approximate Retail Price	Approximate Low Price
Not Available (oven model OH27C4NJ)	$499.00
Not Available (cooktop model BE34B2BJ)	$189.00

Litton 880 is a top-of-the-line, built-in, over-and-under combination microwave/electric unit. The top oven is a 1.2-cubic-foot touch-control microwave with programmed cooking and variable power that lets you use full power or several other choices—warm, defrost, simmer, etc. The conventional lower electric oven is self-cleaning. Both ovens have black glass doors. The optional companion cooktop is a modular unit similar to a grill range. With it you can use (two at a time) any of seven interchangeable modules—grill, two different electric elements, griddle, rotisserie, smoothtop, or cutting board. **Specifications: Overall Dimensions: Height,** 49¾″ (oven), 4″ (cooktop); **Width,** 26¾″ (oven), 30⅜″ (cooktop); **Depth,** 23¾″ (oven), 21″ (cooktop). **Oven Dimensions:** Not Available. **Microwave Oven Capacity:** 1.2 cu. ft. **Microwave Oven Dimensions:** Not Available. **Warranty,** parts and labor, 1 year; magnetron, 5 years.

Approximate Retail Price	Approximate Low Price
Not Available (oven model 880)	$899.00

Modern Maid QCO-480 is a double-oven electrical wall model with a clock-timer. Both ovens are continuous-cleaning and fully automatic, with separate controls and lights. The companion electric cooktop—Modern Maid Model ET-350—has infinite-position heat controls on two six-inch and two eight-inch elements, and a recessed outer edge. **Specifications: Overall Dimensions: Height,** 45¾″ (oven), 3″ (cooktop); **Width,** 23¾″ (oven), 28¾″ (cooktop); **Depth,** 22½″ (oven), 21″

Prices are accurate at time of printing; subject to manufacturer's change.

(cooktop). **Oven Dimensions:** Not Available. **Warranty:** parts and labor (oven and cooktop), 1 year.

Approximate Retail Price	Approximate Low Price
Not Available (oven model QCO-480)	$599.00
Not Available (cooktop model ET-350)	$219.00

Whirlpool RDE6300 has an electric continuous-cleaning oven with two oven racks and a window in the removable door. The unit has a clock-timer and an oven light. The two six-inch and two eight-inch elements are equipped with infinite-setting controls.
Specifications: Overall Dimensions: Height, 27⅜"; **Width,** 28⁹⁄₁₆"; **Depth,** 19³⁄₁₆". **Oven Dimensions:** Not Available. **Warranty,** parts and labor, 1 year.

Approximate Retail Price	Approximate Low Price
$437.00	$409.00

Also Recommended

White-Westinghouse KB451A is a double-oven wall unit. It has two continuous-cleaning ovens, both with black glass doors, oven lights, signal lights, and look-in windows. It also has a digital timer. The companion cooktop is Model KP530A, which features infinite-position elements—two six-inch and two eight-inch. Controls are front-mounted. This unit is a good one, but it's too expensive to qualify as a "Best Buy." **Specifications: Overall Dimensions: Height,** 45⅛" (oven), 7½" (cook-top); **Width,** 25" (oven), 33⅝" (cooktop); **Depth,** 23¾ (oven), 20⅝" (cooktop). **Oven Dimensions:** Not Available. **Warranty,** parts and labor, 1 year.

Approximate Retail Price	Approximate Low Price
$620.00 (oven model KB451A)	$519.00
Not Available (cooktop model KP530A)	$219.00

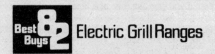 **Electric Grill Ranges**

Jenn-Air F100 is a free-standing electric grill range that comes with standard grill and optional conventional element cooktop unit. Available accessories include a rotisserie, a griddle, a deep-fryer, a shish kebab, and a smoothtop—this selection is what makes the Jenn-Air range the darling of deluxe kitchen remodelers. It's an expensive unit, but its built-in internal ventilating system and convection oven make it very versatile.
Specifications: Overall Dimensions: Height, 36"; **Width,** 29¹⁵⁄₁₆"; **Depth,** 25¾". **Oven Dimensions:** Not Available. **Warranty,** parts and labor, 1 year.

Approximate Retail Price	Approximate Low Price
Not Available	$965.00

Prices are accurate at time of printing; subject to manufacturer's change.

Whirlpool RHE396PP is a free-standing electric grill range with a grill module and two surface elements—one four-inch and one eight-inch. The self-cleaning oven has a light, two oven racks, and black glass door with window. Accessories available for use with this unit include a rotisserie, a griddle, a cutting board, and an alternate surface unit (one six-inch and one eight-inch element).
Specifications: Overall Dimensions: Height, 46⁹⁄₁₆″; **Width,** 30″; **Depth,** 25⁵⁄₁₆″. **Oven Dimensions:** Not Available. **Warranty,** parts and labor, 1 year.

Approximate Retail Price	Approximate Low Price
$917.00	$789.00

Also Recommended

Tappan 13-1581 is a built-in electric grill with modular cooktop that will also accept a griddle, elements, a smoothtop surface, a rotisserie kit, or a cutting board. A vent pulls smoke and odors out of the kitchen. A good companion built-in wall oven would be Model 11-4170, a self-cleaning single oven loaded with good features.
Specifications: Overall Dimensions: Height, 29¹⁄₁₆″ (oven), 4″ (cooktop); **Width,** 25¼″ (oven), 21⁹⁄₁₆″ (cooktop); **Depth,** 22⁹⁄₁₆″ (oven), 20³⁄₁₆″ (cooktop). **Oven Dimensions:** Not Available. **Warranty,** parts and labor, 1 year.

Approximate Retail Price	Approximate Low Price
$390.00	$359.00

Best Buys 82 Smoothtop Electric Ranges

General Electric JBP87G, best overall among ceramic smoothtop ranges, is a self-cleaning model. It has a black glass door with a window, two oven shelves, a digital clock, an automatic oven timer, surface element "on" indicators, a storage drawer, and a fluorescent cooktop light. Two six-inch and two eight-inch infinite setting elements are below the one-piece ceramic top.
Specifications: Overall Dimensions: Height, 47¾″; **Width,** 27⅞″; **Depth,** 27″. **Oven Dimensions:** Not Available. **Warranty,** parts and labor, 1 year.

Approximate Retail Price	Approximate Low Price
Not Available	$799.00

Prices are accurate at time of printing; subject to manufacturer's change.

Refrigerators

L IKE MANY APPLIANCES TODAY, the refrigerator is a product used daily, but given little thought unless it fails. Although the appliance itself may not look different, significant changes have found their way into refrigerator models in recent years, and these changes affect both your operating costs and the convenience you can expect from a new refrigerator.

The major changes in refrigerator design reflect our national commitment to energy conservation. Manufacturers have been working on models that do more while using less energy. Today, the emphasis is on "life-cycle costs." Refrigerators last a long time—about 13 to 15 years—so extra money spent initially on an energy-efficient model will pay dividends in lower electrical bills for many years.

Your Guide to Energy Costs

THE FEDERAL GOVERNMENT has been working to set minimum energy standards for household appliances, but there is now some question as to whether these standards will ever be imposed. From the consumer's point of view, however, there has been one positive step: Manufacturers are now required to place on each refrigerator a label detailing a variety of energy information, and this can help you to compare operating costs of different models and choose the one best suited to your needs.

Most of the major energy advances in refrigerator design are already incorporated into the models now available. In the cabinet and door, manufacturers are using heavier, foamed-in-place polyurethane insulation and plastic liners to reduce energy consumption. On middle and top-of-the-line models, more efficient compressor motors and more efficient evaporator heat exchangers also save energy. New door designs prevent cold air leakage; this offers a side benefit in the form of deeper door shelves. New and better door seals are still another energy-efficient way to keep the cold air inside the refrigerator, where it belongs.

Closing the Door on Energy Waste

MOST REFRIGERATORS have door heaters that prevent condensation in humid weather. Many new units have a switch to turn off the door heater when it's not needed—or to turn it on only when it is needed—and this can cut your refrigerator's energy use 10 percent or more. Some manufacturers have replaced the door heater altogether with a loop or coil design that carries hot refrigerant gas around the door to prevent condensation.

CONSUMER GUIDE®

Electronics Jog Your Memory

THE USE OF electronic controls has been showing up in many appliances, including refrigerators. Whirlpool recently introduced a top-of-the-line, three-door model with an electronic LED (Light-Emitting Diode) display that flashes symbols to advise the owner of certain conditions—that it's time to make new ice, that the interior temperature is too warm or the door ajar, or simply that everything is working right. A Kenmore unit from Sears, which is also made by Whirlpool, offers the same feature, except that the Sears model flashes words.

In the future, electronics may perform other functions on a refrigerator. There are plans for using electronics to defrost freezer sections on demand, based on need rather than on a set-time or set-cycle basis. This would reduce energy consumption on automatic-defrost models.

How Big a Unit Do You Need?

BUYING A BIGGER refrigerator than you need is a waste of money; you'll be paying purchase and operating costs for space you don't use. As a rule of thumb, figure on 8 to 10 cubic feet of fresh food space for a family of two, adding one cubic foot for each additional family member. The freezer section should measure three cubic feet for two people, with another cubic foot for each extra family member.

Of course, you may modify this general rule to suit your living habits. If you shop frequently, you may be able to manage with less space; if you cook in advance or entertain often, you may need more. Keep in mind your needs for both fresh food and freezer space. And don't forget that the design of your kitchen may impose some limits on your choice; for example, a side-by-side unit with its narrow doors frequently works well in a narrow kitchen.

What Are the Styles to Choose From?

HERE ARE THE basic refrigerator styles available for you to choose from:

Single-Door. Single-door units, which usually have a very small interior freezer, are the least expensive to buy and to operate, but selection is limited and they normally have to be defrosted. A new type of single-door refrigerator appeared several years ago—the "all-refrigerator" refrigerator, which offers large capacity (generally about 16 cubic feet) but has no freezer, and is designed for consumers who own a separate freezer. This may sound more attractive at first than use would bear out, unless your freezer also happens to be in the kitchen.

Two-Door Top-Mount. The two-door top-mount, the most popular model, has two horizontal doors—one for the fresh-food section and a smaller one for a freezer mounted on the top. The freezer accounts for about one-fourth to one-third of total capacity. These units are available in a variety of sizes (the larger ones have automatic defrost), and they continue to offer the best value for the money, especially in terms of energy performance.

Two-Door Bottom-Mount. In a two-door bottom-mount refrigerator, the freezer section is at the bottom, and usually has a shelf and/or basket that slides out. This type is considered to be inconvenient by some people, and is less popular than the two-door, top-mount design.

Two-Door Side-By-Side. Refrigerators with two full-length vertical doors generally come in larger sizes than top-mounts, and are a little more expensive to buy. Total capacity usually comes to at least 19 cubic feet, and the freezer takes up one-third to one-half of this. This larger freezer capacity is what makes side-by-side models popular.

Three-Door Side-By-Side. The freezer section on a three-door side-by-side is split horizontally and has two doors, one opening to a small compartment for frequently used items, the second to a larger compartment that holds items for long-term storage. The extra door adds to the price. Less common is the three-door bottom-mount style, which has twin vertical doors to the refrigerator and the freezer underneath.

Compacts. These single-door units have less than 10 cubic feet capacity. They aren't very efficient, and we haven't included any compacts in our selection. They are popular mostly as luxury or specialty items for use in offices, bars, and dormitory rooms.

Details Make a Difference

BECAUSE REFRIGERATORS last a long time, it makes good sense to give some extra thought to features that will serve you well over the life of the unit. Here's a rundown on the features you'll find:

Bins and Crispers. Steel bins are durable; plastic bins are light and easy to clean. Either way, be sure there are stops to prevent the bins from being pulled all the way out unintentionally.

Egg Holders. This may be a tray molded to fit to the eggs, or a bin that can hold up to two dozen eggs.

Fresh Food Shelves. Fully adjustable cantilever shelves are best because they're the most flexible. Fixed or partially adjustable shelves can limit storage options. Plastic is a good all-around shelf material. Glass is attractive and easily cleaned, but breakable. A heavy wire grid is durable and is easy to see through, but also easy to spill through and not always easy to clean. Wire is the most common, and is considered the most practical by many consumers.

Door Shelves. Most refrigerators have fixed shelves, with compartments for butter and cheese and an egg holder. A few models are equipped with cantilever shelves or adjustable bins in the doors.

Freezer Shelves. Most freezer door shelves can hold at least juice cans. Top-mounts may have one or two shelves in the freezer door, while side-by-sides generally have several. A shelf inside a top-mounted unit (either a small partial-width or a full-width shelf) helps you organize your freezer. Side-by-sides generally offer a bin for bulk items in the freezer.

Icemakers. You certainly want removable ice bins, but an automatic icemaker may be an unnecessary extra-cost feature. If you don't need an icemaker now but think you might in the future, compromise with a freezer section that is prewired and plumbed for an add-on icemaker.

1. Type of appliance and capacity.

2. National average cost for electricity upon which the estimated annual energy cost figure is based.

3. Estimated annual operating cost for the model in this size range that costs least to operate.

4. Scale showing lowest and highest estimated operating costs for models within this size range. These models represent different brands, not just those of the company listed in the upper right-hand corner.

5. Where the estimated annual cost of this particular model falls in comparison to all other models in this size.

6. Warning that it is unlawful to remove label.

7. A grid to help determine more closely the customer's operating cost based on local utility rates and use habits.

8. Suggests that the customer ask salesperson or utility for local utility rates.

9. Cautions that the customer's cost will not necessarily be the same as the cost figure given above.

10. Estimated annual operating cost for the model in this size range that costs most to operate.

11. All brands and models compared in the scale on this label fall within this capacity range.

12. All model numbers are listed if the label applies to more than one model.

13. Name of manufacturer and model number of the appliance on which the label appears.

14. Estimated annual operating cost for this model.

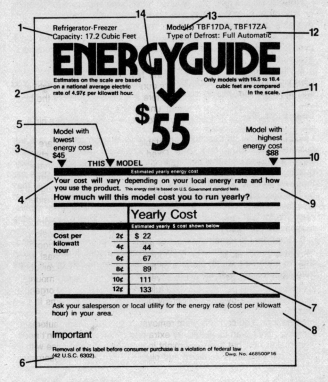

1 — Refrigerator-Freezer
Capacity: 17.2 Cubic Feet

14

13 — Model(s) TBF17DA, TBF17ZA
Type of Defrost: Full Automatic — 12

ENERGYGUIDE

2 — Estimates on the scale are based on a national average electric rate of 4.97¢ per kilowatt hour.

Only models with 16.5 to 18.4 cubic feet are compared in the scale. — 11

$55

5 —

Model with lowest energy cost $45

3 — ▼

THIS ▼ MODEL

Model with highest energy cost $88

▼ — 10

Estimated yearly energy cost

4 — Your cost will vary depending on your local energy rate and how you use the product. This energy cost is based on U.S. Government standard tests.

How much will this model cost you to run yearly? — 9

		Yearly Cost
		Estimated yearly $ cost shown below
Cost per kilowatt hour	2¢	$ 22
	4¢	44
	6¢	67
	8¢	89
	10¢	111
	12¢	133

Ask your salesperson or local utility for the energy rate (cost per kilowatt hour) in your area. — 7

8

Important

6 — Removal of this label before consumer purchase is a violation of federal law (42 U.S.C. 6302).

Dwg. No. 468500P16

Controls. Separate controls for the freezer and fresh-food sections are preferable. Some manufacturers also offer a separate control for the meat keeper, but this feature is like a lot of product features today—it only makes sense if you're sure you'll use it.

Defrost. The most economical way to defrost a refrigerator is to do it yourself. The partial-defrost or cycle-defrost method takes care of the fresh-food section automatically but leaves the freezer to you. Fully automatic defrost for both fresh-food and freezer sections boosts both purchase price and operating cost, but you will probably feel, as many people do, that the convenience is well worth paying for—no one enjoys defrosting a refrigerator.

Power Savers. For top energy savings, get a refrigerator with a switch to turn the door heater down or off, or one with a loop or coil system that prevents condensation around the door.

Liners. The inside wall of a refrigerator is either metal or plastic. Metal is tougher; plastic liners can be damaged if not treated properly. But plastic liners are now almost universally used because they are more energy-efficient.

Rollers. Rollers help greatly when moving the appliance for cleaning or any other purpose. They are standard on large refrigerators, and available as an option on smaller models.

Colors. White is still the standard color for refrigerators, but gold, avocado, coppertone, and almond (the "in" color) units are commonly available.

Styling. Textured steel fronts on refrigerators are becoming very popular; this pebblelike surface hides fingerprints and minor marks. You can also get trim kits to custom-decorate your refrigerator doors.

Best Buys '82

LISTED BELOW, in descending order of total cubic capacity, are our selected "Best Buy" and "Also Recommended" models. Our "Best Buys" are those units that best meet our standards of energy-efficiency, quality, value, and convenience. The "Also Recommended" units are those we consider to be the next best products on the market—they may be fine products, but too expensive for many people; or they may be a little less energy-efficient than the "Best Buys," or have fewer convenient interior features. In our profiles of individual models we indicate the reason for our rating.

It's important to remember that our "Best Buy" or "Also Recommended" designation applies only to that particular model. It doesn't mean that we endorse a whole product line or that other models by the same manufacturer are just as good.

Single-Door Refrigerators

Sears Kenmore 46G61111N (11.0 cubic feet total capacity) is a manual-defrost single-door model that gives you economy both when you buy it and while you use it. The refrigerator section is 9.96 cubic feet, with another 1.04 cubic feet in the freezer. It's an economy model with some good features—an interior light, two full-width adjustable steel shelves, four door shelves, an egg tray, a crisper, and two plastic ice trays. It is available in white only, and has a plastic liner.

Specifications: Height, 59⅞″; **Width,** 23⅝″; **Depth,** 25″; **Total Capacity,** 11.0 cu. ft.; **Shelf Capacity,** not available; **Warranty,** parts and labor, 1 year; compressor system (parts and labor), 5 years.

Approximate Retail Price	Approximate Low Price
$320.00	Not Available

 Two-Door Top-Mount Refrigerators

Whirlpool EHT221MK (22.3 cubic feet total capacity) is a big model with 7.57 cubic feet in the freezer section and 14.68 cubic feet of refrigerator space. The model has a power-saving heater control switch. Textured steel doors hide fingerprints, scratches, and dents. Other quality features include porcelain-on-steel liners, two adjustable door shelves, four half-width adjustable shelves, twin porcelain crispers, and rollers.

Specifications: Height, 65⅞″; **Width,** 32¾″; **Depth,** 32″; **Total Capacity,** 22.3 cu. ft.; **Shelf Capacity,** 29.8 sq. ft.; **Warranty,** parts and labor, 1 year; sealed system (parts and labor), 5 years.

Approximate Retail Price	Approximate Low Price
$862.00	$759.00

General Electric TBF17DB (17.2 cubic feet total capacity) has plenty of insulation and other energy-saving features, including a switch to reduce power to the door heaters. It offers 4.73 cubic feet of freezer space and 12.47 cubic feet of refrigerator space. A special "food life extension" system consists of one low-humidity bin for fruits and bulk meats and two-high humidity bins—one for leafy vegetables (it has an adjustable humidity control) and one for storing unwrapped snacks, cheese, and meat. This unit has four adjustable cantilever half-width refrigerator shelves and a shelf in the freezer section. The deep door shelves in both

Prices are accurate at time of printing; subject to manufacturer's change.

compartments are convenient. A similar refrigerator without the food life extension system is Model TBF17SB.

Specifications: Height, 64"; **Width,** 30½"; **Depth,** 30¹⁵⁄₁₆"; **Total Capacity,** 17.2 cu. ft.; **Shelf Capacity,** 24.3 sq. ft.; **Warranty,** parts and labor, 1 year; compressor system (parts and labor), 5 years.

Approximate Retail Price	Approximate Low Price
Not Available	$533.00

Sears Kenmore 46G61771N (17.0 cubic feet total capacity) is a high-efficiency model with an energy-saving switch to turn off the door heaters when you don't need them. This model has textured steel doors, porcelain enamel interior, three half-width adjustable shelves, two deep door shelves for larger items, one smaller shelf, and automatic defrost. It has twin crispers and a compartment with humidity control. It also has a slide-out egg bin. The unit has 4.75 cubic feet in the freezer, and 12.25 cubic feet of refrigerator space. This model is available through the Sears catalog only.

Specifications: Height, 65⅞"; **Width,** 32¾"; **Depth,** 29"; **Total Capacity,** 17.0 cu. ft.; **Shelf Capacity,** not available; **Warranty,** parts and labor, 1 year; compressor system (parts and labor), 5 years.

Approximate Retail Prices	Approximate Low Prices
$690.00 (White)	Not Available
$700.00 (Other colors)	Not Available

Amana ESRFC-16E (16.2 cubic feet total capacity) offers high energy efficiency. We found the adjustable shelf arrangement and door shelf layout very convenient. The separate controls for freezer and fresh food sections are a plus, as are the meat keeper, twin crispers, and automatic defrost. This model has 12.41 cubic feet of refrigerator space, and a relatively small freezer section—3.79 cubic feet.

Specifications: Height, 66⅜"; **Width,** 28"; **Depth,** 31⅜"; **Total Capacity,** 16.2 cu. ft.; **Shelf Capacity,** 23 sq. ft.; **Warranty,** parts and labor, 1 year; sealed system components and food compartment liner (parts and labor), 5 years.

Approximate Retail Price	Approximate Low Price
$790.00	$659.00

Admiral NT-15A5 (14.6 cubic feet total capacity) has good space distribution—4.14 cubic feet in the freezer and 10.43 cubic feet for fresh food. The refrigerator section has three shelves, of which two are adjustable. There's no freezer shelf; it would be an added convenience to have one. The freezer door has a shelf and can rack. This economy unit has automatic defrost, twin crispers, a meat keeper, and a removable egg tray. The two refrigerator door shelves are deep.

Specifications: Height, 60"; **Width, Depth,** 29¹⁄₁₆"; **Total Capacity,** 14.6 cu. ft.; **Shelf Capacity,** 17.7 sq. ft.; **Warranty,** parts and labor, 1 year; compressor and food liner (parts), 5 years.

Approximate Retail Price	Approximate Low Price
$650.00	$499.00

Prices are accurate at time of printing; subject to manufacturer's change.

Hotpoint CTF14EB (14.2 cubic feet total capacity) is a well-built refrigerator in a smaller size. This model has 4.58 cubic feet of freezer space and 9.62 cubic feet for fresh food storage. Two adjustable full-width refrigerator shelves, three refrigerator door shelves, a freezer shelf, and two freezer door shelves permit flexible storage. This automatic-defrost top-mount refrigerator has an energy-saver switch to turn off door heaters. It also has twin crispers, a meat keeper, and rollers.
Specifications: Height, 61"; **Width,** 28"; **Depth,** 29³/₁₆"; **Total Capacity,** 14.2 cu. ft.; **Shelf Capacity,** 20.5 sq. ft; **Warranty,** parts and labor, 1 year; compressor system (parts and labor), 5 years.

Approximate Retail Price	Approximate Low Price
Not Available	$499.00

White-Westinghouse RT146D (14.0 cubic feet total capacity) has a 3.4-cubic-foot freezer section and 10.6 cubic feet of refrigerator space. The refrigerator has three adjustable wire shelves, two deep door shelves, twin crispers, a covered adjustable meat pan, a butter keeper, and an egg tray. The freezer section has a full-width shelf with a can rack and a shelf in the door. This frost-free model also has an energy-saver switch to reduce energy consumption of the door heaters.
Specifications: Height, 63³/₁₆"; **Width,** 28"; **Depth,** 26⁷/₈"; **Total Capacity,** 14.0 cu. ft; **Shelf Capacity,** 16.6 sq. ft.; **Warranty,** parts and labor, 1 year; sealed refrigerator system (parts), 5 years.

Approximate Retail Price	Approximate Low Price
$590.00	$523.00

Also Recommended

General Electric TBF21DB (20.8 cubic foot total capacity) is a large unit with 6.97 cubic feet of freezer space, and 13.83 cubic feet in the refrigerator. Automatic defrost, twin crispers, a meat keeper, and compartments for cheese and butter are good features; we also liked the adjustable freezer shelf. The unit has a power-saving switch to turn down door heaters, and GE's storage compartments with humidity control. We think this unit is a bit expensive for its size.
Specifications: Height, 66"; **Width,** 30½"; **Depth,** 30¹⁵/₁₆"; **Total Capacity,** 20.8 cu. ft.; **Shelf Capacity,** 27.1 sq. ft.; **Warranty,** parts and labor, 1 year; compressor system (parts and labor), 5 years.

Approximate Retail Price	Approximate Low Price
Not Available	$619.00

Admiral NT-19B6 (18.6 cubic foot total capacity) is an automatic-defrost model with 12.93 cubic feet of refrigerator space and 5.67 cubic feet of freezer storage with a shelf. Three of the four wire shelves in the fresh food section are adjustable, and the door shelf arrangement is quite good. The refrigerator has twin crispers and a meat keeper. This is among the best top-mount models in the 18- to 19-cubic-foot range, but we don't consider that it has the top quality construction that we look for in a "Best Buy."

Prices are accurate at time of printing; subject to manufacturer's change.

Specifications: Height, 65½"; **Width,** 31½"; **Depth,** 27⅝"; **Total Capacity,** 18.6 cu. ft.; **Shelf Capacity,** 25.2 sq. ft.; **Warranty,** parts and labor, 1 year; compressor system and food liner (parts), 5 years.

Approximate Retail Price

Approximate Low Price

$760.00 .... $569.00

Whirlpool EHT171HK (17.2 cubic foot total capacity) is a high-efficiency model with 4.75 cubic feet of freezer space and 12.42 cubic feet of fresh food storage. It's an automatic-defrost unit, with a freezer shelf and three half-width adjustable interior refrigerator shelves. This unit has dual controls, textured-steel reversible doors, twin crispers, and a meat pan. It's a good unit in a popular size, but for overall value doesn't quite meet our "Best Buy" standards.

Specifications: Height, 65⅞"; **Width,** 32¾"; **Depth,** 29"; **Total Capacity,** 17.2 cu. ft.; **Shelf Capacity,** 22.7 sq. ft.; **Warranty,** parts and labor, 1 year; sealed system (parts and labor), 5 years.

Approximate Retail Price

Approximate Low Price

$682.00 .... $589.00

 Two-Door Bottom-Mount Refrigerators

Amana ESBFC-16D (16.2 cubic feet total capacity) has 5.42 cubic feet of freezer space and 10.78 cubic feet in the refrigerator. Bottom-mounts were popular about 15 years ago, and some consumers still prefer them. This is an expensive unit, but it comes with a bulk item basket (something not found in top-mounts), half-width adjustable shelves, dual controls, and rollers.

Specifications: Height, 66⅜"; **Width,** 28"; **Depth,** 31⅞"; **Total Capacity,** 16.2 cu. ft.; **Shelf Capacity,** 22.5 sq. ft.; **Warranty,** parts and labor, 1 year; sealed system and food compartment liner (parts and labor), 5 years.

Approximate Retail Price

Approximate Low Price

$850.00 .... $703.00

Also Recommended

Whirlpool EHB191MK (18.7 cubic foot total capacity) is a bottom-mount with automatic defrost that has two half-width doors to the 12.84-cubic-foot refrigerator section. The refrigerator has three half-width adjustable shelves, twin crispers, adjustable door shelves, and adjustable meat pan. The freezer, with 5.88 cubic feet of space, has a bulk item basket and a shelf that slides out. The unit has porcelain enamel liners and textured steel doors. Bottom-mount refrigerators are very expensive. If you want to spend the money on a bottom-mount we think you'd do better with the two-door "Best Buy" Amana Model ESBFC-

Prices are accurate at time of printing; subject to manufacturer's change.

16D. This Whirlpool model costs more than the Amana, and it doesn't match it for quality of construction.
Specifications: Height, 65⅞"; **Width,** 32¾"; **Depth,** 29"; **Total Capacity,** 18.7 cu. ft.; **Shelf Capacity,** 24.7 sq. ft.; **Warranty,** parts and labor, 1 year; sealed system (parts and labor), 5 years.

Approximate Retail Price   Approximate Low Price
$899.00 .... $779.00

 Two-Door Side-By-Side Refrigerators

General Electric TFF-24ZB (23.7 cubic feet total capacity) has 8.76 cubic feet of freezer space, which is almost as much as many small chest freezers provide. The freezer compartment has four interior shelves, five door shelves, and a storage basket. The 14.94-cubic-foot refrigerator section has three adjustable shelves and five adjustable door shelves. This model has GE's "food saver" humidity control compartments, and the half-width vegetable bins are convenient. Dual controls, rollers, and good energy performance for such a big unit are additional reasons for this GE model receiving a "Best Buy" rating.
Specifications: Height, 66¼"; **Width,** 35¾"; **Depth,** 30½"; **Total Capacity,** 23.7 cu. ft.; **Shelf Capacity,** 26.9 sq. ft.; **Warranty,** parts and labor, 1 year; compressor system (parts), 5 years.

Approximate Retail Price   Approximate Low Price
Not Available $1,019.00

Hotpoint CSF22EB (21.9 cubic feet total capacity) has four adjustable fresh food shelves and four door shelves in the 14.98 cubic-foot refrigerator. It has twin crispers and an automatic energy-saving system that prevents moisture. The 6.92-cubic-foot freezer side has five door shelves, juice can rack, four interior shelves, and a removable basket. It also has an ice storage bucket, three easy-out ice trays, and is equipped for an optional automatic icemaker. This no-frost unit has rollers, and interior lights in both the freezer and refrigerator sections.
Specifications: Height, 66¼"; **Width,** 33"; **Depth,** 31"; **Total Capacity,** 21.9 cu. ft.; **Shelf Capacity,** 26.0 sq. ft.; **Warranty,** parts and labor, 1 year; compressor system (parts and labor), 5 years.

Approximate Retail Price   Approximate Low Price
Not Available $750.00

Sears Kenmore 46G61141N (19.1 cubic feet total capacity) is a moderately priced and energy-efficient automatic-defrost model. A power-saver switch turns off door heaters during periods of low humidity. The 6.34-cubic-foot freezer has six door shelves, slide-out bulk basket, removable interior shelves, and light. The 12.76-cubic-foot

Prices are accurate at time of printing; subject to manufacturer's change.

refrigerator section has a porcelain enamel interior, three full-width adjustable epoxy-coated steel shelves, twin crispers, and removable egg bin.

Specifications: Height, 65⅞"; **Width,** 32¾"; **Depth,** 29"; **Total Capacity,** 19.1 cu. ft.; **Shelf Capacity,** not available; **Warranty,** parts and labor, 1 year; sealed system (parts and labor), 5 years.

Approximate Retail Prices　　　　　　　　　　　**Approximate Low Prices**
$760.00 (white) .... Not Available
$770.00 (other colors) .... Not Available

Whirlpool EHD191MK (19.0 cubic feet total capacity) is best overall among the better values in side-by-side models, with 6.35 cubic feet in the freezer and 12.65 cubic feet in the refrigerator. It has an energy-saving door heater control switch, automatic defrost, dual controls, porcelain steel interior, porcelain twin crispers (one is a meat keeper), textured steel doors, and rollers. Adjustable fresh-food and freezer shelving and adjustable door shelves in the freezer should suit most needs.

Specifications: Height, 65⅞"; **Width,** 32¾"; **Depth,** 29⅛"; **Total Capacity,** 19.0 cu. ft.; **Shelf Capacity,** 24.9 sq. ft.; **Warranty,** parts and labor, 1 year; sealed system (parts and labor), 5 years.

Approximate Retail Price　　　　　　　　　　　**Approximate Low Price**
$906.00 .... $736.00

 Best Buys 82 Three-Door Side-By-Side Refrigerators

White-Westinghouse RS218A (21.0 cubic feet total capacity) has automatic defrost. The three textured-steel doors include one vertical door to the 12.8-cubic-foot refrigerator section and two to the 8.2-cubic-foot freezer side. This freezer can hold as much as a small chest freezer. The small freezer door allows access to frequently used items—like ice—without allowing cold air to escape from the larger part of the freezer. Door storage and interior shelf adjustment are above average in convenience and flexibility. The refrigerator has four adjustable shelves and five door shelves. The lower freezer has three shelves and a basket, and three shelves in the door.

Specifications: Height, 64½"; **Width,** 33"; **Depth,** 29⅜"; **Total Capacity,** 21.0 cu. ft.; **Shelf Capacity,** 27.7 sq. ft.; **Warranty,** parts and labor, 1 year; sealed refrigeration system (parts), 5 years.

Approximate Retail Price　　　　　　　　　　　**Approximate Low Price**
$1,040.00 .... $919.00

Prices are accurate at time of printing; subject to manufacturer's change.

Freezers

IN RECENT YEARS, freezers have become synonymous with savings. When food prices jumped wildly, freezer sales did the same. But for many consumers the freezer is really a convenience product, and should be purchased as such. Yes, you probably can save money by buying food, especially meats, on sale and stocking the freezer. But this potential saving has to be weighed against both the initial price of the freezer and the cost of electricity to operate it.

Energy Label Helps You Choose

LIKE PRODUCERS of other major appliances, freezer manufacturers anticipated that the federal government would introduce new energy conservation standards. Although these standards may not now be enforced, manufacturers have already made energy-saving improvements. Most freezers have door heaters to prevent condensation in humid weather. Many new units have a switch to turn off the door heater when it's not needed—a feature that can cut energy use by 10 percent or more. Some models also now feature more efficient motors and compressors, thicker insulation, and better door gasketing to keep cold air in.

An energy label, one like the accompanying sample, now appears on all freezers. The information on the label can help you calculate the comparative energy-efficiency of one model versus others of the same size. The estimated annual cost—expressed in dollars per year—lets you compare operating costs. Although the estimated annual cost is based on a national average price for electricity, the label also provides a grid with a range of prices (on a per-kilowatt-hour basis) so that you can calculate the cost of operating a freezer in your area. Given a freezer's long lifespan—up to 20 years—the reduced cost of operating an energy-efficient unit can more than make up for any additional expense at time of purchase.

Chest or Upright: Pros and Cons

YOU CAN CHOOSE either an upright or a chest freezer. Each type has its pros and cons. An upright offers the convenience of front-door loading and takes up less floor space than a chest model; so it's a good choice if you want to have your freezer in the kitchen where floor space is limited. A chest freezer is less expensive than an upright of comparable size, and it holds more food. However, it's less convenient because it takes up more room, and goods have to be stacked rather than shelved and are therefore not so accessible. A chest freezer is a

1. Type of appliance and capacity.

2. National average cost for electricity upon which the estimated annual energy cost figure is based.

3. Estimated annual operating cost for the model in this size range that costs least to operate.

4. Scale showing lowest and highest estimated operating costs for models within this size

range. These models represent different brands, not just those of the company listed in the upper right-hand corner.

5. Where the estimated annual cost of this particular model falls in comparison to all other models in this size.

6. Warning that it is unlawful to remove label.

7. A grid to help determine more closely the customer's operating

cost based on local utility rates and use habits.

8. Suggests that the customer ask salesperson or utility for local utility rates.

9. Cautions that the customer's cost will not necessarily be the same as the cost figure given above.

10. Estimated annual operating cost for the model in this size range that costs most to operate.

11. All brands and models compared in the scale on this label fall within this capacity range.

12. All model numbers are listed if the label applies to more than one model.

13. Name of manufacturer and model number of the appliance on which the label appears.

14. Estimated annual operating cost for this model.

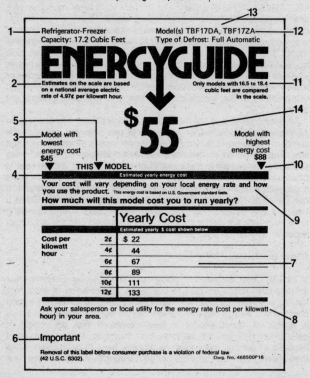

325

good choice for a basement where floor space isn't a problem, and for long-term storage (meat in bulk, for instance). An upright in the kitchen is convenient for everyday use. Decide how you're going to use the freezer and you'll know which kind to choose.

How large a freezer do you need? A freezer that's too large will be inefficient and costly to operate. But a freezer that's too small will defeat its own purpose and cause you a lot of frustration. A good rule of thumb is to allow about three cubic feet of freezer space for each family member. Add another two cubic feet for special purposes, and two or three more if you plan to freeze garden produce or prepare a lot of meals in advance.

Little Things That Help a Lot

ENERGY EFFICIENCY, style, and capacity are important, but they're not the only considerations when you buy a freezer. Here's a rundown on other features to look at:

Baskets. Baskets are useful for bulk items. Chest freezers usually have one or more sliding baskets for easier access to total freezer space. Uprights usually have just one basket at the bottom of the unit.

Door Shelves. Doors on chest freezers—because they swing up—have no shelves. Many upright models offer shelves that will accommodate a great number of items, plus some special storage devices—juice can racks, for example. Shelves that accommodate the widest variety of items are the best choice.

Controls. The freezer does its best work at 0° F or slightly below. Some models have controls that let you vary the temperature, but a properly designed freezer doesn't need controls.

Defrost Systems. Chest freezers only come with manual defrost, but a few upright models are available with automatic defrost. On an upright, automatic defrost will probably add about $100 to the purchase price and between 15 and 20 percent a year to operating costs. It's for you to decide if the convenience automatic defrost delivers is worth the extra cost.

Drain. Manual defrost units usually have a drain at the bottom of the unit with a length of hose attached to feed defrost water into a pan or, better yet, remove it via a floor drain. Some small chest freezers don't have a drain, because the amount of water produced during defrosting is small; a drain isn't really necessary.

Indicator Light. This small light, usually in red or orange, tells you the freezer is on. It may seem a frivolous extra, but it could save you the cost of your freezer's contents if the unit stops functioning for any reason. Many freezers are put in out-of-the-way places, so an indicator offers a quick check at a distance.

Interior Light. An interior light can help you find what you're looking for, but whether it is a necessity depends on where you put the freezer. In a kitchen, an interior light may be unnecessary. But in a dark basement it can be very useful.

Locks. A lock on your freezer is a very important feature if you have young children in your home who may be tempted to climb inside and get trapped. The best type is a key-eject lock that pops out when it's unlocked.

Styling. Some makers of upright freezers offer, as an option, decorator kits for wallpaper or paneling for the door. Textured steel is popular because it helps hide marks and fingerprints. If you're buying a chest freezer, your choice is limited to all white or white body with a woodgrain vinyl-clad top.

Best Buys '82

OUR SELECTION OF "Best Buys" and "Also Recommended" upright and chest freezers follows. Units are listed in descending order of size—those with the largest freezing space listed first. Our choices are based on energy-efficiency, convenience, and design. Remember that a "Best Buy" or "Also Recommended" designation applies only to the particular model in question; it doesn't mean that we necessarily recommend other models in the same product line or from the same manufacturer.

 **Upright Freezers**

General Electric CA21DA (21.2 cubic feet) is big enough to handle large storage needs. Four of the unit's five interior shelves have fast-freezing action; one is adjustable. This freezer has a sliding bulk-item basket, excellent door shelf spacing (six shelves including two juice can racks), a key-eject lock, an indicator light, and a handy drain for the manual defrost system.

Specifications: Height, 70⅛"; **Width,** 32"; **Depth,** 29⅝"; **Capacity,** 21.2 cu. ft.; **Warranty,** parts and labor, 1 year; compressor system (parts), 5 years.

Approximate Retail Price	Approximate Low Price
Not Available	$529.00

White-Westinghouse FU218C (21.2 cubic feet) is a big manual-defrost unit with a defrost drain. It has a textured steel door, interior light, six door shelves, and five interior shelves (one is adjustable). The glide-out storage basket is convenient. Other features include a cold control, indicator light, and key-eject lock. This unit uses a loop design to prevent door sweating.

Specifications: Height, 70"; **Width,** 32"; **Depth,** 26⅜"; **Capacity,** 21.2 cu. ft.; **Warranty,** parts and labor, 1 year; compressor system (parts), 5 years.

Approximate Retail Price	Approximate Low Price
$600.00	$559.00

Prices are accurate at time of printing; subject to manufacturer's change.

Hotpoint FV16CA (16.1 cubic feet) is an upright manual-defrost model with a drain, and a very convenient drop-front bulk storage retainer. The door has five shelves, including one juice can rack; there are three refrigerated shelves and an interior light. This model also has a cold control and built-in lock. The door stop is a good feature.
Specifications: Height, 59⅛"; **Width,** 32"; **Depth,** 31⅝"; **Capacity,** 16.1 cu. ft.; **Warranty,** parts and labor, 1 year; compressor system (parts and labor), 5 years.

Approximate Retail Price	Approximate Low Price
Not Available	$430.00

Gibson FV16M6W (16.0 cubic feet) is a manual-defrost upright with a good drain system. It has a lock, and good interior shelf distribution—five door shelves, slide-out basket, and four interior shelves (one is adjustable) providing more than 18.7 square feet of shelf area. The unit has interior and indicator lights. This is a good unit at a competitive price.
Specifications: Height, 59"; **Width,** 28⅜"; **Depth,** 28⅝"; **Capacity,** 16.0 cu. ft.; **Warranty,** parts and labor, 1 year; compressor system (parts), 5 years.

Approximate Retail Price	Approximate Low Price
Not Available	$449.00

Whirlpool EEV163F (15.9 cubic feet) is a quality unit with textured steel doors and a porcelain enamel interior. It also has a key-eject lock, indicator light, and interior light. Shelf arrangement—both in the door (four shelves and two juice can racks) and the interior (three shelves and a bulk item basket)—is excellent. The manual-defrost system has a drain. This model has a cold control, and a power-saver control.
Specifications: Height, 66"; **Width,** 29¾"; **Depth,** 31⅝"; **Capacity,** 15.9 cu. ft.; **Warranty,** parts and labor, 1 year; sealed system (parts and labor), 5 years.

Approximate Retail Price	Approximate Low Price
$501.00	$439.00

General Electric CA13DA (13.3 cubic feet) is a smaller manual-defrost unit, but it offers good door shelf arrangement. The interior design with three full-width shelves makes it easy to see and reach frozen foods. The four door shelves include a juice-can rack. The unit's economical price accounts for its lack of a drain, lock, or indicator light. This is an excellent basic unit but, because it doesn't have a lock, it's not suitable for households with young children.
Specifications: Height, 54⅝"; **Width,** 28"; **Depth,** 29⅝"; **Capacity,** 13.3 cu. ft.; **Warranty,** parts and labor, 1 year; compressor system (parts and labor), 5 years.

Approximate Retail Price	Approximate Low Price
Not Available	$399.00

Also Recommended

Sears Kenmore 47G31166N (15.6 cubic feet) is an automatic-defrost model that compensates for the frost-free feature with extra insulation. It

Prices are accurate at time of printing; subject to manufacturer's change.

has six deep door shelves, three interior shelves (one is adjustable), porcelain-on-steel liners, interior light, cold control, indicator light, textured steel door, and key-eject lock. This is one of the best automatic-defrost models around, but you'll still save more with a manual-defrost unit and that is why we don't give this a "Best Buy" rating.

Specifications: Height, 66"; **Width,** 29¾"; **Depth,** 30⅛"; **Capacity,** 15.6 cu. ft.; **Warranty,** parts and labor, 1 year; sealed system (parts and labor), 5 years.

Approximate Retail Price	Approximate Low Price
$520.00	Not Available

Admiral F-15C6 (15.2 cubic-feet) is a new manual-defrost model that uses a loop design to eliminate the need for door heaters. This unit has convenient storage in four interior shelves, four well-spaced door shelves with two juice can racks, and a retainer basket for bulk items. It has a key-eject lock, an interior light, a cold control, and a defrost drain. The cabinet and door are of textured steel. This new unit needs a track record to establish reliability, but it has the design features we look for.

Specifications: Height, 60"; **Width,** 30"; **Depth,** 26¾"; **Capacity,** 15.2 cu. ft.; **Warranty,** parts and labor, 1 year; compressor system (parts), 5 years.

Approximate Retail Price	Approximate Low Price
$560.00	$499.00

Amana ESU-13C (13.0 cubic feet) is a small unit with a relatively large price tag. It has been designed for high energy efficiency and will cost less to operate than its lower-priced competitors. This model has a textured steel door, flip-up retainers on the five door shelves (which we liked), four interior shelves, a basket, and a good drain for the manual-defrost system. It also comes with a lock and key. This is a fine unit, but it's too expensive for its size to meet our "Best Buys" standards.

Specifications: Height, 62⅞"; **Width,** 28"; **Depth,** 25⅞"; **Capacity,** 13.0 cu. ft.; **Warranty,** parts and labor, 1 year; sealed system (parts and labor), 5 years.

Approximate Retail Price	Approximate Low Price
$550.00	$469.00

Admiral F-12C5 (12.1 cubic feet) is a newly introduced model. It has five door shelves, three fast-freezing interior shelves, a retainer basket for bulk items, and a cold control. A loop design eliminates the need for a door heater. The cabinet and door are textured steel, and the unit has a key-eject lock. We don't give new models a "Best Buy" rating, however much we like the look of them; this unit needs a year to establish performance, but it incorporates features we like, and looks like a promising addition to the market.

Specifications: Height, 60"; **Width,** 24"; **Depth,** 26¾"; **Capacity,** 12.1 cu. ft.; **Warranty,** parts and labor, 1 year; compressor system (parts), 5 years.

Approximate Retail Price	Approximate Low Price
$520.00	$479.00

Prices are accurate at time of printing; subject to manufacturer's change.

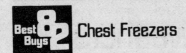 Chest Freezers

Whirlpool EHH180F (18.2 cubic feet) is a large unit built to last. It has three slide-and-store removable baskets—about the best arrangement in big chest freezers. This model has a key-eject lock and indicator and interior lights, making it a unit for out-of-the-way placement. Construction is first-rate.
Specifications: Height (lid open), 62¼"; **Width,** 50¼"; **Depth,** 28"; **Capacity,** 18.2 cu. ft.; **Warranty,** parts and labor, 1 year; sealed system (parts and labor), 5 years.

Approximate Retail Price   Approximate Low Price
$527.00... $449.00

Amana C-15B (15.0 cubic feet) is a manual-defrost model with a convenient drain. A divider and a sliding basket allow you to arrange frozen foods to suit your needs. Other good points are the key-eject lock, an interior light, and a cold control.
Specifications: Height (lid open), 60⅝"; **Width,** 41½"; **Depth,** 30⅝"; **Capacity,** 15.0 cu. ft.; **Warranty,** parts and labor, 1 year; sealed system (parts and labor), 5 years.

Approximate Retail Price   Approximate Low Price
$500.00... $439.00

Sears Kenmore 47G11098N (9.0 cubic feet) was judged the best overall of smaller chest freezers. A textured steel lid helps to hide marks and fingerprints, and the unit has a power-interruption indicator light. This model comes with a cold control, and key-eject lock.
Specifications: Height (lid open), 60½"; **Width,** 37⅛"; **Depth,** 27¾"; **Capacity,** 9.0 cu. ft.; **Warranty,** parts and labor, 1 year; sealed system (parts and labor), 5 years.

Approximate Retail Price   Approximate Low Price
$310.00... Not Available

Also Recommended

Gibson FH10M4W (10.07 cubic feet) has a removable sliding basket. Although it's a manual-defrost unit, it doesn't have a drain; this is true of most small chest freezers. The unit is equipped with a key-eject lock. This is a compact design for tight places, and it's our second choice as an alternative to our Sears Kenmore Model 47G11098N "Best Buy."
Specifications: Height (lid open), 56⅜"; **Width,** 41"; **Depth,** 23¾"; **Capacity,** 10.0 cu. ft.; **Warranty,** parts and labor, 1 year; compressor system (parts), 5 years.

Approximate Retail Price   Approximate Low Price
Not Available.. $379.00

Prices are accurate at time of printing; subject to manufacturer's change.

Dishwashers

THE DISHWASHER—yesterday's luxury appliance—has become a necessity for many people today. Working homemakers and consumers challenged by solo household maintenance chores welcome the relief from cleanup tasks that a dishwasher affords. There's a wide selection of dishwashers available—you can choose from over 25 brands ranging in price from about $250 to more than $500. And since the model you choose will last 8 to 10 years, the decision merits careful thought.

Base Model Choice on Kitchen Space

DISHWASHERS CAN be built in or portable, and kitchen space will probably dictate your choice between these two styles. If you plan to move, you may want to compromise with a convertible—a portable model that can be built in later.

A built-in dishwasher attaches permanently to water and electrical lines, and is the most convenient to use; it requires only loading, switching on, and unloading. It leaves floor space free but does deprive you of one of your kitchen cabinets; the unit fits into the cabinet space. A portable dishwasher connects to the sink faucet with a hose (it should also be connected to a grounded outlet with a power cord) and drains through a hose into the sink. As the name suggests, you can move it around. Most portables have a flow-through valve that lets you draw water from the faucet while the machine is in operation.

If a portable unit is front-loading, it is likely to be designed for conversion to a built-in unit. Top-loaders are the true portables but are not in great demand; although they often cost less, this advantage is offset by a smaller capacity and less convenience in loading.

Energy Label Gives Clues to Costs

IN KEEPING WITH federal regulations, all new dishwashers must now display an energy label that gives approximate energy costs for use with either a gas or an electric water heater as the hot water source. Unfortunately, dishwasher detergents don't work well below 140°F, which means a good deal of hot water goes into an efficient cleaning job. This hot water consumption accounts for most of a machine's energy use, and there is little manufacturers can do about it.

In response, however, to projected federal energy standards (which may not now be implemented), manufacturers have introduced energy-saving features, including shorter rinse-and-dry cycles and alterations in tub design. On many units you'll now find a cycle that uses less hot water

1. Type of appliance and capacity.

2. National average cost for electricity upon which the estimated annual energy cost figure is based.

3. Estimated annual operating cost for the model in this size range that costs least to operate.

4. Scale showing lowest and highest estimated operating costs for models within this size range. These models represent different brands, not just those of the company listed in the upper right-hand corner.

5. Where the estimated annual cost of this particular model falls in comparison to all other models in this size.

6. Warning that it is unlawful to remove label.

7. A grid to help determine more closely the customer's operating cost based on local utility rates and use habits.

8. Suggests that the customer ask salesperson or utility for local utility rates.

9. Cautions that the customer's cost will not necessarily be the same as the cost figure given above.

10. Estimated annual operating cost for the model in this size range that costs most to operate.

11. All brands and models compared in the scale on this label fall within this capacity range.

12. All model numbers are listed if the label applies to more than one model.

13. Name of manufacturer and model number of the appliance on which the label appears.

14. Estimated annual operating cost for this model.

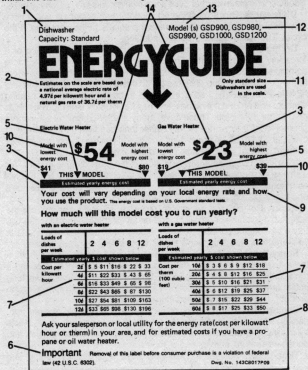

CONSUMER GUIDE®

to clean lightly soiled dishes. Manufacturers call it an "energy-saving" cycle, which is the new way of describing what used to be called the "short wash" cycle.

Two years ago, KitchenAid introduced a unit that internally heats water to between 140° and 150°F. This independent heating system ensures thorough cleaning, while allowing the consumer to save overall household energy by lowering the temperature setting on the central water heater. Other manufacturers have introduced similar heating systems in some models.

Look for Features That Count

DISHWASHERS COME with many features; some good, others not very significant. Here's a rundown on those to look for:

Cycles. A dishwasher may have from two to eight cycles or more. Seldom will you need more than three: a short wash (now called "energy-saving" by some manufacturers); a normal wash; and a pots-and-pans cycle. You might find a rinse-and-hold cycle convenient. Sanitizer and plate-warmer cycles are nice but raise the purchase price.

Dispensers. Buy a machine with a detergent dispenser and a rinse dispenser that automatically release the agents at the right time in the cycle. The rinse agent prevents spotting.

Drying Systems. Dishwashers come with either a convection or a forced-air drying system. The convection system—which is more common—relies on heat rising naturally from a radiant heating element in the bottom of the tub. The forced-air system, which uses a relatively high level of energy, has a blower to force the air over the heating element and around the dishes, and has traditionally been considered to do a better, faster job. These days, many energy-conscious consumers choose to let their dishes air-dry rather than use heat during the drying cycle, and with this option in mind you needn't let the drying system play a major part in your choice of a dishwasher.

Interiors. Porcelain enamel on steel is the most durable material for dishwasher tubs. Stainless steel runs a close second, but it's not commonly used. Some "specialty" materials—like General Electric's one-piece plastic (over metal) interior—also have merit.

Racks. Roll-out and adjustable racks are most convenient, but the adjustable feature is normally found on top-of-the-line machines. If you buy a top-loading portable, look for racks that lift up when you open the lid. Whatever you buy, look for a removable silverware basket.

Spray-Washing Action. The best washing action comes from a three-level spray assembly that has arms at the top and bottom and a turret to help spray the upper rack. Units with two-level spray-washing action (arms at the top and bottom) also do a good job. One-level action probably won't provide satisfactory cleaning.

Styling. Most dishwashers come with interchangeable colored front panels; some machines even lend themselves to special visual effects by means of a decorator kit or black glass kit. Some convertibles and portables feature cutting board tops.

Time-Delay. Several models now have a time-delay setting that allows you to delay washing for up to eight hours. This is practical for consumers who get a price break for using off-peak power, and it's a feature that we believe will become more important in the future.

Doing Dishes the Energy-Conscious Way

IF YOU WANT to save energy, CONSUMER GUIDE® magazine offers these tips: Run the dishwasher only when it's full, and use the short wash or energy-saving cycle if your dishwasher has one. If your machine has a power-saver switch to cut out the powered drying cycle, use it; you'll have to wait for your dishes to "air dry," but you'll save about 10 percent on energy. Finally, prewashing wastes hot water. Don't do it unless you must—a simple scraping is usually good enough.

Best Buys '82

THE FOLLOWING selections of "Best Buy" and "Also Recommended" models have been chosen in keeping with our criteria of value, convenience, and energy-efficiency; they are listed alphabetically within each category. Remember that a "Best Buy" designation applies only to the model listed; it doesn't necessarily apply to other models made by the same manufacturer, or to an entire product line.

Best Buys 82 Built-In Dishwashers

Admiral DU-18B5 is a space-saver model that fits into a standard 18-inch-wide cabinet space. It has a pots-and-pans cycle, normal wash, short wash, two rinse-and-hold options (for dishes and for pots and pans), and a plate warmer. An energy-saving button lets dishes air dry. This unit has two-level spray-washing action and a safety lock; the porcelain interior, "power-on" light, and removable silverware basket are good features.
Specifications: Height, 33¾"; **Width,** 17⅝"; **Depth,** 22½"; **Heating Element Wattage,** 750; **Volts,** 110-120; **Water Use, Regular Wash,** not available; **Warranty,** parts and labor, 1 year.

Approximate Retail Price	Approximate Low Price
$340.00	$220.00

General Electric GSD900X has push-to-start controls and a choice of five cycles, including power scrub. An energy-saving option eliminates heated drying on both pots-and-pans and normal cycles. The unit has GE's long-life (10-year warranty) tub and door. It has three-level spray-washing action, sound insulation, deep racks, and a pack of interchangeable, reversible door panels.

Prices are accurate at time of printing; subject to manufacturer's change.

Specifications: Height, 34″; **Width,** 24″; **Depth,** 26¼″; **Heating Element Wattage,** 700; **Volts,** 110-120; **Water Use, Regular Wash,** 10.3 gal.; **Warranty,** parts and labor, 1 year; tub, 10 years.

Approximate Retail Price	Approximate Low Price
Not Available	.... $399.00

Hotpoint HDA780 offers six cycle options; three basic cycles (power scrub, normal, and short wash) can be set with or without drying. It has three-level spray-washing action, convection drying system, rinse dispenser, porcelain enamel interior, and reversible front color panels (five colors). A kit for custom fronts is available.

Specifications: Height, 33⅞″ (min.); **Width,** 23⅞″; **Depth,** 25¾″; **Heating Element Wattage,** 700; **Volts,** 110-120; **Water Use, Regular Wash,** 11.4 gal.; **Warranty,** parts and labor, 1 year.

Approximate Retail Price	Approximate Low Price
Not Available	.... $300.00

KitchenAid KDP-20 is a durable, quality unit with two-level spray-washing action, four cycles including a new low-energy cycle, indicator lights, porcelain interior, and steel frame. An internal heating element heats the water in the unit to the 150°F washing temperature and to 165°F for a sanitized final rinse. The built-in water heater saves energy by reducing demand on a standard water heater. Powered drying can be used with or without heat.

Specifications: Height, 34½″; **Width,** 24″; **Depth,** 25¹³⁄₁₆″; **Heating Element Wattage,** 700 (2); **Volts,** 115; **Water Use, Regular Wash,** 11.5 gal.; **Warranty,** parts and labor, 1 year; motor (parts), 5 years; tub and inner door (parts), 10 years.

Approximate Retail Price	Approximate Low Price
Not Available	.... $589.00

Maytag WU500 provides three-level spray-washing action and three cycles plus a rinse-and-hold option. A low-energy regular wash cycle uses 20 percent less hot water than the regular wash cycle. You can select powered drying action or the more energy-efficient "air" (non-heated) drying. A unique rack arrangement—called dual deep racks—is the answer to heavy loads with too many big items to fit on one rack. The porcelain enamel interior is a good feature.

Specifications: Height, 34 to 35½″; **Width,** 24″; **Depth,** 24¹⁄₁₆″; **Heating Element Wattage,** 750; **Volts,** 110-120; **Water Use, Regular Wash,** 11 gal.; **Warranty,** parts and labor, 1 year; all parts, 2 years; cabinet (against rust) and spray mechanism (parts only), 5 years.

Approximate Retail Price	Approximate Low Price
Not Available	.... $459.00

Sears Kenmore 65G7014N is an economy model with three-level spray-washing action and a forced-air drying system—a switch allows you to turn off the heating element and run the forced air alone to dry dishes. Sound insulation and a porcelain enamel interior are good features for an economy model, and the concealed pushbuttons (behind

Prices are accurate at time of printing; subject to manufacturer's change.

a sliding panel) will be appreciated in homes with young children. The unit has seven cycles; including normal wash, light wash, rinse-and-hold, and pots-and-pans cycles.

Specifications: Height, 34 to 34½"; **Width,** 23⅞"; **Depth,** 25"; **Heating Element Wattage,** 750; **Volts,** 110-120; **Water Use, Regular Wash,** not available; **Warranty,** parts and labor, 1 year; tub and inner door (parts and labor), 5 years.

Approximate Retail Price	Approximate Low Price
$440.00	Not Available

Whirlpool SHU-7004 has nine cycle options, with energy-saving air-dry on four of them. This model has dual-level spray-washing action and a washing option that uses an internal heating element to raise the water temperature to about 150°F. It has a porcelain interior, side racks that are about 50 percent higher than usual to accommodate large items, an in-the-door silverware basket, and reversible door panels giving a choice of four colors.

Specifications: Height, 34⅛"; **Width,** 23¾"; **Depth,** 26"; **Heating Element Wattage,** 800; **Volts,** 110-120; **Water Use, Normal/Light,** 9.0 gal.; **Warranty,** parts and labor, 1 year.

Approximate Retail Price	Approximate Low Price
$445.00	$399.00

Also Recommended

General Electric GSD1000S has nine cycle options and a rack arrangement that is bigger and more flexible than most. The model has three-level spray-washing action, a heated drying cycle (the heat can be turned off to save energy), and heavy insulation. GE's one-piece plastic interior should resist cracking in normal use. Water consumption is lower than that found on many competitive units, but this model's high price takes it out of our "Best Buy" range.

Specifications: Height, 34½"; **Width,** 24"; **Depth,** 26¼"; **Heating Element Wattage,** 700; **Volts,** 110-120; **Water Use, Regular Wash,** 10.3 gal.; **Warranty,** parts and labor, 1 year; tub, 10 years.

Approximate Retail Price	Approximate Low Price
Not Available	$499.00

Whirlpool SHU-5004 gives you nine cycle options including four automatic cycles. It has convection drying, but a power-saving option allows you to set three cycles without drying. A wash feature will, when set, use an internal heating element to raise the water to the proper washing temperature. The porcelain interior and semi-concealed latch are good features. Although it doesn't qualify as a "Best Buy," this is a worthwhile model.

Specifications: Height, 34⅛"; **Width,** 23¾"; **Depth,** 26"; **Heating Element Wattage,** 800; **Volts,** 110-120; **Water Use, Regular Wash,** 9.0 gal.; **Warranty,** parts and labor, 1 year.

Approximate Retail Price	Approximate Low Price
$415.00	$369.00

Prices are accurate at time of printing; subject to manufacturer's change.

White-Westinghouse SU500D, between its pushbuttons and its dial, gives you 11 cycle options. A power-saver switch cuts out the drying part of the cycle. Although we cannot rate it a "Best Buy," this model has many good features, including a porcelain enamel interior, dual-level spray-washing action, rinse agent dispenser, and sound insulation. Its low water consumption—9.1 gallons for the normal cycle—is its most notable attribute and puts it in our "Also Recommended" category.
Specifications: Height, 34¼"; **Width,** 24"; **Depth,** 25"; **Heating Element Wattage,** 760; **Volts,** 110-120; **Water Use, Regular Wash,** 9.1 gal.; **Warranty,** parts and labor, 1 year.

Approximate Retail Price   Approximate Low Price
$400.00 .... $369.00

 Convertible/Portable Dishwashers

Hotpoint HDB820 offers seven cycles, including an energy-saving short-wash cycle. On all but the rinse-and-hold cycle you can eliminate the powered drying phase. Quality features are the three-level spray-washing action, porcelain interior, and an easy-to-use faucet connector that allows you to use the faucet even when the dishwasher is hooked up to it. The top, in cherry veneer, is an attractive detail.
Specifications: Height, 36¾"; **Width,** 24⅜"; **Depth,** 25"; **Heating Element Wattage,** 700; **Volts,** 110-120; **Water Use, Regular Wash,** 11.4 gal.; **Warranty,** parts and labor, 1 year.

Approximate Retail Price   Approximate Low Price
Not Available $334.00

KitchenAid KDI-60 possesses many of the quality features found on the "Best Buy" KDP-20 built-in model from KitchenAid. It has the same porcelain interior, two-level spray-washing, sturdy construction, and internal heating action designed to save energy by reducing the demand on your home's primary water heater. You can use the powered drying cycle with or without heat. Though expensive to buy, this is a quality machine that can help hold down your utility costs.
Specifications: Height, 36"; **Width,** 24"; **Depth,** 26¹¹⁄₁₆"; **Heating Element Wattage,** 700 for heating water and 800 for drying; **Volts,** 115; **Water Use, Regular Wash,** 12 gal.; **Warranty,** parts and labor, 1 year; motor (parts), 5 years; tub and inner door (parts), 10 years.

Approximate Retail Price   Approximate Low Price
Not Available $619.00

Maytag WC300 is an economy convertible with enough features to make it a good value. It has a porcelain enamel tub, and offers a heavy wash cycle, regular cycle, and rinse-and-hold cycle. You can save

Prices are accurate at time of printing; subject to manufacturer's change.

power by turning off the heating element during the drying period. This unit has been redesigned to use less hot water than earlier Maytag units. It comes with a wood cutting board top and heavy-duty casters, and can be built-in with an optional conversion kit.

Specifications: Height, 36½"; **Width,** 24"; **Depth,** 27"; **Heating Element Wattage,** 750; **Volts,** 110-120; **Water Use, Regular Wash,** 11 gal.; **Warranty,** parts and labor, 1 year; on all parts, 2 years; cabinet (against rust) and spray mechanism (parts only), 5 years.

Approximate Retail Price	Approximate Low Price
Not Available	$475.00

Sears Kenmore 65G70051N—among the best of the middle economy-priced convertible/portables—has four cycles (plus a light wash), two-level spray-washing action, a hose compartment, and a five-foot cord. It also has several quality features usually found only on more expensive models: porcelain interior, forced-air drying, and a power-saver switch to shut off the heating element during the drying period.

Specifications: Height, 37¼"; **Width,** 24½"; **Depth,** 26¾"; **Heating Element Wattage,** 750; **Volts,** 110-120; **Water Use, Regular Wash,** not available; **Warranty,** parts and labor, 1 year; tub and inner door panel (parts and labor), 5 years.

Approximate Retail Price	Approximate Low Price
$360.00 (white)	Not Available
$370.00 (other colors)	Not Available

 Portable -Only Dishwashers

Sears Kenmore 65G71561N is a narrow (18 inches) unit for small kitchens, with seven cycles including a pots-and-pans cycle and a light-wash cycle that saves hot water. It has two-level spray-washing action. Quality features include a porcelain enamel interior and a switch to turn off the heating element. The rack arrangement is good, and efficient loading is possible despite the narrow configuration.

Specifications: Height, 35¾"; **Width,** 18"; **Depth,** 26⅛"; **Heating Element Wattage,** 750; **Volts,** 110-120; **Water Use, Regular Wash,** not available; **Warranty,** parts and labor, 1 year; tub and inner door panel (parts and labor), 5 years.

Approximate Retail Price	Approximate Low Price
$320.00 (white)	Not Available
$330.00 (other colors)	Not Available

Prices are accurate at time of printing; subject to manufacturer's change.

Garbage Disposers

CHANCES ARE your kitchen's daily wastes include such tough items as apple cores, corncobs, and bones. So a garbage disposer needs to be tough to do its job every day without jamming or making a lot of noise.

Basically, garbage disposers use a grind wheel driven by a motor to grind up food waste. Disposer prices start from about $60 to $75 at the budget end of the line, and peak at about $200. That may seem like a big jump, but the extra price can give you a lot—a heavy-duty motor (½-horsepower or more), a higher proportion of good-quality corrosion-resistant materials (like stainless steel), and important safety features. For durability, efficiency, and reliability, CONSUMER GUIDE® magazine recommends that you select a disposer from the mid- to top-of-the-line range.

Jamming of the grinding mechanism can be a frustrating problem with inexpensive low-power units. Heavy-duty machines, on the other hand, usually have an anti-jam system that automatically unclogs trapped wastes, which is one of the features that justify a higher price. The system may work by reversing the direction of the grinding action, or by applying jolts of power to the machine. Either way, it's a big advantage in terms of convenience and safety: Because the machine can unclog itself, you won't be tempted to free it by sticking your hand or a utensil into the mechanism—both highly undesirable procedures.

Almost every kitchen sink can be fitted with a disposer. Even so, you should check local building codes before making the installation. If you have a septic tank, check with a local plumber or other expert before installing a disposer.

Continuous- or Batch-Feed?

DISPOSERS COME in two types—batch-feed and continuous-feed. Both work well and safely when used properly. The main difference is the way you load the machine.

With a batch-feed model, you load the unit with food waste (usually about a quart), then insert a cover that also includes the start switch. Once you turn the disposer on, the cover locks in place, and you cannot add more waste without stopping the unit.

On a continuous-feed disposer, a remote wall switch turns the machine on and off. You must run cold water continuously (hot water softens grease, which will later harden again and clog the system) while using the disposer. A safety cover or lid, which you can remove and replace easily while the motor is still running, lets water run into the unit and also keeps waste from flying out. As the name implies, you can continuously feed this type of food waste disposer. A word of caution —when the safety cover is removed, waste can fly out and dishcloths and other objects can fall in.

There is no price advantage to either type. Because they have their own wiring, batch-feed units cost more to buy but less to install. The reverse is true for the continuous-feed variety; they cost less to buy and more to install, because you also need a wall switch. At today's service charges, plan to spend (if you're making a first installation) about $50 to install a batch-feed model and $75 to $100 for a continuous-feed unit. Do-it-yourself instructions generally are good, so you might consider putting in a replacement yourself.

Most garbage disposers are directly wired to a wall switch, but many manufacturers also offer at least one model with a grounded power cord, which is good news if you have a suitable electrical outlet under the sink (or a switch outlet, if the disposer is continuous-feed). If you don't already have such an outlet, we suggest you stay with a standard model.

When replacing a broken or worn-out disposer, we think it's best to stick with the same type (batch- or continuous-feed), because installation will be easier. Of course, if you've been displeased with your original choice, you may want to change to another type.

Base Your Choice on Performance Features

BEWARE OF FEATURES that make a disposer look better without making it work better. This is one product in which cosmetic beauty counts for nothing, except pushing the price up. Once installed under the sink, a disposer's charm rests completely on performance. Take note of the following features when making your choice:

Anti-jam System. A worthwhile feature for both convenience and safety, the system can clear jams by applying power jolts to the machine or by reversing the unit's direction. Both work well. Reversing features can add to the life of the unit by reducing stress on the motor.

Corrosion Resistance. CONSUMER GUIDE® magazine recommends disposers using stainless steel or corrosion-resistant alloys for the key parts.

Motor. Larger motors mean more power for the job at hand and better endurance under heavy use. The ⅓-horsepower motors of less expensive units are more liable to jam than the ½- to ¾-horsepower motors used in better models.

Mounting System. We've looked for what manufacturers call quick-mounting systems; better units have them. (Quick-Click, Quick-Connect, Fast-Mount, Quick-Lock, and so on are manufacturers' own names for the same thing.) They keep installation costs down, and no special tools are needed—a plus for do-it-yourselfers.

Sound Insulation. Sound-insulated units are more expensive but can be worth the extra cost, especially if you have a stainless steel sink. The insulation (rubber or plastic foam in many cases) helps dampen vibration to plumbing lines and reduces noise.

Dishwasher Drain. If you have or plan to install a dishwasher, make sure the disposer has a side opening for a dishwasher drain hose. This makes dishwasher installation easier and eliminates potential water backup problems.

Best Buys '82

CONSUMER GUIDE® magazine stresses solid construction and corrosion-resistance in this review of currently available garbage disposers. Special attention is given to disposers from manufacturers that offer a full range of models. Our "Best Buys" are models that combine the best features at the best prices in a given price range. Remember that a "Best Buy" or "Also Recommended" designation applies only to the model listed—not to a full product line or to other models by the same manufacturer. Models are listed alphabetically within each category.

 Batch-Feed Disposers

General Electric GFB910 batch-feed disposer was judged the best of the medium-priced models. It has a heavy-duty ½-horsepower motor and is ruggedly constructed. This model has automatic overload protection and sound insulation that includes a drain-line cushion to minimize noise transfer to plumbing lines. Key components are made from stainless steel or corrosion-resistant alloys.
Specifications: Drain Diameter, standard; **Volts,** 115; **Mounting,** quick-mounting; **Warranty,** parts and labor, 1 year.
Approximate Retail Price   Approximate Low Price
Not Available $169.00

In-Sink-Erator 17 is a stainless steel model with automatic reversing operation and a special wrench to clear persistent jams. This unit uses corrosion-resistant alloys for key components, and the ½-horsepower motor provides enough driving force to prevent frequent jamming. The design has proven to be one of the more efficient and durable grinding methods. Sound insulation rounds out features that make this model the best among the more economical of those in the medium-price range.
Specifications: Drain Diameter, standard; **Volts,** 115; **Mounting,** quick-mounting; **Warranty,** parts and labor, 1 year; parts only, 5 years.
Approximate Retail Price   Approximate Low Price
Not Available $149.00

KitchenAid KWS-200 is a quality model with sound insulation and automatic overload protection; key components are made of stainless steel and cast iron. An electronic reversing mode is backed up by a jam-clearing system that provides 120 jolts per second at the touch of a button to clear any persistent jam. The ½-horsepower motor can handle

Prices are accurate at time of printing; subject to manufacturer's change.

heavy loads. This unit was judged the best of the high-priced disposers. **Specifications: Drain Diameter,** standard; **Volts,** 115; **Mounting,** quick-mounting; **Warranty,** parts and labor, 1 year; parts only, 5 years.

Approximate Retail Price	Approximate Low Price
$210.00	$189.00

Also Recommended

Maytag FB20 is a solidly constructed, medium-price batch-feed unit, that features motor overload protection (manual reset), dishwasher drain, and sound insulation shield. Key components are made of stainless steel. The unit isn't subject to frequent jamming, and its ½-horsepower motor can handle most heavy loads. In the price range, however, we prefer the General Electric GFB910 to this model for overall value. **Specifications: Drain Diameter,** standard; **Volts,** 115; **Mounting,** quick-mounting; **Warranty,** parts and labor, 1 year; parts only, 2 years; corrosion failure, 5 years.

Approximate Retail Price	Approximate Low Price
Not Available	$179.00

 Continuous-Feed Disposers

General Electric GFC810 is the continuous-feed version of top-rated batch-feed Model GFB910, and was judged the best continuous-feed model among the middle-priced units. The unit has a heavy-duty ½-horsepower motor and is ruggedly constructed, with automatic overload protection, and sound insulation that includes a drain-line cushion to minimize noise transfer to plumbing lines. Key components are made of stainless steel or corrosion-resistant alloys. **Specifications: Drain Diameter,** standard; **Volts,** 115; **Mounting,** quick-mounting; **Warranty,** parts and labor, 1 year.

Approximate Retail Price	Approximate Low Price
Not Available	$149.00

In-Sink-Erator 77 is the continuous-feed version of Model 17, and is judged the best among the economical medium-priced units. It has upper and lower sound insulation, automatic reversing to clear jams, and a ½-horsepower motor; key components are made of stainless steel. This unit has a special sound baffle design that keeps noise at a minimum. It also has a dishwasher drain and a special wrench to clear persistent jams. **Specifications: Drain Diameter,** standard; **Volts,** 115; **Mounting,** quick-mounting; **Warranty,** parts and labor, 1 year; parts only, 5 years.

Approximate Retail Price	Approximate Low Price
Not Available	$125.00

Prices are accurate at time of printing; subject to manufacturer's change.

KitchenAid KWI-200, the continuous-feed version of Model KWS-200, is a quality model with durable construction, and has sound insulation and automatic overload protection. Key components are made of stainless steel and cast iron. An electronic reversing mode is backed up by a jam-clearing feature that provides 120 jolts per second at the touch of a button to clear any persistent jam. The ½-horsepower motor can handle heavy loads. This unit was judged the best of the high-end models of disposers.

Specifications: Drain Diameter, standard; **Volts,** 115; **Mounting,** quick-mounting; **Warranty,** parts and labor, 1 year; parts only, 5 years.

Approximate Retail Price   Approximate Low Price
$200.00 .... $179.00

Waste King SS8000, a unit with a high price tag but an equally high reliability rating, is one of the better-made models available, and was judged one of the two best units in the high-price category. Key components are made of stainless steel and corrosion-resistant alloys. A ¾-horsepower motor makes this a brute of a unit, capable of grinding even bones without strain. Sound insulation and overload protection are standard. The model also has a rubber connection to absorb vibrations.

Specifications: Drain Diameter, standard; **Volts,** 115; **Mounting,** quick-mounting; **Warranty,** parts and labor, 1 year; parts only, 5 years; selected corrosion-resistant parts (parts only), 20 years.

Approximate Retail Price   Approximate Low Price
$260.00 .... $223.00

Also Recommended

Maytag FC20 is the continuous-feed version of Model FB20. It is soundly constructed, and features motor overload protection (manual reset), dishwasher drain, and sound insulation shield. Key components are made of stainless steel. The unit isn't subject to frequent jamming, and its ½-horsepower motor can handle most heavy loads. In the price range, however, we prefer the General Electric Model GFC810 for overall value.

Specifications: Drain Diameter, standard; **Volts,** 115; **Mounting,** quick-mounting; **Warranty,** parts and labor, 1 year; parts only, 2 years; corrosion failure, 5 years.

Approximate Retail Price   Approximate Low Price
Not Available $159.00

Tappan Sinkmaster 800 is a continuous-feed unit with a ½-horsepower motor. Key parts are of stainless steel or corrosion-resistant alloys and the unit is sound-insulated. This isn't the best unit on the market, but it is a good product and has the advantage of being readily available through catalog companies and hardware stores, in areas where it might be difficult to find other disposers.

Specifications: Drain Diameter, standard; **Volts,** 115; **Mounting,** quick-mounting; **Warranty,** parts and labor, 1 year.

Approximate Retail Price   Approximate Low Price
Not Available $75.00

Prices are accurate at time of printing; subject to manufacturer's change.

Trash Compactors

W E SPEND A GOOD deal of time finding ways to make life easier. The trash compactor is the result of such effort; it's a product that takes some of the burden out of disposing of trash. The device works by crushing the air out of bulky refuse, reducing the heap to about a quarter of its original size. A typical family stacks up three to four bags of trash a week—about 30 pounds in weight. With a compactor, that 30 pounds can fit into one neat bundle.

Two Ways to Smash the Trash

COMPACTORS CRUSH TRASH with one of two kinds of mechanical action: a ram-screw method, or a combination scissor-jack and ram-screw. Both methods have the desired effect and rate comparably on most points, so this difference shouldn't play a large part in your choice. Whirlpool, who introduced the trash compactor and is the leading producer, uses the ram-screw method.

The style you select—built-in, free-standing, or convertible—depends on your space situation. Because most compactors are installed in the kitchen, where space is limited, CONSUMER GUIDE® magazine reviewed more built-in units than free-standing or convertible models. You might choose a free-standing unit for a basement or garage. If you are remodeling and are still uncertain of where the compactor might end up, then a convertible unit might be a good choice. Whatever your need, there is a "Best Buy" to meet it.

Safety, Styling, Sweetening the Scent

HERE ARE FEATURES you'll find on available compactors:

Deodorizers. Nothing truly "deodorizes" a large amount of trash, but deodorizing systems (both automatic and manual) can help minimize the problem and are worth having. Whirlpool and other manufacturers favor solid air fresheners placed in compartments in the compactor. To control odor, it's best to put only dry waste in the compactors and to channel wet garbage through a garbage disposer or dispose of it separately.

Locks. Locks are a safety measure to prevent children from playing with the powerful—and, in little hands, potentially hazardous—machinery. Both key-locks and removable on/off knobs are available, with the latter being the preferred style; you can't turn the machine on without a knob. Of course, having removed the knob, you'll have to keep it where you can find it and the children can't.

Styling. Most manufacturers provide compactors in a choice of colors. If you're looking for a built-in unit, choose one that comes with replaceable front panels so that you can alter the color if you change your kitchen decor. Many companies also make decorator kits, allowing you to brighten up the compactor front with paneling, wallpaper, or other personal touches.

Containers. Containers—receptacles in which the trash is held inside the compactor—are round or rectangular. The round bucket type is a little easier to handle when full than the rectangular basket kind.

Container Access. A good compactor lets you get at the container easily, without unnecessary bending or maneuvering. The most convenient units have an automatic slide-out drawer or swing-out bucket activated by a toe-bar. This automatic feature costs extra, but it is worth the money when you are trying to open the drawer and your hands are full. Nonautomatic compactors have a pull-out drawer, side-opening door, or a half-door that tilts from the top.

Best Buys '82

OUR "BEST BUY" and "Also Recommended" trash compactors follow; they are listed alphabetically within each category. We believe that our selections represent the best available products in terms of value, durability, and efficiency. Remember that a "Best Buy" designation applies to that model only and doesn't necessarily apply to other models made by the same manufacturer, or to an entire product line.

 Trash Compactors

General Electric GCG900 can be used free-standing, built-in under a counter, or anywhere there is a 15-amp grounded circuit. This model is our top-rated unit at the high end of compactor offerings and is above-average in convenience, with an easy-opening door for access to the loading bucket. Safety features are good; a key/knob prevents unauthorized operation. The model has a storage compartment above the compactor door, an automatic deodorizer system, reversible mountings for the swing-out door, and a reversible color front panel in wheat or almond colors.

Specifications: Height, 34½"; **Width,** 14⅞"; **Depth,** 18"; **Container,** round; **Loading,** swing-out bucket; **Warranty,** parts and labor, 1 year.

Approximate Retail Price   Approximate Low Price
Not Available $449.00

Sears Kenmore 65G41508N is tops among the budget-priced compactors. It can be built-in under a counter or used as a free-standing unit. Safety features are above average; the unit has a combination safety key-lock and start-stop system, as well as a misload warning light. Considered one of the easier units to clean, the almond-colored machine has a textured steel top, and a solid deodorizer compartment.

Specifications: Height, 34⅜″; **Width,** 15″; **Depth,** 24″; **Container,** rectangular; **Loading,** slide-out drawer; **Warranty,** parts and labor, 1 year.

Approximate Retail Price	Approximate Low Price
$290.00	Not Available

Whirlpool SHC-8004 is a built-in model that is convenient, safe, and practical. One of the unit's best features is its foot-touch-bar container-access system. The unit has a special bag caddy and efficient sound insulation. The slide-out drawer has a drop-down side to ease removal of a full bag of compacted trash. The unit also has a solid deodorizer compartment and comes with a six-color pack of reversible front panels. It is definitely the leader in moderately priced trash compactors.

Specifications: Height, 34½″; **Width,** 15″; **Depth,** 24³⁄₁₆″; **Container,** rectangular; **Loading,** toe-activated slide-out drawer; **Warranty,** parts and labor, 1 year.

Approximate Retail Price	Approximate Low Price
$353.00	$319.00

Also Recommended

KitchenAid KCS-100C is a top-of-the-line unit that can be built-in or left free-standing. It has two forms of access—a tilt-down door and a large-capacity slide-out drawer. The model has a fan-assisted air system that includes a charcoal filter. For safety, it has a key-lock and separate start and stop buttons. The front panels come in popular colors, and there's an optional trim kit. It's a very well-built unit, but too expensive to rank as a "Best Buy."

Specifications: Height, 35″; **Width,** 17¾″; **Depth,** 23¹¹⁄₁₆″; **Container,** rectangular; **Loading,** tilt-down door, slide-out drawer; **Warranty,** parts and labor, 1 year.

Approximate Retail Price	Approximate Low Price
$500.00	$479.00

Whirlpool SHC-4500 is a free-standing model—it cannot be built in later—in the middle price range. It comes with a pull-out drawer with a drop side for easy unloading, a solid deodorizer compartment, a four-color pack of reversible front panels, and a textured steel top. It's a basic, no-frills unit that's made to last.

Specifications: Height, 34⅜″; **Width,** 15″; **Depth,** 24³⁄₁₆″; **Container,** rectangular; **Loading,** pull-out drawer; **Warranty,** parts and labor, 1 year.

Approximate Retail Price	Approximate Low Price
$329.00	$299.00

Prices are accurate at time of printing; subject to manufacturer's change.

Clothes Washers

CHOOSING A WASHER is among the most basic home appliance decisions facing the modern consumer. Models come in all sizes and with capabilities to suit everyone, from the family with half a dozen kids to the jeans and T-shirt set. And compact machines that fit in small spaces keep more and more people out of the weekly social hour at the laundromat.

Don't Pick for Price Only

THE VARIETY OF products available can make it tricky to choose the washer that's right for your household. You're picking a machine that will be around for a while (the average life of a washer is about 10 years), so if you make a mistake you'll have to live with it for a long time. Remember, then, that price isn't the only consideration—design and construction are just as important.

With washing machines, the sturdier units are usually those in the middle or top price ranges; since mid-priced models tend to vary from the more expensive ones only because they have fewer features—especially automatic features—the best overall values tend to be found in the middle price bracket.

Suiting Style to Wash Day Needs

CLOTHES WASHERS COME in several types: full-size top-loading, full-size front-loading, compact, and portable models. Full-size top-loading machines, which are the most popular, can handle from 14 to 20 pounds of laundry (16 is about standard), fed into the unit through the lid on the top; an agitator forces water through the clothes. With a full-size front-loading (or tumble-type) machine, loads of 16 or 18 pounds are put in through a door in the front, and a tumbling action does the cleaning. Front-loaders are seen more in Europe than in the U.S.—here they are found mainly in commercial use. Currently, this type of washer is made only by White-Westinghouse.

Compact washers—smaller versions of the full-size machines—have become popular in recent years. Front- and top-loading compacts offer capacities of 8 to 12 pounds, and fit well in smaller homes, condominiums, and apartments—some even fit snugly under a counter.

Portable washers, with five- to eight-pound capacities, are the smallest laundry appliances, and many of them (especially the smaller ones) really aren't up to tough washing chores. Some compacts are called "portable," but a true portable connects to a faucet and usually requires moving the clothes from a wash chamber to a spin drum.

Look for Safety, Energy Clues

WHEN YOU'RE CHOOSING a washer, look for the Underwriters' Laboratories seal, which tells you that the unit meets current safety standards. Safety features are important, especially when you have young children around. Some washers have a lid switch that stops the agitator or spin action when the lid is opened. Other washers have automatic locks that prevent the lid being opened during the spin cycle.

Almost 90 percent of the energy used in washing clothes goes into heating the water. Rinsing a typical load with cold instead of warm water can reduce energy consumption by about 8 percent. In fact, most manufacturers are making cold-rinse cycles standard. Matching water level to load size is another important way to control energy consumption; on some models, a built-in scale helps you do this. Washers carry an energy label that shows approximate energy use with a gas or an electric home water heater, and this can help you judge the wisest buy. Laundry appliances that help you save energy are worth a little extra on the purchase price.

Washer Features to Watch For

HERE'S A RUNDOWN on features to consider when you're buying a washer:

Cycles. Cycles may be preset (semi-programmed) or fully programmed (automatic). Semi-programmed controls, where you have to set some of your options, give you a more flexible and less expensive unit than a fully programmed one with a button for all types of loads. Semi-programmed machines should still serve you well as fabrics change in the future.

Speeds. Units usually come with two speeds, but there are other combinations. Normal agitate and normal spin, and slow agitate and slow spin, are the combinations you'll probably use most. You can also get normal agitate and slow spin, or slow agitate and normal spin. Two speeds are a smart buy; one-speed machines don't usually provide enough options for the typical user.

Water Levels. Washers with fixed levels give you two, three, or four different level settings as well as "full." On a machine with variable water levels, you can set the level anywhere between low and full; we prefer this system.

Water Saver. In keeping with the times, what used to be called a "suds saver" is now called a "water saver." This feature stores wash water in a separate tub and returns all but the bottom inch or so (where dirt has settled) to the washer to be used again for the next load. Many consumers question using "dirty" water to wash a second or third load, and this feature isn't as popular as it used to be. However, it does save both water and energy.

Water Temperatures. Wash/rinse combinations available are cold/cold, warm/cold, hot/cold, warm/warm, and hot/warm. We recommend the first three, which use cold water for at least one cycle.

Load Balance Stabilizer. Washers use one of two systems to deal

1. Type of appliance and capacity.

2. National average cost for electricity upon which the estimated annual energy cost figure is based.

3. Estimated annual operating cost for the model in this size range that costs least to operate.

4. Scale showing lowest and highest estimated operating costs for models within this size range. These models represent different brands, not just those of the company listed in the upper right-hand corner.

5. Where the estimated annual cost of this particular model falls in comparison to all other models in this size.

6. Warning that it is unlawful to remove label.

7. A grid to help determine more closely the customer's operating cost based on local utility rates and use habits.

8. Suggests that the customer ask salesperson or utility for local utility rates.

9. Cautions that the customer's cost will not necessarily be the same as the cost figure given above.

10. Estimated annual operating cost for the model in this size range that costs most to operate.

11. All brands and models compared in the scale on this label fall within this capacity range.

12. All model numbers are listed if the label applies to more than one model.

13. Name of manufacturer and model number of the appliance on which the label appears.

14. Estimated annual operating cost for this model.

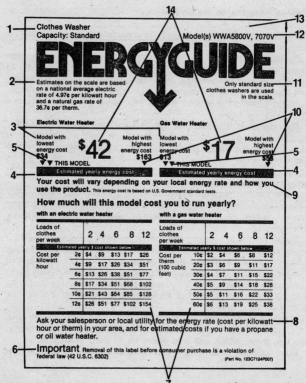

Clothes Washer
Capacity: Standard

Model(s) WWA5800V, 7070V

ENERGYGUIDE

Estimates on the scale are based on a national average electric rate of 4.97¢ per kilowatt hour and a natural gas rate of 36.7¢ per therm.

Only standard size clothes washers are used in the scale.

Electric Water Heater

Model with lowest energy cost
$34

$42

Model with highest energy cost
$163

▼▼ THIS MODEL

Gas Water Heater

Model with lowest energy cost
$13

$17

Model with highest energy cost
$53

▼▼ THIS MODEL

Estimated yearly energy cost

Estimated yearly energy cost

Your cost will vary depending on your local energy rate and how you use the product. This energy cost is based on U.S. Government standard tests.

How much will this model cost you to run yearly?

with an electric water heater

Loads of clothes per week		2	4	6	8	12
Estimated yearly $ cost shown below						
Cost per kilowatt hour	2¢	$4	$9	$13	$17	$26
	4¢	$9	$17	$26	$34	$51
	6¢	$13	$26	$38	$51	$77
	8¢	$17	$34	$51	$68	$102
	10¢	$21	$43	$64	$85	$128
	12¢	$26	$51	$77	$102	$154

with a gas water heater

Loads of clothes per week		2	4	6	8	12
Estimated yearly $ cost shown below						
Cost per therm (100 cubic feet)	10¢	$2	$4	$6	$8	$12
	20¢	$3	$6	$9	$11	$17
	30¢	$4	$7	$11	$15	$22
	40¢	$5	$9	$14	$18	$28
	50¢	$5	$11	$16	$22	$33
	60¢	$6	$13	$19	$25	$38

Ask your salesperson or local utility for the energy rate (cost per kilowatt hour or therm) in your area, and for estimated costs if you have a propane or oil water heater.

Important Removal of this label before consumer purchase is a violation of federal law (42 U.S.C. 6302)

(Part No. 123C7124P007)

with unbalanced loads. A shut-off system turns the unit off and sounds a buzzer. Compensating systems, which we prefer, don't shut off, but reduce spin speed if a load is badly unbalanced.

Safety Features. Safety features that are worth looking for are a lid switch to stop the agitator or spin action when the lid is opened, or a lid lock that prevents anyone from opening the lid during the spin cycle.

Lint Filters. A filter keeps lint from redepositing on clothes. Most models have a lint filter, and many of these are self-cleaning.

Dispensers. Bleach and fabric-softener dispensers are convenient because you don't have to wait around for the right moment to add these agents.

Tub Materials. Washers come with a coated steel, porcelain-on-steel, or stainless steel tub; the latter two are the most durable.

Other Features. Other helpful features include a hand-wash option —a small basket or hand-size agitator for delicate items—and a work surface or control panel light.

Best Buys '82

OUR "BEST BUY" and "Also Recommended" selections follow. The models are listed alphabetically within each category. These are the washers that best meet our criteria of convenience, value, and energy efficiency, and that we believe will give you good service for many years. It's important to remember that a "Best Buy" or "Also Recommended" label on a product refers only to that particular model, and doesn't imply that we endorse a whole line or that other models by the same manufacturer are equally good.

 Full-Size Washers

General Electric WWA8320B is a two-speed, large capacity model that has automatic cycles for regular and permanent press/knit loads. There is also a cycle for extra cleaning. There are four water levels and four wash/rinse temperature combinations—warm/cold, hot/cold, cold/cold, warm/warm. If the load gets off balance, the spin action slows down but the cycle continues until completed. The unit has bleach and fabric softener dispensers, and the basket and top are of porcelain enamel. **Specifications: Height,** 43½"; **Width,** 27"; **Depth,** 25"; **Capacity,** large; **Volts/Amps,** 115/8; **Speeds,** normal and gentle; **Warranty,** parts and labor, 1 year; transmission (parts only), 5 years.

Approximate Retail Price	Approximate Low Price
Not Available	$379.00

Hotpoint WLW1500A is a standard-capacity one-speed economy unit, with cycles for heavy, normal, and lightly soiled loads, and a special

Prices are accurate at time of printing; subject to manufacturer's change.

cycle for permanent press and knits/delicates. You'll find three water-level selections and three wash/rinse temperature combinations (hot/cold, warm/cold, cold/cold). Although this is a one-speed machine, it's a good economy buy.

Specifications: Height, 42½"; **Width,** 27"; **Depth,** 25"; **Capacity,** standard; **Volts/Amps,** 115/15; **Speeds,** normal; **Warranty,** parts and labor, 1 year; drive train (parts), 5 years.

Approximate Retail Price	Approximate Low Price
Not Available	$300.00

Maytag A610 is one of the best machines available. This large-capacity unit has pushbuttons for permanent press, regular, and delicate cycles, and "timed soak" or "soak only" on the dial. It allows four water-level selections and four wash/rinse temperature combinations (hot/warm, hot/cold, warm/cold, cold/cold). This quiet unit has an excellent reliability rating; it's easy to use and offers abundant features, including bleach and fabric softener dispensers.

Specifications: Height, 43⅝"; **Width,** 25½"; **Depth,** 27"; **Capacity,** large; **Volts/Amps,** 115/15; **Speeds,** normal and slow; **Warranty,** labor, 1 year; parts, 2 years; cabinet (against rust) and transmission, 5 years.

Approximate Retail Price	Approximate Low Price
Not Available	$435.00

Sears Kenmore 26G11751N is a standard-size two-speed washer with five cycles (normal, permanent press, knit, delicates, and pre-wash), three water-level selections, and three wash/rinse temperature choices (hot/cold, warm/cold, cold/cold). It has a self-cleaning lint filter, and porcelain enamel lid and basket. The off-balance switch and the safety lid switch are good safety features. A water-saver is an extra-cost option.

Specifications: Height, 43"; **Width,** 24"; **Depth,** 25½"; **Capacity,** standard; **Volts/Amps,** 120/10; **Speeds,** normal and slow; **Warranty,** parts and labor, 1 year; transmission (parts), 5 years; porcelain, 30 days.

Approximate Retail Prices	Approximate Low Prices
$350.00 (white)	Not Available
$360.00 (other colors)	Not Available

Sears Kenmore 26G21711N is a large-capacity two-speed machine with four water-level choices and three wash/rinse temperature combinations—hot/cold, warm/cold, cold/cold. Preset cycles will handle normal, permanent press, knit, delicates, and pre-wash. All cycles use an energy-saving cold rinse. The porcelain enamel wash drum and lid are good features, and there's a fabric softener dispenser. A water saver is optional.

Specifications: Height, 43"; **Width,** 29"; **Depth,** 25½"; **Capacity,** large; **Volts/Amps,** 120/10; **Speeds,** normal and slow; **Warranty,** parts and labor, 1 year; transmission (parts), 5 years; porcelain, 30 days.

Approximate Retail Prices	Approximate Low Prices
$390.00 (white)	Not Available
$400.00 (other colors)	Not Available

Prices are accurate at time of printing; subject to manufacturer's change.

Whirlpool LA7800XK is a large-capacity machine with four water-level selections and six cycles—permanent press, knits, pre-wash, soak, regular, and super wash. You get four wash/rinse temperature options (hot/warm, hot/cold, warm/cold, cold/cold), and bleach and fabric softener dispensers. A water-saver is optional. This model has a porcelain top and lid.
Specifications: Height, 43³⁄₁₆″; **Width,** 29″; **Depth,** 25½″; **Capacity,** large; **Volts/Amps,** 120/15; **Speeds,** normal and slow; **Warranty,** parts and labor, 1 year; motor housing (parts only), 5 years.

Approximate Retail Price   **Approximate Low Price**
$461.00.. $400.00

Also Recommended

General Electric WWA7070B is a standard capacity washer with automatic cycles for regular loads and permanent press and knits. The unit has three wash/rinse temperature combinations—cold/cold, warm/cold, and hot/cold—and four water levels. If the load is unbalanced the cycle slows but does not stop. This three-speed model has a mini-basket for delicate items, fabric softener and bleach dispensers, and porcelain enamel lid and tub. It's a good machine, but we feel that better values are available.
Specifications: Height, 42½″; **Width,** 27″; **Depth,** 25″; **Capacity,** standard; **Volts/Amps,** 115/8; **Speeds,** normal, normal/gentle, gentle.
Warranty, parts and labor, 1 year; transmission, (parts only), 5 years.

Approximate Retail Price   **Approximate Low Price**
Not Available $369.00

Maytag A210 is a standard-size machine with many good features (some found on "Best Buy" Maytag Model A610). It has a soak-only cycle and a timed-soak cycle, and three water-level selections instead of the Model A610's four. The four wash/rinse combinations are hot/warm, hot/cold, warm/cold, cold/cold. This machine is reliable to use and is our second choice in its higher price-range.
Specifications: Height, 43⅝″; **Width,** 25½″; **Depth,** 27″; **Volts/Amps,** 115/15; **Speeds,** normal and slow; **Warranty,** parts and labor, 1 year; parts only, 2 years; cabinet (against rust) and transmission, 5 years.

Approximate Retail Price   **Approximate Low Price**
Not Available $409.00

Speed Queen HA6001 is a large-capacity machine with a lifetime warranty on its stainless steel tub. It has three agitator/spin combinations (normal/fast, normal/slow, and gentle/slow), and preset cycles for regular loads, permanent press, knits, delicates, and pre-wash soak. This model has four water-temperature combinations (hot/cold, hot/warm, warm/cold, cold/cold) and four water levels. The unit has a porcelain cabinet and top, and a bleach dispenser. This quality machine with a good warranty is our alternative choice in the higher price bracket.
Specifications: Height, 42½″; **Width,** 25⅝″; **Depth,** 28″; **Capacity,** large; **Volts/Amps,** 120/15; **Speeds,** fast, normal, and slow; **Warranty,** parts and labor, 1 year; transmission parts, 10 years; stainless steel tub

Prices are accurate at time of printing; subject to manufacturer's change.

(parts), guaranteed for as long as original buyer owns the machine.

Approximate Retail Price **Approximate Low Price**
Not Available $409.00

White-Westinghouse LT570A is a front-loading, middle-of-the-line tumbler washer with standard capacity and cycles for normal, permanent press, knits, and pre-wash soak. It has a porcelain enamel tub and a safety feature that locks the door once the spin cycle has started. The unit has five water-level choices and five wash/rinse temperature combinations—hot/warm, warm/warm, hot/cold, warm/cold, cold/cold. A scale built into the door helps you match load and water level precisely. This is the only full-size domestic front-loader available.

Specifications: Height, 44¾"; **Width,** 27"; **Depth** 25"; **Capacity,** standard; **Volts/Amps,** 120/15; **Speeds,** normal; **Warranty,** parts and labor, 1 year; drive parts, 5 years.

Approximate Retail Price **Approximate Low Price**
$630.00 .... $435.00

 Compact Washers

General Electric WWP1170B offers regular, delicate, and permanent press time cycles. Even though it's a compact—five-pound capacity—it has variable water-level selection. You adjust the water temperature at the faucet and a bypass lever lets you draw water while the washer is in use. This unit is mounted on casters, and can be either rolled out on wash day or permanently installed with an optional kit. Accessories are available for stacking or wall-mounting the companion dryer.

Specifications: Height, 34"; **Width,** 23½"; **Depth,** 24¾"; **Capacity,** compact; **Volts/Amps,** 120/15; **Speeds,** one; **Warranty,** parts and labor, 1 year; transmission (parts only), 5 years.

Approximate Retail Price **Approximate Low Price**
Not Available $375.00

Whirlpool LC4900XK is a small machine but one that's loaded with features. It provides two-speed operation, five cycles, and four water-level selections. The four wash/rinse combinations are hot/warm, hot/cold, warm/cold, and cold/cold. This top-loader can be either permanently installed or rolled out when needed. The porcelain top and lid are quality features.

Specifications: Height, 32½"; **Width,** 23⅞"; **Depth,** 23⅝"; **Capacity,** compact; **Volts/Amps,** 120/15; **Speeds,** normal and slow; **Warranty,** parts and labor, 1 year; motor housing (parts only), 5 years.

Approximate Retail Price **Approximate Low Price**
$419.00 .... $385.00

Prices are accurate at time of printing; subject to manufacturer's change.

Clothes Dryers

WASHDAY USED TO MEAN the pleasing sight of sheets billowing in the wind and the fresh scent of clothes dried on an outdoor clothesline. It's a nostalgic sight—and a splendid way of conserving energy—but an automatic clothes dryer takes up a lot less space than a clothesline, and can be used even when it's raining. And when it comes to conserving another kind of energy (your own), the dryer wins every time.

Laundry Pairs—They're Made for Each Other

LIKE ITS PARTNER, the washer, your dryer is a long-term investment (it should last you 13 years or so), so keep this in mind when you go to buy one. Don't let price be your only guide—construction, design, and adaptability to your present and future needs are just as important. As with washers, the sturdier units are usually found in the medium to high price brackets. A high price may indicate only that a machine has more features—especially automatic ones—than its medium-priced counter-part, so you may well find the best value in this middle price range.

If you're buying a washer and dryer together, it makes sense to buy a pair designed by the manufacturer to be used together—with paired machines, the dryer is usually available in both gas and electric models. We've kept this in mind when making our "Best Buy" recommendations and indicated the washer model each of our selected dryers can be paired with.

Design Changes Cut Dryers' Energy Use

IN RECENT YEARS, dryers have become much more energy-efficient. Electric ignition systems have replaced standing pilot lights on gas dryers. More machines now have an automatic shutoff control to help prevent over-drying—laundry's worst waster of energy. The shutoff systems monitor moisture content in the clothes or in exhaust air, and signal the machine to turn off when drying is completed. Other energy-efficient design changes include improved air flow, better door seals, and increased insulation.

Gas vs. Electric: Cost and Style Difference

GENERALLY, GAS DRYERS cost a little more to buy than electric dryers, but are considerably less expensive to operate. Both gas and electric dryers come in full-size and compact models, and you can also get small-capacity portable electric units. You can't get a portable gas dryer: a burner (with electric ignition) provides the heat; the unit is attached to a gas line and, for safety reasons, vented to the outside. So the installation is permanent.

The full range of electric dryers, including portables, use an electric element as the heat source. Both full-size and compact models require a 220-240-volt grounded electrical circuit; a small-capacity portable can operate on ordinary 110-120-volt household current and can be moved around with relative ease.

Look for the Underwriters Laboratories' seal on electric dryers, and for the blue-flame seal of the American Gas Association on gas dryers. Both seals assure you that a unit meets current safety standards. Especially if you have young children, choose a dryer that has a switch to stop the drum when the door is opened—most do.

We've already said that gas dryers are a lot more energy-efficient than electric dryers. Neither type, however, carries an energy label because, within its category and size range, one model costs pretty much the same to operate as other models. In other words, most gas dryers of a similar size will be similar in energy use, and the same goes for electric models.

Dryer Details Aid Efficiency

ENERGY EFFICIENCY is an important consideration when you're choosing a dryer—but it's not the only one. Here are features to look at when making your decision:

Drying Controls. Dryers usually give you a choice of timed or automatic drying. Timed drying (generally 60 to 90 minutes) is indicated in minutes on the dial; you select the time you think the load will take to dry. Automatic settings are preset to suit certain types of load—for example, regular, permanent press, or delicate. A permanent press cycle has a cool-down period during which the drum continues to turn although the heat is off; this prevents wrinkling. A delicate cycle runs on low heat. We prefer a machine with some preset, or automatic, options because the automatic mode ensures that the dryer runs only as long as necessary.

Dryness Sensor. On some dryers there is also an automatic shutoff device called a dryness sensor, which detects the moisture content of the clothes or of the exhaust air and shuts off the machine when the clothes are dried. This is an excellent safeguard against over-drying, which wastes a lot of energy.

Temperature Selection. This is a feature that allows you to match drying temperature to the kinds of fabric in the load. You may have just two choices—high and low—or a few more in between. It's a good feature, especially when you're drying by time. On some machines, temperature controls and drying controls are linked. On others, they operate separately.

Wrinkle Prevention. This is a system that continues to tumble the load, without heat, intermittently after the end of a cycle. A buzzer also sounds at intervals during this period. Both the tumbling action and the buzzer stop when you open the dryer door. This feature prevents dry clothes from wrinkling if you don't take them out immediately.

Air-fluff Setting. On this setting the machine tumbles the load without heat. It's good for drying (or freshening) items like pillows, comforters, or down jackets. But remember that full drying takes a long time when no heat is used.

Drying Racks. These are small devices (racks or shelves) that fit inside the dryer to hold items like gym shoes, which would otherwise rattle around. If you've got a lot of little boys, you may find this handy.

Lint Filters. An effective lint filter is important to the performance of a dryer. It should be accessible, and easy to remove for cleaning.

Venting. With a gas dryer, venting possible harmful exhaust fumes outside the house is an important safety factor. With an electric dryer it's not so important, but it does prevent hot air and humidity building up inside the house in hot weather. Standard venting is suitable for almost every home. If you are installing your dryer in an extremely tight corner with no clearance behind it or at the sides, ask about venting.

Drum Materials. The drum is the container that holds the laundry. On better machines the drum is made of porcelain enamel on steel, or stainless steel.

Other Features. Other useful features are a drum light that goes on when the door is opened (desirable if the dryer is being installed in a dark area); a panel or worktop light; a switch that stops tumbling action when the door is opened (this is a good safety feature); and a buzzer to signal the end of a cycle.

Best Buys '82

OUR "BEST BUY" and "Also Recommended" dryers follow; they are listed alphabetically within each category. We've selected those that, paired with their companion washers, will give you years of convenient, energy-efficient, and trouble-free laundry service. Remember that a "Best Buy" designation only applies to the model listed; it doesn't necessarily apply to other models made by the same manufacturer, or to an entire product line.

 Full-Size Gas Dryers

Hotpoint DLL1550A is a standard-size gas dryer companion to Hotpoint "Best Buy" Model WLW1500, an economy machine. It has timed drying only, up to 90 minutes, with special settings for permanent press and delicate loads. Temperature selections include normal, low (for knits and delicates), and air-fluff (no heat). There is no automatic operation. This is a well-built no-frills unit that has a porcelain enamel drum. An electric unit with the same features is Model DLB1550A. **Specifications: Height,** 42½″; **Width,** 27″; **Depth,** 25″; **Volts/Amps,**

110-120/6; **Venting,** standard; **Lint Trap Location,** inside door; **Warranty,** parts and labor, 1 year.

Approximate Retail Price   **Approximate Low Price**

Not Available $299.00

Maytag D610, one of the best gas dryers in the higher price range, is a high-quality companion for the Maytag Model A610 washer. It has timed drying for up to 60 minutes, and automatic settings for permanent press and regular loads. You get three temperature choices—regular, delicate, and air-fluff. The end-of-cycle signal can be adjusted in volume, and there's a drum light. This well-built machine is also available in an electric version—the model number is the same.

Specifications: Height, 43"; **Width,** 28½"; **Depth,** 27"; **Volts/Amps,** 110-120/15; **Venting,** standard; **Lint Trap Location,** inside door; **Warranty,** parts and labor, 1 year; parts, 2 years; cabinet (against rust) and tumbler, 5 years.

Approximate Retail Price   **Approximate Low Price**

Not Available $389.00

Sears Kenmore 26G71711N is a good companion to Kenmore's "Best Buy" Model 26G21711N washer. This gas model has automatic settings for permanent press and delicate loads, timed drying up to 60 minutes, and an electronic sensor that shuts off the machine when the load is dry. Other features include two drying temperatures (low for delicates and high for other loads), an end-of-cycle signal, and a wrinkle prevention system that tumbles the clothes at intervals until the door is opened. Model 26G61711N is an electric dryer with the same features.

Specifications: Height, 43"; **Width,** 29"; **Depth,** 27½"; **Volts/Amps,** 220-240/25; **Venting,** standard; **Lint Trap Location,** top; **Warranty,** parts and labor, 1 year.

Approximate Retail Price   **Approximate Low Price**

$290.00 (white) .... Not Available
$300.00 (other colors) .... Not Available

Sears Kenmore 26G71851N is an electric dryer companion to Sears Model 26G11751N washer (a similar electric unit is Model 26G61851N). This model has both timed drying, and automatic drying for permanent press and delicate loads. An automatic sensor shuts off the machine when clothes are dried as selected. There are three temperature selections: high, low, and air-fluff. It also has an end-of-cycle signal.

Specifications: Height, 43"; **Width,** 29"; **Depth,** 25½"; **Volts/Amps,** 220-240/25; **Venting,** standard; **Lint Trap Location,** top; **Warranty,** parts and labor, 1 year.

Approximate Retail Price   **Approximate Low Price**

$280.00 (white) .... Not Available
$290.00 (other colors) .... Not Available

Whirlpool LG7801XK is the companion gas dryer to the Whirlpool Model LG7800XK washer. This unit has timed drying, and automatic settings for permanent press and regular loads. Five temperature levels are selected independently of the timed and automatic operations. An

Prices are accurate at time of printing; subject to manufacturer's change.

automatic sensor shuts off the machine when the load is dry. The unit also has an end-of-cycle signal, a porcelain enamel drum, and a drying rack to keep items like gym shoes from bouncing around inside the machine. The equivalent electric unit is Model LE7800XK.

Specifications: Height, 43³/₁₆"; **Width,** 29"; **Depth,** 27¹³/₁₆"; **Volts/Amps,** 120-240/30; **Venting,** standard; **Lint Trap Location,** top; **Warranty,** parts and labor, 1 year.

Approximate Retail Price	Approximate Low Price
$378.00	$339.00

Also Recommended

Maytag D410, a good match for the Maytag Model A210 washer, is an economical gas dryer with many good features. An automatic control shuts off the unit when clothes are dry, and a buzzer signals at the end of the cycle. This model has timed drying up to 60 minutes at regular or low temperature, and automatic settings for regular, permanent press, and air-fluff loads. This is a good second choice in the lower price range. The dryer is also available in an electric version; the model number is the same.

Specifications: Height, 43"; **Width,** 28½"; **Depth,** 27"; **Volts/Amps,** 110-120/15; **Venting,** standard; **Lint Trap Location,** inside door; **Warranty,** parts and labor, 1 year; parts, 2 years; cabinet (against rust) and tumbler, 5 years.

Approximate Retail Price	Approximate Low Price
Not Available	$359.00

Speed Queen HG6009, the companion for the Speed Queen Model HA6001 washer, is a gas dryer with timed drying, or automatic settings for normal and delicate loads. There are three temperature selections, high, medium, and low, and a no-heat air-fluff setting. Temperature selection is independent of drying action. The end-of-cycle signal has a volume control. This is a heavy-duty unit with one of the better lint filters, and it is our second choice at the higher end of the price range. An electric unit with similar features is Model HE6003.

Specifications: Height, 42½"; **Width,** 26⅞"; **Depth,** 28"; **Volts/Amps,** 110-120/15; **Venting,** standard; **Lint Trap Location,** inside door; **Warranty,** parts and labor, 1 year.

Approximate Retail Price	Approximate Low Price
Not Available	$349.00

White-Westinghouse DG500A is a good companion to the company's Model LT570A washer. This heavy-duty gas model has a porcelain enamel drum, settings for automatic or timed drying; and regular, medium, and low temperature settings. There's also a no-heat, air-fluff setting. Model DE500A is the electric version.

Specifications: Height, 44¾"; **Width,** 27"; **Depth,** 25½"; **Volts/Amps,** 110-120/15 (gas); **Venting,** standard; **Lint Trap Location,** inside door; **Warranty,** parts and labor, 1 year.

Approximate Retail Price	Approximate Low Price
$390.00	$360.00

Prices are accurate at time of printing; subject to manufacturer's change.

Compact Gas Dryers

White-Westinghouse DG170A is the companion gas dryer to the company's Model LT170A washer. It has a high heat setting (which the manufacturer calls "automatic"), a medium heat setting for permanent press loads, or timed drying. In the timed drying mode you have three temperature selections (regular, medium, and low) or air only. This machine has an end-of-cycle signal, and the porcelain basket and interior light are good features on a compact dryer. An optional drying shelf is available. The same features in an electric unit may be found in Model DE170A.

Specifications: Height, 34⅝"; **Width,** 27"; **Depth,** 26¹¹⁄₁₆"; **Volts/Amps,** 110-120/15 (gas); **Venting,** standard; **Lint Trap Location,** inside door; **Warranty,** parts and labor, 1 year.

Approximate Retail Price   Approximate Low Price
$430.00 .... $400.00

 Full-Size Electric Dryers

General Electric DDE7900B is a large capacity electric dryer mate to washer 8320B. It offers four drying selections—high, medium, low, and air-fluff (no heat). A similar model in gas is DDG7980B. The unit has automatic settings for regular or permanent press loads, and an automatic sensor that shuts off the dryer when selected dryness is reached, and a drum light. You can also dry by time. The drum is porcelain enamel.

Specifications: Height, 43½"; **Width,** 27"; **Depth,** 25"; **Volts/Amps,** 115-240/30; **Venting,** standard; **Lint Trap Location,** inside front door; **Warranty,** parts and labor, 1 year.

Approximate Retail Price   Approximate Low Price
Not Available $320.00

Hotpoint DLB1550A is a standard-size electric dryer companion to Hotpoint "Best Buy" Model WLW1500, an economy machine. It has timed drying only, up to 90 minutes, with special settings for permanent press and delicate loads. Temperature selections include normal, low (for knits and delicates), and air-fluff (no heat). There is no automatic operation. This is a well-built no-frills unit that has a porcelain enamel drum. A gas unit with the same features is Model DLL1550A.

Prices are accurate at time of printing; subject to manufacturer's change.

Specifications: Height, 42½″; **Width,** 27″; **Depth,** 25″; **Volts/Amps,** 120-240/24 (electric), 120/6 (gas); **Venting,** standard; **Lint Trap Location,** inside door; **Warranty,** parts and labor, 1 year.

Approximate Retail Price   **Approximate Low Price**
Not Available $269.00

Maytag D610, one of the best dryers in the higher price range, is a good electric companion for the Maytag Model A610 washer. It has timed drying for up to 60 minutes, and automatic settings for permanent press and regular loads. You get three temperature choices—regular, delicate, and air-fluff. The end-of-cycle signal can be adjusted in volume, and there's a drum light. This well-built machine is also available in a gas version—it has the same model number.

Specifications: Height, 43″; **Width,** 28½″; **Depth,** 27″; **Volts/Amps,** 120-240/30 (electric); **Venting,** standard; **Lint Trap Location,** inside door; **Warranty,** parts and labor, 1 year; parts, 2 years; cabinet (against rust) and tumbler, 5 years.

Approximate Retail Price   **Approximate Low Price**
Not Available $359.00

Sears Kenmore 26G61711N is a good companion to Kenmore's "Best Buy" Model 26G21711N washer. This electric model has automatic settings for permanent press and delicate loads, timed drying up to 60 minutes, and an electronic sensor that shuts off the machine when the load is dry. Other features include two drying temperatures (low for delicates and high for other loads), an end-of-cycle signal, and a wrinkle prevention system that tumbles the clothes at intervals until the door is opened. Model 26G71711N is a gas dryer with the same features.

Specifications: Height, 43″; **Width,** 29″; **Depth,** 27½″; **Volts/Amps,** 240/25; **Venting,** standard; **Lint Trap Location,** top; **Warranty,** parts and labor, 1 year.

Approximate Retail Price   **Approximate Low Price**
$290.00 (white) .... Not Available
$300.00 (other colors) .... Not Available

Sears Kenmore 26G61851N is an electric dryer companion to Sears Model 26G11751N washer (a similar gas unit is Model 26G71851N). This model has both timed drying and automatic drying for permanent press and delicate loads. An automatic sensor shuts off the machine when clothes are dried as selected. There are two temperature selections—high and low—and air only (no heat). The unit also has an end-of-cycle signal and a wrinkle prevention system that sounds a buzzer and tumbles the clothes at intervals until the door is opened.

Specifications: Height, 43″; **Width,** 29″; **Depth,** 25½″; **Volts/Amps,** 240/25; **Venting,** standard; **Lint Trap Location,** top; **Warranty,** parts and labor, 1 year.

Approximate Retail Price   **Approximate Low Price**
$280.00 (white) .... Not Available
$290.00 (other colors) .... Not Available

Prices are accurate at time of printing; subject to manufacturer's change.

Whirlpool LE7800XK is the companion electric dryer to the Whirlpool Model LA7800XK washer. This unit has timed drying, and automatic settings for permanent press and regular loads. Five temperature levels are selected independently of the timed and automatic operations. An automatic sensor shuts off the machine when the load is dry. The unit also has an end-of-cycle signal, a porcelain enamel drum, and a drying rack to keep items like gym shoes from bouncing around inside the machine. The equivalent gas unit is Model LG7801XK.

Specifications: Height, 43³⁄₁₆″; **Width,** 29″; **Depth,** 27¹³⁄₁₆″; **Volts/Amps,** 120-240/30; **Venting,** standard; **Lint Trap Location,** top; **Warranty,** parts and labor, 1 year.

Approximate Retail Price

Approximate Low Price

$340.00 .... $309.00

Also Recommended

General Electric DDE6350B is a companion electric dryer to our recommended GE washer 7070B. It has a dryness control on the automatic regular and permanent press cycles; you can also dry by time for up to 60 minutes. The four temperature selections are normal, permanent press, knits and delicates, and air fluff (no heat). The drum is porcelain enamel. This is a good unit, but we prefer our "Best Buy" model for overall value. If you'd prefer a gas dryer, you'll find the same features on GE's DDG6380B.

Specifications: Height, 42½″; **Width,** 27″; **Depth,** 25″; **Volts/Amps,** 115-240/30 (electric), 115/6 (gas); **Venting,** standard; **Lint Trap Location,** inside front door; **Warranty,** parts and labor, 1 year.

Approximate Retail Price

Approximate Low Price

Not Available $285.00

Maytag D410, a good match for the Maytag Model A210 washer, is an economical electric dryer with many good features. An automatic control shuts off the unit when clothes are dry, and a buzzer signals at the end of the cycle. This model has timed drying up to 60 minutes, and automatic settings for regular, permanent press, and air-fluff loads. You can select a regular or low temperature. This is a good second choice in the lower price range. The dryer is also available in a gas version.

Specifications: Height, 43″; **Width,** 28½″; **Depth,** 27″; **Volts/Amps,** 240/30; **Venting,** standard; **Lint Trap Location,** inside door; **Warranty,** parts and labor, 1 year; parts 2 years, cabinet (rust) and tumbler, 5 years.

Approximate Retail Price

Approximate Low Price

Not Available $319.00

Speed Queen HE6003, the companion for the Speed Queen Model HA6001 washer, is an electric dryer with timed drying, or automatic settings for normal and delicate loads. There are three temperature selections, high, medium, and low, and a no-heat air-fluff setting. Temperature selection is independent of drying action. The end-of-cycle signal has a volume control. This is a heavy-duty unit with one of the better lint filters, and it is our second choice at the higher end of the price range. A gas unit with similar features is Model HG6009.

Prices are accurate at time of printing; subject to manufacturer's change.

Specifications: Height, 42½″; **Width,** 26⅞″; **Depth,** 28″; **Volts/Amps,** 120-240/30; **Venting,** standard; **Lint Trap Location,** inside door; **Warranty,** parts and labor, 1 year.

Approximate Retail Price
Not Available .... **Approximate Low Price** $309.00

White-Westinghouse DE500A is a good companion to the company's Model LT570A washer. This heavy-duty electric model has a porcelain enamel tub, options for automatic or timed drying; and regular, medium, and low temperature settings. There's also a no-heat, air-fluff setting. As this is the only front-loading washer on the market, people who choose it will probably also choose this companion dryer. Model DG500A is the gas version.

Specifications: Height, 44¾″; **Width,** 27″; **Depth,** 25½″; **Volts/Amps,** 120-240 or 120-208/30; **Venting,** standard; **Lint Trap Location,** inside door; **Warranty,** parts and labor, 1 year.

Approximate Retail Price
$350.00 .... **Approximate Low Price** $320.00

 Compact Electric Dryers

General Electric DDP1270B is the electric dryer companion to "Best Buy" compact washer WWP1170B. This five-pound capacity model can be set for timed drying up to 120 minutes. It also has an air-fluff setting without heat, and an end-of-cycle signal. Perhaps best of all is the ease with which the DDP1270B can be installed. It will operate off a standard 120-volt household circuit (be sure, however, to put it on a 15 or 20 amp individual circuit), and it does not require venting. An optional rack or wall-mounting kit is available.

Specifications: Height, 34″; **Width,** 23½″; **Depth,** 24¾″; **Volts/Amps,** 120/15 or 20; **Venting,** none required; **Lint Trap Location,** front; **Warranty,** parts and labor, 1 year.

Approximate Retail Price
Not Available .... **Approximate Low Price** $280.00

Whirlpool LE4930XK is the compact electric dryer companion to the "Best Buy" Whirlpool Model LC4900XK compact washer. The unit has automatic settings for regular, permanent press and delicate loads, high and low temperature settings, and a no-heat air-fluff feature. It has an end-of-cycle signal, and automatic door shut-off. It's a simple, easy-to-use unit, and can be stacked or mounted on the wall.

Specifications: Height, 32½″; **Width,** 23⅞″; **Depth,** 21¹⁵⁄₁₆″; **Volts/Amps,** 120-240 or 120-208; **Venting,** 2-way; **Lint Trap Location,** inside, at the back of the drum; **Warranty,** parts and labor, 1 year.

Approximate Retail Price
$282.00 .... **Approximate Low Price** $259.00

Prices are accurate at time of printing; subject to manufacturer's change.

Room Air Conditioners

FROM ONE POINT OF VIEW, buying a room air conditioner is a fairly straightforward matter. You have only one major question to answer: How well does it work? But air conditioners gulp electricity at an alarming rate, so if you're going to pay a high price for the luxury of having one, you might as well buy the model that gives you the most for your money.

Room air conditioners have a basic advantage over central air conditioning in that they cool only a specific area—you aren't paying to cool empty rooms. A lot of people who did go to the expense of installing central air conditioning are now finding that, as energy costs rocket, they can't afford to operate it. So room air conditioners are probably going to become a lot more popular than a central system as an answer to a long, hot summer.

Label Answers Your Energy Questions

ALTHOUGH IT'S STILL up to you to figure how much power you need to cool down your living spaces, the government has done you a favor by mandating that every room air conditioner manufactured after May 1980 must carry an energy label providing the consumer with cost-of-operation information. This label includes a very useful quick-check rating called an Energy Efficiency Ratio (EER)—the higher the EER, the more efficient the machine. Although a unit with a high EER may also carry a high price tag, it will pay you back for your higher initial outlay in lower electricity bills over a period of time. A sample of the energy label, along with an explanation, accompanies this report.

For some time, manufacturers have been expecting the government to set minimum EER levels for room air conditioners. These levels may not now be imposed, but manufacturers have already made energy-efficient improvements in many models. They are using more efficient compressors and fan motors, enlarging the cooled coil surface—the heat transfer area—by using larger coils, and incorporating larger condenser fans to move air across this surface. Many units also now have an energy-saver setting or switch that shuts off the fan motor when the compressor isn't operating; this can reduce energy use by as much as 10 percent.

The Right Size and Style

ALTHOUGH MOST room air conditioners are designed for installation in standard double-hung windows, other units will fit sliding windows, or can be mounted through a wall. Smaller room units draw 7.5 amps and

1. Type of appliance and capacity.

2. Energy Efficiency Ratio (EER) for this model; the higher the EER the more efficient the unit and the lower the cost of operation.

3. Estimated annual operating cost for the model in this size range that costs least to operate.

4. Scale showing lowest and highest estimated operating costs for models within this size range. These models represent different brands, not just those of the company listed in the upper right-hand corner.

5. Where the estimated annual cost of this particular model falls in comparison to all other models in this size.

6. Warning that it is unlawful to remove label.

7. A grid to help determine more closely the customer's operating cost based on local utility rates and use habits.

8. Suggests that the customer ask salesperson or utility for local utility rates.

9. Cautions that the customer's cost will not necessarily be the same as the cost figure given above.

10. All brands and models compared in the scale on this label fall within this capacity range.

11. All model numbers are listed if the label applies to more than one model.

12. Name of manufacturer and model number of the appliance on which the label appears.

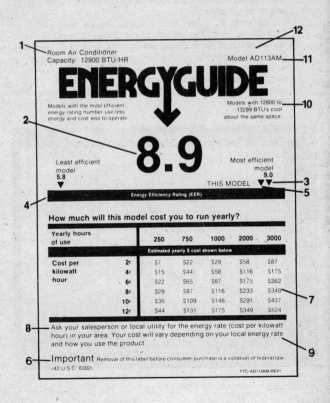

Room Air Conditioner
Capacity: 12900 BTU/HR

Model AD113AM

ENERGYGUIDE

Models with the most efficient energy rating number use less energy and cost less to operate.

Models with 12800 to 13299 BTU's cool about the same space

8.9

Least efficient model
5.8 ▼

Most efficient model
9.0

THIS MODEL ▼▼

Energy Efficiency Rating (EER)

How much will this model cost you to run yearly?

Yearly hours of use		250	750	1000	2000	3000
		Estimated yearly $ cost shown below				
Cost per kilowatt hour	2¢	$7	$22	$29	$58	$87
	4¢	$15	$44	$58	$116	$175
	6¢	$22	$65	$87	$175	$262
	8¢	$29	$87	$116	$233	$349
	10¢	$36	$109	$146	$291	$437
	12¢	$44	$131	$175	$349	$524

Ask your salesperson or local utility for the energy rate (cost per kilowatt hour) in your area. Your cost will vary depending on your local energy rate and how you use the product.

Important Removal of this label before consumer purchase is a violation of federal law
(42 U.S.C. 6302)

FTC-AD113AM-REV1

can operate on a 115-volt line. These can be plugged into a regular household outlet along with other electrical devices (but be careful not to overload the circuit). Large units draw 12 amps and should have a separate regular household line. The largest models require special circuits of 230 or 208 volts. It's important to buy a room unit that's the right size. If the unit is too small, it won't cool the room enough; if it's too big, it won't dehumidify properly, and the room will be uncomfortable and clammy.

With this report we've included a Room Air Conditioner Worksheet to help you determine the proper capacity unit for your living space. Work through the sheet before shopping; you'll have a better idea of your needs. If you have questions, check with your dealer.

Room Air Conditioner Worksheet

I. Estimated Cooling Capacity
1. Find the floor area of the room to be cooled by multiplying its length by its width:
   ___feet long × ___feet wide = _____square feet
2. Find this figure on the left side of the Cooling Load Chart. Now decide which of the following descriptions, A, B, or C, describes the space *above* the room where you plan to put the room air conditioner.
   Band A—Occupied room above room to be cooled.
   Band B—Insulated ceiling and unoccupied attic above room to be cooled.

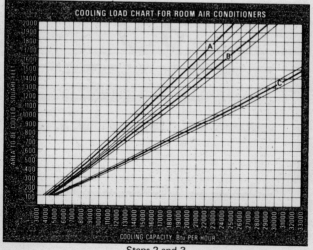

Steps 2 and 3

CONSUMER GUIDE®

Band C—Uninsulated ceiling and unoccupied attic above room to be cooled.

Now, from your square foot figure on the left of the diagram, move horizontally to the right until you intersect the center of Band A, B, or C, depending on what kind of space is above the room.

3. Within the band (that area formed by the two lighter lines on either side of the bold diagonal line), move to the left for a shady exposure, or to the right for a sunny exposure.

4. From this point, move straight down to the bottom of the chart to determine the unadjusted cooling capacity in Btu per hour:
Unadjusted cooling capacity from chart:_____Btuh

5. Find your geographical area on the map that shows the climate factor for your area. Multiply the answer from step 4 (your Btuh figure) by the climate factor:
_____Btuh (from step 4) × ___(climate factor) = _____Btuh

6. If the room is to be cooled primarily at night, and daytime cooling is not important, multiply the answer to step 5 by 0.7. If daytime cooling is important, skip this point.
_____Btuh (from step 5) × 0.7 = _____Btuh

7. The proximity of the room to be cooled to other cooled rooms is important. Measure along the length of wall separating the room to be cooled from other cooled rooms. Multiply this number of linear feet by 30 Btuh; subtract the result from the answer to step 5 or 6. If other rooms are not cooled, skip this point.
a. ___feet × 30 Btuh = _____Btuh
b. ___Btuh (from step 5 or 6) -___Btuh (from a) = _____Btuh

8. If only one person will occupy the cooled room, subtract 600 Btuh from the answer to step 7, 6, or 5. If three or more people will occupy the room, add 600 Btuh for each person over two:
a. One person:___Btuh (from step 7, 6, or 5) −600 Btuh = _____Btuh

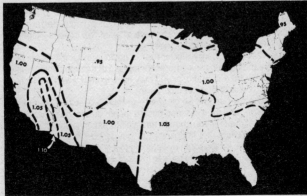

Step 5

b. Two people:____Btuh (from step 7, 6, or 5)

c. Three or more people:____Btuh (from step 7, 6, or 5)
+ ____Btuh (600 for each person over two) = _____Btuh

9. If the area to be cooled includes a kitchen, add 4000 Btuh to the answer from step 8. If it does not, step 8 is your final answer:
____Btuh (from step 8) + 4000 Btuh (if area includes a kitchen) = _____Btuh

The answer to point 8 or point 9 is the approximate cooling capacity you will need. Enter that figure below:
_____Btuh = Estimated Cooling Capacity.

II. Type of installation (check appropriate one):
_____Double-hung window
_____Casement window
_____Sliding window
_____Through-the-wall space

III. Dimensions of window or space:
_____inches high by _____inches wide

IV. Type of circuit available (check appropriate one):
_____115-volt, 15-amp branch circuit (might have other electrical product on this circuit).
_____115-volt, 15-amp isolated circuit (nothing else on circuit).
_____Other. Fill in:_____volt, _____amp.

Performance Features to Look for

WHEN YOU'RE BUYING a room air conditioner, efficiency in both performance and energy use is your most important concern. But there are other factors to consider—like convenience, quiet operation, and good design. Here's a rundown on features to look for:

Air Movement. Look for fully adjustable louvers and vents that will let you adjust air movement in different directions. Avoid units with motor-driven louvers—they're not energy-efficient.

Fan Speeds. Room air conditioners vary from one-speed units to deluxe models with a control that lets you dial a complete range of speeds. The better models usually have at least two speeds—high for fast cooling and low for quiet cooling.

Energy-Savers. Energy-efficient air conditioners usually have fans that turn on and off with the compressor instead of running continuously. This action can be automatic, or you may have to start it with a switch or button. We prefer the automatic kind.

Filters. The filter should be cleaned—or replaced—at the start of the cooling season, and then cleaned once a month during the season. So, make sure that the unit you choose has a filter that is easily accessible.

Sound Insulation. It's impossible to gauge how noisy a room air conditioner will be in one room by listening to it in another. The best way to judge the probable noise level is to investigate the unit's construction. Are the noise-making parts well isolated? Is there adequate sound insulation? A good dealer should be able to advise you.

Thermostat Controls. The thermostatic control, usually a numbered dial, alters the frequency with which the compressor turns on and off. Some thermostatic controls have a fan-only setting that runs without the compressor; this is a good energy-saving feature.

Ventilation. Look for an intake vent and an exhaust vent to allow the machine to bring in fresh air (a sure cure for stale or musty air) and to remove odors and smoke.

Chassis. A room air conditioner consists of the chassis—which is the machinery itself—and the sleeve or cabinet, which encases the machinery. The chassis is either fixed in place so that the whole unit is one piece, or built to slide forward or lift completely out of the cabinet. A sliding chassis is convenient for cleaning and maintenance, and with heavy units in particular, it eases installation problems.

Styling. Most room air conditioners have a simulated-wood front panel. Controls should be behind an access panel; this looks smarter and discourages children from playing with the knobs or dials.

Best Buys '82

THE FOLLOWING ARE our selected "Best Buy" room air conditioners, listed by cooling capacity in Btu's (British thermal units) per hour. Because our ratings are based on efficiency of performance, we haven't included any "Also Recommended" models—if we don't consider a unit a "Best Buy" in terms of performance, we don't want to recommend it at all. Remember that a "Best Buy" rating applies only to one particular model; it does not imply that we endorse a whole product line or that other products by the same manufacturer are equally good.

 5000 Btuh to 7000 Btuh

Sears Kenmore 871059 (EER, 7.5) is a high-efficiency 5000-Btuh unit with excellent air direction, an automatic energy-saver to turn off the fan when the compressor cycles off, and an adjustable thermostat for maximum temperature control. This unit is a bit noisy in operation, but overall it ranks high among the more economical models of its size. **Specifications: Height,** 14½"; **Width,** 20½"; **Depth,** 13⅞"; **Weight,** 51 pounds; **Maximum window width,** 36"; **Watts,** 665; **Volts,** 115; **Amps,** 5.8; **Moisture removal rate,** 1.4 pints per hour; **Fan speeds,** 2; **Air delivery,** 383 cubic feet per minute (high speed); **Warranty,** parts and labor, 1 year; compressor system (parts and labor), 5 years; outdoor case (parts), 10 years.

Approximate Retail Price
$280.00 .... **Approximate Low Price** Not Available

Friedrich SP05F10A (EER, 8.8) is a 5200-Btuh high-efficiency model by a manufacturer that offered high quality, high-efficiency models long before rising energy costs made them popular. This unit has an energy-

Prices are accurate at time of printing; subject to manufacturer's change.

saving switch that turns off the fan when the compressor goes off. Air direction control is excellent. This unit has sound-absorbing insulation, an washable filter, a fan-only setting, and an air exhaust setting. There are cheaper units on the market, but you won't find one that's quieter or of better overall quality.

Specifications: Height, 13¹³⁄₁₆″; **Width,** 22⁵⁄₁₆″; **Depth,** 18⅝″; **Weight,** 108 pounds; **Maximum window width,** 42″; **Watts,** 590; **Volts,** 115; **Amps,** 5.0; **Moisture removal rate,** 1.0 pints per hour; **Fan speeds,** 2; **Air delivery,** 190 cubic feet per minute; **Warranty,** parts and labor, 1 year; compressor system (parts and labor), 5 years.

Approximate Retail Price	Approximate Low Price
$449.00	$426.00

Carrier BK705B1 (EER, 8.7) is a very efficient 5500-Btuh model. It weighs 66 pounds, which is light for a high-efficiency model, and the fixed chassis makes it easy to handle. This unit has sound insulation, an automatic thermostat, good side-to-side air flow control, three fan speeds, and an optional exhaust vent.

Specifications: Height, 13⅞″; **Width,** 20¹⁄₁₆″; **Depth,** 16⁹⁄₁₆″; **Weight,** 78 pounds; **Maximum window width,** 41″; **Watts,** 630; **Volts,** 115; **Amps,** 5.6; **Moisture removal rate,** 1.3 pints per hour; **Fan speeds,** 3; **Air delivery,** 135/180 cubic feet per minute; **Warranty,** parts and labor, 1 year; compressor system (parts), 5 years.

Approximate Retail Price	Approximate Low Price
$414.00	$275.00

Friedrich SS07F10 (EER, 10.2) is a fairly expensive unit in the 7000-Btuh size, but the high EER will give you back lower electric bills. An energy-saving switch cycles the fan on and off with the compressor for more efficient operation. This model also has a five-speed blower fan, a fresh-air intake, an exhaust, and a fan-only setting. The good insulation and the slide-out chassis are features to note. This unit has excellent air direction control and quiet operation.

Specifications: Height, 15¹¹⁄₁₆″; **Width,** 25¹⁵⁄₁₆″; **Depth,** 26½″; **Weight,** 153 pounds; **Maximum window width,** 42″; **Watts,** 685; **Volts,** 115; **Amps,** 6.0; **Moisture removal rate,** 0.6 pints per hour; **Fan speeds,** 5; **Air delivery,** 315 cubic feet per minute; **Warranty,** parts and labor, 1 year; compressor system (parts and labor), 5 years.

Approximate Retail Price	Approximate Low Price
$599.00	$530.00

7000 Btuh to 8000 Btuh

White-Westinghouse AK087E7V (EER, 8.7) is a 7500-Btuh model for sliding windows. This is a high-efficiency model with good four-way air

Prices are accurate at time of printing; subject to manufacturer's change.

direction, an 11-position adjustable thermostat, high and low speeds, a washable filter, and an exhaust vent. The thermostat has a visual marking to show the most efficient operating range. This unit also has an energy-saving setting that cycles the fan and compressor together.
Specifications: Height, 19¼"; **Width,** 14¼"; **Depth,** 23⅞"; **Weight,** 100 pounds; **Maximum window height,** 48"; **Watts,** 860; **Volts,** 115; **Amps,** 7.5; **Moisture removal rate,** 2.2 pints per hour; **Fan speeds,** 2; **Air delivery,** 270 cubic feet per minute; **Warranty,** parts and labor, 1 year; compressor system (parts and labor), 5 years.

Approximate Retail Price   **Approximate Low Price**
Not Available $480.00

 8000 Btuh to 10,000 Btuh

Whirlpool AHF-P80-2 (EER, 8.8), rated best of the 8000-Btuh models, is a high-efficiency machine with hidden controls, a 12-position thermostat, and an exhaust vent. It has good two-way air direction control, and the three-speed fan operates either continuously or in an energy-saving mode, which turns the fan on and off with the compressor. The slide-out chassis is convenient.
Specifications: Height, 15"; **Width,** 22¹¹⁄₁₆"; **Depth,** 22¾"; **Weight,** 106 pounds; **Maximum window width,** 38"; **Watts,** 905; **Volts,** 115; **Amps,** 7.5; **Moisture removal rate,** 2.3 pints per hour; **Fan speeds,** 3; **Air delivery,** not available; **Warranty,** parts and labor, 1 year; sealed system (parts and labor), 5 years.

Approximate Retail Price   **Approximate Low Price**
$473.00 .... $370.00

Amana ES9-2MS (EER, 9.3) is an 8500-Btuh model with a refrigerant muffler that makes it one of the quietest units available. It's very well built and has plenty of sound insulation. The fan and compressor cycle together for efficient operation, and the eight-position thermostat has a fan-only setting. Air direction control is good, and the model also has an exhaust vent and a fresh-air setting.
Specifications: Height, 15⅜"; **Width,** 24"; **Depth,** 23"; **Weight,** 143 pounds; **Maximum window width,** 42"; **Watts,** 915; **Volts,** 115; **Amps,** 7.5; **Moisture removal rate,** 1.9 pints per hour; **Fan speeds,** 2; **Air delivery,** 265 cubic feet per minute; **Warranty,** parts and labor, 1 year; sealed system (parts and labor) and specified major parts (parts only), 5 years.

Approximate Retail Price   **Approximate Low Price**
$500.00 .... $419.00

Prices are accurate at time of printing; subject to manufacturer's change.

Friedrich SSO9F10 (EER, 10.5) is a 9200-Btuh model with one of the highest EERs available. It has a power-saving switch to cycle the fan and compressor together for more efficient operation, a five-speed blower fan, a fresh air intake, an exhaust, and a fan-only setting. This model has excellent air direction control and is very quiet in operation.
Specifications: Height, 15¹¹⁄₁₆″; **Width,** 25¹⁵⁄₁₆″; **Depth,** 26½″; **Weight,** 157 pounds; **Maximum window width,** 42″; **Watts,** 875; **Volts,** 115; **Amps,** 7.5; **Moisture removal rate,** 1.5 pints per hour; **Fan speeds,** 5; **Air delivery,** 300 cubic feet per minute; **Warranty,** parts and labor, 1 year; compressor system (parts and labor), 5 years.

Approximate Retail Price	Approximate Low Price
$674.00	$597.00

 Over 10,000 Btuh

Sears Kenmore 872149 (EER, 9.6) is a 14,000-Btuh model that delivers high efficiency at a competitive price. The unit has excellent air control and air distribution; it also has an energy-saver mode to cycle the fan and compressor together, an eight-position adjustable thermostat, a fresh-air intake, an exhaust, and hidden controls. A slide-out chassis makes it easy to handle, and it can be installed through the wall.
Specifications: Height, 18¾″; **Width,** 25⅞″; **Depth,** 28¹³⁄₁₆″; **Weight,** 163 pounds; **Maximum window width,** 40″; **Watts,** 1460; **Volts,** 115; **Amps,** 12; **Moisture removal rate,** 4 pints per hour; **Fan speeds,** 3; **Air delivery,** 383 cubic feet per minute; **Warranty,** parts and labor, 1 year; compressor (parts and labor), 5 years.

Approximate Retail Price	Approximate Low Price
$550.00	Not Available

Amana ES218D-3ML (EER, 8.5), judged best among the units between 15,000 and 20,000 Btuh, is a 17,400/17,600-Btuh model with an exhaust and a fresh-air intake, isolated components for reduced noise and vibration, an eight-position thermostat, and excellent air distribution. Like most of the big units, the ES218D-3ML requires an electrical supply of 230 or 208 volts. This model will cost you a little more to buy, but it is a good value and will serve you well.
Specifications: Height, 17⅛″; **Width,** 26½″; **Depth,** 30⅞″; **Weight,** 245 pounds; **Maximum window width,** 44″; **Watts,** 2095/2050; **Volts,** 230/208; **Amps,** 9.0/9.8; **Moisture removal rate,** 5.25 pints per hour; **Fan speeds,** 3; **Air delivery,** 475 cubic feet per minute; **Warranty,** parts and labor, 1 year; compressor system (parts and labor), and specified major parts (parts only), 5 years.

Approximate Retail Price	Approximate Low Price
$780.00	Not Available

Prices are accurate at time of printing; subject to manufacturer's change.

Nonprescription Drugs

AMERICANS SPEND HUNDREDS of billions of dollars every year on nonprescription medication—the cough syrups, cold remedies, antacids, stimulants, and laxatives you can buy at your neighborhood drugstore or supermarket. Over $700 million a year is spent on pain relievers alone, and the figure for cold and cough remedies is even higher.

What do we get for all this money? In many cases we get safe, effective medication. Over-the-counter (OTC) drugs will relieve a minor headache, soothe an upset stomach, suppress a cough, and stop the itching from a rash. There are limits to their effectiveness however. They will not cure a cold or an ear infection (although they can relieve some of the symptoms), and they won't make a rash from poison ivy go away any sooner (but they may make you more comfortable for its duration). Some OTC products are no more effective than a sugar pill or a cup of coffee. Any of them could be dangerous if used improperly or for too long a time, and they can conceal the symptoms of serious disease, thereby delaying needed professional treatment.

Consumers are understandably confused when confronted by the hundreds of OTC remedies on drugstore shelves, and all too often are guided in their buying decisions to pick up the package with the name made familiar by advertisements on television or in magazines. Yet drug advertising, like advertising for other products, conveys what the manufacturer wants you to know, rather than what you need to know to make a purchasing decision.

The Food and Drug Administration (FDA) is now reviewing all the over-the-counter drugs on the market to ensure that they are safe and effective. It is evaluating OTC drug product labels to make sure that they are clearly written and contain useful information; it is assessing all the ingredients used in OTC products and removing those that cannot be proven effective. It is regulating dosages and restricting advertising claims. However, this review is not yet complete, and until it is, the OTC marketplace will undergo many changes as products are removed, package labels are rewritten and advertising is reworked.

Once the FDA review is completed, purchasing nonprescription drugs should be a little less confusing. Until then, follow these guidelines when you're looking for a cough syrup, an antacid, a pain reliever, or any other OTC product:

Use single-ingredient products to treat the symptoms you have. Avoid multiple-ingredient products intended to treat a variety of symptoms. A good example of such a product is the cold remedy that combines aspirin or acetaminophen (and sometimes both) to relieve achiness and fever, a decongestant to help relieve a stuffy nose, a cough suppressant to stop a cough, and an antihistamine, which is of dubious value for any cold symptoms. If your only symptom is a stuffy nose, all you need is the decongestant. By taking the other drugs, you're risking additional side effects and possible drug interactions. Moreover, such multiple-ingredient products are almost always a good deal more expensive than single-ingredient products.

What if you have a fever and a stuffy nose? Take plain aspirin or acetaminophen for the fever and a product that's pure decongestant for your nose. That way, when the fever goes down, you can stop taking the analgesic while continuing to take the decongestant for as long as is necessary. You won't be locked in to taking possibly unnecessary medications.

Study the label on the drug before you buy it. You're going to have to read the label to find out how many ingredients the product contains and which symptoms it's intended to treat. Read a little farther to find out if this drug is the one for you. OTC drug labels should include, in addition to the name, type, and purpose of the drug, dosage instructions, special warnings, and directions for its use. The label should include the drug's expiration date, the date beyond which the drug should not be used. Look for an explanation of the maximum safe dosage and any possible side effects. If you have any questions, ask your pharmacist.

It is not mandatory that manufacturers list quantities of ingredients for some products; however, we feel that you deserve to know what's going into your body when you take an over-the-counter medication. Only when the manufacturer supplies a complete listing of the amounts of the active ingredients can you make a true price comparison. We believe such a listing is advisable for every OTC remedy.

Look for generics. The buyer of nonprescription drugs can often save money by buying nontrademarked brands. Generic aspirin will no doubt be less expensive than the Bayer brand, and generic acetaminophen will cost less than that sold under the Tylenol name. If you're shopping in a chain store, look to the house brands for the best buys. The FDA has assured us that there are no major differences between most brand-name drugs and their generic equivalents. In fact, the same manufacturer often supplies the basic chemical to several different drug companies, some of which will sell the drug under their own trade names, while others will sell the identical drug generically.

Buying Nonprescription Drugs

THE GUIDELINES listed above can be helpful, but you also need to know which OTC ingredients are effective. In the next few pages, we discuss different categories of OTC medication—from acne remedies to wart removers—and recommend those products with the most effective formulation in each category. Trade name products mentioned will begin with a capital letter; generics, with a lower-case letter.

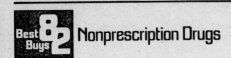

Acne Remedies

OTC ACNE REMEDIES open blocked skin pores. The most effective ingredient in such remedies is benzoyl peroxide. Because these products also remove some of the surface of the skin, they can be irritating. If you find a product too irritating, ask your pharmacist to recommend one with a lower concentration of benzoyl peroxide, or try using the product less often. See a doctor if your acne is inflamed—red, swollen, and painful.

Recommended: benzoyl peroxide; Clearasil; Dry and Clear lotion or cream; Oxy-5; Oxy-10; Stri-Dex B.P.; Topex

Allergy Remedies

IF YOU'RE TREATING an allergy, try the least expensive form of the antihistamine chlorpheniramine maleate that your pharmacy carries. Chlorpheniramine is the antihistamine most likely to be effective without causing excessive drowsiness.

Recommended: chlorpheniramine maleate; Chlor-Trimeton

Antacids

ANTACIDS ARE one exception to the "buy single-ingredient products" rule. Look for an antacid that is a combination of salts of aluminum and magnesium. Aluminum salts can be constipating; magnesium has laxative effects. Taken together they generally counteract each other's side effects. Liquid antacids are superior to tablets or wafers because the ingredients in liquid medications have been ground into fine particles. If you use tablets or wafers, be sure to chew them thoroughly and drink a glass of water afterward. Do not self-medicate for indigestion or sour stomach for more than two weeks or if the symptoms seem especially severe; call your doctor.

Recommended: Gaviscon liquid; Kolantyl; Maalox; Maalox #1; Maalox #2

Antinauseants

CHOOSE AN OTC ANTINAUSEANT containing an antihistamine to prevent motion sickness. Do not self-medicate if you suspect your nausea is due to pregnancy. Nausea and vomiting due to food intolerance is self-limiting and generally needs no medication; you'll feel better as soon as the offending food is out of your system. Also, do not self-medicate if you continue vomiting for two or three days, notice blood in the material vomited, or if you have severe abdominal pain or a headache.

Recommended: Bonine; dimenhydrinate; Dramamine; Dramamine Jr.; Marezine; meclizine hydrochloride

Appetite Suppressants

THE MOST EFFECTIVE OTC appetite suppressants contain phenyl-propanolamine hydrochloride, but they are effective only for a week or two at a time. For a long-term weight loss program, you can use these products effectively by taking them for up to two weeks at a time with one-week intervals between, or you can take them from Monday through Friday with weekends "off." These products should be used only as a supplement to a nutritionally balanced, low-calorie diet. They do not, of themselves, cause weight loss. Remember, you should consult your doctor before beginning any diet.

Recommended: Ayds; Control; Dietac tablet, liquid, or maximum strength capsule; P.V.M.

Athlete's Foot and Jock Itch Remedies

CHOOSE A TOLNAFTATE PRODUCT to treat these fungal infections. The cream, gel, or liquid forms are more economical than spray forms. In addition, sprinkle the powder form into your shoes, socks, or undercloth-ing to help keep the affected area dry. If the condition does not improve in three weeks, see your doctor.

Recommended: Aftate; Tinactin

Body Lice Remedies

THESE OTC PRODUCTS are just as effective as prescription medica-tion for treating an infestation of body lice. After using them as directed, use a fine-toothed comb to remove dead insects and eggs from the hair. Or apply a solution of equal parts of vinegar and water to the hair and then shower. These products should not be used more frequently than indicated on the label, and care should be taken that none of the solution gets in the eyes. Do not use on children unless your doctor approves. If the condition does not respond quickly, see your doctor.

Recommended: A-200 Pyrinate; Barc; Rid

Burn and Sunburn Remedies

OTC PRODUCTS sold for the treatment of minor burns and sunburn are local anesthetics; that is, they relieve pain at the burned area. They can be effective, but try a cold water soak before resorting to OTC medication for a minor burn. Soak the burned area in cold water or apply cloths soaked in cold water to the affected area. Do not use ice water. This procedure will cool the area, relieve pain, and limit swelling. You can also take aspirin to relieve pain. If you want to use a local anesthetic,

look for one that contains at least 20 percent benzocaine. Severe burns require professional treatment.
Recommended: Americaine

Canker Sore and Fever Blister Remedies

PRODUCTS SOLD over the counter to treat canker sores and fever blisters do not significantly hasten healing, but they do relieve pain. Look for a product containing carbamide peroxide, which releases oxygen in the mouth. The oxygen cleanses the area, reduces inflammation, and relieves pain.
Recommended: Gly-Oxide

Corn and Callus Removers

PRECUT PADS AND PLASTERS impregnated with salicylic acid are recommended to remove painful corns and calluses. Placed over the corn or callus, such products cushion the painful area while the acid softens the dead skin cells that form the corn or callus. These products should not be used by people with diabetes or poor circulation. To prevent the formation of corns and calluses, be sure your shoes and socks fit well.
Recommended: any of Dr. Scholl's medicated pads or discs

Cold Remedies

AVOID MULTIPLE-INGREDIENT products; treat only the symptoms you have. If you feel feverish or achy, take aspirin or acetaminophen. Either will make you more comfortable. Decongestant tablets will provide long-lasting relief of nasal congestion without irritating nasal membranes. Generic pseudoephedrine hydrochloride (or Sudafed brand) is the oral decongestant of choice. For rapid relief of nasal congestion, use topical decongestant spray or drops. Sprays are preferred for most people; drops are better for small children. Use of these products should be restricted to three or four days; used for a longer period, they are likely to cause rebound congestion, leaving you more congested than you were before you began using them. Products containing oxymetazoline hydrochloride (Afrin, Duration) have the longest duration of action.
Recommended: acetaminophen; Afrin; aspirin; Duration; pseudo-ephedrine hydrochloride; Sudafed

Cough Remedies

CODEINE AND DEXTROMETHORPHAN are proven effective cough suppressants available in OTC cough remedies. Because codeine is a narcotic, it is available for sale without a prescription only in combination products. Therefore, to reduce the frequency and severity of a cough due to a cold, look for a product listing dextromethorphan as the only active ingredient. Dextromethorphan is safe, causes few side effects, and is generally considered to be as effective, or very slightly less effective, than codeine.

Recommended: Benylin DM; Pertussin 8-Hour Cough Formula; Silence Is Golden

Dandruff Shampoos

SELENIUM SULFIDE is the most effective ingredient in nonprescription dandruff remedies. Selenium sulfide shampoos slow the growth of scalp cells, thereby lessening the number of dandruff flakes. Do not use these products more frequently than directed on the label, and discontinue use if irritation occurs.

Recommended: selenium sulfide; Selsun Blue

Dental Anesthetics

TO RELIEVE THE PAIN of a toothache until you can get to a dentist, you can take aspirin or acetaminophen. OTC products intended specifically for the relief of pain of toothache, teething, or sore gums generally contain a local anesthetic. If you want to use one of these products, look for one with a high concentration of benzocaine. Such products are the most economical and effective. The substance may be in either liquid or ointment form. If you have a cavity, put the anesthetic on a piece of cotton and insert the cotton into the cavity. To relieve gum pain, rub the agent on the gums.

Recommended: Benzodent

Diarrhea Remedies

ACUTE DIARRHEA, that which lasts only a day or two, usually does not require medication. The best thing for you to do if you have acute diarrhea is to drink extra fluids (eight to ten glasses of water a day) to prevent dehydration. If diarrhea persists for more than two or three days, see your doctor. If you feel you must take medication choose a mixture of kaolin and pectin. These are the most economical and the safest.

Recommended: kaolin with pectin; Kaopectate

Eardrops

USE NONPRESCRIPTION eardrops to soften hardened earwax or to dry out the ear (a good preventive measure for those prone to swimmer's ear). Products containing carbamide peroxide and glycerin will serve both purposes. Do not self-treat severe or persistent earaches.

Recommended: Debrox; Murine

Eyedrops

OVER-THE-COUNTER eyedrops can be used to wash a foreign object from the eye (as long as it is not embedded), to ease irritation, or to lubricate dry eyes. Isopto Plain eyedrops are recommended for these uses.

Recommended: Isopto Plain

First Aid Products

APPLYING A FIRST AID product to a minor cut or abrasion is usually not necessary. Washing with soap or water will most likely prevent infection. If you do choose to dress such a wound, use an antibiotic ointment. These ointments are also used to treat the skin disease impetigo. Do not use such products for either purpose for more than four or five days, and do not use them on large areas of the body.

Recommended: Baciguent; Mycitracin; Neo-Polycin; Polysporin

Hemorrhoidal Preparations

THE MOST EFFECTIVE OTC hemorrhoidal preparations contain hydrocortisone, a steroid hormone. Until recently, these products were available only by prescription, but now you can purchase hydrocortisone over the counter in strengths up to 0.5 percent. When using these products to treat hemorrhoids, be sure to follow directions carefully and do not apply more frequently than directed. Any hemorrhoids that do not respond within several days or that are bleeding profusely should be seen by a doctor.

Recommended: Cortef Acetate; Dermolate

Laxatives

TO TREAT OCCASIONAL constipation, choose a bulk-forming laxative. These laxatives have fibers from seeds or other parts of plants that cannot be digested or absorbed by the body but do, however, have a high affinity for water. When they come in contact with water in the intestine, they swell, thus increasing the bulk of material in the intestine. They also produce a gel that lubricates the bowel to ease evacuation. These laxatives are gentle and cause few side effects. The only precaution about their use is that they must be completely mixed with water before they are swallowed.

Recommended: Metamucil; Modane Bulk; Serutan

Muscular Pain Remedies

MUSCULAR PAIN REMEDIES reduce soreness due to overexertion, cold weather, or arthritis by increasing the flow of blood to the muscle, thereby producing warmth. Choose a cream or an ointment containing a salicylate. Such products can be rubbed into the skin vigorously, and the rubbing itself will add to the therapeutic effect. Before applying these products, soak the sore muscle in hot water for 15 to 20 minutes to further alleviate the pain. Application of heat, moist or dry, is also helpful for relieving muscular aches.

Recommended: Ben-Gay; Icy Hot Balm; Icy Hot Rub

Pain Relievers

MOST OTC PAIN RELIEVERS are primarily aspirin or acetaminophen; some have added ingredients—commonly caffeine, antihistamines, or antacids. No test has ever shown that such a combination of ingredients is more effective than an equivalent dose of plain aspirin or acetaminophen, and these combinations are almost always a great deal more expensive. Aspirin or acetaminophen is treatment of choice for all minor aches and pains, including sore muscles, menstrual cramps, toothaches, and the discomforts of a cold or the flu.

Aspirin reduces inflammation, although for some people it causes stomach irritation; acetaminophen is not effective for pain associated with inflammation, but it does not irritate the stomach. If you're treating pain associated with inflammation (that of arthritis, for example), choose aspirin. Choose acetaminophen if aspirin upsets your stomach. If you have a headache and an upset stomach (a common combination of symptoms due to overindulgence in alcohol), use acetaminophen for the headache. Aspirin should not be used by people who have asthma, peptic ulcers, or blood-clotting disorders, and people with diabetes or gout should use it carefully.

Recommended: acetaminophen; aspirin

Poison Ivy/Poison Oak Remedies

TO RELIEVE THE ITCHING of a rash due to poison ivy or poison oak, try soaking the affected area in hot water. You could also apply a cloth that has been wrung out in hot water to the affected area. This treatment may provide relief for several hours. In addition, use ordinary calamine lotion on the blisters. Although calamine lotion dries to form a pink crust on the skin, it is effective in relief of itching, and it is likely to be less irritating than products containing local anesthetics, antihistamines, or antiseptics.

Recommended: calamine lotion

Rash Remedies

YOUR BEST BUY among rash remedies depends upon the rash you are treating. If you have prickly heat, try Aveeno Colloidal Oatmeal bath. To prevent diaper rash, apply Vaseline petroleum jelly as a protectant before putting on a fresh diaper. Hydrocortisone acetate, a topical steroid sold under the brand names Cortaid and Dermolate, is useful for inflammatory rashes. Such rashes are characterized by pain, a sensation of heat, redness, and swelling. Steroids do relieve inflammation, thus also relieving itching, but relief occurs only after a day or two of use. Because they do not provide immediate relief, many people apply them more often than recommended, thereby increasing the risk of suffering an adverse reaction. We recommend that if you use topical steroids, do so cautiously and follow directions carefully.

Recommended: Aveeno Colloidal Oatmeal bath; Cortaid; Dermolate; hydrocortisone acetate; Vaseline petroleum jelly

Sleep Aids

OTC SLEEPING TABLETS contain an antihistamine such as pyrilamine maleate. Antihistamines have not been proven effective as sleep-inducers at the dosages used in OTC sleeping aids, and they commonly cause side effects such as blurred vision, dizziness, dry mouth, and palpitations. Increasing the dosage, of course, increases your risk of side effects. If a minor ache or pain is keeping you awake, try acetaminophen or aspirin. Otherwise, try to identify and correct the cause of your sleeplessness.
Recommended: none

Stimulants

NONPRESCRIPTION STIMULANTS contain caffeine in dosages ranging from 100 to 200 mg. One cup of brewed coffee contains 100 to 150 mg of caffeine. If you feel you need a stimulant, try drinking a cup of coffee, tea, or a cola beverage.
Recommended: none

Vitamin/Mineral Supplements

DIETARY DEFICIENCIES of vitamins are uncommon in the United States. Most people who have vitamin deficiencies should be under a doctor's care. They should not be self-medicating with OTC vitamin/mineral supplements. Certain people (pregnant and nursing women, infants, alcoholics, people with certain diseases) do have increased nutritional needs and may benefit from dietary supplements. If you think you need extra vitamins, consult your doctor to see if a true deficiency exists.
Recommended: the generic product providing the dosages suggested by your doctor

Wart Removers

OTC WART REMOVERS usually contain salicylic or acetic acid, and they remove tissue from the wart a little at a time. Do not try to remove a wart that is oozing fluid or one that has changed color, shape, size, or texture. These symptoms may signal serious disease; call your doctor right away. Do not attempt to remove a wart on your face; you may cause permanent scarring. Never treat warts yourself if you are diabetic or have a disease that impairs your circulation.
Recommended: Compound W; Wart Off

Index